Pro-Democracy Contention in Hong Kong

SUNY series in New Political Science
—————————
Bradley J. Macdonald, editor

Pro-Democracy Contention in Hong Kong

Relational Dynamics between the Umbrella Movement and the Anti-Extradition Protests

FRANCIS L. F. LEE

SUNY
PRESS

Published by State University of New York Press, Albany

For information, contact State University of New York Press, Albany, NY
www.sunypress.edu

Library of Congress Cataloging-in-Publication Data

Name: Lee, Francis L. F., author.
Title: Pro-democracy contention in Hong Kong : relational dynamics between the
    Umbrella Movement and the Anti-Extradition Protests / Francis L. F. Lee.
Description: Albany : State University of New York Press, [2024] | Series:
    SUNY series in New Political Science | Includes bibliographical references and
    index.
Identifiers: ISBN 9798855801088 (hardcover : alk. paper) | ISBN 9798855801101
    (ebook) | ISBN 9798855801095 (pbk. : alk. paper)
Further information is available at the Library of Congress.

Contents

List of Illustrations   vii

List of Abbreviations   xi

Acknowledgments   xiii

Chapter 1. Introduction   1

Chapter 2. The Umbrella Movement   27

Chapter 3. The Mongkok Civil Unrest   61

Chapter 4. Localism Facing the Voting Public   91

Chapter 5. Ideological Brokerage and Articulating
            Hong Kong's Future   125

Chapter 6. State Repression and Affective Depolarization   159

Chapter 7. The Anti-ELAB Protests   189

Chapter 8. Conclusion   231

Appendix: Research Methodologies   257

Notes   269

References   277

Index   301

Illustrations

Figures

3.1 Street map of Mongkok and location of major incidents during the Mongkok civil unrest. 71

7.1 No. of posts on LIHKG mentioning "no severing of ties." 194

7.2 No. of posts on LIHKG mentioning "black police." 196

7.3 No. of posts on LIHKG mentioning "leading the wind" and "air-conditioned strategist." 197

7.4 Posters promoting the code of conduct for actions toward different types of shops. 202

7.5 No. of posts containing the phrase *five demands* on LIHKG. 209

7.6 No. of posts containing *Liberate Hong Kong* and *Revolution of Our Time* on LIHKG. 211

7.7 No. of posts on LIHKG mentioning Hong Kong independence. 217

Tables

2.1 Demographics and party support of Umbrella Movement participants in Admiralty and Mongkok. 38

2.2 Views about self-mobilization and perceptions of the foundation of the Umbrella Movement. 39

2.3   Correlations between sense of belonging to Hong Kong and
      China and perceived foundation of the Umbrella Movement.   41

2.4   Actions undertaken by the Umbrella Movement participants.   43

2.5   Predicting engagement in confrontational actions.   44

3.1   Simplified chronology of major happenings and incidents
      during the Mongkok civil unrest.   70

4.1   Naming of the Mongkok civil unrest in different newspapers. 94

4.2   Mentions and descriptions of actors and actions in the
      Mongkok civil unrest under different event labels.   96

4.3   Identification of causes, responses, and suggested solutions. 97

4.4   Public attitudes toward the Mongkok civil unrest in March
      2016.   115

4.5   Public attitudes toward radical actions in March 2016.   118

4.6   Predicting public attitudes toward the Mongkok civil unrest. 120

5.1   Support for possible post-2047 arrangements for Hong Kong
      (2016 and 2017 surveys).   148

5.2   Public attitudes regarding Hong Kong independence (survey
      in March 2016).   149

5.3   Attitudes toward independence by age, education, and
      attitudes toward the Mongkok civil unrest (survey in
      March 2016).   151

5.4   Predicting attitudes toward Hong Kong independence
      (survey in March 2016).   153

6.1   Citizens' ratings of political factions in 2016 and 2019.   181

6.2   Regression analysis of ratings of factions and polarization. 184

7.1   Protest participants' perceptions of representativeness of
      movement slogans.   195

7.2   Agreement with statements related to radical protests.   199

7.3 Solidarity with and guilt feelings toward militant protesters.   205

7.4 Demands indicated in posters associated with protest
     events, July 28, 2019, to January 19, 2020.   212

7.5 Predicting percentage of LIHKG posts mentioning
     Hong Kong independence.   219

7.6 Attitudes toward one country, two systems.   221

7.7 Self-proclaimed political inclination among the protesters.   224

7.8 Self-proclaimed political inclination and protest attitudes
     (December 8, 2019).   226

A.1 Basic information about population surveys belonging to
     CCPOS's Hong Kong Public Opinion and Political
     Development Program.   260

A.2 List of interviewees on the Mongkok civil unrest.   262

Abbreviations

Anti-ELAB	Anti-Extradition Law Amendment Bill
CCP	Chinese Communist Party
CCPOS	Center for Communication and Public Opinion Survey
CHRF	Civil Human Rights Front
CLO	Chinese Liaison Office (official full name: Liaison Office of the Central People's Government in the Hong Kong Special Administrative Region)
COI	Commission of inquiry
DP	Democratic Party
FCC	Foreign Correspondents Club
FEHD	Food and Environmental Hygiene Department
HCT	Hawkers Control Team
HKI	Hong Kong Indigenous
LegCo	Legislative Council
LSD	League of Social Democrats
NPC	National People's Congress
NSL	National Security Law
OCLP	Occupy Central for Love and Peace
RTHK	Radio Television Hong Kong
SAR	Special Administrative Region

Acknowledgments

This book is based on years of research on prodemocracy protests in Hong Kong. Some of the research data employed were derived from my own work; some data were collected specifically for the purpose of writing this book. But a substantial part of the research data utilized in several chapters come from collaboration with various colleagues. They are thus the first ones I need to thank here. Prof. Joseph Chan was a mentor and the person who invited me to join him to study the July 1, 2003, protest in Hong Kong, and that became the starting point of my study of contentious politics. Our collaboration would later extend to studies of the Umbrella Movement and Tiananmen commemoration. Data from these projects are incorporated, to different extents, into the present book. In 2019, I had the pleasure to collaborate with a group of energetic and talented young colleagues—Dr. Edmund Cheng, Dr. Gary Tang, and Dr. Samson Yuen—as well as a group of even younger graduate students on a range of studies about the Anti-Extradition Law Amendment Bill protests. Not only did we conduct a large number of protest onsite surveys, but we also conducted in-depth interviews, focus groups, and digital data analysis. Dr. Liang Hai, my colleague at the Chinese University of Hong Kong, offered crucial expertise to help me tackle a vast amount of digital data.

However, this book is not so much about the Umbrella Movement and the Anti-ELAB protests than about what happened in between the two peaks of protest mobilization and what connected the two. Substantively, it represents an attempt to move beyond analyzing the peaks of mobilization in order to more properly examine a "movement" instead of individual "moments." Practically, this is made possible by the opportunities offered to me over the years to engage in other relevant research work, which gave me access to meaningful materials and data. Most notable is a research project initiated by a collective composed of academics, journalists, and civil society actors who originally aimed at producing an unofficial report about the Mongkok civil unrest in 2016. The project started in early 2019. The Anti-ELAB protests inevitably presented a huge distraction, but the project continued, and the relevant research work was completed none-theless. Subsequent political changes in the city had complicated the issue of whether and how the results of the project can be presented in more public-oriented form (as originally intended), but there are solid data from the project for serious academic analysis. I have to thank the people who brought me into the project at the beginning as well as all the people who were involved in it, even though it is no longer convenient to recognize many of them by name.

In addition to being a researcher working in the areas of political com-munication and contentious politics, I am also a citizen living through the changes in the city. Over the years, many ideas, arguments, and "hypotheses" were developed through sheer observations of ongoing political dynamics and conversations with friends inside or outside the academia. To give just one anecdote. In late February 2016, I was taking a more or less routine evening walk with my wife around a small artificial lake in our residential area. Our conversation turned to current events. At one point, she said that if she were still living in New Territories East (as she was when she grew up), she would have voted for Edward Leung in the by-election happening at that time. Edward Leung was the localist candidate and a protagonist of the Mongkok civil unrest (and he will be a major figure in a couple of chapters in this book). I was surprised, and I reminded her that she was very angry about the protester violence when the Mongkok civil unrest occurred just three weeks previously. She said something, if my memory can be relied upon, along the lines of Leung being reflective and sincere in the way he addressed the public since the Mongkok clashes. My wife never became a localist, though she did hold negative attitudes toward the so-called leftards. This anecdote (and others) probably had strongly influenced the way I approach public attitudes toward localism: members of the public were not reacting to the articulated localist discourses that ardent political observers and young activists were familiar with; they were responding to what appeared to them at the interface where the localists and the public met. This remains my view, and it is an important working assumption informing this book's account of the mainstreaming of localism.

This is just one anecdote. And of course, conversations and interactions with others do not always result in ideas that I would cling to over time.

There were certainly occasions when my ideas and "working hypotheses" were challenged by the arguments, observations, stories, and/or information provided by friends and acquaintances (and obviously, sometimes by subsequent happenings in the political arena or simply by the empirical data derived from systematic research). I thank all those people who gave me insight and inspiration through formal and informal conversations in different settings.

As a Hong Kong researcher, I hope this book can serve to document arguably the most important time period in the contemporary history of contentious politics in the city. The basic documentation function of academic works seems to be increasingly significant in an era and a context where political power has a larger and larger influence on the definition of reality and the determination of "facts." Certainly, as its author is a communication and social movement scholar, this book is after all written and developed as a piece of academic work addressing general conceptual issues in the study of contentious politics and political change. I believe the Hong Kong case can offer important insights into a significant number of theoretical issues including, among others, the relational dynamics in movement development, what movement actors actually do in the so-called abeyance period, the interaction between social movements and the public, and the relationship between elections and protests in a hybrid regime. Hopefully all readers can find something meaningful in it.

Chapter 1

Introduction

In the early morning hours of September 28, 2014, after twenty months of public debates and preparation, Occupy Central for Love and Peace began in Hong Kong after a week of student protests. Within twenty-four hours, the police's firing of eighty-seven canisters of tear gas into the protesting crowd triggered mass participation and protester improvisation (M. S. Ho, 2019; Tang, 2015). The action was turned into a multisite, prolonged occupation of public roads in three districts in Hong Kong known as the Umbrella Movement. Many participants engaged in a form of prefigurative politics and attempted to materialize their ideals about civic life in the occupied areas (Pang 2020), while protest actions extended to other city spaces and cyberspace (Lee & Chan, 2018; Wang et al., 2019). The protest called for "genuine universal suffrage." The state, however, did not make any meaningful concession. It adopted a strategy of attrition (Yuen & Cheng, 2017) and utilized the counterframes of the rule of law, public nuisance, and foreign intervention to undermine the legitimacy of the movement (Hargreaves, 2015; Lee & Chan, 2018). The occupation ended after seventy-nine days. It was the largest and longest-lasting civil disobedience campaign in Hong Kong.

Five years later, an even bigger and longer-lasting protest movement occurred. Beginning as an opposition to the Hong Kong government's attempt to amend the Fugitive Ordinance, which would have allowed the government to extradite suspected criminals to Taiwan and mainland China, the protest evolved into an antiauthoritarian uprising calling for not only the retraction of the bill but also investigation into police abuse of power and democratization (Lee, Yuen et al., 2019). Instead of occupying public space, protest tactics diversified (e.g., Chan & Pun, 2020; Lee & Fong,

2023; Li & Whitworth, 2023a). The movement was also marked by a trend of radicalization. Protesters' use of force escalated from throwing bricks to throwing Molotov cocktails. The government shelved the amendment bill, but it did not make any further concessions. Collective actions died down after the COVID-19 outbreak in early 2020 and the establishment of the National Security Law in June of the same year.

The Anti-Extradition Law Amendment Bill (Anti-ELAB) Movement was sometimes referred to as Umbrella Movement 2.0 (V. Chow, 2019). There are certainly similarities between the two movements: both were large scale, lasted for a significant period of time, had democratization as their core demand, and had (to different extents) several core features of contemporary networked social movements, such as being decentralized, horizontal, and digitally enabled (Castells, 2012; Cheng & Lee, 2023).

However, there are also significant differences between the two peaks of mobilization. For this book, three differences can be pointed out at the beginning. First, the two movements enjoyed rather different levels of public support. Hundreds of thousands of people participated in the Umbrella Movement, but among the general public, there was never a clear majority supporting the occupation. An opinion poll in October 2014 conducted by the Center for Communication and Public Opinion Survey (CCPOS) at the Chinese University of Hong Kong showed that the percentages of people supporting and opposing the occupation stood at 37.8 percent and 35.5 percent respectively (Lee & Chan, 2018: 151). This was the only public opinion survey during the entire movement period registering more supporting citizens than opposing citizens. In contrast, a series of surveys conducted by CCPOS in the second half of 2019 showed that, throughout the period, supporters of the Anti-ELAB Movement vastly outnumbered opponents. In November 2019, for example, the percentages of Hong Kong citizens supporting and opposing the Anti-ELAB Movement stood at 62.3 percent and 18.0 percent, respectively (CCPOS, 2020: 82).

Second, related to the first point, the Hong Kong public exhibited a high degree of tolerance toward radical tactics during the Anti-ELAB Movement. Historically, Hong Kong's public culture had long been dominated by an order imagery (Ku, 2007). Although the trend of movement radicalization had already started in the 2000s (Cheng, 2014), radicalization progressed slowly. The Umbrella Movement itself can be considered as a case of radicalization with self-restraint (Lee and Chan, 2018: 50–74). It was a civil disobedience campaign coupled with principled nonviolence. Even with such self-restraint, the Umbrella Movement was considered by many citizens as too disruptive. During the Anti-ELAB Movement, in contrast, the public exhibited high levels of sympathy, if not necessarily support, toward radical actions. CCPOS's survey in September 2019 showed that 55.7 percent of the respondents agreed with the statement "when large-scale peaceful protests fail to make the government respond, it is understandable for protesters to carry out radical actions." In November, the percentage stood at 68.4 percent (CCPOS, 2020: 88).

Third, the Umbrella Movement was marked by significant internal conflicts and tension. The main organizers and the moderate democrats were mainly stationed in the Admiralty occupied site, whereas the Mong-kok occupied area was dominated by the more militant "localists" (Yuen, 2019). The localists' adversarial framing against the democrats and the student leaders (Law, 2019), and the distrust between the two factions in general, hampered the movement's ability of making coherent and effective strategic decisions (A. Chow, 2019). The Anti-ELAB Movement, in contrast, was marked by a high degree of solidarity between the moderates and the militant protesters (Lee, 2020). Solidarity can have its limits and problems: internal tensions and conflicts became more conspicuous as time went on; an overemphasis on solidarity could undermine the movement's ability to control the process and degree of radicalization (Lai & Sing, 2020); solidarity could be hegemonic and suppressive toward internal dissent (P. S. Y. Ho, 2020); and so on. Nonetheless, even these critical reflections were premised on the presence of a high degree of solidarity in the Anti-ELAB Movement that was nonexistent in the Umbrella Movement.

There are various ways to explain the above differences between the two movements. For example, the repertoires of contention adopted by the two movements could have influenced public support. The continual occupation of public roads in the Umbrella Movement had indeed caused significant degrees of inconvenience to people living close to the occupied sites, whereas the more spatially and temporally dispersed actions in the Anti-ELAB Movement might have helped limit public backlash. Besides, there was a strong majority opinion against the amendment bill in the first place, while the same level of public support behind the original demand of the Umbrella Movement did not exist.[1] Put generally, one might treat the two movements as comparable cases and try to identify the factors that might account for their differences.

However, this book does not adopt the comparative approach. After all, the Umbrella Movement and the Anti-ELAB Movement were two "moments" belonging to the same, more broadly defined prodemocracy movement in Hong Kong. The two occurred in a temporal sequence, with one happening five years after the other. When treated as two moments of the same movement, the question becomes: How did the prodemocracy movement in Hong Kong evolve between 2014 and 2019 so that the second outburst of social mobilization took up its characteristics?

This framing of the overarching question motivating this book shall bring us to the question of movement continuity, which will be discussed in the next section. Here, once we look beyond the peaks of mobilization, another difference between the Umbrella Movement and the Anti-ELAB protests should be highlighted: the Umbrella Movement was preceded by years of high-profile protests, whereas the Anti-ELAB Movement was preceded by a period of low levels of social mobilization.

To be specific, in the years immediately before the Umbrella Movement, Hong Kong had experienced the Anti-Express Railway protests in late 2009 and early 2010, as thousands of protesters surrounded the Legislative Council (LegCo) Building to protest against the government's plan to build a railway linking Hong Kong to the express rail system in mainland China (Yung & Chan, 2011).[2] In 2012, the Anti-National Education campaign was formed (Wang, 2017). A summer of mobilization against the government's plan to turn national education into a required subject for high school students culminated in a protest in front of the government headquarters, participated in by 120,000 citizens (according to the organizers). In October 2013, the Hong Kong government refused to offer a new free television broadcasting license to the company HKTV. Tens of thousands of citizens congregated in front of the government headquarters to protest against the decision.

In contrast, social mobilization was largely subdued in 2017 and 2018. It was not because of the absence of controversial political decisions or policies. In late 2016 and 2017, six legislators were disqualified and expelled from the LegCo by the Hong Kong court, following a verdict based on the National People's Congress's interpretation of the Basic Law. In the same year, the Hong Kong government proposed a colocation arrangement at the Hong Kong terminus of the express rail. The arrangement would allow the application of mainland Chinese laws in an area inside the terminus. Critiques argued that it would create the precedent of the transfer of territorial jurisdiction to mainland China. In 2018, the Hong Kong government announced the Lantau Tomorrow Vision, an ambitious development project involving the reclamation of seventeen hundred hectares of land and an estimated cost of over HKD600 billion (around USD80 billion). Critiques questioned the cost of the project, pointed out the environmental impact, and opposed the "economic development at all costs" mindset underlying the policy. Nonetheless, despite the presence of fervent public criticisms, protest rallies or marches associated with such controversies were participated in by at most only a few thousand people.

Opinion surveys captured the sense of inefficacy: On a five-point Likert scale, Hong Kong citizens' agreement with the statement "Hong Kong people's collective action can improve the society" dropped substantially from around 3.2 in March 2014 to lower than 2.8 in January 2018; agreement with the statement "Hong Kong people's collective action can have huge influence on public affairs" dropped from around 3.5 to slightly above 3.0 in the same time period (Lee, 2018b). This sense of powerlessness was reflected in the writings of commentators. Cultural critic Ah-Guo (2019) titled his book *Hong Kong's Loss of Voice*. The book started with an in-depth report on ordinary citizens' news avoidance. When the government proposed the amendment to the Fugitive Ordinance in early 2019, large-scale protests did not arise immediately. In the months before the outburst, commentators sometimes wrote about why young people were *uninterested* (e.g., W. L. Wong, 2019).

Given the scenario described above, how can we understand the linkage between the Umbrella Movement and the Anti-ELAB protests? How can we make sense of the fact that prodemocracy protests in Hong Kong had seemingly undergone a period of demobilization yet reemerged in the second half of 2019 with a transformed tactical repertoire, a higher level of sustained public support, and a stronger sense of solidarity?

By tackling such questions, this book aims at contributing both to Hong Kong and China studies as well as to social movement studies and political sociology in general. For Hong Kong and China studies, much has been written about each of the two peaks of mobilization in 2014 and 2019, but there has been a bias toward the "moments of madness" (Liu, 2017) in the literature. Certainly, when analyzing the Umbrella Movement or the Anti-ELAB protests, scholars would typically contextualize the events and comment on the possible consequences of the protests, but only a few scholars have tried to offer more elaborate accounts of how the two peaks of mobilization can be understood in relation to each other. Ming-sho Ho (2020) discussed what activists in the Anti-ELAB Movement had learned from the Umbrella Movement, and Cheng and Yuen (2024) posited that the events and happenings between 2014 and 2019 had led to threat alignment among various activist groups, which explained the increased level of cohesiveness of the Anti-ELAB Movement. Nonetheless, such analysis remains rare, and at the end of this book, I will explicate how my analysis contributes substantially to current knowledge on the topic.

Beyond the local context, this book engages in dialogues with research on several interrelated theoretical issues in the study of social movements. One fundamental issue is how to understand movement continuity, or the linkage between peaks of social mobilization. As will be explicated below, this book takes up the concept of movement abeyance but examines it through articulating it with the relational perspective in social movement studies and the notion of critical events. Summarized into an overall statement, this book attempts to offer a case study of *how the relational dynamics among key political actors during a period of movement abeyance, together with the occurrence of distinctive event clusters, not only facilitated movement continuity but also contributed to movement transformation.*

The following parts of the chapter thus discuss the concept of abeyance, the relational approach, and the role of events in movement evolution. The discussions will provide the general conceptual guideposts and a broad analytical framework. Afterwards, the notion of localism in Hong Kong, a key aspect of the movement dynamics to be examined in this book, will be discussed. The introduction will end with a chapter outline and some notes about data.

Theoretical Building Blocks

Movement Abeyance

Social movements tend to capture the most public attention at their peaks of mobilization marked by large-scale mass participation and dramatic performances. In between the peaks or distinctive waves of mobilization, movements might not be conspicuous, but that does not mean that movements just "die." Taylor's (1989) seminal analysis of abeyance highlights how social movements may survive periods when the social and political environment is unfavorable or even hostile toward mobilization. The crux to survival, according to Taylor, is the formation of abeyance structures through which activists can maintain their goals, identities, and networks. Writing at a time when resource mobilization theory (McCarthy & Zald, 1977) was a dominant perspective in social movement research, her analysis centered on the significance of social movement organizations. Surviving movement organizations, in the case she examined, are typically marked by longevity of the participation by the core activists, strong commitment to the movement's values and ideals, the tendency to turn inward and become more exclusive in terms of membership, centralized leadership for providing organizational stability, and alternative cultural frameworks for providing security and meanings so that activists' commitment can be sustained.

Numerous subsequent studies about movement abeyance similarly centered on the role of core social movement organizations (Drago, 2021; Gade, 2019; Holland & Cable, 2002; Valiente, 2015), but they also pointed toward important variations in the characteristics of surviving movement organizations under different social and political contexts. For instance, Holland and Cable (2002) noted that not all five factors identified by Taylor (1989) are equally important in explaining the abeyance process of grassroots organizations. Valiente (2015) discussed movement abeyance in authoritarian states. She noted that, in autocracies, movement organizations and activists from the previous wave of mobilization are likely to have been repressed. Hence newly formed organizations are crucial for the construction and maintenance of abeyance structures. Besides, social movement organizations in democracies typically narrow down their range of goals in times of abeyance due to reduced levels of available energies and resources. But in nondemocracies, Valiente (2015) argued, groups and organizations during abeyance are unlikely to focus on single goals as they have the incentive to tie their issues to the broader pursuit of regime change.

Beyond social movement organizations, other scholars have noted how movement abeyance can be facilitated or achieved by processes and mechanisms in other social and cultural arenas, including the formation of safe spaces and the activities by decentralized actors (Cassegard, 2023), the organization of flash mob actions (Gyimesi, 2021), intergenerational transmission of ideologies inside families (Veugelers, 2015), the establishment of activist media (Newth, 2022), or simply everyday life in general (Yates, 2015). In Hong Kong, Lee, Chan, and Chen (2021) noted the role social media can play in movement abeyance. Once young people get connected with activists, politicians, and political groups via social media platforms, the connections are unlikely to disappear after the peak of mobilization. The weak ties maintained through such networks can continue to serve as information channels. Their analysis of survey data obtained in early 2019, months before the outburst of the Anti-ELAB protests, shows that university students who used social media to larger extents held more positive evaluations of the Umbrella Movement, and both social media use and evaluations of the Umbrella Movement positively related to protest potential.

This book does not tackle something as broad as "everyday life politics." The focus will be on a series of networked actors in the abeyance process. In fact, the typical formation of movement campaigns has changed significantly in the past decades with changes in political culture and the rise of digital technologies. Many contemporary protest movements were characterized by decentralization, horizontalism, and apparent leaderlessness (Bennett & Segerberg, 2013; Flesher Fominaya, 2020; Tufekci, 2017). Conventional movement organizations are still part of these movements, but they are mixed with new types of informal groups, bottom-up coordination by ordinary citizens, and influential individual actors (Cheng & Lee, 2023). Moving beyond the peak of mobilization, the array of informal groups formed during or immediately after the peak of mobilization, as well as individual public figures or networked microcelebrities (Tufekci, 2013), could play important roles in the abeyance process. What sustains movement abeyance can be a networked abeyance structure.

In addition to what constitutes the abeyance structures, another question to consider is what actors can achieve during the abeyance period. Early analysis of movement abeyance focuses on sustainability and survival (Bagguley, 2002; Taylor, 1989; Sawyer & Meyers, 1999); that is, the abeyance structures are important for the task of preserving the goals, identities, and networks of a movement. In fact, this is also what Hong Kong scholars tended to focus on when they evoked the idea of movement abeyance. For example, researchers have noted that, after the Umbrella Movement, there was the formation of a range of professional associations (Lam, 2018; Ma & Cheng, 2023), community associations (Chung, 2021), and self-proclaimed localist groups (Kaeding, 2016). Many of them would play significant roles in the Anti-ELAB Movement in 2019 (Cheng & Yuen, 2024). This is a classic argument about how the earlier peak of mobilization contributed to the formation of new mobilizing structures, which become part of the basis for subsequent mobilization.

However, other scholars have pointed out that movement actors sometimes have to do more than merely preserve resources and identities. Surviving the period of low levels of mobilization could require movements to reconsider their framing of the issue at hand. There could be a need to develop "retention frames" to retain the commitment of the core activists (Marullo, Pagnucco & Smmith, 1996; Mooney & Hunt, 1996). Geha (2019) highlighted the need for activists to rethink their strategies and tactics. Jacobsson and Sorborn (2008) argued that, after facing a period of demobilization, frustration could arise. Therefore, movements in abeyance need to find ways to rebuild collective agency. Similarly, Zihnnioglu (2023) argued that, if a movement is to prepare for the next wave of mobilization, merely keeping the core activists is inadequate. There is a need to maintain "activist capital" among the public.

Such studies not only enrich our understanding of the array of goals and tasks for activists during abeyance; they also point toward the fact that abeyance is about both continuity and transformation. As strategies are reconsidered and frames are altered, it would not be surprising for the next wave of mobilization to take up new characteristics and espouse somewhat different ideas and ideologies. Movement abeyance can be both generative and preservatory.

What changes occur during the period of abeyance should not be determined solely by what happens inside the movement. Here, one limitation of the literature of movement abeyance is its typical assumption of noninteraction between the movement and the environment during abeyance. Taylor's (1989) original analysis argued that movements tend to turn inward when the environment is hostile. Sawyers and Meyers (1999) argued that withdrawing from mobilization is not necessarily advisable for movement groups during abeyance. There could be opportunities in specific policy arena even when the environment is generally unfavorable. Withdrawal from mobilization could therefore result in missing the opportunities. Sawyers and Meyers's (1999) analysis, nonetheless, does contain the same assumption about the withdrawal of social movements from attempts to mobilize the public and influence the government during abeyance.

Nevertheless, in reality, movement actors do not necessarily stop or minimize their interactions with the state and the public even in a hostile environment. Reconsideration of strategies and tactics may lead them to take other forms of actions and interact with political institutions in alternative ways, such as through participating in elections or taking their challenges to the court. Without issuing calls for mass protests, movement actors may continue to communicate with their supporters and the public by speaking to and through the media. As Sawyers and Meyers (1999) noted, studies of movement abeyance can be rather equivocal on whether movement behavior during periods of low levels of mobilization is merely the consequence of a hostile environment, or if it is ultimately a matter of choice by movement actors. Movement actors can certainly exercise their agency and opt to continue interacting with the public and the state in various ways. This book thus sees abeyance as a period in which movement actors could still be interacting with other actors in a relational field. This takes us to the relational approach in analyzing movement evolution.

The Relational Approach

The relational approach to social movement analysis emphasizes the dynamic and contingent evolution of social movement phenomena through the complex interactions among a range of actors in a relational field (della Porta, 2014, 2018). Compared to earlier theories in social movement research such as the political process model, the relational approach emphasizes the importance not to treat other actors merely as static "context" variables (Bosi, 2008). The state, for instance, is not a static political opportunity structure. Its strategies and reactions to social movements—for example, concession, repression, attrition, cooptation, and so on—influence the choices of movement actors. Similarly, the public is not a group of bystanders who have a fixed favorable or unfavorable attitude toward protests. Movement actors and the state can appeal to public support continually. Public approval or disapproval could be expressed through elections, participation in protests and counterprotests, opinion polls, and news media representations. Depending on the public's reactions, both activists and the state may need to adjust their frames and strategies.

To engage in a relational analysis, therefore, requires one to identify the core actors involved in a study and attempt to reconstruct their interactional dynamics so as to produce a causal narrative capable of explaining specific outcomes. To give a couple of more recent examples in the East Asia region, M. S. Ho (2023) analyzed the rise of the pronuclear movement in Taiwan in the 2010s by referring to how the state, the antinuclear movement, the pronuclear movement, and the environmental movement at large interacted with each other. The success of the pronuclear movement was explained in terms of its ability to take advantage of the antinuclear movement's withdrawal from street politics and the internal fragmentation of the environmental movement in Taiwan. Thompson and Cheng (2023) examined antigovernment protests in Hong Kong and Thailand in 2019 and 2020. They argued that the antigovernment pushbacks can be understood as the result of how protest movements responded to evolving public sentiments and, especially in Thailand, the state's infiltration into civil society.

In an attempt to construct a more systematic and generalizable framework for relational analysis, Alimi and colleagues (2012) argued that movement dynamics can be analyzed by distinguishing among four arenas of interactions: (1) interaction between the movement and the state (including its various agents such as the police), (2) interaction between the movement and the broader social environment, (3) interaction between the movement and its countermovements, and (4) interaction within the movement itself, such as the interaction between the moderate and radical flanks. The four arenas are related to each other. Interactions in one arena can influence the interactions in the others. Lee, Yuen, and colleagues (2022) have employed the framework to examine the relational dynamics behind radicalization in the Anti-ELAB Movement in Hong Kong.

This book largely follows this framework, though it focuses primarily on three instead of four arenas of interaction: (1) the interaction between the state and the prodemocracy movement, (2) the interaction between the prodemocracy movement and public opinion, and (3) the interaction between the moderate and radical flanks of the prodemocracy movement. The interaction between movement and countermovements is not singled out due to two interrelated considerations. First, in the Hong Kong context, one might question whether there has been an independent countermovement against the prodemocracy movement. Countermobilization was actively promoted by the state as part of its "united front" strategies, and the countermovement groups were typically sponsored by the state in various ways (Chan & Junker, 2021; Cheng, 2020; Yuen & Cheng, 2020). One might therefore see movement-countermovement interactions as part of movement-state interactions. Second, to the extent that the countermovement was mobilized by the state in response to prominent mobilization by the prodemocracy movement, direct interactions between the prodemocracy movement and its countermovement would be less prominent in the period of movement abeyance. The need for countermobilization is weak when level of prodemocracy mobilization is low.

Following the above paragraph, at least four major actors are identified: the state, the movement's moderate camp, the movement's radical camp, and the public. It is worth noting at this point that throughout this book, the terms *radical* and *radicalization* do not carry normative assumptions about the justifiability of specific groups, actions, or discourses. Being radical means deviating from the prevailing social norms to larger extents or demanding more fundamental social and political changes (Beck, 2015). What is seen as radical is therefore also context specific (Acconero, 2013).

None of the four actors identified above is unitary. The public obviously is composed of individuals with different political orientations. The moderate and the radical camps of a movement are composed of groups and activists. There can be subtle but significant differences among actors presumably belonging to the same camp. Actors who are otherwise in the same camp may prefer different strategies when interacting with others. Such internal heterogeneities of the actors are particularly important given our emphasis on the role of networked actors in movement dynamics. Even the state is, theoretically speaking, composed of various institutions or subunits. There can be "hawkish" and "dovish" actors within the state who relate to the prodemocracy movement somewhat differently.

The above consideration also implies that the boundaries separating the actors can be porous and malleable. The significance of some activists or groups may be better understood when they are treated as located between two groups of actors, instead of belonging to either one. For the present book, when analyzing the relationship between the moderate and radical camps of the prodemocracy movement, I will pay particular attention to a group of ideological brokers who negotiated the relationship between the two camps.

In social movement studies, there is a body of literature on the radical flank effect (Haines, 1984; McCammon et al., 2015; Schifeling & Hoffman, 2019). The emergence of the radical flank can have positive and negative consequences on the movement that it belongs to. On the negative side, it might cost the movement its public support if citizens reject the use of violence or other radical means. On the positive side, the radical flank may force the state to consider its approach and try to work with the moderate flank in order to marginalize the radical groups. From a relational perspective, whether the positive or negative radical flank effects prevail would depend on the strategies adopted by the actors. Put in simplified terms, the state's basic options are (1) to coopt the moderate groups and divide and rule or (2) to reject the movement holistically as the latter radicalizes. For the moderate and radical flanks of the movement, the question is whether they should attempt to reconcile with each other and build alignment, or they should try to maintain a boundary between them and differentiate from each other. At the same time, the state, the moderate groups, and the radical groups would need to respond to their supporters and the public.

Nevertheless, as already noted, neither the moderate nor radical flank of a movement is a coherent and undifferentiated entity. There could be actors belonging to the moderate camp who might prefer a more conciliatory stance toward the state and distance themselves from the radicals, and there could be actors who prefer to reconcile and align with the radical groups in order to build a stronger opposition force. Similarly, different actors within the radical camp or even different actors within the state might have different preferences. Between any two actors, which type of interactions or relationships prevail could depend on how each of the two actors relate to the other actors in the relational field. For instance, for the moderate groups, whether distancing themselves from or aligning themselves with the radicals is more appealing would depend on whether the state is willing to negotiate with them and make meaningful concessions to their demands, as well as their interpretations of how the public is responding to the rise of radicalism. Alignment and confluence between the moderate and radical flanks should be most likely when the state closes down political opportunities even for the moderate groups and when the public does not react as negatively to radicalism as one might originally suspect.

While the relational approach emphasizes ongoing interactions among actors, there could be times when the ways actors interact with each other shift abruptly and substantially. This would happen when important events occur. The notion of events is often a component in social movement analysis following the relational approach (e.g., Alimi, 2007, 2016; Sanches, 2022). Yet it is also a significant concept in itself that deserves explication.

Events and Movements

It is widely recognized that dramatic, contingent, and unpredicted events could significantly alter the trajectory of a social movement or social and historical development in general. Social historian William Sewell (1996, 2005) argued that historical change was seldom incremental, and "historical temporality is lumpy, uneven, unpredictable, and discontinuous" (Sewell, 2005: 9). Transformative events can alter structures fundamentally, leading to new trajectories of development. In social movement studies, Staggenborg (1993) put forward the notion of "redefining critical events" as contextually dramatic happenings that lead to significant shifts in public and elite perceptions of reality. As perceptions shift, actors adjust their strategies and interactions with others, thus setting new relational dynamics in place.

This is why events often feature prominently in relational analysis of social movements. The significance of events has been embedded in studies of many different kinds of movements. Scholars on transnational mobilization have noted the significance of events in creating people's diasporic imagination (Koinova, 2018; Sokefeld, 2006). Nuclear disasters such as the incidents in Chernobyl, Three Mile Island, and Fukushima created suddenly imposed grievances among people and provided impetus to the antinuclear movement in various countries (Bernardi et al., 2018; M. S. Ho, 2023; Walsh, 1988). Other scholars have examined the significance of critical events in the trajectories of the women's movement (Kay & Ramos, 2017), antiracism protests (Espeland & Rogstad, 2013), aboriginal mobilization (Ramos, 2008), and others.

The critical events identified by scholars in specific studies vary in terms of whether they are external or internal to social movements and the kind of changes they initiate. Some studies examined how social and political events generate movement mobilization or significantly alter movement interactions (Espeland & Rogstad, 2013; Meyer & Staggerborg, 1996). Some examined how a significant event within a protest campaign alters the course of the campaign. This is the sense in which Rosa Parks's action and the ensuing Montgomery bus buycott was often considered a critical event in the American civil rights movement. By the same token, state repression is sometimes treated as an event creating new protest dynamics (Grimm & Harder, 2018; Hess & Martin, 2006; Shultziner, 2018). Some studies treated large-scale protests themselves as events that alter the course of political development. Uncu (2016) treated the 2013 Gezi protests in Turkey as a critical event in this sense. Writing before the Anti-ELAB Movement, Chingkwan Lee (2019) pinpointed the 1967 riots, the 1989 protests in support for the Beijing Student Movement, the 2003 July 1 protest, and the Umbrella Movement as four transformative events in an eventful history of Hong Kong's political change.

There is no definitive method to ascertain which event should be seen as important enough to be singled out as "critical." The notion of an event can be considered a sensitizing concept that one can utilize to construct meaningful accounts of movement trajectories. Nonetheless, there are several theoretical principles in the analysis of events. The first is the significance of interpretations. As McAdam and Sewell put it: "[transformative events] *come to be interpreted as* significantly disrupting, altering, or violating taken-for-granted assumptions governing routine political and social relations. In so doing, they serve to dramatically rachet up (or down in the case of demobilizing events—for example, the Tiananmen Square massacre) the shared sense of uncertainty (with its partisan variants, 'threat' and 'opportunity') on which all broad episodes of contention depend" (2001: 110, emphasis added).

The significance of interpretation implies the possibility of contestation, as different parties could try to offer competing interpretations serving varying interests. Hess and Martin (2006), for example, discussed how authorities typically try to manage public discourses after repression events to prevent backfire. Authorities may try to cover up the repression, blame the target of repression, reinterpret the event, produce authoritative assessments of the event, and intimidate participants and witnesses. Movement activists, in response, need to counter these strategies through communicating information to the public, humanizing the protesters, producing persuasive accounts by credible witnesses, and exposing biases in formal inquiries. Whether backfire occurs is the result of "a credibility battle over whose version of the facts of the repressive event and whose legitimating/delegitimating frame is correct" (p. 264). Vicari (2015) showed a similar process of "outrage management" by political authorities after the violent protest events during the 2001 Anti-G8 Summit in Genoa.

Second, while the occurrence of events is contingent, postevent interpretations are also contingent upon available opportunities and the happening of other events. As della Porta (2020) explicated, after the occurrence of major protest events that shock and expose the cracks of the society, there would be a period of vibration. New norms and identities can emerge, and chance encounters can play a role in shaping the outcome. For a concrete example, as Lee and Chan's (2011) study of the 2003 July 1 protest in Hong Kong showed, after the half-a-million-strong protest forced the Hong Kong government to shelf the national security legislation, the Hong Kong society seemingly "returned to normal." However, the District Council elections held in November of that year allowed another expression of public opinion. As the democrats won a major victory, commentators interpreted the electoral results as a manifestation of the "July 1 effect." In other words, the presence of an election only a few months after the protest offered an institutionalized opportunity for public opinion to be expressed, and the expressed public opinion was interpreted in a way so that the significance of the July 1 protest was confirmed.

Third, as Bosi and Davis (2017) argued, saying that events are contingent does not mean that events are "spontaneous or random flukes of history." "On the contrary, [many important] events would never have happened if it had not been for the sustained, concerted and determined action of the people behind them" (p. 224). Emphasizing the causes and agency behind critical events is important to prevent the concept from becoming a magical wand thrown out to explain social change arbitrarily. One way to understand agency in critical events is to understand the extent to which and the ways in which people may have been preparing themselves for the contingencies. There is a difference between planning for something and preparing for something. A person taking first aid materials with her on a hiking trip is not planning to get hurt; she is getting herself prepared for the contingency. Yet such preparation significantly shapes what would happen if the contingency does arise. In the 2014 Sunflower Movement in Taiwan, Ho (2018) noted that, while street protesters had to improvise when the protest leaders were trapped inside the Legislative Yuan, the improvisation was led mainly by the more experienced activists. Protest experience allowed those activists to respond to the situation effectively.

Given the above considerations, this book pays particular attention to how an important protest event is associated with other subsequent happenings and incidents to form an event cluster, which shapes its significance and consequences. Here, an event cluster can be defined as the occurring of several social and political events in close temporal proximity so that the significance of the original event is crystalized through the happening of the other events. More specifically, similar to Lee and Chan (2011), the "clustering" of major protests and subsequent elections constitutes an important part of the analysis in this book. The 2015 District Council election was an occasion in which the significance of the Umbrella Movement was contested and constructed. The District Council election in November 2019 played a highly important role in consolidating people's understanding of where the public stood in relation to the Anti-ELAB Movement. In addition, this book sees the 2016 Mongkok civil unrest as another important protest event that happened between the Umbrella Movement and the Anti-ELAB protests. Yet the significance of the Mongkok civil unrest cannot be properly understood without examining the subsequent LegCo by-election, which happened merely three weeks after the protest. Analysis of the Mongkok civil unrest would also illustrate the argument that an unpredicted protest event could be related to activists' preparation, though not planning.

A VERY BRIEF SUMMARY

In sum, the analysis in this book addresses a process of movement abeyance. But instead of focusing on inward-looking movement organizations as the mainstay of abeyance structures, the emphasis will be placed on the presence of an array of actors and the continual interactions among them. Following a relational approach, the analysis will pay particular attention to the interaction between the state and the prodemocracy movement, between the moderate and radical flanks of the movement, and between the prodemocracy movement and the general public. Yet the main actors are not treated as singular entities. Within the moderate and radical camps of the movement, in particular, there can be actors favoring different strategies, trying to align with other actors in different ways. There could also be actors playing the role of brokers between the two camps, instead of simply belonging to either side. Finally, both the Umbrella Movement and the 2016 Mongkok civil unrest are highlighted as significant protest events that influenced subsequent interactions among the actors. However, they are not treated as "stand-alone events." Instead, the protest events and the subsequent elections are treated as forming event clusters, with the elections being crucial in shaping how actors evaluate the significance of the earlier protests.

As such, the analysis is not based merely on a straightforward application of the existing concepts of abeyance, relational dynamics in multiple arenas, and critical events onto the case of Hong Kong between 2014 and 2019. The analysis also aims to make general theoretical contributions through emphasizing the possibly generative character of the abeyance process, the role of ideological brokers in shaping movement interactions, and the notion of event clusters in understanding how critical events matter.

Understanding Localism in Hong Kong

Since one of the major differences between the Umbrella Movement and the Anti-ELAB Movement is the latter's higher level of radicalism, and a core aspect of the analysis is the rise of the radical flank of Hong Kong's prodemocracy movement, the emergence of localism in Hong Kong in the 2010s is an important part of the book's account. Hence it would be useful to provide relevant background and clarify this book's approach to the phenomenon of localism.

Conventional analysis of Hong Kong after World War Two would note that the city developed as a refugee society with population growth spurred by the political chaos in mainland China. The refugees lacked affective attachment to the place (Hughes, 1968). A distinctive local identity emerged mainly in the 1970s, supported by the economic takeoff, the growing up of the second generation of the postwar refugees, and the growth of local popular culture (Tsang, 2003). Nevertheless, the early development of Hong Kong people's local consciousness was intricately articulated with their Chinese identity. For Law (2018), youngsters in the 1970s had no obvious ideological basis for them to develop their perspectives on the pressing issues arising from colonial reality. They thus resorted to Chinese interest and identity as the bases of their claims.

However, continual social and economic development of Hong Kong strengthened Hong Kong people's sense of superiority over their mainland "relatives." Hong Kong popular culture started to portray mainland Chinese as the other, either as threats to social order or as ignorant rural residents overwhelmed by capitalist modernity (Ma, 1999). Meanwhile, the 1989 Beijing student movement deepened the distrust of Hong Kong people toward the Communist Party (Lee & Chan, 2021). But on the eve of the handover, Mathews (1997) still noted that Hong Kong people tended to see themselves as "Chinese plus something." The "something" can refer to material affluence, support for democracy, or higher levels of civility. In other words, the Hong Kong identity at the time still did not involve a rejection of Chineseness. In surveys, when people were asked to rate their identification with Hong Kong and China separately, the two were positively correlated (Steinhardt et al., 2018).

The relationship between Hong Kong and China took a significant turn in 2003, when five hundred thousand citizens protested against national security legislation and government incompetence in general. The outburst of social energies would sediment into various forms in subsequent years, including the rise of the New Preservation Movement (Ku, 2012) and the group of progressive localists behind it (Chen & Szeto, 2015). The progressive localists espoused leftist liberalism and antidevelopmentalism. They saw democracy as involving not only the direct elections of government leaders, but also grassroots participation in policymaking (Law, 2019). They appealed to young people's turn to postmaterial values and quest for local identity (Lee, 2018c; Ma, 2011; Wong & Wan, 2009). Nonetheless, the local identity forged by the progressive localists still did not involve antagonism against China as its core component.

Meanwhile, after the 2003 July 1 protest, the Chinese government became more proactive in building its united front in the city and promoting Hong Kong citizens' national identification. It attempted to help Hong Kong to resolve its economic crisis through policies such as the Individual Visitors Scheme, which opened the floodgate for Chinese tourists, and the Closer Economic Partnership Agreement between Hong Kong and the Guangdong Province. While such policies brought some benefits to the local economy, negative impact on social life emerged and became more serious by the end of the 2000s. Conflicts between local citizens and mainlanders arose on both resource distribution issues (e.g., availability of hospital services and milk powder) and symbolic and cultural matters (e.g., shopkeepers' differential treatment of Hongkongers and mainland tourists) (Lam, 2020; So & Ip, 2019). Public discontent was expressed through various kinds of protests (Chan & Chan, 2017).

In more theoretical language, Lee (2019) argued that, by the 2010s, Hong Kong people were reacting against the trends of dedemocratization in the political realm, colonization of the lifeworld in the social realm, and subsumption in the economic realm. Fong (2017) contended that China had been acting as a centralizing state adopting a range of incorporation strategies toward the city. Commentators started using the term "mainlandization" to describe the threat facing Hong Kong (Kong, 2017). Ferments of a new kind of localism arose. Chen and Szeto (2015) called it the anti-China path to localism. Law (2019) described them as radical right-wing localists who espoused radicalism, populism, and ethnic struggles against mainlandization. By the early 2010s, in Hong Kong's public discourse, the term *localist* would mainly refer to this new range of actors. In addition to criticizing China, the right-wing localists also engaged in adversarial framing against the democrats and the progressive activists, seeing the latter as being ineffective, too moderate, or even the willing accomplice of China's control over Hong Kong (Law, 2019; Ortmann, 2020). The distrust between the localists and the democrats sowed the seeds for the lack of effective leadership in the Umbrella Movement.

People who found the new localism appealing tended to be highly frustrated by how the Umbrella Movement ended. The aftermath of the Umbrella Movement thus witnessed the formation of new localist groups headed by young people with little political experience, most notably Youngspiration and the Hong Kong Indigenous (HKI). Localism became not only a sentiment or loosely organized discourse shared by a group of citizens but also a (weakly) institutionalized political force encompassing an identifiable set of political groups, activists, and prominent public figures who self-proclaimed to be localists. The challenge posed by localism to both the state and the democrats thus intensified (e.g., Lee & Chan, 2021: 210–16).

The rise of localism as an increasingly pervasive sentiment and a political force spurred a range of academic writings (e.g., Kaeding, 2017; Kwong, 2016; Ip, 2020; Lo, 2019; Yuen & Chung, 2018; Veg, 2017). Some of these writings focus on the "right-wing localists" and explicate how they differ from other parts of the prodemocracy movement. Notably, some of these authors were aligned with progressive localism and expressed a critical attitude toward the right-wing localists. Ip (2020), for instance, criticized what he called the nativists for putting forward "remote visions or indeterminate futures without any concrete plan" (p. 67).

While such analyses capture certain aspects of the kind of localism arising at the time, attempts to outline the frames offered by the "right-wing localists" as a group may create a misleading image of the presence of a coherent entity. As Ip (2020: 76) also presciently put it: "[The surge of nativism] creates a sort of political activism characterized by 'atomisation' of movements participated by individual activists, small associations and even ad hoc working groups. What holds them together is often a set of symbols. A bunch of commentators, primarily active on the Internet, further whip up fear, justify the nativists' actions, define the field of possibilities." The array of networked actors may not share the same framing of their struggles. Highlighting the most toxic aspects of right-wing localism, such as its ethnocentrism, xenophobia, and inclination toward violence, is unlikely to shed light on how localism attracted the support from a larger and larger proportion of citizens over the years.

The appeal of localism might be more intuitively explained by the point that, if the term is defined broadly to refer to the prioritization of the interests of the local society when they come into conflict with the interests of the nation (or the global society), then "local people" would be prone to support localism. Hong Kong has been governed under the framework of "one country, two systems" since the transfer of sovereignty. The formulation of one country, two systems itself presumes the presence of certain local institutions and culture that need to be preserved (Lui, 2020). The conflict between the proregime politicians and the democrats can be understood in terms of whether "one country" or "two systems" is emphasized. In addition to striving for democratization, the prodemocracy movement has been working to defend Hong Kong's autonomy and existing civil liberties (Lui, 2003; Ma, 2005). As Hui and Lau (2015: 352) put it when discussing the Umbrella Movement: "Active participants of the [movement] are more or less against interventions from Beijing. In that light, all factions of the democratic movement in Hong Kong are localists."

Along this line of thinking, Lo (2019) identified five groups of localists: the nationalistic, the liberal, the progressive, the confrontational, and the separatist. The five groups encompass the full spectrum within the prodemocracy movement, with the first two groups referring to the "old guards," and the last two groups referring to the localists emerging in the 2010s. Lam (2018), discussing post-Umbrella Movement developments in civil society, treated localism as "a range of political positions that prioritize the welfare of the locals" (pp. 72–73). Such positions can be articulated with nativism, cosmopolitanism, and even multiculturalism. She discussed three strands of emerging localist organizations since the mid-2010s, including community-oriented groups, professional associations, and political organizations.[3] Nonetheless, many associations appearing in Lam's (2018) analysis might not label themselves localists.

Obviously, understanding localism in such broad terms can help understand the appeal of the label. It can help explain why certain members of the moderate democrats did pick up the label of localism. But when all factions in the prodemocracy movement are seen as localists, the term also becomes detached from how it functioned in actual political discourses.

In between a focus on the most radical nativists and an all-encompassing definition of localism, other authors attempted to identify the common characteristics shared by groups generally understood as localists. The study by Ng and Kennedy (2019) is illustrative. They examined media reports, documents, and interview materials related to fifteen localist groups. They found three common characteristics: regionalism, populism, and radicalism. That is, these groups emphasized the distinctive culture and identity of a subnational region vis-à-vis the nation-state; they criticized the elites as corrupted and saw politics as a struggle to express the people's will; and they were willing to call for actions that deviate from current norms and pursue goals that require fundamental changes in power structure.

Nevertheless, even Ng and Kennedy's (2019) approach has limitations. The exercise can capture the common characteristics of a set of groups within a definite period of time, but there is no guarantee that the groups would not shift or rearticulate their ideologies in important ways. In fact, their article acknowledges that, by around 2017 and 2018, certain developments "have drawn some localist groups away from certain aspects of radicalism and populism" (p. 133). In this case, should one stick to the definition of localism as radical populist regionalism and treat those groups who adjusted their ideologies as no longer belonging to the localist camp? But what if those groups continue to identify themselves as localists?

The various ways to explicate the notion of localism reviewed above were all useful for the various authors' own purposes. For this book, however, neither a narrow focus on "right-wing localism" nor an overly broad definition would be appropriate. Even attempting to identify the common core of self-proclaimed localist groups could be problematic because of this book's emphasis on the dynamic evolution of protest movements. Instead, we may understand the term as being loosely associated with a range of "initial meanings," including the distinctiveness of the Hong Kong identity, the need to prioritize Hong Kong people's interests, a willingness to consider and adopt more confrontational protest actions, and so on. Yet it is simultaneously a floating signifier, in the sense that different actors may articulate the meaning of the term somewhat differently, and what the signifier refers to can be constantly negotiated and redeveloped in association with ongoing political dynamics.

Nonetheless, treating localism as a floating signifier does not entail that any meanings can be arbitrarily assigned to it. Four considerations should be kept in mind when examining localism's multivocality. First, at any given point in time, the range of credible and plausible meanings to be attributed to a floating signifier could be bounded. If we take the metaphor of "floating" seriously, we should acknowledge that floating typically involves slow motions over a limited amount of space within a short period of time, though it carries the possibility of an object traveling a long way over a long period of time. Indeterminacy of meanings is bounded in the short run but theoretically unbounded in the long run.

Second, while different groups may attribute different meanings to a signifier, there can be forces driving the meaning of a signifier to move toward a specific direction. Actors do not attribute meanings to a label because of their whim. Keywords are articulated in specific ways because of people's convictions or strategic considerations. For example, Ho's (2022) analysis of the Facebook pages of three localist groups found a shift from ethnonationalism to civic nationalism over time. This can be understood as the groups' attempt to respond to public criticisms. Localists might rearticulate their discourses in order to appeal to the public, respond to critics, differentiate themselves from the moderate camp, or avoid state repression.

Third, not everyone has equal influence and credibility in the contestation of meanings. As recent scholarship on networked social movements pointed out, the absence of central leaders does not entail equality among all networked actors (Cheng & Lee, 2023; Liang & Lee, 2023). Leaders, defined broadly as people who exert relatively stronger influence on others, inevitably exist. Some localist figures might have become media icons and enjoyed disproportionate influence on people's perceptions of what localism is. Others might have particularly high levels of cultural capital that allow them to put forward claims convincingly. Focusing on the prominent "leaders" should remain a sensible research strategy.

Fourth, no matter what the activists said about localism, how the public understands localism is a separate issue. For instance, it was pointed out that the localists often criticized the moderate democrats' tactics as ineffective. However, analyzing a survey of university students, Tang and Chung (2018) found no evidence that self-proclaimed localist supporters would reject conventional movement activities such as peaceful rallies. While activists can selectively articulate what localism is, people can also take up the localist discourses selectively.

Many academics have highlighted how localism was only loosely defined. Yuen and Chung argued that localism is "an amalgam of ideas and action logics assembled sequentially through events and discursive constructions" (2018: 19). This book also understands localism as developing dynamically through the interactions among actors who varied in terms of convictions, influence, and strategic choices. A key argument to be ventured is that localism underwent a process of mainstreaming in Hong Kong through such interactional dynamics. That is, in the years between the Umbrella Movement and the Anti-ELAB protests, the discourse of localism was smoothened in ways that made it more acceptable to the mainstream public, while the mainstream public had also become more receptive to certain ideas espoused by the localists.

Chapter Outline and Methodological Notes

This introductory chapter has put forward the key research question to be addressed, explicated the theoretical underpinnings as well as expected contributions, and provided background discussions on localism in Hong Kong. Chapter 2 will begin the analysis with the Umbrella Movement. The chapter will first explicate the relational dynamics—both within the prodemocracy movement and between the movement and the state—that led to the occupation campaign. It then discusses the formation and dynamics of the Umbrella Movement itself, especially the division and tension between the Admiralty and the Mongkok occupied areas, which was mapped onto the democrats-localists divide. The chapter will then discuss the movement's internal conflicts toward its end and the "residual actions" carried out by some protesters after the eviction of all occupied areas. The chapter will end by examining the performance of the "Umbrella soldiers" in the 2015 District Council elections.

Continuing the discussion of post–Umbrella Movement developments, chapter 3 will begin with the rise of localist groups and new forms of militant actions, especially the HKI and the "reclamation" campaigns. The core of the chapter will offer an account of the Mongkok civil unrest, informed by Snow and Moss's (2014) theoretical explication of spontaneity in protests. Three aspects of the event will be highlighted for discussion: the question of leadership (i.e., if any organizer was "in charge"), the question of preparedness versus planning (i.e., the sense in which actors did not plan the event but were "prepared" for it), and the question of policing (i.e., how protest policing shaped the dynamics of the unrest).

Chapter 4 will begin by examining media reactions toward the Mongkok civil unrest, illustrating that the action was apparently universally condemned for its violence. Yet the event was followed by a LegCo by-election in which the leader of the HKI, Edward Leung, participated as a candidate. The chapter will examine Leung's performance and affective framing in the election. It will analyze how his electoral performance, including a "surprisingly good" result, was interpreted in media discourses. The chapter will end with an analysis of survey data obtained one month after the Mongkok civil unrest, which illustrates public ambivalence toward the event and protest violence in general.

Chapter 5 will examine the negotiation of the relationship between the localists and the democrats since 2016 and up to mid-2019. The analytical focus will center on the role of ideological brokers who, intentionally or not, served as bridges between the democrats and the localists. The chapter will examine the role of the political party Demosisto, which articulated the notion of democratic self-determination, and the works of a prominent public affairs commentator. The chapter will end with another analysis of survey data illustrating why and how the notion of democratic self-determination rhymed with the political values and orientation of the Hong Kong public.

Chapter 6 will address the interaction between the state and the pro-democracy movement between 2016 and 2019. It will illustrate how the state exercised indiscriminate repression of the moderate democrats and the localists in those years. The core of the chapter will examine electoral repression through disqualification of legislators and legal repression through court cases related to the Mongkok civil unrest and the Umbrella Movement. The chapter will end by illustrating the trend of affective depolarization between the supporters of the two camps, thus paving the way for intramovement solidarity during the Anti-ELAB protests.

Chapter 7 will discuss the Anti-ELAB Movement. Consistent with the relational approach, the developments between 2014 and 2019 were not "independent variables" influencing the movement mechanically. Rather, they provided significant input into the relational dynamics inside the Anti-ELAB

Movement. The chapter will examine several major themes, including the continual evolution of movement solidarity, the evolution of the slogan "Liberate Hong Kong, Revolution of Our Time" as a broker frame, and the extent of localist identification and proindependence sentiments among the protesters. Together, these analyses will illustrate the completion of the mainstreaming of localism during the Anti-ELAB protests.

Chapter 8 will conclude the book by comparing how the book's account is similar to and yet different from existing works that addressed the relationship between the Umbrella Movement and the Anti-ELAB Movement. It will offer summary discussions on the core theoretical themes and contributions made by the study. It will end with a brief discussion of the happenings in Hong Kong since the establishment of the new National Security Law (NSL) in 2020 and whether and how the approach adopted in this book might be applied to post-NSL Hong Kong.

The brief descriptions of the chapters hint at the range of contributions the book shall make in addition to the core theoretical themes already discussed. For example, chapter 3 will further elaborate on how critical events can be considered as contingent yet not arbitrary. Activists can get themselves "prepared" even though the occurrence of the event remains unpredicted and shocking. Chapter 4 will discuss the notion of affective framing by movement actors. It will argue that political actors may frame a situation and their actions not only by offering a rational diagnosis and prognosis but also by appealing to people's moral sentiments and affect. Chapter 5 will conceptualize the role of ideological brokers in the negotiation between factions in a social movement. Chapter 6 will explicate the notion of legal repression, and Hong Kong offers a pertinent case study of how an authoritarian state can appropriate legal procedures originating from the West (e.g., the common-law system) for the purpose of political control. Chapter 7 will extend extant analysis of the Anti-ELAB Movement, offering an analysis of the dynamic emergence of broker frames in a networked protest.

This book does not come from a single project designed to examine the topic. It is instead based on a range of data and materials obtained through different endeavors over the years. In early 2019, the author was invited to participate in a collaborative effort by a group of academics and civil society actors who wanted to reconstruct the happenings of the Mongkok civil unrest in 2016. Thirty-eight in-depth interviews with different types of participants and observers were conducted. The interview data constituted the basis for the analysis in chapter 3. As part of that project, the author also conducted analysis of media reactions to the civil unrest, as well as a qualitative analysis of the court verdicts in the riot cases associated with the event. These become the basis of parts of chapter 4 and chapter 6, respectively.

The author has, over the years, conducted research on the Umbrella Movement (Lee & Chan, 2018), the Anti-ELAB protests (e.g., Lee, Yuen, et al., 2019; Lee, Yuen, et al., 2022), and Hong Kong people's collective remembering of Tiananmen (Lee & Chan, 2021). Data from these research efforts—including protest onsite surveys, focus group discussions, media analysis, and in-depth interviews—constituted the bases for Chapter 2 and Chapter 7. Such data will also be drawn upon as supplementary materials in the other chapters when appropriate. Chapters 4 to 7 make use of a range of public opinion surveys conducted by the author or his colleagues at the CCPOS at the Chinese University of Hong Kong.

Some additional research and analysis were conducted specifically for the book, including the analysis of Edward Leung's framing efforts in the 2016 LegCo by-election (chapter 4), and an analysis of the writings by Joseph Lian, a prominent author who were closely connected with the democrats yet highly sympathetic toward localism (chapter 5). Eight in-depth interviews with key political actors were conducted to derive supplementary materials for the analysis in several chapters (chapters 2, 5, and 6).

The book, therefore, is based on research materials derived over the years using methods ranging from in-depth interviews and opinion surveys to textual analysis of media materials and court rulings. Appendix A provides further information about the methodologies involved in the various kinds of studies. Admittedly, to the extent that much of such research was not designed for the purpose of this book, some of the analyses could be considered as secondary data analysis. However, the range of materials and analysis is wide and should be able to sustain the account given in the following pages.

Chapter 2

The Umbrella Movement

The Umbrella Movement, generally understood as lasting between September 28 and December 15, 2014, is a redefining critical event in the political history of Hong Kong. While the Umbrella Movement marks the beginning of the time period (2014 to 2019) that is the focus of this book, the emergence of the movement needs to be understood in relation to the historical trajectories that led to its formation and character. The Umbrella Movement was preceded by nearly twenty months of public debates surrounding the proposal of Occupy Central for Love and Peace (OCLP), during which the idea of civil disobedience was widely discussed and contested in the public arena. Put into the posthandover development of the prodemocracy movement in Hong Kong, OCLP can be regarded as the moderate democrats' response to movement radicalization since the late 2000s. In terms of movement-state interaction, OCLP signified the last attempt by the moderate democrats to pressure the Chinese government to return to the negotiation table, and the actual staging of the occupation campaign signified the end of the engagement approach adopted by the moderates.

The plan of OCLP was interrupted by a series of contingent happenings in late September 2014. The interaction between protesters and the police led to the formation of a multi-site and prolonged occupation that came to be called the "Umbrella Movement" or "Umbrella Revolution." Since the sustained occupation of public roads was unplanned, once the danger of immediate police eviction dissipated, protesters were left largely on their own to further improvise and experiment. In the process, competing understandings of the meanings and norms of protests and various imaginations of the future of Hong Kong were developed. The Mongkok occupation, in particular, became the site dominated by activists with localist orientation. It became the place where activists engaged in transgressive contention (McAdam et al., 2001; Yuen, 2018) and challenged the norms represented by the Admiralty occupation. The Mongkok occupation not only heavily influenced the dynamics during the Umbrella Movement; its legacy significantly shaped the subsequent development of the prodemocracy movement.

This chapter provides an account of the Umbrella Movement. There has already been a substantial literature on the campaign, including several book-length accounts and edited volumes (Cai, 2017; Cheng & Ma, 2020; Lee & Chan, 2018; Lee & Sing, 2019; Pang, 2020). This chapter does not aim at a comprehensive examination of the Umbrella Movement. In line with the relational approach, it tries to first explicate how the Umbrella Movement resulted from both intramovement dynamics and movement-state interactions in the preceding years. The chapter will then discuss the Umbrella Movement itself, with a focus on the distinction and relationship between the Admiralty and Mongkok occupations. Doing so will help highlight how the Umbrella Movement, through the Mongkok occupation, paved the way for the growth of localism after 2014. The chapter will also discuss the development of contentious politics in the immediate aftermath of the Umbrella Movement with a brief discussion of "shopping protests" in Mongkok and the participation of the "Umbrella Soldiers" in the District Council elections in 2015.

Within-Movement and Movement-State Interactions before the Umbrella Movement

Social movements addressing local issues in Hong Kong are generally understood as arising in the 1970s when civic groups and activists took advantage of the newfound political opportunities to push for social changes (Lui & Chiu, 2000). According to Lam (2004), the political culture of Hong Kong in the 1980s and 1990s was marked by the coexistence of a culture of depoliticization with a nonnegligible degree of activism. Many Hong Kong people tended to see politics as dirty and politicians as self-interested individuals who do not genuinely care about the public's interests, but level of protest participation was by no means low.

As political opportunities continued to expand due to governance reform by the colonial government and the negotiation of Hong Kong's future began, a political society came into being (Kuan, 1998). Immediately after the transfer of sovereignty in 1997, Hong Kong suffered from a serious economic downturn due to the Asian Financial Crisis. Protest became a prominent means through which social and economic grievances were expressed. By 2000, Hong Kong was described by the international media as a city of protest (Chandler, 2000).

Nevertheless, even with such developments, it remained a huge surprise to observers when five hundred thousand people took to the street on July 1, 2003, to protest against national security legislation and government incompetence. The protest changed the Chinese government's approach to govern the city, which Tai (2009) described as a change from "one country in passive voice" to "one country in active voice." It marked the beginning of various incorporation strategies trying to integrate the city more tightly into the nation (Fong, 2017).

Meanwhile, the 2003 July 1 protest had two significant impacts on the city's protest culture. First, given its success in forcing the postponement of national security legislation, the protest contributed to the rise of Hong Kong people's collective efficacy, that is, belief in their capability to effect social change through acting collectively (Lee, 2006). This sense of efficacy, together with the expansion of mobilizing structures through the formation of new protest groups, political parties, and online media, fueled the growth of social mobilization. By the early 2010s, Lee and Chan (2013) argued that Hong Kong was showing signs of becoming a movement society (Meyer & Tarrow, 1996), where protests were routinized, normalized, and widely accepted by the media and the public as a legitimate means to strive for one's goals. Second, the peaceful character of the July 1 protest was hailed in public discourses as signifying the high quality of Hong Kong people (Lee & Chan, 2011). Being peaceful, rational, and nonviolent was valorized into an ideal, codified by the Cantonese phrase *woleifei*. This would remain the dominant protest norm for the prodemocracy movement up to at least the Umbrella Movement.

However, the presence of a dominant norm does not entail the absence of ferments that push the boundary of acceptable protest actions. Several interlinked developments led some activists to question the conservatism of the extant protest culture. First, routinization implies predictability. Therefore, as protests became more routinized, they became less capable of disrupting people's sense of reality and creating shocks. It also means that the same kind of protest actions could become less effective over time. Second, while academics or long-time activists might understand that protest movements typically achieve outcomes only by sustained activities over a long period of time, the "immediate success" achieved by the July 1 protest might have established an unrealistic yardstick. That is, some activists and citizens might become relatively easily frustrated by the lack of immediate success of their protest activities, leading to an instrumental urge to seek more effective forms of actions.

Third, in line with the development of new social movements since the 1980s in Europe (Melucci, 1989) and the shift from dutiful citizenship to self-actualizing citizenship norms (Bennett, 2008), new groups of young activists, such as the progressive localists in the New Preservation Movement (Chen & Szeto, 2015), were eager to find ways to express their ideas and identities in more powerful manners. In this process of looking for innovative practices, young activists were inspired by protesters in other countries. The performance of the Korean farmers during the 2005 Anti-WTO protests in Hong Kong, in particular, taught the Hong Kong media and protesters a "lesson" of how dramatic direct actions can be staged (Leung, 2009).

As a result of these factors, major protest campaigns between 2005 and 2012 in Hong Kong typically featured some form of direct action. Occupation and laying siege to key buildings were recurrent features in campaigns such as the Star Ferry and Queen's Pier protests in 2005 and 2007,[1] the Anti-Express Railway protest in 2009 and 2010, and the Anti-National Education Campaign in 2012 (Cheng, 2016: 392). The occupation and siege involved in such protests differed from the occupation in the Umbrella Movement in that the space being occupied was small, and the occupation did not last long. For example, when the police moved in to end the occupation of the Queen's Pier in 2007, seventeen activists chained themselves together. They were taken away by the police and arrested. Their action was meant to signify their sacrifices in face of state coercion. Such protests were more disruptive than peaceful marches, and they "inflicted costs on the state" (Cheng, 2016: 395–96), but they did not deviate from the norm of nonviolence. As Kwong (2016: 432) illustrated, while the number of demonstrations rose from about two thousand per year around year 2005 to more than seven thousand in 2012, numbers of protest-related arrests had remained low between 2006 and 2013.[2]

The low number of arrests can be understood not only in relation to the relative mildness of the protest tactics, but also in relation to the character of protest policing in that period. Since the 1970s and 1980s, the Hong Kong police has been developed into a professional and resourceful unit enjoying high levels of public trust (Lo, 2016). Even in the case of the Anti-WTO protests in 2005 when the Hong Kong police had to face the "threat" of foreign protesters whose tactics might not be entirely peaceful, they adopted a largely conciliatory approach (K. K. L. Ho, 2019). In fact, the relationship between protest organizers and the police in Hong Kong used to be cooperative. In the prelude to the 2005 Anti-WTO protests, a representative of the Confederation of Trade Union in Hong Kong, which was the main coordinator for the protests to be held during the WTO conference, even drew suspicion from the Korean protesters because of her seemingly close contact with the police force (Lee, 2008). Certainly, the police's refrain from using force could become more difficult to maintain as protest tactics became more confrontational. When occupations, sieges, and blockades became more common, the police "reacted by increasing their numbers, repeatedly using violence and leading charges against the protesters" (Cheng, 2016: 396).

For the prodemocracy movement, the pressure to expand their repertoire of actions and reevaluate the norms of nonviolence was also rooted in the slow progress of democratization. The National People's Congress (NPC) ruled out, in a decision made in 2004, direct elections of the chief executive of the Hong Kong government in 2007. In December 2007, the NPC decided that direct election of the chief executive of Hong Kong could be conducted in 2017. Prodemocracy politicians and academics suspected that Beijing would establish procedures for preselecting candidates, but they varied in their judgments of what steps to take to ensure the institutionalization of meaningful direct elections. A serious split within the prodemocracy movement emerged in the debates surrounding the 2012 political reform proposal.

It should be noted that, even before the rise the localist groups in the 2010s, there had long been tension between the "moderates" and the "radicals" within the prodemocracy camp. In the early posthandover years, when the Democratic Party (DP) was by far the largest prodemocracy party in the city, the tension was one between the "mainstream faction" and the "Young Turks" within the party (Ma, 2001). The Young Turks left the DP and joined other political groups and parties in subsequent years. Party fragmentation, driven by the proportional representation system in LegCo elections (Carey, 2017), continued through the 2000s (Ma, 2020). The DP, for instance, won nine of the twenty directly elected seats in the LegCo elections in 1998. In 2008, although the number of directly elected seats had increased to thirty, the DP won only seven, whereas the Civic Party and the League of Social Democrats (LSD), two prodemocracy parties formed in year 2005 and 2006, won four and three seats respectively. The

LSD, in particular, represented the "radical wing" within the prodemocracy movement at the time.

The controversy surrounding political reform in 2012 arose against the above background of party fragmentation. In 2005, chief executive of Hong Kong Donald Tsang had put forward a political reform proposal. The proposed changes were regarded as minimal or even trivial, and the proposal did not contain any timetable for the direct elections of the chief executive and the whole legislature. Since a political reform proposal required the support from two-thirds of the legislature to be passed, the democrats had enough votes to reject the proposal, and they did so in December 2005. Subsequently, in 2007, the Hong Kong government issued a green paper on the development of the political system in Hong Kong. It was followed by the aforementioned NPC decision in December 2007 that Hong Kong could have popular elections of the chief executive in 2017, whereas the electoral methods for the chief executive and LegCo elections in 2012 can also be adjusted. Based on the NPC decision, Donald Tsang put forward, in year 2010, another political reform proposal for the 2012 elections.

The content of the 2010 proposal did not differ too substantially from the 2005 proposal. The most important changes include the expansion of the selection committee for the chief executive from having eight hundred members to having twelve hundred members, but the number of nominations required for a candidate to stand in the CE election remains at one-eighth. Besides, the proposal expanded the legislature from sixty to seventy seats, with five more directly elected seats and five more seats for the functional constituencies. The additional functional constituency seats would be returned through the District Council. More precisely, an election would be held among the district councilors in order to return six members to the legislature (the five new seats plus the one functional constituency seat already assigned to the District Council before the reform).

Most prodemocracy parties and politicians were against the proposal, again seeing the changes as inadequate. In late 2009, the Civic Party and LSD had already proposed the Five-District Referendum campaign. The idea is to have one directly elected legislator resigning from each of the five geographical constituencies, thus forcing the government to hold by-elections in all districts in Hong Kong. The by-elections could then be taken—at least symbolically—as a public referendum on political reform.

The Hong Kong and Chinese governments emphasized that the by-elections were by no means a public referendum. More importantly, the DP also objected to the Five-District Referendum campaign. The party made two main arguments against the campaign: (1) the campaign carries the risks of losing existing seats; (2) even if all five seats are won, the result would not be recognized as a referendum result by the state.

Underlying the divide between the DP and the proponents of the referendum campaign was the former's preference for having dialogue with the Chinese government. According to veteran member and former chairperson of DP Lee Wing-tat, three considerations drove the DP to prefer "communication" at that time. First, given the rejection of the 2005 political reform proposal, the DP worried that a second consecutive rejection would lead the Hong Kong government to put aside political reform completely. Second, political development could be path dependent. The DP saw the possibility of small changes setting the path toward bigger changes in the future. Third, there had never been any chance for prodemocracy political parties in Hong Kong to directly negotiate with the Chinese Central Government. The chance appeared at that time, and the DP wanted to try.[3] Sociologist Chan Kinman, who participated in the negotiation on the 2012 political reform, expressed similar thoughts. For him, since the timetable for direct election was already set, one could aim at keeping the dialogue and building trust in order to strive for the best outcome for 2017. Besides, back in 2010, China itself was liberalizing. Critical journalism and civil society organizations were growing in the mainland (Lei, 2018; Tweets, 2014). In fact, Chan Kinman himself was well-known for his work on civil society development in China. At that historical juncture, dialogue seemed possible.[4]

In the negotiation, the DP proposed certain revisions, the most important of which is that the five new functional constituency seats would not be returned by voting among the district councilors. Instead, eligible voters who do not belong to any other functional constituencies would be eligible to vote in the so-called Super District Council functional constituency. This essentially allows all eligible voters to have two votes—one in the geographical constituencies and one in a certain functional constituency. Practically, if the five new seats were returned through voting by the district councilors, the progovernment parties were likely to get the majority of the seats due to their dominance in the District Council. But when millions of eligible voters could participate, the prodemocracy camp was likely to win the majority of the seats. The difference between the government's original proposal and the DP's amendment might only be one more seat for the democrats, but the DP could at least present it as an improvement benefitting the prodemocracy camp.

The DP's proposal was adopted by the government, and the 2012 reform passed the legislature with support from the DP. However, the concession was indeed very minor, and the DP's decision to support the government turned themselves into targets of attack. In the 2012 LegCo elections, the DP won only four seats through direct elections. Their vote share in direct elections was 13.65 percent, which was almost 7 percent lower than their vote share in 2008.

The election result was a serious setback for the DP and the "engagement approach" adopted by the moderates. Adding to the frustration was the perception that the Chinese government was trying to undermine the DP through supporting the radical groups in the prodemocracy camp. Although there was no available evidence to validate the suspicions, such suspicions deepened the distrust within the prodemocracy movement. Moreover, as Lee Wing-tat recalled, during the negotiation on the 2012 reform, Chinese officials promised the DP that there would be continual communication between the two sides. The promise did not materialize. It led the DP to start questioning the utility of the engagement approach.

Chan Kinman experienced similar frustrations and disillusion. He recalled that, after the 2012 political reform was passed, the Chinese Liaison Office organized two group visits to Beijing for prodemocracy academics and politicians in Hong Kong. But his impression was that the officials they met in Beijing seemingly did not know about the purpose of the trips. There were some exchanges of viewpoints but no follow-up afterwards. Meanwhile, after the 2012 elections, the DP was unwilling to continue to engage the Chinese government. Chan's thought was that, if even the DP would not engage with the Chinese government, no one would. He started to look for alternative ways to push the prodemocracy movement ahead.

This development explained why Chan Kinman reacted positively when fellow academic, legal scholar Benny Tai raised the idea of occupy central in a newspaper op-ed piece published in January 2013. Benny Tai suggested that the public can stage an occupation campaign in the financial district of Central if the procedures for the 2017 elections do not meet the standard of meaningful democratic elections. The proposal raised eyebrows partly because Tai himself has long been regarded as a moderate academic. In retrospect, Tai's role in proposing the idea of occupy central was a part of the rise of legal activism in Hong Kong since the 2000s (Lee, 2017). Within a couple of months, Tai was joined by Chan Kinman and Reverend Chu Yiu-ming. They initiated the OCLP Campaign.

According to Chan Kinman, the original aim of OCLP was to try to force the Chinese government and the moderate democrats to get back to the negotiation table. However, learning from the experience of the 2012 political reform controversy, in which the moderates alienated many supporters of the prodemocracy movement, Chan thought that negotiation with China could not begin until the campaign had gone through a process to achieve a consensus on what political reform proposals to put forward. He thus refused to privately talk to the Hong Kong government or representatives from Beijing in the early stage of the OCLP campaign. Instead, drawing upon the theories and practice of deliberative conventions originated from the United States (Fishkin, 1995), OCLP conducted a series of deliberation days. The deliberation days were aimed at allowing supporters of the occupation campaign to achieve a common understanding of the goal of OCLP and on what kinds of electoral arrangement would be seen as acceptable. The deliberation process was followed by a public vote in June 2014 (Shen, 2020).

Between January 2013 and September 2014, Hong Kong entered a critical discourse moment (Gamson & Herzog, 1999) as the society debated about the merits and justifiability of civil disobedience. The OCLP campaign became the site where forces of radicalization and deradicalization contested and negotiated. On the one hand, in response to criticisms from the progovernment elites, the government, and the relatively conservative sector of the prodemocracy movement, the discourses of OCLP had become more moderate over time (Lee & Chan, 2018: 50–74). On the other hand, even before the occupation began, the OCLP initiators already found it difficult to handle the challenge of radicalization. The relatively radical groups strongly mobilized their supporters to join the deliberation days. On the last deliberation day, the participants had to select three proposals regarding the electoral arrangement in 2017, which would then be put forward for public voting. All three selected proposals were relatively "radical" ones—they all contain the element of civil nomination, that is, a procedure allowing ordinary citizens to nominate candidates to run in the election.[5] More politically moderate proposals without the component of civil nomination were voted out (Shen, 2020).

If the deliberation days were designed to be a platform through which a wide range of ideas would be produced and then put forward for further public selection, then the purpose was not achieved at the end. This shows the difficulties of exercising effective leadership amidst tensions between groups with vastly different orientations. Such difficulties and tensions would only become even more serious after the occupation began.

On August 31, 2014, the Chinese government announced the framework for the 2017 chief executive election. Within the framework, any candidate would need to obtain support from more than half of the members of the nomination committee in order to stand in the election, and only two to three candidates would be allowed to run. Given the overwhelming dominance of proregime people in the nomination committee, the framework made it virtually impossible for any prodemocracy politicians to run in the election. Many citizens might even doubt if, under the NPC framework, public figures who are politically "centrists" and yet have good public standing would be easily ruled out. The gap between the NPC decision and the OCLP's proposal is gigantic. Chan Kinman recalled that when the leaders of OCLP tried to restart discussion with the government in summer 2014 after the deliberation days, he quickly realized that Beijing had already made its decision. For Chan, China showed its hands through the August 31 NPC decision. The occupation would have to go ahead.

The Occupation and the Admiralty-Mongkok Divide

The OCLP leaders originally chose to start the occupation on the National Day of October 1. While there might be various reasons behind the choice, starting the occupation on the beginning of a two-day public holiday would reduce the disruption caused by the occupation. In the mind of the OCLP initiators, the occupation would involve people sitting down and logging arms, while the police could evict the occupation by taking them away one by one. They did not plan to resist police eviction, and the original prediction was for the occupation to end within a few days.[6]

Other political actors did not follow the script, however. The Hong Kong Federation of Students (the federation of university students) and Scholarism (an activist group formed by high school students) initiated a week-long class strike beginning on September 22. In the late evening of September 27, during a rally in front of the government headquarters in Admiralty, a group of student protesters rushed into the "Civic Square," the enclosed space in front of the government headquarters.[7] Clashes with the police ensued, and a group of student activists were arrested. In response, the OCLP initiators announced the beginning of OCLP in the early morning hours of September 28. Beginning from the morning of September 28, more and more citizens tried to access Admiralty to support the student groups and the OCLP. But the police surrounded the protesters in front of the government headquarters, thus cutting off the linkage between the protest leaders and supporters on the street. As the number of supporters swelled, the pedestrian pathways became overcrowded. Some citizens breached the police cordon lines and inadvertently started the occupation of public roads. At around 6:00 p.m., the police fired tear gas into the protesting crowd. It backfired and led many citizens who were watching the events on television to come out to join the protest (Tang, 2015).

The police continued to fire tear gas intermittently at night, but still to no avail. Some protesters suggested starting occupation in other districts in order to make an immediate eviction impossible. The suggestions were shared via online forums. Occupation started in Causeway Bay, Wanchai, Mongkok, and Tsim Sha Tsui. Within a few days, the occupation campaign settled down into having three occupied areas: Admiralty, Mongkok, and Causeway Bay. The international media dubbed the protest the *Umbrella Revolution*, referring to how protesters used umbrellas to protect themselves against the police. The activists changed the label to *Umbrella Movement* in order to signify that they were not trying to overthrow the regime. (Yet some participants and activists would continue to prefer the term *Umbrella Revolution*.)

Paradoxically, while the Mongkok and Causeway Bay occupations were improvised in an attempt to defend the Admiralty occupation, the presence of multiple occupation sites allowed the preexisting tension between different factions of the prodemocracy movement to map onto the spatial division of the occupation campaign. It allowed people with different predilections and inclinations to gather at different sites, and it facilitated the formation of distinctive ethos and identities through protesters drawing upon the cultural, social, and symbolic resources associated with the places (Yuen, 2018).

The distinction and relationship between the Admiralty and the Mongkok occupations significantly influenced not only the evolution of the Umbrella Movement, but also post-Umbrella Movement protest activism in Hong Kong. It is therefore important to explicate their characteristics and differences here by drawing upon onsite survey data and materials provided by other scholars in their accounts. Tables 2.1 to 2.4 present the results derived from a protest onsite survey conducted in the occupied areas in early November 2014. Table 2.1 shows that the Mongkok occupiers were primarily males, whereas the Admiralty occupation was participated by a roughly equal number of males and females.[8] The Mongkok occupiers were better educated, partly because there were more current university students in the area. Besides, a higher proportion of the Mongkok occupiers saw themselves as belonging to the lower class. This is consistent with the fact

Table 2.1a–c Demographics and party support of Umbrella Movement participants in Admiralty (N=272) and Mongkok (N=288)

Table 2.1a. Demographics

Demographics	Admiralty	Mongkok
Gender*** (% Female)	51.5	30.2
Education*** (% Tertiary)	55.8	66.3
University Students ** (% Yes)	16.2	23.1
Socioeconomic status***: % Lower or grassroots	40.4	50.8
Socioeconomic status***: % Middle class	58.0	38.5
Age: 25 or below	44.7	51.1
Age: 26 to 40	39.7	35.9

Table 2.1b. Support for political parties: Moderate democrats

Moderate democrats	Admiralty	Mongkok
Democratic Party	3.7	3.1
Civic Party*	17.6	10.5
ADPL	1.1	1.0
Labor Party	6.6	3.7
Confederation of Trade Union	1.5	2.4

Table 2.1c. Support for political parties: Radical democrats/localists

Radical democrats/localists	Admiralty	Mongkok
League of Social Democrats	9.6	11.2
People Power	8.8	11.9
Civic Passion**	4.8	12.9

Note: ***p < .001; **p < .01; *p < .05 in a cross-tabulation exercise with Chi-square test.
Source: Created by the author.

that Mongkok itself is a grassroots residential area, whereas Admiralty is a business district.

In terms of support for political groups or parties, a higher percentage of participants in Admiralty were supporters of political groups or parties belonging to the moderate camp of the prodemocracy movement. The percentage of supporters of Civic Party, a political party formed in 2005 mainly by a group of legal professionals, was significantly higher in Admiralty than in Mongkok. Further analysis would show that 25.7 percent of the respondents in Admiralty supported one of the listed moderate parties or groups, whereas only 14.6 percent of respondents in Mongkok did so. In contrast, higher percentages of respondents in the Mongkok survey reported being supporters of the three listed radical parties. Civic Passion, a party adopting a right-wing localist stance, was particularly influential in Mongkok.

Consistent with the differences in participants' party support, table 2.2 shows that, when asked whether "local interests," "universal values," and "democratization of China" constituted the foundation of the Umbrella Movement, participants in Admiralty emphasized universal values to the largest extent, whereas participants in Mongkok emphasized local interests to the largest extent. Meanwhile, table 2.2 also shows how participants in the two occupied areas viewed the notion of "self-moibilization," that is, mobilization among ordinary citizens themselves as opposed to mobilization

Tables 2.2a–b. Views about self-mobilization and perceptions of the foundation of the Umbrella Movement (Admiralty N=272; Mongkok N=288)

Table 2.2a.

Foundation of the movement	Admiralty	Mongkok
Local interests***	4.27	4.57
Universal values	4.34	4.46
Democratization of China	3.35	3.25

Table 2.2b.

Views on self-mobilization. Self-mobilization	Admiralty	Mongkok
makes the movement purer***	3.89	4.18
helps avoid the movement to be kidnapped***	3.74	4.09
leads to loss of focus***	2.99	2.61
leads to loss of leadership***	3.22	2.99

Note: Entries are mean scores on a five-point Likert scale. ***p < .001; **p < .01; *p < .05 in an independent samples t-test.

Source: Created by the author.

by formal organizations. The survey contained two statements about the possible benefits and two statements about the possible downsides of self-mobilization. Participants in both areas tended to see self-mobilization positively. They agreed that self-mobilization makes the movement "purer" and helps prevent the movement from being hijacked (by politicians). When compared to each other, participants in Mongkok agreed with the positive statements to an even larger extent. Participants in Mongkok also tended to disagree with the two negative statements, whereas participants in Admiralty were more willing to acknowledge the potential problems of self-mobilization, especially the loss of effective leadership.

Chung's (2015) ethnographic account of the Mongkok occupation can corroborate and add nuances to the findings here. He noted that the Mongkok occupation did not have a clear power hierarchy. In the Mongkok occupation, "one was empowered not by his reputation, political stance or identity, but by how long he had been staying and how much he has been contributing to the community" (p. 12). Nevertheless, Chung's point about the absence of a clear power hierarchy in Mongkok cannot be taken at face value. Saying that one can be empowered by how long one has been staying and how much one has contributed implies the possibility of an alternative hierarchy developed based on alternative criteria. As scholars studying decentralized movements have shown (Flesher Fominaya, 2020; Tufekci, 2017), inequality in influence and power inevitably exists in seemingly leaderless movements. What table 2.2 shows is the Mongkok participants' rejection of conventional movement leadership, but the Mongkok occupation could still be dominated by specific groups to a certain extent.

Interestingly, while the Mongkok occupation was often understood as dominated by the localists, when the onsite survey asked the respondents to evaluate their sense of belonging to Hong Kong and to China, respondents from the two areas did not differ from each other significantly. On a 0-to-10 scale, respondents in Admiralty had a mean score of 7.54 on sense of belonging to Hong Kong, while the corresponding mean score for the Mongkok respondents was 7.55. The two scores were virtually the same. For sense of belonging to China, respondents in Admiralty and Mongkok had mean scores of 2.49 and 2.20, respectively. The Mongkok respondents did score lower on sense of belonging to China, but the two mean scores were not statistically different from each other. Participants of the Umbrella Movement shared the common affective attachment to Hong Kong and the common detachment from China.

However, participants in the two areas might articulate what "Hong Kong" means differently. Table 2.3 shows how a sense of belonging to Hong Kong, a sense of belonging to China, and perceived importance of local interests, universal values, and democratization of China correlated with each other for the two groups of participants. There are clear and meaningful distinctions. For participants in Admiralty (table 2.3a), a sense of belonging to Hong Kong is positively and significantly correlated to a sense of belonging to China. It also correlates significantly and positively to perceived importance of universal values as the foundation of the Umbrella Movement. Besides, perceived importance of local interest correlates positively and very strongly with perceived importance of universal values. It also correlates significantly with perceived importance of democratization of China. At the same time, perceived importance of universal values correlates positively and significantly to perceived importance of democratization of China. On the whole, the Admiralty participants' conceptions of local interest and Hong Kong identity are intertwined with the idea of universal

Tables 2.3a–b. Correlations between sense of belonging to Hong Kong and China and perceived foundation of the Umbrella Movement

Table 2.3a.

Admiralty (N=249 to 260)	1	2	3	4	5
1. Sense of belonging to HK	1.00				
2. Sense of belonging to China	.27***	1.00			
3. Importance of local interests	.10	−.08	1.00		
4. Importance of universal values	.13	.01	.48***	1.00	
5. Importance of democratization of China	.25	.19**	.14*	.29***	1.00

Table 2.3b.

Mongkok (N=274 to 284)	1	2	3	4	5
1. Sense of belonging to HK	1.00				
2. Sense of belonging to China	.13*	1.00			
3. Importance of local interests	.05	−.19**	1.00		
4. Importance of universal values	.02	.03	.11	1.00	
5. Importance of democratization of China	−.10	.22***	−.06	.25***	1.00

Note: Entries are Pearson correlation coefficients. ***p < .001; **p < .01; *p < .05.

Source: Created by the author.

values, and they are also compatible with a sense of belonging to China and perceived importance of democratization of China.

In contrast, as shown in table 2.3b, among the Mongkok participants, the relationship between a sense of belonging to Hong Kong and a sense of belonging to China is much weaker, though it remains statistically significant. There is no significant positive relationship between a sense of belonging to Hong Kong and perceived importance of universal values. Perceived importance of local interests relates significantly negatively to a sense of belonging to China. Besides, perceived importance of local interests does not relate significantly to perceived importance of universal values and perceived importance of democratization of China. The correlation coefficient for the relationship between perceived importance of local interests and perceived importance of democratization in China is even negative in sign. On the whole, among the Mongkok participants, local interests are dissociated from universal values, and there are signs of an antagonistic relationship between an emphasis on local interests and concerns with China's development. These findings point to an emerging form of anti-China localism.

Beyond what the participants believed and perceived, one of the most significant differences between the two occupied areas is the more tension-filled and conflictive atmosphere in Mongkok. Various authors have noted the valorization of valiant resistance in the Mongkok occupation (Chung, 2015; Yuen, 2018). In the onsite survey, when asked whether they have undertaken specific types of actions, the Admiralty and Mongkok occupiers did not differ from each other significantly on participation in nonconflictive actions, such as joining civic lectures, giving materials to participants, donating money, or discussing movement directions. However, as shown in table 2.4, significantly higher proportions of the Mongkok occupiers had participated in handling counterprotesters, protecting the occupied area when the police took action, and setting up blockades, though level of participation in confrontational actions in Admiralty was also substantial.

In addition to overall frequencies of participation, there were also differences in the factors explaining individual-level participation in confrontational actions in the two occupied areas. Table 2.5 shows the results of a logistic regression analysis using demographics, perceived importance of the three values, a sense of belonging to Hong Kong, and support for one of the three radical political parties to predict whether a participant had joined at least one of the three confrontational actions listed in table 2.4b.

In Admiralty, none of the demographic factors explained participation in confrontational activities. Instead, supporters of radical parties were more

Tables 2.4a–b. Actions undertaken by the Umbrella Movement participants (Admiralty N=272; Mongkok N=288)

Table 2.4a.

Non-confrontational	Admiralty	Mongkok
Discuss movement directions	43.6	44.9
Deliver materials or maintain order	55.7	60.1
Join civic lectures or seminars	59.3	55.1
Give materials to participants	68.5	65.9
Make donations	13.2	10.8
Support the movement outside the occupied areas*	57.9	48.0

Table 2.4b.

Confrontational	Admiralty	Mongkok
Set up blockades**	26.4	38.2
Handle anti-occupy citizens***	36.3	53.0
Protect the area when the police take action**	52.4	63.5
At least one of the three confrontational actions	60.4	73.3

Note: ***p < .001; **p < .01; *p < .05 in a cross-tabulation exercise with Chi-square test.
Source: Created by the author.

likely to participate in confrontational actions. Interestingly, Admiralty occupiers who perceived universal values to be more important were more likely to have participated in confrontational actions. In contrast, among the Mongkok participants, ideational factors and party support did not explain participation in confrontational actions. Rather, three demographic factors predicted the dependent variable: males, less-educated individuals, and younger people were more likely to have participated in confrontational actions.

One way to interpret the differences is that in Admiralty, participants engaged in confrontational actions only if they had strong beliefs in what they saw as the most important value foundation of the movement or they were receptive toward confrontational acts. But in Mongkok, engagement

Table 2.5. Predicting engagement in confrontational actions

	Admiralty	Mongkok
Gender (Female = 2)	0.70	0.48*
Age	0.99	0.97*
SES	1.10	0.82
Educational level	0.81	0.44*
Support radical party	2.40*	1.39
Sense of belonging to Hong Kong	1.08	1.08
Importance of local interests	0.82	0.90
Importance of universal values	1.56*	1.07
Importance of democratization of China	1.01	0.94
Model Chi-Square	17.76*	17.84*
Nagelkerke R^2	0.104	0.111
N	222	227

Note: Entries are odd ratios. ***$p < .001$; **$p < .01$; *$p < .05$.

Source: Created by the author.

in confrontations was treated as "normal." Therefore, ideational factors and support for radical parties did not constitute significant predictors. The remaining issue is only whether individuals were biographically inclined to engage in confrontations.

Certainly, the differences between Admiralty and Mongkok in terms of prevalence of physical confrontations need to be understood as the result of not only the characteristics of the occupiers but also the interactions between the occupiers, other actors, and the environment. In popular cultural imagination as well as in reality, Mongkok was a district with a significant presence of triad societies. During the occupation, some of the counterprotests were apparently perpetrated by gangsters (Varese & Wong, 2017). Besides, Chung wrote about his experience and observations of police actions during the occupation as follows: "I have been staying in both territories and the way the police dispersed the crowd was totally different in level of cruelty. In Admiralty, some police would advance at a speed that people could have sufficient time to fall back, but in Mongkok, all the police advance with their batons in hands hitting everyone really hard" (2015: 14). Therefore, occupiers in Mongkok engaged in physical conflicts more frequently partly because there were the opportunities and the needs to do so.

Conflicts between protesters and the police or counterprotesters did not happen all the time, but the tense atmosphere in the Mongkok occupation could be maintained by the participants' exercise of (self-)discipline. A major difference between the Admiralty and Mongkok occupations was the extent to which participants were engaging in prefigurative politics, that is, whether and how the participants tried to experimentally realize their political ideals "here and now" (A. Chow, 2019). In Admiralty, a self-study area was constructed. People saw themselves as "villagers." Some even cultivated plants. They tried to materialize their ideas of community life. In Mongkok, "villagers" were not welcomed (Chung, 2015). People were adamant that the occupation was an act of resistance. One illustrative incident occurred in early October when some participants tried to initiate the playing of mahjong and table tennis. The activities drew heavy criticism from and were stopped by some other occupiers, who thought that the activities would turn the occupation into a carnival and dissolve the spirit of resistance (Pang, 2020).

For the Umbrella Movement, the emergence of Mongkok as a transgressive contention made the already difficult tasks of the movement leaders even more difficult. In one anecdote recounted by Alex Chow (2019: 46), a leader of the Hong Kong Federation of Students during the Umbrella Movement, when the movement leaders considered in late October to conduct a "square voting" on whether the movement should resume negotiations with the government, there were differences in opinions regarding whether the voting should cover the Mongkok and Causeway Bay occupation sites. Obviously, not including Mongkok and Causeway Bay would be an act of exclusion, but it was unclear if the Mongkok occupiers would welcome "square voting" in the first place.[9] As the occupation continued to evolve, achieving consensus between Mongkok and Admiralty became less and less likely. The problem of tactical freeze was deepened.

Equally or even more important is the possible long-term impact of the Mongkok occupation. The occupation was not only a site where people who already shared certain ideas opted to congregate; it was also a site where people could be socialized and brought into the emerging movement of localism. Here, the story of Aaron (pseudonym) is illustrative. Aaron was interviewed in 2018 for the author's research on collective remembering of Tiananmen in Hong Kong. At the time of the interview, Aaron was a university student leader and a self-proclaimed localist. He participated in the Umbrella Movement when he was a high school student. He originally spent time primarily in Admiralty. He remembered discussing with others about issues such as what democracy and civil society are. But ultimately, what influenced him the most was his experience in Mongkok. As he recalled:

> Because I knew that the Mongkok occupation was about to be evicted, so I went there to try to help, and at that time my ideology had already been shifting toward the Mongkok side. [. . .] After I went there, the conflicts had already started. There were fights, and I was standing among the protesters. But the fighting was not nonstop. There were times when the two sides just confronted each other without taking action, and you could chat and eat and drink. I talked to another protester, and I remember he said: "From now on, it will no longer be a binary opposition between the pan-democrats and the proestablishment; the localists will emerge."

In Aaron's recollection, Admiralty was a peaceful utopia constructed by the participants, whereas Mongkok was "really a place of resistance [. . . where] people were thinking about how to continue to fight." He vividly described a seemingly minor but illustrative incident that happened one night in Mongkok:

> First of all, the police would harass you, and then you felt that there was a sense of brotherly loyalty in Mongkok. I remember very well that, one night when I was sleeping, suddenly there were something like siren sounds from police vehicles. It was deep at night, and everyone had slept. But I was woken by the sound. So I left my tent to see what was happening. And at that moment I saw many people in the occupation leaving their tents at the same time. People were picking up gears and weapons. They were like getting prepared for a battle. At that moment I felt people were indeed engaging in a resistance.

Aaron thought the spirit of resistance was what Hong Kong people needed. "It's not about violence; it is when you are violated by others, you have to stand up and use your body to stop the invasion by an institution."

Aaron's story illustrates a few points. First, he did not arrive at Mongkok as a blank sheet of paper. He recalled that he was already leaning toward Mongkok before shifting his station. Given how people moved between the occupied areas and the prevalence of digital and social media communications, getting acquainted with localist ideas and discourses was not premised on staying in Mongkok. Second and nonetheless, the Mongkok occupation remained highly significant because it constituted the place in which people could interact and socialize with each other in an emerging community. Third, Aaron was convinced of the "correctness" of the localists not because of a well-developed discourse about Hong Kong's situation. It was not a matter of having a persuasive diagnosis and prognosis. It was primarily an affective experience grounded in the ambience of the Mongkok occupation. Instead of what social movement researchers used to call "cognitive liberation" (McAdam, 1982), what Aaron experienced was an affective or emotional imprint.[10]

Of course, not all Mongkok occupiers were equally deeply influenced by the experience and turned themselves into localist activists in subsequent years. Interestingly, Charles (pseudonym), another localist student activist the author interviewed in 2018, recalled his discontent with the Admiralty occupation because of the absence of an atmosphere of resistance there. But he was not satisfied with Mongkok either. He thought that, even in Mongkok, people seemed to have nothing to do other than waiting for things to happen. Charles shared Aaron's inclination to look for "resistance," though they varied in their evaluation of whether the Mongkok occupation came close to their imagination of what resistance is.

In addition to individual variabilities, the analysis in the previous pages about the Mongkok occupation also needs to be qualified in a few ways. First, the Mongkok occupation was not monopolized by localist-oriented activists and participants. In fact, as there were rumors about how the localists in Mongkok were "attacking" movement participants of other political orientations, some nonlocalist political parties and groups also set up their own "stations" in Mongkok in order to monitor the situation. Second, as Yuen (2018) explained, Mongkok was a grassroots community, and as shown in table 2.1, there were more self-identified lower-class citizens in Mongkok. This was another aspect of the Mongkok occupation's identity. However, while valiant resistance and grassroots orientation supplemented each other in the early stage of the Mongkok occupation, the two came into conflict in the later stages of the Umbrella Movement. Third, not everyone and everything in Mongkok can be simply classified as "localist" or not. An example is Lau Siu-lai's Mobile Democracy Classroom. Lau was a college instructor who set up a "mobile classroom" in the Mongkok area and offered free lectures to the occupiers. She proclaimed herself to be a localist, though she was treated as a pretender by many localist youngsters.

Therefore, one should not essentialize the Mongkok experience, and the malleability of what localism meant should be kept in mind. Nevertheless, the Mongkok occupation indeed exhibited certain distinctive characteristics, and it was a place where the localist experience and imagination had a chance of being developed. It was where some young people got their first taste of what valiant resistance meant. The occupation added a new layer of meanings to the set of already rich cultural and symbolic resources associated with the place. It is not entirely coincidental that a civil unrest would occur in Mongkok a little more than a year later.

End of the Umbrella Movement and the *Gauwu* Protests

Despite the use of tear gas by the police on September 28 and occasional conflicts between protesters and counterprotesters in subsequent weeks, the occupation had gone on largely smoothly and peacefully. There was a scandal about police misconduct occurring on October 15. Seven police officers, after a protester-police confrontation, took a protester to a corner of a park and beat the protester, who was lying on the ground without the ability to self-defend. The incident was captured by a television camera crew. The use of tear gas and the "seven policemen incident" illustrated the higher tendency—when compared to the past—of the police to use coercive tactics to handle protests in 2014, which was the result of a gradual change toward more confrontational protester-police interactions over the years (K. K. L. Ho, 2021). However, the police largely refrained from using coercive tactics after mid-October. Police-protester clashes would not occur again until the protesters escalated their actions toward the end of the occupation. Police nonaction signified the state's strategy of attrition (Yuen & Cheng, 2017). Instead of stopping the occupation immediately, the state let the occupation lose steam and public support as time passed.

As part of the strategy of attrition, the state and its agents, including the progovernment media and politicians, promoted three counterframes. They argued that the occupation was the result of the intervention of foreign forces who tried to instigate a color revolution, emphasized the public nuisance caused by the occupation and the suffering of citizens, and criticized the occupation for breaching the rule of law (Lee & Chan, 2018).

The rule of law frame and the public nuisance frame, in particular, were effective in undermining the legitimacy of the occupation. In official discourses, the rule of law was defined merely in terms of rule following and the willingness to bear the legal consequences of one's actions (Hargreaves, 2015). This contrasts with the conceptualization of the rule of law promulgated by Benny Tai, initiator of the OCLP campaign and a legal scholar by trade. For Tai (2012), the rule of law includes the idea of constraining power by law and achieving justice through law. Nevertheless, the state's "thin theory" of the rule of law is easy for the public to understand. Wong's (2020) analysis of survey data showed that concern with the Umbrella Movement's impact on the rule of law was one of three major factors explaining public opposition to the occupation campaign. Meanwhile, throughout the OCLP campaign, the initiators indeed emphasized that willingness to bear the legal consequence of one's actions is a core component of civil disobedience. Shen's (2019) analysis found that the Mongkok occupation had developed a law-defying frame, but a law-abiding frame remained dominant within the activists stationing in Admiralty. It was difficult for the activists to counter the rule of law frame promulgated by the state.

Similarly, it was difficult for the movement to counter the public nuisance frame because the prolonged occupation of public roads in a few busy districts in Hong Kong had indeed caused inconveniences to citizens' everyday lives. The public nuisance frame was played up in the news media when aggrieved citizens went to the protest site to criticize the occupiers. One might suspect that those aggrieved citizens were mobilized by the progovernment forces, but it does not diminish the effect of the impression produced. In an opinion survey conducted by the CCPOS at Chinese University of Hong Kong in November 2014, 67.4 percent of the respondents believed that the protesters should evacuate all their occupied areas. Only 13.9 percent answered "should not." In the survey in early December, 76.2 percent of the respondents thought the protesters should evacuate. Notably, in both surveys, the level of support for the Umbrella Movement still stood at 33.9 percent (CCPOS, 2014). In other words, toward the end of the occupation, many movement supporters also believed that the occupiers should retreat to avoid further alienating the public.

As already noted, the Umbrella Movement suffered from a lack of effective leadership. The movement had attempted to establish various legitimacy mechanisms, such as a five-party platform to facilitate collaboration among the participating parties (Kwok & Chan, 2017). However, the mechanisms never fully resolved the problem of decision-making. The movement entered a stalemate and suffered from a tactical freeze. By November, the leading student groups were under pressure to escalate the action. In late night of November 18, a group of militant protesters tried to break into the Legislative Council Building. Several prodemocracy politicians tried to stop the action in vain. The police dispersed the protesters with pepper spray.

The clash continued until the early morning hours of November 19. After the event, the moderate democrats made an announcement to condemn violent actions. The militant protesters and their supporters, in return, criticized the democrats for severing ties with other protesters. The controversy exacerbated the internal conflict of the Umbrella Movement. Nonetheless, facing the continual stalemate and after the clearance of the Mongkok occupation on November 25 and 26,[11] the pressure for the protest leaders to escalate the actions continued to accumulate. On November 30, the Hong Kong Federation of Students called for besieging the Government Headquarters. Violent clashes between the police and the protesters occurred at night. The plan to besiege the Government Headquarters failed.

On December 1, three members of Scholarism staged a hunger strike, but it was far from capable of reenergizing the movement. As Cai (2020) argued, escalation of actions in the Umbrella Movement occurred only when the movement was already losing momentum. Activists and supporters started to prepare for the seemingly inevitable end of the occupation. On December 2, the three initiators of OCLP surrendered themselves to the police in a move to showcase their willingness to bear the legal consequence of their acts of civil disobedience. On December 11, the police evicted the Admiralty occupation. The protesters returned to the original script of OCLP. Hundreds of occupiers sat down on the ground and let the police to take them away without forceful resistance, and 247 persons were arrested. Four days later, the Causeway Bay occupation was evicted, thus ending the seventy-nine-day campaign.

The Causeway Bay eviction on December 15 was usually treated as the end of the Umbrella Movement, but actions directly related to the Umbrella Movement actually continued for a significant period of time. After the Admiralty eviction, a group of activists continued to stage an "occupation" in an area in front of the Legislative Council Building for months. They called the place "New Tim Mei Village" (Tim Mei is the name of the road in front of the East Wing of the Government Headquarters). The action could be considered as a continuation of the prefigurative politics initiated during the Umbrella Movement (Pang, 2020). The police allowed the "occupation" to go on as it did not cause any disruption to public order or citizens' everyday life. The occupation ended in late June, 2015, after the LegCo voted down the government's political reform proposal.

Meanwhile, a very different type of action continued in Mongkok. After the police ended the Mongkok occupation, a group of protesters started the *"gauwu* protest." *Gauwu* is the homophone of the Mandarin phrase *gou-wu*, which literally means "shopping." The use of the phrase was related to a television news story in summer 2014 on a progovernment rally against the plan of OCLP. When the reporter asked a rally participant what she was doing, the participant said *"gou-wu."* The absurdity of the answer seemingly confirmed prodemocracy citizens' belief that progovernment groups often paid people—Hongkongers or travelers from the mainland—to participate in their rallies, and the progovernment rally participants often did not know what they were joining. Then, in November 2014, when the Umbrella Movement was moving toward the end, chief executive of the Hong Kong government CY Leung encouraged people to go shopping in order to support the Hong Kong economy, which was purportedly damaged by the occupation campaign. Protesters thus claimed that they were responding to the chief executive's call to shop.

Gauwu protests were not organized by any groups or organizations. Citizens simply congregated at a designated time and place in Mongkok to begin the action. They would move around the shopping area in Mongkok and shout *"gauwu"* or "I want to *gauwu"* repeatedly. As Gan described, "Protesters thronged the streets of Mongkok, ostensibly to shop, but in reality, to display their dissatisfaction with the government and to see if they could re-take the streets" (2017: 167). *Gauwu* protest, at least when it began in late November 2014, thus combined several characteristics. It was initially understood as partly an attempt to look for opportunities to restart the occupation. The police also understood the protest action as such. Hence, they employed harsh and coercive tactics, including the use of batons and pepper spray, to control the crowd. Besides, the actions were disruptive to the businesses in Mongkok. The degree of disruption depended on the details of the actions, such as when they started and ended, and whether the protesters entered specific shops collectively.

Nonetheless, *gauwu* protest also has its lighthearted aspect. It is first of all a mockery of the mainlander interviewed by television and an ironic yet subversive response to the call by the chief executive. Each of the two Cantonese words *gau* and *wu* is multivocal. *Gau* can refer to a vulgar word for penis, and in young people's parlance, it is often used as an adjective to describe the silliness and pointlessness of an act. *Wu* can refer to a meaningless sound. *Gauwu* thus can be understood as the pointless emission of a meaningless sound. This in turn can be understood as the protesters' self-mockery. Gan (2017) argued that the protest evoked humor's potency and constituted "an irreverent revoicing that wrests control away from dominant discourses" (p. 163).

Gauwu protests were therefore ambivalent in their aims and character. Nevertheless, as time passed, people came to realize that the possibility of restarting the occupation was slim, and further disrupting people's everyday life and the businesses of local shops could only further alienate the public. Hence the *gauwu* protest became more and more like a form of performance art. On Facebook, a public page titled "9wu Freedom" was set up in late November 2014.[12] One can clearly see that the page was run by people of the localist camp based on its language (e.g., Umbrella Revolution), targets of criticisms (i.e., including the moderate democrats), and materials shared. The page was very active throughout December 2014, reporting on the *gauwu* protests occurring at the time. But the frequency of postings declined by the turn of the year. Then, a post published by the page on January 26, 2015, said: "Put it simply, everyone knows that the leftards have hijacked *gauwu*." *Leftard* is the derogatory term the localists used to describe the moderate democrats and progressive activists. The statement shows that, at least from the perspective of the administrator of the Facebook page, the nature of the protest has changed from being an act of defiance to being something more formalistic, if not merely for fun.

Gauwu protests would go on for a long period of time. On August 21, 2017, a group of prodemocracy politicians and activists organized a public forum in Mongkok and commemorated the one thousandth day since the beginning of *gauwu* protests.[13] After all, sustaining *gauwu* protests required only the occasional congregation of twenty to thirty people to engage in the act of walking around and chanting the *gauwu* slogan. But as Gan put it, by September 2015, "while [*gauwu*] continues to remain a colourful spectacle, it is contained to a street in Mongkok and is becoming more a curiosity, a remnant of a seemingly pointless protest, much as the street occupations of the Umbrella Movement eventually became" (2017: 170).

The brief history of *gauwu* protests illustrated the Umbrella Movement participants' eagerness to find ways to continue their struggle after the end of occupation. It also shows how ordinary citizens' self-mobilized protest activities sustained the significance of Mongkok as a space for resistance. In fact, into 2015, instead of *gauwu*, the majority of activists and Umbrella Movement supporters were trying to find other means of political engagement. This included participation in elections.

Umbrella Soldiers in the 2015 District Council Elections

Around the world, it is not uncommon for activists and politicians to try to bring the political energies mobilized through protest campaigns into the electoral arena. Many European countries witnessed the formation of movement parties, which can be defined as "coalitions of political activists who emanate from social movements and try to apply the organizational and strategic practices of social movement in the arena of party competition" (Kitschelt, 2006: 280). An exemplar is the Podemos in Spain, which was founded in 2014 in the aftermath of the Spanish Indignados (Flesher Fominaya, 2020; Vittori, 2017). Meanwhile, with or without the presence of movement activists, postprotest elections could serve as a test of the extent to which the protest movement garnered public support. In Hong Kong, the District Council elections in November 2003, a few months after the 2003 July 1 protest, helped demonstrated public support for the democrats and thus confirmed the political implications of the protest (Lee & Chan, 2011). This is why, when an election does occur during or after a major protest movement, the movement and the election can be regarded as forming an event cluster.

After the Umbrella Movement, the District Council elections were held in November 2015. Although the District Council is only a local level consultation body without much actual political power, financial resources are associated with District Council seats. Winning the District Council elections, for political groups and parties, can help build community networks, connections with voters, and media and public recognition. Notably, at the end of the Umbrella Movement, many activists turned to local communities as the site for "deep cultivation" (Lam, 2018; Yuen & Mok, 2023). Participating in the District Council elections was consistent with their approach. Not surprisingly, a significant number of candidates associated with the Umbrella Movement appeared in the 2015 District Council elections. Many of them, as Mok (2020) showed, were motivated by the desire to prove that the Umbrella Movement did enjoy public support.

The news media called the candidates associated with the Umbrella Movement the "Umbrella Soldiers" and put them forward as a main point of observation. A search on the electronic news archive Wise News shows a total of 426 articles mentioning both "District Council elections" and "Umbrella Soldiers" on eight local newspapers[14] in November 2015. In comparison, only 75 articles from the same eight newspapers mentioned both "District Council elections" and "the localist faction" in the same period. That is, at least before the end of the election, the Umbrella Soldiers, instead of the localists, were the focal point. This is partly because the Umbrella Soldiers encompassed a wider range of candidates exhibiting different political inclinations. This is also partly because the term helped signify a group of "political newcomers." Their novelty fitted the basic news value underlying conventional journalism. Nonetheless, depending on the political inclination of the media outlets, the Umbrella Soldiers could be treated as either a breath of fresh air or an emerging threat.

Most media accounts put the number of Umbrella Soldiers in the election at slightly more than fifty. It is impossible to have a precise and definite number because not all identified Umbrella Soldiers called themselves as such, and not all self-proclaimed Umbrella Soldiers would be accepted by others as such. Throughout the electoral campaign, there were debates among the prodemocracy candidates about "fake Umbrella Soldiers." There were even conspiracy theories regarding how some self-proclaimed Umbrella Soldiers might be agents paid by the state to divide the prodemocracy votes.

What is noteworthy about the Umbrella Soldiers is that many of them deliberately downplayed the Umbrella Movement and political issues in general in their electoral campaigns. The most notable example is Youngspiration, a localist group formed in 2015 after the Umbrella Movement by a group of young activists. They sent out nine candidates to contest in the District Council elections, but the electoral platforms of all nine candidates did not mention the Umbrella Movement or any political matters at all. The platform put onto the official election website by Youngspiration member Yau Wai-ching, for instance, only included "resuming ferry service connecting Hung Hom and Wan Chai" (Hung Hom being the district where she ran), "relaxation of seat numbers of minibuses," "concerning the [bus] route rationalisation upon completion of [metro] extension," and "to propose to set-up a community hall and dock museum." The platform also included the slogan Hongkongers, Let's Win Together. Only the slogan hinted at a localist political stance, while the other four are all typical district-level and mostly livelihood matters. Interestingly, it was her opponent, progovernment politician Priscilla Leung who stated "adamantly opposed to Occupy Central" on her electoral platform.[15]

The self-restraint exercised by many of the Umbrella Soldiers during the election can be understood as based on their recognition of two facts. First, the District Council is indeed a local-level consultation body addressing mainly community and livelihood issues. "Politicizing" the District Council election may not be an appropriate strategy if one seriously attempts to win. Second, although some Umbrella Soldiers might want to use the election to showcase public support for the Umbrella Movement, they also needed to face the reality that many ordinary citizens indeed did not support the movement. They would risk alienating the politically neutral citizens if they played up protest-related themes too prominently. In early November, chairperson of Youngspiration Baggio Leung, when responding to the media about why their platforms did not indicate their localist stance, said that an election platform should indicate what the candidate can achieve after being elected, and he did not write "Hong Kong independence" onto his election platform because it could not be achieved even if he wins the election.[16]

Baggio Leung did not deny his own political stance. Hence it was not a matter of the candidates completely hiding their political views. They were just trying not to emphasize politics. As political scientist Ma Ngok explained in a newspaper article at the time:

> [When the Umbrella Soldiers] met the District Council elections, they quickly discovered a contradiction: the contradiction between the logic of citizen protest movement and the logic of electoral campaigning. The above-mentioned "Umbrella Soldiers" did not have much innovation. An important reason is that they understood the necessity to have their platforms, campaigning methods, and political roadmap acceptable to the majority if they want to win. Even if they have innovative ideas or radical stances or tactics, they have to follow the mainstream in the electoral contest. (Ma, 2015)

Electoral participation, in other words, can deradicalize under certain conditions. Even if the candidates' real beliefs do not change, they at least have to perform in a more "mainstream" manner. This is an important point to which chapter 4 and chapter 6 will return.

In the end, it was generally recognized that eight Umbrella Soldiers won. Overall, according to Lam (2017), the number of seats taken by the progovernment camp decreased from 311 in the 2011 District Council elections to 298, whereas the prodemocracy camp, including the Umbrella Soldiers, gained 22 additional seats compared to 2011. Since the elections were to return a total of 431 District Councillors, the shift was not substantial. The progovernment camp still won the majority of the seats.

Nonetheless, many commentators interpreted the election results as a "small victory" for the democrats. As one author put it: "The voter turnout of this District Council election reached 47 percent, which is a historical high. The pan-democrats gained 25 additional seats when compared to the last election, and eight 'Umbrella Soldiers' won unexpectedly. Many of the losing independent prodemocracy candidates also gained good numbers of votes. All these seem to demonstrate positive recognition of the Umbrella Movement" (Fong, 2015).[17] More systematic academic research in subsequent years would show that the Umbrella Movement might actually have undermined public support for prodemocracy candidates in the 2015 District Council elections. Wang and Wong (2021), in particular, analyzed constituency-level voting data and found that the vote shares of prodemocracy candidates were lower in constituencies physically closer to the occupation sites. Assuming that distance from the occupied areas is related to the degree to which everyday life was disrupted, their findings suggest that the inconvenience caused by the occupation had dampened people's support for the democrats at the voting booth. Of course, one cannot expect media commentators to respond to election results by conducting such advanced analysis. Rather, commentators had to construct immediate, reasonably convincing, and meaningful interpretations of the results. Such interpretations can affect how political actors understand the electoral outcome and potentially shape their subsequent decisions and strategies (Hershey, 1992; Kelly, 1983; Mendelsohn, 1988). In the 2015 District Council elections, in addition to the idea of a small victory for the democrats, another interpretation was that the results signified the rise of localism.

Treating the elections as signifying the rise of localism involved the discursive acts of re-grouping and boundary drawing. Authors have to put several results together to generate an overall interpretation and explain away results that might challenge the interpretation by acts of exclusion. For re-grouping of results, political scientist Ivan Choy (2015) was the most systematic. Titling his article, "District Council election results might lead the democrats to adjust their political stance," he grouped together four electoral outcomes: (1) the better-than-expected performance of the Umbrella Soldiers, (2) the loss of prodemocracy candidates who still emphasized communication with the Chinese Central Government, (3) the success of the political group Neo Democrat (winning fifteen seats with sixteen candidates), the campaign of which centered on several "local issues" and antimainlandization, and (4) the good performance of those democrats who belonged to moderate parties but exhibited a more hardline stance toward mainland influence in Hong

Kong. The grouping of results provided the basis for his prediction that a new generation of democrats who emphasize "the local" and who are more receptive toward valiant resistance would become more vocal and influential in the prodemocracy camp.

Meanwhile, to sustain the idea of the rise of localism, one has to dismiss the relevance of the losses suffered by other localist candidates. Commentator Lai Jak-fan wrote: "The moderate localist Neo Democrat won a major victory. [. . .] Together with the 70,000 votes won by the 'Umbrella Soldiers,' all these show the awakening of local consciousness [. . .]. These localists, who are really rooted in Hong Kong, are fundamentally different from the fake localists, such as Civic Passion [and others], who hoist the flag of valiant localism but really care about getting money" (2015). Lai emphasized the "moderate" character of the "real" localists who performed well in the election. By distinguishing between the "real" and "fake" localists, the validity of interpreting the election outcome as signifying the rise of localism was not only defended but also further specified: the election witnessed the rise of *moderate* localism. Similar emphasis on the success of *moderate* localists was apparent in the writings of other commentators.

Interpretations of electoral outcomes did not emerge arbitrarily. They have to be grounded in some facts and are rooted in the authors' political predilection. For instance, writers for the Communist-sponsored *Wen Wei Po* and *Ta Kung Po* did not draw any distinction between the Umbrella Soldiers who won and the radical localists who lost. For the progovernment media, all Umbrella Soldiers were radicals. They thus presented the electoral outcome as signifying a threat for Hong Kong. Meanwhile, both Ivan Choy and Lai Jak-fan quoted above were well-known figures having close ties with the moderate democrats. Their writings are illustrative of the moderate democrats' reaction to the election results: they recognized the rise of a group of young political actors with ostensible "localist" orientation, but they tried to draw a line between the moderate and the radical actors. The former were individuals that they could align with, while the latter had to be rejected. Interpretations of election results thus signified how political actors were negotiating their relationships with others.

Not all authors agreed with the "rise-of-localism" interpretation. Political scientist Yep Kinman (2015) noted the Umbrella Soldiers' self-restraint and the fact that many of them did not emphasize any "localist themes." Hence their victories should not be attributed to their ideologies. Nonetheless, rise of localism remained the more common interpretation. A search in Wise News using "District Council election" and ("local consciousness," "local discourse," or "local thinking") would return eighteen articles from eight newspapers in the eight days between November 23 and 30, while there were only two articles matching the keyword set in the three weeks before the election day. The 2015 District Council elections and the postelection interpretations helped constructed the rise of localism as a phenomenon.

Concluding Remarks

This chapter has reviewed the prelude, occurrence, and immediate aftermath of the Umbrella Movement. The Umbrella Movement occurred against the background of two intertwined interaction dynamics: the emerging trend of radicalization within the prodemocracy movement and the "bankruptcy" of the moderates' attempt to engage the state. The occupation was both planned and unplanned. It was originally meant to be a highly disciplined act of civil disobedience lasting for only a few days, but a series of contingent incidents altered the formation of the campaign. The emergence of multiple occupation sites empowered the movement by facilitating more participants to join the action, but it aggravated the problem of decentralization and the tension between the moderate and radical factions. The Mongkok occupation, in particular, became a place where young protesters looking for more forceful forms of protest actions could experience an atmosphere of valiant resistance. It became a place where protesters could be socialized into the ethos of the emerging localism.

After the end of the occupation, protests did not immediately disappear. People energized by the Umbrella Movement tried different ways to continue their resistance and/or exert influence on politics and society. Some continued with small-scale nondisruptive occupations, and some engaged in innovative forms of protests. Despite its limitations, the *gauwu* action had made Mongkok a persistent site of political contestation.

Meanwhile, part of the political energies was channeled into the electoral arena. Theoretically, it is emphasized that the impact of a redefining critical event does not arise merely from the "nature" of the event. The impact also depends on subsequent happenings and people's interpretations of such happenings. In Hong Kong, while the 2003 July 1 protest was followed by a major victory by the democrats in the District Council elections in November of the same year, the Umbrella Movement was followed by what can at most be interpreted as a "small victory" by the democrats and the Umbrella Soldiers in the District Council elections in 2015. Nonetheless, through regrouping the results and drawing boundaries, the rise of localism was constructed in the mainstream media as the main "lesson" that one could learn from the results of the election.

Nevertheless, the rise of localism was not treated as the same as the rise of radicalism. The electoral process can be deradicalizing because the candidates need to appeal to the majority, and postelection interpretations emphasized the diverging fate of the moderate (or real) localists and the radical (or fake) localists. In fact, while the localist groups had adopted adversarial framing and heavily criticized the moderate democrats during the Umbrella Movement, internal disputes within the prodemocracy camp were subdued during the 2015 District Council elections. Looking at the results of the 2015 District Council elections and the postelection interpretations, one might find a seeming willingness on the part of the moderate democrats and part of the localist camp to reconcile with each other. The electoral arena had promoted a specific type of relational dynamics between the two camps of the prodemocracy movement.

However, back on the streets, in addition to the playful *gauwu* protests, more confrontational actions were carried out throughout 2015 by other newly formed political groups. These political groups and their militant and controversial actions helped them attract media attention and gain notoriety in the process. The development of militant protests would culminate in the Mongkok civil unrest on the first day of Chinese New Year in 2016. This is the subject of the next chapter.

Chapter 3

The Mongkok Civil Unrest

This chapter focuses on the Mongkok civil unrest, alternatively dubbed Fishball Revolution by the protesters and their supporters and a riot by the government. It occurred on the first day of the Chinese New Year in 2016. The Mongkok civil unrest happened in a single night. It did not capture as much international attention when compared to the long-lasting and spectacular Umbrella Movement in 2014 and the Anti-ELAB protests in 2019, but it was a significant event that appeared in many academic accounts of the development of protest politics and localism in Hong Kong. During the clash between the police and the protesters that night, protesters threw bricks and glass bottles at the police, and a police officer fired two warning shots toward the sky at one point. This level of use of force from the two sides might not raise any eyebrows by international standards, and it was far from comparable to the level of violence during the Anti-ELAB protests in 2019. But given Hong Kong's protest culture and emphasis on social order, it was hugely shocking to the local public at the time.

As the end of the last chapter recounted, although the emerging localists in the early 2010s in Hong Kong generally tended to believe in the need of forceful resistance through militant tactics, some localist actors and groups did turn to the electoral arena in 2015. They exercised self-restraint by not highlighting their more radical political views in order to appeal to the mass public. After the District Council elections in 2015, many commentators interpreted the results in a way to emphasize public receptiveness toward *moderate* localism. Yet the Mongkok civil unrest—together with the LegCo by-election held weeks after the incident—altered media and public perceptions again. The unrest and the by-election also directly contributed to the prominence of the Hong Kong Indigenous (HKI) and its leaders, Wong Toi-Yeung and Edward Leung. Edward Leung, who participated in the 2016 LegCo by-election as a candidate, would become an icon in Hong Kong's public arena in the years that followed. His campaign slogan in the by-election—Reclaim Hong Kong, Revolution of Our Time—would become a main protest slogan during the Anti-ELAB protests in 2019.

Despite its significance, there have not been systematic studies about the Mongkok civil unrest. The event typically received passing mentions in scholarly narratives about the rise of localism. Even Yuen and Chung's (2018) "eventful analysis" of the rise of localism could give the event only a rather brief account. A chapter-length account of the event was given by Lo (2016), but his study focuses specifically on protest policing. His description of the happenings during the protest event itself is based only on media materials.

Of course, the aim of analyzing the Mongkok civil unrest in detail goes beyond the provision of a more thorough description of the event itself. Within the context of this book, the HKI was one of the most important localist groups emerging after the Umbrella Movement, and the Mongkok civil unrest was the most consequential contentious action understood to be led by the localists. A close analysis of the HKI and the Mongkok civil unrest can allow us to better understand the formation, characteristics, and limitations of the localist movement in that period. More specifically, drawing upon Snow and Moss's (2014) theorization of spontaneity in protests, this chapter will show how localist protests were often both organized and unorganized. Hence this chapter shall also contribute to more general theoretical understandings of spontaneous protests.

The following begins with a background discussion about the formation of localist groups after the Umbrella Movement, the basic characteristics of the HKI, and the confrontational "reclaim actions" in 2015. The main body of the chapter will offer an account of the Mongkok civil unrest by drawing upon materials from the media, court proceedings, and thirty-eight in-depth interviews with participants and onsite observers.

New Localist Groups and Spontaneous Protests

Before examining the Mongkok civil unrest, it is important to further explicate the social movement scene after the Umbrella Movement, introduce the HKI, and examine the notion of spontaneous protests.

Generally, extraordinary protest events are often associated with the outbursts of huge amounts of social and political energies. Such energies will typically be sedimented in various ways, including the formation of new groups and organizations (della Porta, 2020). The debate surrounding national security legislation and the subsequent July 1 protest in Hong Kong in 2003, for example, triggered the public participation and activism of numerous members of the legal profession. Several prominent legal professionals formed the Article 45 Concern Group[1] in late 2003. In 2006, the group became the Civic Party, which would continue to be one of the two most important prodemocracy political parties in the city in the next fifteen years.

Not all new organizations survive over time, but even those organizations that dissipated relatively quickly can be the platforms through which new politicians or activists began their public career. For instance, 7.1 People Pile was another new but short-lived group formed in August 2003 by young activists. Members of the group who were political newcomers at the time included a couple of activists who would later play prominent roles in the New Preservation Movement in the mid-2000s. There was also Alvin Yeung, who would later become one of the most prominent prodemocracy politicians in the 2010s.

The Umbrella Movement, unsurprisingly, also had its organizational outgrowth. Lam (2018) noted the formation of three main types of groups and organizations after the occupation campaign: (1) associations formed by liberal-oriented practitioners in various professions, (2) community associations focusing on promoting democracy and addressing issues in local communities, and (3) political groups active in both protest and electoral politics. Many of these associations and organizations were manifestly localist in orientation, for example, through their self-identification as localists, their critique of mainlandization, and/or their discursive emphasis on Hong Kong people as a distinctive ethnic group. Ng and Kennedy's (2021) analysis of what constitutes localism in the mid-2010s included three localist community groups and five localist political groups. All three community groups—Kowloon East Community, Tin Shui Wai New Force, and Tung Chung Future—were formed in late 2014 when the Umbrella Movement was drawing to a close. Among the five political groups examined by Ng and Kennedy (2021), four were formed after the Umbrella Movement: the HKI (formed in 2015), Youngspiration (formed in 2015), Demosisto (formed in 2016), and the Hong Kong National Party (formed in 2016).

For the present discussion, the important point to note is the informal character of many of these emerging groups and organizations. The HKI is exemplary in this regard. A commentary article published in February 2016, more than one year after the establishment of the group, wrote that the group neither registered as an organization under the Societies Ordinance nor registered as a company. The political group had no publicized party constitution. There was no information about how its leadership was elected or selected, no information about its structure and organization, and no formal bank account (Yeung, 2016). According to K, a core member of the group,[2] the group indeed had no internal structure. It was, in K's words, "like a club" with people sharing similar interests and views. Individuals were connected with each other via a mobile messaging group, and whoever joined the mobile messaging group became a member. The group would gather regularly in an apartment corented by the members. Wong Toi-Yeung, a prominent leader, told a reporter in mid-March 2016 that the group had about fifty members (Nam, 2016). According to K, members could join meetings and discuss policy directions and activities. They were required to pay 300 Hong Kong dollars for the signature blue jacket bearing the name of the HKI, and then another 100 to 200 dollars per month to support the group.

Because of the informality, K noted that people could "jump in and out." That is, sometimes people just left the group by posting a message, explaining their reasons for leaving. Sometimes, some people who had left the group would want to return. Whether accepting a returnee would be decided through discussion among the members in a meeting. The group's culture thus emphasized equality and the absence of hierarchy, both internally and externally (i.e., in the group's relationship with other protesters). As a news report in March 2016 stated: "One can initiate; one can participate; one can speak. But 'to represent' and 'to lead' are taboos. Although many protesters could be seen following the ones in blue jackets whenever the latter appeared, Wong Toi-Yeung emphasized that the group did not intend to lead the protesters. 'Every protester needs independent thinking. If the blue jackets lead protesters into the wrong way, protesters need to remain critical instead of blindly believing in organizations'" (Nam, 2016). However, as Freeman's (1972) classic discussion about the US feminist movement pointed out, movements that emphasize horizontality and the absence of structures may end up with the de facto presence of leadership and hidden hierarchy. The HKI can be a case in point. As the group became visible to the media, someone had to speak on their behalf. Wong Toi-Yeung became the group's spokesperson. On the one hand, the title of *spokesperson*, instead of *chairperson*, was deliberately chosen in order to signify the absence of "leaders," and Wong became the spokesperson—according to K—merely because he was willing to take up the position that others did not want to take up. But on the other hand, Wong did become the "de facto leader" over time. He had some public recognition even before the establishment of the HKI because he was arrested during the Umbrella Movement. When other groups wanted to contact the HKI, they would contact Wong. Wong also hosted an online program via YouTube. Besides, those around Wong knew that he—a freelance internal designer by trade—sacrificed substantially because he lost a lot of jobs due to his activism. Therefore, Wong was well respected among his peers.

The small size of the group, its public visibility (through the blue jackets), the lack of formal structure and hierarchy, the emphasis on a culture of equality, and yet the inevitable presence of de facto leadership are important characteristics to keep in mind for understanding the role of the HKI in various protest actions. This range of characteristics contributed to the emergence of spontaneity in the protest actions they initiated.

The notion of spontaneous protest is often used to refer to protests that were not planned by formal organizers but emerged from the bottom up through the simultaneous decisions made by many individuals and the interaction dynamics spreading through informal networks. Spontaneity was an important aspect of many historical movements such as the Tiananmen Square protests in China and the protests in East Germany in 1989 (Opp et al., 1995; Zhao, 2001). The notion has appeared more frequently in academic writings since the early 2010s, probably partly because of the rise of digitally mediated connective action and decentralized networked social movements (Bennett & Segerberg, 2013; Castells, 2012). Nevertheless, several authors have questioned whether protest movements hailed by people as exemplars of spontaneous protests were indeed as spontaneous as observers regard them to be (Flesher Fominaya, 2015; Pilati et al., 2019).

Against this background, Snow and Moss (2014) offered a systematic framework for analyzing spontaneity in protests. In their explication, actions and events can be spontaneous in the sense that they "are not thought through in a deliberative fashion in advance of their occurrence" (p. 1123). Yet spontaneity does not entail lack of rational thinking. Spontaneous actions can still be driven by strategic concerns, but the cognitive process associated with spontaneous actions is compressed in time. Spontaneity does not entail the complete lack of planning or organizing. It can be an element intervening into a planned protest and altering its course. Protest events can therefore be "organized but not entirely organized" (p. 1139).

Snow and Moss (2014) outlined four conditions that facilitate the emergence of spontaneity. First, spontaneous actions are more likely to arise when the organizer of a protest has a nonhierarchical instead of hierarchical structure because the culture of nonhierarchical movements "valorize openness, innovation, and experimental forms of collective action" (p. 1128). Second, spontaneous actions are more likely to arise when the situation is ambiguous. Ambiguity, in turn, can result from the breakdown of scripts, the dissolution of scripts at the end of a planned action, or the emergence of nonscripted stand-offs between protesters and counterprotesters or the police. Third, spontaneity is based on priming and framing. The lines of action that emerge "are not random but are dictated, in part, by prior priming experiences or cues and their recency" (p. 1134). Cognitions that are at the top of people's heads and affect already strongly felt by people influence their onsite improvisation. Fourth and finally, spontaneity is shaped by ecological factors, that is, the "spatial configurations and arrangements, whether natural or built, that affect patterns of human settlement and interaction" (p. 1136).

Given the framework, it is not difficult to see why spontaneity tended to feature prominently in protests initiated by the HKI. The HKI is a nonhierarchical organization. The actions initiated by the group (and other emerging localist groups) often involved an element of experimentation with new tactics, about which there was no existing, well-developed "script" understood by the participants. Yet it does not mean that the actions and interactions constituting the protest activities occurred completely randomly, as they could be shaped by prior protest experiences, existing frameworks of understanding, and spatial and ecological factors. While the next section will illustrate how these considerations could help us understand the Mongkok civil unrest, the same considerations are useful for understanding the series of "reclaim actions" conducted by the HKI in 2015. A brief discussion of the reclaim actions can provide further background for understanding the HKI and the Mongkok civil unrest.

The reclaim actions refer to a series of protests targeting mainland tourists and parallel traders in various districts in Hong Kong in 2015 and 2016. Such actions had their precedents before the Umbrella Movement. In September 2012, a group of local citizens initiated the "reclaim Sheung Shui station" action. About three hundred people responded to the call for action and congregated at the train station in Sheung Shui, the town close to the border with mainland China, to confront people suspected to be conducting parallel trading activities. The action was repeated several times in later months. Meanwhile, starting from February 2014, netizens self-mobilized to engage in protest activities in Canton Road, an area in the shopping district Tsim Sha Tsui, against mainland tourists. The netizens described their action as an attempt to "expel the locusts," with locusts being the derogatory term used to refer to mainland tourists and immigrants who were considered as swarming over and devastating Hong Kong.

The above pre-Umbrella Movement activities often did not have clear organizers. The actions were highly controversial. Many prodemocracy citizens questioned the justifiability of targeting tourists directly and the appropriateness of using dehumanizing language. The confrontational protests often resulted in skirmishes between the protesters and their targets or citizens disturbed by the actions. Nevertheless, supporters of such actions believed that they were compelled to radicalize because only more confrontational actions could force the government to respond.

Therefore, the reclaim actions in early 2015 were not entirely a tactical innovation. Localist groups were adopting a protest tactic developed in the most recent years. On February 8, 2015, Civic Passion, the HKI, a student group, and a local community group initiated the Reclaim Tuen Mun action to protest against parallel traders. Around five hundred people participated. On February 15, the HKI participated in the Defend Shatin action, in which protesters walked around the major shopping mall in the Shatin district and confronted the tourist shoppers. On March 1, Civic Passion and the HKI initiated the Reclaim Yuen Long action to protest against parallel trading activities and Hong Kong's tourism policy. Skirmishes ensued between the protesters and a group of local residents who disagreed with the protest actions. On March 8, similar protest activities occurred in Sheung Shui, Shatin, and Tuen Mun simultaneously.[3]

The protest in Tuen Mun on March 8 generated an incident that put the already controversial action into disrepute. During the action, a group of protesters surrounded a middle-aged woman on the street. The woman was carrying a little girl and a piece of luggage. The protesters thus identified her as a parallel trader, but the woman insisted that she was not. The woman even opened her luggage to prove her case. The protesters and the woman shouted at each other, and the little girl was scared and started to cry. The whole incident was captured in a video, which went viral on the Internet.[4] Citizens who commented on the matter online were generally highly sympathetic toward the little girl and criticized the protesters severely.

The Incident put the HKI into the spotlight. In a media interview, Wong Toi-Yeung explained his stance: "[Reporters] asked me whether we would apologize to the public. But those who shouted [at the woman] and those who engaged in skirmishes were not members of our group, why do I need to apologize? And almost every media outlet asked if I would condemn the action. I won't. This is because we understand what the protesters were doing. [. . .] I only represent my organization. I do not represent all protesters" (quoted in Nam, 2016). A few points can be made about the crying girl incident and Wong's response. First, the controversial incident could be considered as arising partly due to the ambiguity of the protest situation. The reclaim action did not have a clear script; that is, other than the general idea of going to shopping malls and onto the street to drive away parallel traders and tourists, it was not entirely clear exactly what protest participants were supposed to do, how they were supposed to identify the parallel traders, and how they were supposed to act when their targets or bystanders reacted to their protests. The action ostensibly required the participants to improvise as the interaction at the protest site unfolded.

Second, the improvised speeches and actions did not come from nowhere. Protesters' reactions during the incident were based on existing discourses about and affect toward the negative impact of the influx of mainlanders on Hong Kong people's everyday life. For instance, at one moment of the confrontation in the crying girl incident, the woman claimed that her daughter was studying in Hong Kong. A protester immediately criticized her for consuming Hong Kong's public resources. That is, while the woman tried to make the point that she was not a tourist, in the eyes of the protester, she immediately became identified as a new immigrant who took away public resources from Hong Kong people. The response from the protesters was driven by ideas and affect that were already prominent among the protesters given the social context.

Third, the incident arose also partly due to the ecological factor that, in a shopping mall or on the street, there was no simple method for the protesters to accurately determine who was a parallel trader and who just happened to be carrying luggage and may not even be a tourist. The protesters might rely on subtle cues ranging from how people look and dress, but they can easily identify the wrong target.

Fourth, the culture of equality emphasized by the HKI compelled them not to claim leadership. But despite how the HKI positioned itself, the group was indeed a main initiator of the action. Hence, they were identified by the media as the spokespersons for the protests. In other words, the group was held accountable—in the sense of being responsible for giving an account—for the reclaim actions. Yet their ability to provide a coherent account was limited by their self-positioning as nonleaders, as well as by the fact that the protesters' onsite actions were indeed largely spontaneous. This could lead the public to perceive the group as irresponsible.

The reclaim actions thus both enhanced the public recognition and solidified the controversial image of the HKI. In any case, the reclaim actions subsided after the protest on March 8, 2015. The next time the group came under a strong media spotlight, it would be associated with a protest event that was even more controversial, but similarly marked by the presence of a strong degree of spontaneity.

Reconstructing the Mongkok Civil Unrest

After providing the background of the emergence of the HKI and their reclaim actions in 2015, we can now turn to the Mongkok civil unrest. Methodologically, thirty-eight in-depth interviews were conducted between March 2019 and September 2020 to obtain the experiences and observations of people who were at the protest site in the night when the unrest occurred. The interviewees can be categorized into participants, observers, and journalists. Twelve interviewees were participants in the protest; that is, they engaged in the clashes with the police that night, though their participation might be restricted to specific time periods inside the whole event. Twenty-one interviewees were observers, people who were there and witnessed different parts of the event. They did not engage in the clashes with the police (or at least not after the beginning of intensive clashes). Five interviewees were journalists. Obviously, they were observers too, but they were also carrying out a professional duty. So they were treated as a separate category. All interviewees remained anonymous. The methodological appendix includes additional information about the interviews.

The major aim of the interviews was to gather information about the details of the happenings in the protest event, the interviewees' observations about the actions of various parties, and their thoughts and feelings during the event. Of course, memories are not necessarily a reliable guide to reality, especially since the memories were collected three to four years after the original event. Therefore, the following account was also based on media materials and documents from the court cases associated with the Mongkok civil unrest. These latter documents were often the basis for basic facts about the protest that night. Nevertheless, the interviewees' accounts remain highly useful because the details and views they provided could aid the proper interpretations of the happenings throughout the protest event.

Based on court proceedings and media materials, table 3.1 offers a simplified chronology of the Mongkok civil unrest, and figure 3.1 offers a street map showing the area where the various clashes throughout the night

Table 3.1. Simplified chronology of major happenings and incidents during the Mongkok civil unrest

Time	Incident / Happenings	Brief description
Early evening	1. The night market started	The night market started in the early evening hours in Portland Street of Mongkok
9:00 p.m.	2. Arrival of the HKI	About 10 members of the HKI arrived at Portland Street at around 9 p.m.
10:00 p.m.	3. Taxi incident	A taxi drove into Portland Street and hit an old man; a group of citizens surrounded the taxi, and police officers arrived to handle the matter
11:45 p.m.	4. Elevated platform incident	About 250 police officers arrived at the juncture of Portland Street and Shandong Street and put forward an elevated platform
1:30 a.m.	5. Confrontation and negotiation	Protesters and police officers stood off against each other at the intersection of Portland Street and Shandong Street
1:30–1:45 a.m.	6. Clash at Portland Street	Clashes between protesters and the police at the intersection of Portland Street and Shandong Street
2:00–2:30 a.m.	7. Firing of warning shots	A traffic police officer fired warning shots toward the sky at Argyle Street
2:30–3:30 a.m.	8. Clashes at Nathan Road	Protesters congregated on the two sides of Nathan Road. Some protesters began burning objects on the street. Clashes with the police ensued.
3:30–4:30 a.m.	9. Clashes at Shandong Street	Clashes intensified, and protesters continued to throw bricks and various objects at the police.
4:30–8:00 a.m.	10. Clashes at Garden Street	About fifty members of the police's Special Tactical Contingent arrived at the scene as protesters engaged in guerrilla battles with the police around the area of Fa Yuen Street, Soy Street, and Sai Yee Street

Source: Created by the author.

Figure 3.1. Street map of Mongkok and location of major incidents during the Mongkok civil unrest. The numbers marked on the map refer to the numbered incidents in table 3.1. *Source:* Created by the author.

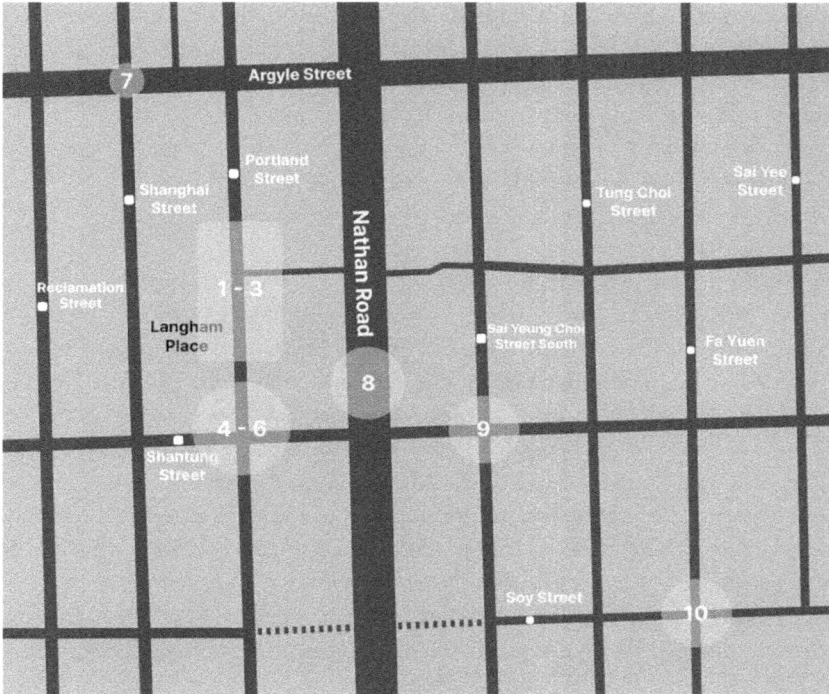

occurred. The court proceedings separated the night's events into a number of distinctive "incidents." Based on the interview materials and the factual happenings, it is believed that the Mongkok civil unrest can be meaningfully reconstructed as involving three stages. In the first stage, conflicts have not started. It was a night market on the first day of Chinese New Year, though activists were there to prepare to defend the hawkers in case officers from the Food and Environmental Hygiene Department (FEHD) or the police attempted to evict the night market. This is the period between the early evening hours to around 11:00 p.m. The second stage refers to the period between the beginning of confrontations on the site and the police officer's firing of warning shots. The latter more or less coincided with the time Edward Leung was arrested. This is the period from around 11:45 p.m. to 2:30 a.m. The third stage involves intensified police-protester clashes. This period began at around 2:30 a.m. and ended at around 8:00 a.m., when the whole unrest was brought under control.

The following pages attempt to provide a thick description—that is, a description that would highlight the social and theoretical import—of the happenings at these three stages of the Mongkok civil unrest. It will be followed by an overall discussion of the key characteristics of the protest event following Snow and Moss's (2014) framework.

BACKGROUND OF STREET HAWKING IN HONG KONG AND PRELUDE TO THE CIVIL UNREST

Before the event evolved ultimately into violent police-protester clashes, it was originally meant to be a festive evening with street hawkers forming a night market selling cooked food alongside Portland Street in Mongkok. A brief history of street hawkers in the city and their symbolic significance can help put the event into perspective. Street hawkers emerged in Hong Kong as early as the 1870s. By 1946, there were more than seventy thousand hawkers in the city (Rewal, 2018). From the 1960s to the 1980s, street hawkers constituted an important part of the city's informal economy during the process of economic modernization (Smart, 1989). Working as a street hawker was, for some grassroots citizens, a means to start their small businesses. For others, the flexibility of working as a street hawker allowed them to earn extra income to compensate for their low wages. While the street hawkers sold a wide range of goods, for many ordinary citizens, purchasing cooked foods as snacks from street hawkers was part of everyday life. Curry fishball, in particular, was among the most common and popular street snacks.

An informal market formed by street hawkers was part of the urban landscape, and it offered a range of unique cultural experiences to ordinary citizens and even tourists. As Smart (2006) recounted (quoted by Rewal, 2018: 293): "One of the exciting features of daily life in the 1980s was the instantaneous disappearance of an entire street market when spotters observed the Urban Services Department Hawker Control Squad arriving. As long as bystanders could avoid the hurtling cooked food carts, particularly those bearing vats of boiling oil, the scattering of hawkers like a flock of pigeons was an amusing side-show." The scenario described by Smart (2006) was called *jau-gwai* in Cantonese, which literally means "running ghosts." It is part of the cultural memory of citizens old enough to have experienced such scenarios. However, not unlike other developed cities around the world, the Hong Kong government has, over the decades, tightened its regulation of street hawkers in the name of urban governance, public order, safety, and sanitation (Marinelli, 2018). The selling of cooked food on the street, in particular, was banned. But given the aforementioned value of street hawking, the government policy could be criticized for eroding the chances for citizens to use informal means as a path to self-employment. As Smart and Smart (2017: 450) asked at the end of their analysis of the process of "formalization" in Hong Kong: "Is eradicating informality a reasonable goal in a place where income inequality has soared to one of the highest levels among rich countries?" Culturally, the eradication of street hawkers could also be seen as an example of how aspects of the local grassroots lifestyle were undermined or even eliminated by the government's pursuit of "development." Given how the issue relates to the livelihood of grassroots citizens and to local culture, it is understandable that the hawker issue would attract the attention of the emerging localist groups.

Nonetheless, the elimination of street hawking was incomplete. In the early 2000s, under the economic downturn triggered by the Asian financial crisis in 1997, the Hong Kong government decided to adopt a more flexible approach to manage street hawkers. The Hawkers Control Team (HCT) was given the discretionary power to determine when, where, and under what conditions street hawking would be allowed. Chan (2018) described the Hong Kong government's approach as a case of informality from above through which "legal and spatial ambiguities have been constructed to organize and discipline urban space" (p. 440). Meanwhile, his ethnographic studies of a night market in another district in the mid-2010s found that hawkers would develop strategies to handle the situation. For example, one specific strategy was "giving face" to the HCT: hawkers would hide their products and stopped doing business when the HCT arrived, and they expected their respect to the HCT to be reciprocated, even though the HCT remained in control of whether to enforce restrictions or not.

Certain "conventional practices" were developed within this space of ambiguity and informality. In the late 2000s and early 2010s, regularly operating night markets with street hawkers selling cooked foods could still be found in a few residential areas in the city. By the mid-2010s, in several grassroots districts, including Mongkok, it was not uncommon for street hawkers to form a night market and run their businesses during Chinese New Year, hoping that the HCT would ignore them during such festive times.

Against this background, the HKI engaged the hawker issue starting in 2015. Before the Chinese New Year, they wrote a proposal to the FEHD, suggesting the department to allow the formation of a night market of street hawkers during the festival, and saying that the group would help maintain order and clean up the place afterward. The government did not respond. Then, during the first three nights of the Chinese New Year, the HKI went to Mongkok to help coordinate the operation of the informal night market. Nam described the 2015 experience as follows:

> When the FEHD people went to Portland Street, the hawkers went hiding in the small alleys. [The HKI] helped escort the hawker carts to escape, and they confronted the FEHD people. When police officers arrived at the scene with police dogs, they formed a human chain to defend the area. When the police left and there was no longer any action to clear the night market, they set up their own booths to seek donations. In the early morning hours, when all people had gone, they cleaned up the Portland Street. (Nam, 2016)

The 2015 experience was important because it suggests what could have been the case and what could have been in the mind of the members of the HKI when they decided to go to Portland Street again in 2016. The above description of the happenings in 2015 does not deviate too substantially from Chan's (2018) finding that hawkers in informal night markets tended to "give face" to the HCT and go into hiding when the latter arrives, with the implicit expectation that the HCT would just leave after "performing" their duty. The description also shows that the action of the HKI was guided by only a vague and general "script": they were supposed to be there to help coordinate the night market, try to protect the hawkers when government and police officers took action, and clean up the place at the end. The core of the action was ostensibly to protect the hawkers, but there could not have been a clear script regarding exactly what to do because there was uncertainty regarding the actions of the law enforcement.

As a matter of fact, in 2016, the decision to go to Mongkok to support the hawkers was itself somewhat ad hoc. By January 2016, the HKI had already participated in the LegCo by-election to be held in late February. According to interviewee A01, the group originally did not intend to address the hawker issue again because of the lack of time. While some hawkers contacted the group a few days before the Chinese New Year, there was no immediate consensus of whether the group should do anything. The situation changed only in the night of February 7, when activist Lau

Siu-lai was arrested at another night market in the Sham Shui Po district. As interviewee A01 recalled, Wong Toi-Yeung said "let's go" in their messaging group in the morning of February 8. By 12:30 p.m., the HKI published a Facebook post calling upon people to join and support the night market on Portland Street that night. In addition to the HKI, Lau Siu-lai herself was released by the police and decided to shift to Mongkok to support hawkers. She issued a call to action on her Facebook page at around 5:00 p.m. At around 8:26 p.m., Agnes Chow of Scholarism also issued a Facebook post suggesting people to go to Mongkok.

Given the calls issued by activists of different political orientations, many social movement supporters and journalists went to Mongkok that night. Among the thirty-eight interviewees of the project, twenty-four attended the night market. Most of the interviewees acknowledged that the calls issued by Edward Leung and Lau Siu-lai were part of the reason they went. Yet many of them also stated that going to Mongkok was not meant to be a political act. As one interviewee put it when asked if he was concerned about the hawker issue: "Actually people went there that day not because they were concerned about the issue. They just went there to eat. I had a friend who ran a street stall that night, so I was supporting him. It was very relaxed. [. . .] I don't think there was a big political interest there."

Therefore, the night market was festive yet peaceful when it started, according to interviewee B17, who arrived early to help the hawkers to set up their stalls. Interviewee B10 recalled that he arrived at Mongkok at around 8:00 to 9:00: "At the beginning it was just holiday atmosphere. People said *kung hei fat choi* to each other. Just be happy during the New Year." Interviewee B02 arrived at the scene after 9:00 p.m. He recalled that the hawkers and other people had already occupied the part of Portland Street in front of Langham Place, a major shopping mall. "There were just too many people; it was impossible not to occupy the road." Yet there was no sense of danger at the beginning. Portland Street is not a main road in the district. Its "occupation" in the night hours would not cause serious traffic problems. Interviewees B13 and A08 recalled that, during the period when the night market remained peaceful, members of the HKI were maintaining order and clearing rubbish on the street.

Nevertheless, numerous interviewees also opined that they were aware of the *possibility* of conflicts. Both B03 and B17 said that, because some of the hawkers were social activists, they anticipated that there could be sporadic, minor conflicts that night. Some interviewees who had more protest experiences said that they had the psychological preparation for the occurrence of conflicts, and they were prepared to help if conflicts did arise. "Helping" could include protecting the hawkers when the government officers or the police attempted to evict the night market, or it could refer to providing support for arrested hawkers. Some other interviewees opined that, given the arrest of Lau Siu-lai in the previous night, they predicted that arrests and small-scale conflicts could occur. But they treated the night market during Chinese New Year as a local tradition that needed to be defended. Hence, they still wanted to support the hawkers. No one predicted the scale of the conflict that eventually arose.

The first tension-filled moment occurred shortly after 9:00 p.m., when officers of the HCT arrived. Supporters on the site surrounded and booed the officers, preventing them from executing their work. Interviewee B05 recalled that, when he arrived at Portland Street, Wong Toi-Yeung was standing on top of something and speaking through a loudspeaker. "The atmosphere was a bit tense. The FEHD people were outnumbered." According to information from court proceedings, the HCT left Portland Street at 9:50 p.m. and called the police to help. After the HCT left, the festive atmosphere of the night market resumed, and citizens continued to queue up and purchase at the hawkers' stalls.

Up to this point, there was still no sign of serious conflicts to come. Instead, one interviewee who belonged to the HKI opined: "My personal observation on the site was that different people were protecting the hawkers according to their own understanding. In fact, by 10:00 p.m., after the FEHD people left, the HKI had finished its job." This opinion from the interviewee corroborates with the point that there was no concrete and detailed script for people in the night market to follow. Many people shared the goal of protecting the hawkers, but they did so according to their own understanding of what needed to be done. Yet the response could also be read as implying the presence of a general and simple script: when the HCT arrived, activists and supporting citizens were supposed to outnumber them and "boo them off." The job could be considered done when the HCT was driven away, with the hope that the latter would then turn a blind eye given the occasion of the Chinese New Year.

Stand-off and the Beginning of Police-Protester Clash

The atmosphere on Portland Street turned tense again at 10:00 p.m., when a taxi drove into the street and reportedly hit an old man. This is dubbed "the taxi Incident" in later court trials related to the Mongkok civil unrest.

Interviewee B08 recalled that a few individuals were very angry and repeatedly patted the front of the taxi. A team of police officers of the patrol subunit arrived. They attempted to stand around the taxi to block off the surrounding citizens, but even more people became agitated when they saw the police. According to interviewee B02, the police demanded that the citizens disperse, but people refused to do so and booed the police instead. Some individuals started shouting "black police"—a derogatory term referring to suspected collusion between the police and criminal gangs. One interviewee recalled that Wong Toi-Yeung used a loudspeaker to suggest people make way and allow the taxi to leave. Another interviewee corroborated with the account: "The first time the police came [due to the taxi incident], many people rushed forward to shout 'black police.' It wasn't Wong Toi-Yeung who did not make way [for the taxi]; other people did not. Because it occurred suddenly. People were eating, and then suddenly the police arrived. The emotions changed immediately. [. . .] After the police left the scene, people cheered. The mood returned, and people started buying beers and foods again." The taxi incident was merely accidental and did not result in sustained conflicts, but it already illustrated the tendency of people to react emotionally to the presence of the police and thus the potential volatility of the situation. It also illustrated the delicate relationship between the HKI and the night market participants. Some participants joined the night market because of the call by the HKI. The group had the capacity to mobilize its own members and supporters, but it did not have the capacity to dictate the happenings on the site.

After the taxi incident, the night market remained peaceful for another hour. According to court materials, at around 11:45 p.m., about 250 police officers arrived at the intersection of Portland Street and Shandong Street. They set up an elevated platform. The arrival of a large number of police officers immediately altered the atmosphere of the night market again. Many people stood in front of the police in an attempt to stop the police from marching into Portland Street. The police requested the citizens to leave the road and return to the pedestrian way, but this only flustered the mood of the crowd further.

The night market participants' protest experience shaped their interpretations of and responses to the appearance of the police. Interviewee B02 recalled that the atmosphere turned tense very quickly, "I felt that the majority of people were familiar with this kind of scenario." Interviewees A05, A06, and A07 all mentioned that, according to their experience during the latter stages of the Umbrella Movement, the use of elevated platforms by the police signified a "serious situation." The interviewees started to think that the police would forcefully evict the night market. Interviewee B02 opined that the police suddenly were in full gear, "They went up to what we called the 'fort,' [. . .] and I don't know why they had to hold their shields. It is so obviously a very negative [development]."

There is no detailed information about the rationale or plan of the police action, and the participants' interpretation might not be entirely accurate. But such interpretations constituted the background to understand people's actions at that moment. Video recordings of the event showed that some people moved potted plants from the roadside to the center of the road. Some threw the plants and the mud toward the police. Others threw plastic bottles. The police showed their red flag with the words Stop Charging or We Use Force. There were also people asking others to calm down and stop throwing things at the police, but to no avail. Some police officers used pepper spray and batons against the agitated people. The scene became rather chaotic. The mobile stalls of a few hawkers fell over.

According to Interviewee B06, the use of pepper spray by the police did force a truce because many of the protesting night market participants were hurt and had to move to the roadside to receive treatment. But even as the skirmishes stopped, a stand-off had already been formed. The crowd broke into two groups. One group stood in the middle of Portland Street and confronted the police; the other stood on the roadside to observe. At the front of the group confronting the police were members of the HKI in their blue jackets and holding their self-made shields. There were people throwing things at the police occasionally from the back. The police continued to warn the crowd and asked people to leave, whereas Wong Toi-Yeung stood at the top of a van and asked the police to leave via a loudspeaker.

The formation of the stand-off could be regarded as the point when a protest event emerged. It was also the point when the HKI took up a "leading" role at the site. It does not mean that all night market participants were willing to follow the group's instructions, and it also does not mean that the HKI tried to become the leader. Interviewee A01 noted, "I felt that Wong Toi-Yeung's words and deeds were trying to maintain people's morale. There was no concrete content or direction given. Just to maintain a voice [. . .] and there were many different views there." Interviewee B21 also said that, according to his observation, Wong Toi-Yeung kept talking to other people on the site, but there were arguments and debates. That is, people did not simply listen to Wong.

Nonetheless, the HKI became the de facto leader on the site partly due to the presence of a sizable number of visible group members (due to their blue jackets), and partly due to their preparedness (e.g., the self-made shields). As Edward Leung was at the time a candidate in the 2016 LegCo by-election, the group also had the option of conducting an election march. According to Hong Kong law, an election candidate can conduct an election march without prior approval by the police if the number of participants is lower than 30. At 12:27 a.m., the HKI announced on its Facebook page that Edward Leung would exercise his right as an election candidate to conduct an election march at the Mongkok night market, and the post called upon people to go to Mongkok to support the action. On Portland Street, members of the HKI brought out flags with the group's name and started preparing for the march.

According to interviewee A01, the HKI apparently thought that starting an election march could ease the tension that was building up at the site. The group thought that the marching team could stand between the police and the protesting citizens, and the police would refrain from using force. This could protect the citizens on the street. The interviewee also noted that the HKI actually had just conducted an election march in Sheung Shui the previous month.

However, it is not entirely clear how one could expect the election march to resolve the tension on the site. The action could not last long. The police might not stop the march, but they also did not have reasons to leave because of it. The protesting citizens also held different views regarding the action at that point. Interviewee B03 recalled that some social movement activists on the site disliked the decision made by the HKI. Interviewee B17 was involved in the earlier skirmishes with the police. But when the election march was announced, he returned to the roadside from the center of the street because he felt the HKI had already dominated the site, and he did not intend to join their action.

In other words, regardless of the intention of Edward Leung and Wong Toi-Yeung, a main effect of the election march was reinforcing the status of the HKI as the de facto leader of the emerging protest action, though it would remain so without the actual capability of controlling and directing the actions of other people on the site. The police also identified Wong Toi-Yeung as the person to negotiate with, but the negotiation process was repeatedly disrupted by other citizens. The police told Wong that they had the duty to maintain public order. Wong replied that, if the police left the site, the crowd would also disband. At one point, the police officer asked Wong if they had the ability to control the crowd, and the surrounding crowd shouted: "No! No! No!" The negotiation failed. Interviewee A08 opined that the crowd was angry toward the police because they thought that the earlier taxi incident already resolved in a collaborative manner. The return of the police was a breach of mutual trust. Interviewee B03, who was watching the negotiation, opined that Wong Toi-Yeung was too confrontational when dealing with the police. At that moment, she and her friends were predicting that things would inevitably run out of control.

At around 1:30 a.m., members of the Police Tactical Unit arrived with shields and batons. At 1:34 a.m., a police officer went to the top of the elevated platform and issued a formal warning, stating that the crowd was participating in an unauthorized assembly. The police requested people to leave via Argyle Street within ten minutes. The police then issued further warnings three and six minutes later, respectively, stating that the police would forcefully evict the place if people did not leave voluntarily. But members of the HKI and other protesting citizens still congregated in front of the police's defense line.

At 1:45 a.m., as recorded by the police via video, Wong Toi-Yeung shouted, "Three, two, one, go," and members of the HKI charged into the police's defense line with their self-made shields in hand. The police responded by using pepper spray and batons. This was the beginning of intensive and sustained police-protester clashes. Edward Leung and many protesters fell to the ground because of the police's use of force. The protester crowd retreated, though people at the back still kept throwing objects at the police. According to materials from court proceedings, about five hundred citizens and three hundred police officers were involved in this initial clash. The police pushed forward from Shandong Street toward Argyle Street. Various interviewees opined that the initiation of the clash came all of a sudden. None of our interviewees could provide a convincing and confident account of what triggered the HKI to charge. Edward Leung himself also did not predict Wong to really order people to charge. During the court trial of his case, Leung told the court that he responded to Wong's call to charge by saying "Charge? How?"

Interviewee C04, who was a photojournalist, recalled that the police moved forward quickly once the clash started. This was because the crowd was loose, and people quickly receded to Argyle Street. The police took control of the part of Portland Street in front of the shopping mall Langham Place. Edward Leung was hit by a police baton during the conflict and fell to the ground. His glasses had been knocked off, and he was taken away by his peers. Emotions were boiling among the crowd retreated to Argyle Street. At 2 a.m., some protesters tried to build a roadblock with rubbish bins and cardboard at the intersection of Argyle and Shanghai Streets. There was a small group of traffic police on Argyle Street, and several protesters tried to attack them. One of the traffic police officers fell to the ground, and numerous protesters moved forward to throw objects at the traffic police officers.

At 2:05 a.m., one traffic police officer took out his gun and fired a shot into the sky. He then pointed his gun toward the protesters. The protesters stopped the attack. The traffic police officer fired a second shot into the sky. The protesters moved backward, though there were still people throwing objects toward the direction of the police. A large group of police officers then arrived at Argyle Street and escorted the traffic police officer away. At more or less the same time, Edward Leung arrived at Argyle Street. He attacked a police officer there. The police then arrested Leung at the intersection of Argyle and Shanghai Streets.

The Subsequent Clashes in the Early Morning Hours

The firing of warning shots constituted another turning point of the event. People at different locations might have different immediate reactions to the incident. Interviewee C03 happened to be in a position behind the traffic police officer. As she saw the crowd rushing forward, she felt that the police officer was in real danger. Therefore, she actually felt relieved when the police fired the warning shots, and the protesters stopped. However, more typically, protesters and observers were shocked and angered. Interviewee B21 had taken a video clip on the site immediately after the incident. In the clip, although the protesters had stopped attacking, their emotions ran extremely high. People pointed their fingers at the police officer who fired the warning shots. Some started discussing how to fight back.

The effect of the warning shots rippled outward. Interviewees B03 and B17 recalled that they heard a bang from afar, though at the beginning they did not realize that it was a gun shot. They were shocked when they knew that the police had opened fire, and they started seeing more people congregating in Mongkok. Interviewee B03 described: "There were many people on the pedestrian way. Many young people. Everyone was looking at their mobile devices. Some wore masks, and you knew they would like to [. . .] do something."

Among our thirty-eight interviewees, six arrived at Mongkok only after the police's firing of the warning shots. Those interviewees concurred that the news of the warning shots led them to go to the protest site because they thought firing of real bullets, even only into the sky, had "crossed the bottom line" of acceptability.

Meanwhile, as Edward Leung was arrested and Wong Toi-Yeung had disappeared from the scene, the protest evolved into another stage where no persons or groups dominated the proceedings. According to our interviewees, the blue jackets of the HKI had also disappeared by that time, though no one could be sure if members of the group had largely left, or if they had joined the subsequent clashes after changing clothes.

At 2:30 a.m., protesters gathered on the two sides of Nathan Road, the main road of Mongkok. There were people setting bonfires by burning miscellaneous objects at a couple of road intersections. The protesters also occupied the large intersection between Argyle Street and Nathan Road and clashed with the police there. Some protesters dug up the bricks from the pedestrian pathways and threw them at the police; there were also protesters pulling out buckets filled with glass bottles and throwing the glass bottles at the police. The police dispersed the crowd with force, and the media captured images of protesters covered in blood. At around 3 a.m., a large group of protesters clashed with the police again. The protesters threw bricks and glass bottles. Several police officers were injured. The police tried to drive the protesting crowd toward Sai Yeung Choi Street, but the protesters outnumbered the police. At 3:30 a.m., antiriot police arrived. The police started to successfully push the crowd toward the direction of Sai Yeung Choi and Shandong Streets.

Several interviewees opined that the protesters did not have clear formation or defense lines. They mainly threw bricks and other objects at the police. When individual police officers were isolated, some protesters would go forward to attack. When the conflict entered periods of stalemate, protesters tried to set up bonfire and roadblocks. Some dug up and collect bricks from the pedestrian pathways. The throwing of bricks dug up from the pedestrian pathways was a "tactical innovation" as it has never occurred in past protests in Hong Kong. Nonetheless, several interviewees noted that discussions of how protesters could dig up bricks from the roadside and use them in protests had existed online for some time before the Mongkok civil unrest. Interviewee B10 witnessed how protesters threw bricks on Soy Street: "Very movie-like, the police charged forward, the protesters retreated, and then suddenly the police moved backward and the bricks were flying. This happened at least three or four times. [. . .] Then you heard the sound of the bricks hitting the police shields; it was like the sound during a torrential rain." For Interviewee A02, the use of bricks signified the "resistance consciousness" of the protesters. He noted that the protesters were already throwing various objects during the clash at Portland Street earlier in the night. Later, the protesters wanted to generate actual harm and injuries. Hence, they started using bricks.

The police were apparently underprepared. At 4:00 a.m., intensive police-protester clashes occurred on Shandong and Soy Streets. The police in Shandong Street tried to push toward Sai Yeung Choi Street, but the protesters continually threw bricks at them. Protesters surrounded isolated police officers, whereas there were protesters subdued and arrested. The police failed to push toward Sai Yeung Choi Street and had to regroup on Nathan Road.

As the scene became increasingly chaotic, a few journalists were also inadvertently attacked by both sides of the conflict. Around 3:45 a.m., a newspaper reporter went up to a bus parked alongside Nathan Road to take pictures. He was driven down the bus and then pushed onto the ground by police officers. About half an hour later, a journalist from Radio Television Hong Kong (RTHK) and a cameraman of Television Broadcasting Ltd. were attacked by the protesters. The cameraman sustained a stab wound in his hand.

At around 4:30 a.m., fifty members of the police's Special Tactical Contingent arrived at Mongkok. By that time, the protesters were scattered throughout the area of Fa Yuen Street, Soy Street, and Sai Yee Street. The protesters started using guerrilla tactics against the police. Interviewee A11 recalled that, after 4 a.m., the protesters no longer had any numerical advantage. Nevertheless, it remained difficult for the police to gain immediate control of the whole area.

Notably, Mongkok itself has many roads and streets crisscrossing each other (as shown in figure 3.1). It was relatively easy for protesters to disperse and regroup. Clashes continued to arise in many different places. In numerous intersections, bricks were dug up, and road signs were removed by the protesters. The protesters transported the bricks using rubbish bins on the roadside. Various bonfires were set. The police tried to call upon the fire department to extinguish the bonfires, whereas the protesters attempted to block the fire trucks from getting to the area. At around 6:00 a.m., another standoff occurred at the intersection of Fa Yuen and Soy Streets. Protesters attempted to set fire on an empty taxi. The police tried to disperse the crowd and arrest the protesters. The protesters threw bricks again, hitting a television news cameraman in the head.

Around that time, there were discussions among some protesters regarding whether they should start a Mongkok occupation. As interviewees A08 and A12 recalled, some protesters thought that if there were enough people staying and defending the occupation into the morning hours, there would be other protesters coming over to support. However, the number of protesters was declining at that moment. Interviewee A11 noted that, after a whole night of conflict with the police, many protesters were very tired and left the place. The declining number of protesters undermined the confidence of those who remained on the site. In the end, the idea of starting an occupation was dropped. Even more protesters left Mongkok. At 7:00 a.m., the police issued another warning on Soy Street. The Special Tactical Contingent ran at the protesters and arrested several of them. This was the last notable clash between the police and the protesters. By 8:00 a.m., most protesters had left the site. The police drove away the remaining ones on Sai Yee Street. The Mongkok civil unrest came to an end.

THE MONGKOK CIVIL UNREST AS A SPONTANEOUS PROTEST

The previous subsections have narrated the various incidents constituting the Mongkok civil unrest, which can be understood as a spontaneous protest. As Snow and Moss (2014) pointed out, spontaneity and organization should not be seen as entirely incompatible with each other. Instead, protests can be organized and yet not fully organized, planned but at the same time not entirely planned. The Mongkok civil unrest can be a case in point. The event was generally understood by the media and the public as led by the HKI. But different from the reclaim actions in 2015, the HKI could not be regarded as the initiator of the event. The event originated merely as a Chinese New Year night market, and the HKI were called upon to help maintain order. The group even did not make the decision to participate until the last moment.

Certainly, the HKI indeed played an indispensable role in the event. The group did not "plan" or "organize" any protest actions. But since the night market was indeed technically illegal, one could see the probability of actions on the part of government officers or the police. An arrest of an activist had also just occurred at another night market in the previous evening. What the group did was to prepare themselves for what might happen. Hence, they brought their self-made shields and flags, and they had the option of the election march in mind. These preparations allowed them to become the de facto leader when protest actions emerged. To the extent that they exercised leadership, the role was not preassigned but emerged through the interaction dynamics at the protest site.

Nevertheless, the leadership by the HKI was contested. The group did not have the capability to direct the action of the whole crowd. In fact, given the internal culture of the HKI, the group also emphasized that it did not represent all people at the night market. Once the intensive conflict started, the group's key leader was arrested within a relatively short period of time, whereas "newcomers" arrived at Mongkok to join the action. As Snow and Moss (2014) noted, the absence of a hierarchical organization with effective leadership provides the first condition of the rise of spontaneity.

Besides, much of the action on the night was largely unscripted. The original idea was to protect the night market against intrusion by the HCT. The activists seemingly had a very general script in mind: they predicted that the HCT would arrive, but if people at the night market could outnumber the officers and drive them away, then hopefully the government department would not insist on evicting the market because it was the Chinese New Year. To a certain extent, the happenings on Portland Street before 10 p.m. did follow this general script. Even the accidental "taxi incident" did not turn the situation out of control: the arrival of police officers was greeted with boos and jeers, but the police officers and the activists collaborated. The officers left afterward, leading some activists to believe that their job was done.

Therefore, when police officers reemerged, it could be considered as creating what Snow and Moss (2014) called "script dissolution," which occurs when "the [scripted part of the] event has ended and there is no additional script for subsequent action" (p. 1131). From the perspective of the night market participants, the HCT had left, and the taxi incident was resolved. The reemergence of police officers was unnecessary. At that point, the situation became highly ambiguous. People needed to improvise.

Certainly, the situation could have looked very different from the perspective of the police. The present study did not have access to the police's thinking and tactical plans. But in the immediate aftermath of the civil unrest, media reports did raise questions about the appropriateness of police tactics. Lo (2016: 205) bluntly stated that the police "did miscalculate the entire situation in several aspects." He summarized various complaints and criticisms against the police:

> A number of front-line police officers complained to the mass media that their commanders failed to give proper orders, because the commanders who asked them to stand still with their protective shield actually adopted a controversially defensive posture, especially when the rioters kept throwing bricks, engaged in arsonist attack and countered the police by throwing broken flower pots. Some police officers even said that their use of pepper spray had actually worsened the standoff with the protestors, that the deployment of traffic police officers without anti-riot training was a fault made by commanders, that the police intelligence team responsible for detecting the moves from localists through Internet surveillance failed to provide accurate intelligence to front-line officers in Mongkok, that many police constables were actually on vacation and that the hurried way in which the 150-member Special Tactical Unit was assembled first at Fanling and then sent to Mongkok at 6 am, all demonstrated the lack of detailed calculation, meticulous risk assessment and crisis preparation by the police force. [. . .] Clearly, the police command had underestimated the impacts of helping the [Food and Environmental Hygiene Department] to clear the hawkers away from Portland Street. (Lo 2016: 206–7)

In other words, the police did not have a clear and sensible script in mind either regarding what needed to be done. Admittedly, following the above analysis of the Mongkok civil unrest, the police could not have detected the plan of the localist activists beforehand because the localist activists did not really have a "plan." In any case, the actions of specific police officers—most notably the firing of warning shots—could have been as spontaneous as many of the actions of the protesters.

Nonetheless, as Snow and Moss (2014) as well as Ho (2018) emphasized, spontaneous or improvised acts were not random. They were shaped by existing frames, ideas that were already primed, emotions that were prominent given the political context, and ecological factors such as the spatial environment of a protest site. Specifically, a strongly negative attitude toward the police was already shared by many night market participants even before the police appeared and any conflicts occurred. Whenever the police appeared, even during the taxi incident when the police officers were merely trying to resolve an accident more or less professionally, the atmosphere at the night market turned tense. This fits with what Snow and Moss (2014) called "emotional priming" (cf. Anisin, 2016; Bray et al., 2019). Besides, the participants' protest experiences served as the basis for them to interpret the actions and intentions of the police, and apparently new tactics such as the digging up of bricks from the pedestrian pathway had already been discussed for some time among the more militant protesters in the online arena. No one planned to use the new tactic that night, but militant protesters have been preparing themselves for more forceful resistance and violent confrontations with the police.

Last but not least, the fact that the event occurred in Mongkok matters, even though it is not easy to prove or pin down its influences and implications. For instance, numerous protesters arrived at Mongkok only after the news of police-protester clashes was spread via social media. Physically, Mongkok was literally at the center of the Kowloon Peninsula. It was easy for people from around Hong Kong to quickly arrive there. As mentioned in the analysis, the physical character of the district was conducive to the use of guerilla warfare style tactics by the protesters. Culturally, the district had taken up protest-related significance given the Mongkok occupation during the Umbrella Movement and the *gauwu* protests in 2015. The idea of "defending Mongkok" could have easily struck a chord with those who were participants in the previous protest events. The area itself could have primed the kind of cognitions and emotions that drove the protesters into more confrontational actions. In fact, the protesters in the Mongkok civil unrest did deliberate about the possibility of starting another occupation, though the idea was dropped because the protesters were already losing steam. Nevertheless, the Mongkok civil unrest had allowed the most radical undercurrents in the social movement sector to be expressed in a way that shocked the entire society.

Concluding Remarks

This chapter has analyzed the Mongkok civil unrest against the background of the rise of new localist groups and militant protest tactics since 2015. While the District Council election in 2015 was taken as signifying the possible appeal of a moderate form of localism, the Mongkok civil unrest seemingly confirmed the continuation of the trend of movement radicalization. It set up a new benchmark of what militant resistance means. The throwing of bricks did signify a distinctive new level of violence—a flying brick hitting someone's head can indeed result in very serious injuries and possibly death.

Theoretically speaking, the analysis in this chapter emphasized the notion of spontaneity. The underlying concern is to understand the extent to which and the sense in which the protests typically associated with the localists were organized and led by them. One important point that emerged from the analysis is the distinction between planning and preparing. In the context of the present analysis, to plan a protest event is to spend the effort to systematically work out a course of action to follow so that the protest can occur and be conducted successfully. To prepare, in contrast, refers to the effort to equip oneself with the resources, capabilities, and/or ideas that would help one to handle various kinds of contingent situations.

The line between planning and preparing, admittedly, may not always be clear, and the two are certainly not mutually exclusive. People can work out a course of action to follow and simultaneously equip themselves for handling various contingencies. The analytical distinction resides mainly in two points. First, preparation does not necessarily involve the prescripting of actions to take; very often, preparation merely gives people a wider range of options when they are requested by the situation to improvise. Second, people construct detailed plans for events that will definitely occur or events that they would like to bring into being, but people often need to get themselves prepared for highly uncertain and undesired happenings.

Past research on spontaneous protests has typically focused on the extent to which a protest is planned or deliberately organized. But in protests as well as in everyday life, people may engage in a range of actions not because they are planning to do something but because they have to ensure their readiness to face certain possible, and often undesired, scenarios. If a person brings with him or her certain protecting equipment to a protest site, it does not entail that the person desires physical confrontations to occur and intends to engage in it; it could be a means just to ensure one's own safety if confrontation does arise. (By the same token, professional journalists going to a protest site where serious physical confrontations are likely to occur also have to equip themselves with protective gears.) However, whether and what kinds of preparation people make would certainly influence the dynamics of a protest event because they shape the range of options people have when contingent incidents occur.

Return to the case under examination here, the HKI played an important role in the Mongkok civil unrest, but they were not the organizers or leaders in the conventional sense. They did not provide a script for fellow protesters, and they did not have the capacity to direct the action of many protesters on the site. This is symptomatic of the relationship between the new localist groups in the 2010s and their supporters in general. De facto protest leadership inevitably arose, though the effectiveness of such leadership is constrained by a culture emphasizing horizontality and the absence of centralized leadership.

In any case, in both the Mongkok civil unrest and the reclaim actions analyzed in the early parts of this chapter, the visibility and preparedness of the HKI did lead the media and the law enforcement to treat them as the leaders. As a result, the group had to take up certain responsibilities, including responsibilities for the spontaneous actions of the protesters (especially those in the early morning hours) that they did not command. In the case of the reclaim actions, it only meant the need to respond to media queries related to the crying girl incident. In the Mongkok civil unrest, it meant the need to bear the legal consequences associated with the event.

Of course, being treated as one of the leading groups in the emerging localist faction was not one-sidedly detrimental to the interests of the HKI and its key figures. After the Mongkok civil unrest, Edward Leung and the HKI became the most prominent "public faces" of localism in Hong Kong. No matter whether they wanted to do so or not, they became the main interpreter of localism in the public arena. They had the task of articulating what localism is, justifying militant protest actions, and putting forward their vision of Hong Kong's future. Held almost immediately after the Mongkok civil unrest, the LegCo by-election became the platform through which this task was done, and Edward Leung's performance during the by-election would significantly shape the public image of localism and the significance of the Mongkok civil unrest.

Chapter 4

Localism Facing the Voting Public

When the Mongkok civil unrest occurred, the city had not seen a protest event with such a level of physical violence for decades. As to be illustrated in this chapter, immediately after the Mongkok civil unrest, media outlets and politicians on all sides converged to condemn the violence in the event. It seems that the Hong Kong public was far from ready to embrace such confrontational protest actions.

As a matter of coincidence, the Mongkok civil unrest was immediately followed by a LegCo by-election in late February. Edward Leung was a candidate in the election. Given the single-seat, single-vote system in place for the by-election, virtually no observers saw any chance for Leung to win. However, the occurrence of the Mongkok civil unrest and Leung's role in it added spice to the electoral contest. The situation gave Leung a degree of media and public attention that he would not have had otherwise. Leung had the burden of explaining the protesters' actions and justifying the need of militant actions, but he also had an opportunity to articulate a version of localism that might appeal to the public.

Leung seemed to have grasped the opportunity successfully. On February 28, 2016, only three weeks after the Mongkok civil unrest, Edward Leung won 66,524 votes, or 15.38 percent of all casted votes. It was far from enough to win the contest—the winning candidate, Alvin Yeung of the prodemocracy Civic Party, won 37.19 percent of the votes. Yet the result surprised most observers and analysts, especially given the highly negative media reactions to the protest event earlier in the month. LegCo elections require campaigning throughout a constituency with a large geographical size. More than 15 percent of the popular vote could be regarded as a great result for any inexperienced candidate not backed by a well-oiled electoral machine. Leung's performance in the by-election thus created a conundrum: How can we understand the appeal of Edward Leung in the by-election? Was there a quick shift in public opinion toward militant protests and localism over the month?

This chapter argues that a key part of the answer to the above questions resides in how Edward Leung articulated a softened form of militant localism in the 2016 by-election. It was softened in the sense that, despite an emphasis on militant actions, Leung exercised discursive self-restraint when explicating his position to the public. He was willing to adjust his views over the course of the campaign. As a result, the radical edges of localism were smoothened to a certain extent. It was softened also in the sense that Leung deliberately positioned himself as "the weak" who had made huge personal sacrifice for the city he loved. The strength of Leung's articulation arguably resided in its affective, rather than cognitive, appeal. The majority of the Hong Kong public might not have wholeheartedly embraced Leung's account, but in response to the softened form of militant localism, many citizens might start developing more sympathetic, if not necessarily supportive, attitudes toward the localists.

To provide an account of the shifting public reception to Edward Leung, the HKI, militant protests, and localism in the month of February 2016, this chapter begins with a brief analysis of the immediate media reactions to the Mongkok civil unrest. The core of the chapter then adopts a framing perspective (Gamson, 1995; Snow & Benford, 1988) to examine Edward Leung's discourses in the by-election. It delineates the diagnostic, prognostic, adversarial, and affective framings involved, and it discusses how Leung seemingly adjusted and revised his articulations over the course of the campaign. The chapter then draws upon a population survey conducted in March 2016 to demonstrate public opinion toward the Mongkok civil unrest. It shows that a significant degree of ambivalence toward militant actions had already existed in public attitudes at the time.

Media Reactions to the Mongkok Civil Unrest

A prominent tradition of research on media coverage of social protests argued that the mainstream media, embedded in the dominant political economic structure of a society, are agents of social control who tend to delegitimize protests (Chan & Lee, 1984; McLeod & Hertog, 1998). Research in Hong

Kong up to the early 2000s also noted a strong emphasis on social order in the city's public culture. Hence media discourses about social protests could quickly turn negative once protests became disruptive (Ku, 2007). However, as social protests became more prominent and routinized (Meyer & Tarrow, 1998), research in various countries around the world has also shown more variegated protest coverage. Instead of a consensual condemnation of disruptive protests, media with different political and ideological stances tend to cover the same protest differently (Cottle, 2008; Harlow & Johnson, 2011; Lee, 2014). Did Hong Kong newspapers of different political predilection cover the Mongkok civil unrest differently? Or did all media outlets demonstrate the same judgment?

We can begin by looking at how the news media labeled the event (see methodological appendix for information about methods). While this book uses the term *Mongkok civil unrest* to refer to the event, localist supporters tended to call the event the *Fishball Revolution*, whereas the government branded the event a riot. Notably, there is no one-to-one correspondence between English and Chinese words. Civil unrest might be translated as *sou-lyun* or *dong-lyun* in Chinese, whereas the stronger word *riot* could be translated as *bou-lyun*, *bou-dong*, or *sou-lyun*. In Chinese, the word *bou* literally means violence. Hence the terms *bou-lyun* or *bou-dong* conveyed a stronger sense of condemnation when compared to *sou-lyun*. In addition, the media might use the less value-laden phrases *chung-dat* (i.e., conflict) or simply *si-gin* (i.e., incident) to refer to the event.

Table 4.1 summarizes the number of articles appearing on nine newspapers between February 10 and 19 that contain the various possible names of the event. Specifically, the six names were *Mongkok bou-lyun*, *Mongkok bou-dong*, *Mongkok sou-lyun*, *Mongkok chung-dat*, *Mongkok si-gin*, and *yu-daan-gaak-ming*, that is, *Fishball Revolution*.

The nine papers were grouped into three categories. *Apple Daily* was the most strongly prodemocracy newspaper in Hong Kong, whereas *Ming Pao* was professional and somewhat liberal-oriented. Past research on protests in Hong Kong treated the two as relatively supportive toward the prodemocracy movement (e.g., Lee & Chan, 2018). On the other side of the spectrum, *Ta Kung Pao* and *Wen Wei Po* were two communist-sponsored newspapers in the city. They were strongly supportive toward the government. The other five were grouped together as centrist / conservative newspapers. They could be placed in-between the prodemocracy and pro-Communist papers, but media researchers in Hong Kong had pointed out that, given the singular power structure in Hong Kong, these centrist newspapers actually tended

Table 4.1. Naming of the Mongkok civil unrest in different newspapers

	bou-lyun	bou-dong	sou-lyun	chung-dat	si-gin	Fishball
Liberal / Prodemocracy						
Apple Daily	6	1	106	8	16	17
Ming Pao	13	4	25	61	18	12
Centrist / conservative						
HK Economic Journal	9	2	73	8	17	8
HK Economic Times	40	1	1	4	6	1
Sing Pao	25	41	6	3	2	3
Oriental Daily	124	2	10	1	4	6
Sing Tao Daily	70	10	54	21	13	3
Pro-Communist						
Ta Kung Pao	152	4	14	4	10	9
Wen Wei Po	212	14	24	0	9	6
Total	651	79	307	107	93	65

Note: Articles were searched using the phrase *Mongkok xxxx*, with *xxxx* being one of the first five labels, and the Chinese phrase for Fishball Revolution. Entries refer to the number of articles appearing in the newspaper between February 10 and 19, 2016, that contained the various possible names of the event. The total number refers to total number of articles that contain at least one of the six names. All numbers were derived from the electronic news archive Wise News.

Source: Created by the author.

to be politically conservative, especially on sensitive political matters (Fung, 2007).

As table 4.1 shows, the newspapers indeed differed from each other systematically in their choice of labels. *Apple Daily* used Mongkok *sou-lyun* overwhelmingly,[1] as it appeared in 106 articles, whereas *bou-dong* and *bou-lyun* appeared in only 1 and 6 articles, respectively. *Ming Pao* also seldom used *bou-dong* and *bou-lyun*. It used Mongkok *chung-dat* most frequently. At the other end of the spectrum, *bou-lyun* appeared in 212 articles on *Wen Wei Po* in the ten-day period, while *sou-lyun* appeared in only 24 articles. Similarly, *bou-lyun* appeared in 152 articles on *Ta Kung Pao*, whereas *sou-lyun* appeared in only 14 articles.

Three of the five centrist/conservative newspapers also tended to use *bou-lyun* much more frequently. The exceptions are *Sing Tao Daily*, which used *bou-lyun* and *sou-lyun* more or less equally frequently, and *Hong Kong Economic Journal*, which primarily used *sou-lyun* to name the event.

Nonetheless, the between-newspapers differences are bounded. With the exception of *Ming Pao*, the choice of names was between *bou-lyun* and *sou-lyun*. *Fishball Revolution* appeared only sporadically, and it appeared mainly in the writings of commentators or when news reports quoted how the international media covered the event.

Based on the results in table 4.1, the articles were differentiated into: (1) those that primarily employed *bou-lyun* or *bou-dong* and (2) those that primarily employed *sou-lyun* or other names. It can be expected that different ways to name the event would be associated with different emphases when the event was described. Table 4.2 summarizes the findings from the relevant analysis. When mentioning actors, articles employing the two types of names did not differ from each other substantively in terms of whether the police, the hawkers, or the HKI were mentioned. Nevertheless, an important difference exists in the way the protesters were named. Nearly 60 percent of articles using *bou-lyun* or *bou-dong* to name the event used the phrase *bou-tou* (thugs) to refer to the protesters who engaged in violent actions, whereas only about 30 percent of articles using *sou-lyun* or other names for the event used the phrase *bou-tou*. Articles using *sou-lyun* or other names for the event were more likely to use the more value-neutral term *si-wai-je* (*i.e.*, protester or demonstrator) to name the citizen participants in the clash.

In addition, naming of the event was systematically associated with mentioning of the actions by the protesters and the police. Articles calling the event *bou-lyun* or *bou-dong* were more likely to mention the throwing of bricks, arson, and physical assaults on police officers committed by some of

Tables 4.2a–c. Mentions and descriptions of actors and actions in the Mongkok civil unrest under different event labels (*bou-lyun* or *bou-dong* N=690; *sou-lyun* or others N=371)

Table 4.2a. Actors

	bou-lyun or *bou-dong*	*sou-lyun* or others
Police	56.7%	54.7%
Hawkers	19.6%	18.3%
The HKI / Localists	27.0%	27.5%
Leung Tin-Kei (i.e., Edward Leung) / Wong Toi-yeung	11.3%	15.1%
bou-tou (thug)	58.0%	29.4%
si-wai-je (protester)	18.6%	34.8%

Table 4.2b. Protestors' use of force

	bou-lyun or *bou-dong*	*sou-lyun* or others
Throwing bricks	20.0%	17.0%
Arson	25.7%	13.5%
Attacking police officers	27.7%	20.2%

Table 4.2c. Police's use of force

	bou-lyun or *bou-dong*	*sou-lyun* or others
Firing shots	12.0%	18.1%
Pepper spray	2.6%	4.3%
Elevated platform	0.6%	3.5%

Note: Entries are percentages of articles employing the event name that mentioned the actor or action.

Source: Created by the author.

the protesters, whereas articles calling the event *sou-lyun* or *chung-dat* were more likely to mention the police's firing of warning shots, use of pepper spray, and the use of an elevated platform during the standoff. However, the differences are not substantial in size. One might also note that mentioning of protesters' use of force was more frequent than mentioning of police's use of force, regardless of how the event was labeled.

The analysis further examines whether the articles made any claims about the causes of the event and claims about what needed to be done in response to the event, that is, what scholars called "diagnostic" and "prognostic framing" (Snow & Benford, 1988). Table 4.3 summarizes the findings based on an inductive identification of the major diagnoses and prognoses offered. Articles calling the event *bou-lyun* or *bou-dong* were somewhat more likely to evoke the notions of radicalism, separatism, and pro–Hong Kong independence sentiments when discussing the cause of the event. In contrast, articles calling the event *sou-lyun* were more likely to point toward public grievances, social contradictions, and governance problems when explaining the event. Nonetheless, both sets of articles were more or less equally likely to tie the event to the rise of localism. Besides, even in articles calling the event *sou-lyun*, radicalism was the second most frequently evoked idea when explaining the protest. There are both differences and underlying commonalities between the two sets of articles.

Tables 4.3a–b. Identification of causes, responses, and suggested solutions (*bou-lyun* or *bou-dong* N=690; *sou-lyun* or others N=371)

Table 4.3a. Causes of the event.

	bou-lyun or *bou-dong*	*sou-lyun* or *others*
Localist / localism	36.7%	40.0%
Radicalism	30.0%	20.2%
Separatism / Hong Kong independence	18.0%	12.9%
Social contradictions / public grievances	7.2%	15.4%
Governance problems	10.0%	16.4%
Localist / localism	36.7%	40.0%

Table 4.3b. Reactions and suggested solutions.

	bou-lyun or *bou-dong*	*sou-lyun* or *others*
Condemnation	38.0%	35.6%
Legal punishment / bringing to justice	20.0%	8.9%
Antimask-wearing law	1.3%	1.3%

Note: Entries are percentages of articles employing the event label that made specific causal attributions or mentioned specific reactions or possible solutions.

Source: Created by the author.

The pattern is similar when prognostic framing is concerned. Table 4.3b shows that articles calling the event *bou-lyun* or *bou-dong* were more likely to emphasize the need to bring the rioters to the court and punish them with an appropriate level of severity. In contrast, articles calling the event *sou-lyun* were more likely to mention the need to set up an independent commission of inquiry to understand the root causes of the outburst. Nevertheless, even when the event was called *sou-lyun*, the idea of having an independent commission of inquiry, something the colonial Hong Kong government did in the aftermath of the 1967 urban riots, was mentioned in fewer than 10 percent of the articles. More importantly, the differences between the two groups of articles were overshadowed by the fact that, in both sets of articles, condemning the protesters' actions was the most frequently registered reaction. For example, the lead paragraph of the front-page coverage by *Apple Daily* on February 10 read:

> The new year for Hong Kong began with a blood-shedding clash. On the first day of the Chinese New Year, the eviction of street hawkers led to a riotous clash between the police and the people. Police officers chased and hit the protesters and fired a warning shot twice, while protesters led by the localists threw bricks and glass bottles in return. [. . .] Chief Executive Leung Chun-ying described the incident as "*bou-lyun*" and called the protesters *bou-tou*. Pro-establishment political parties and groups followed and condemned the event. Pro-democracy political parties also condemned the violence, but at the same time blamed Leung Chun-ying for leading to the outburst of grievances. At least 125 people were injured. The police had hitherto arrested 61 people, who are expected to be charged for rioting.

The coverage did not one-sidedly blame the protesters. It highlighted the government's attempt to frame the event as a serious riot committed by thugs. The description of the happenings on the night even implicitly posited the police as the ones initiating the violent clash. However, the paragraph also conveyed the point that the government, progovernment politicians, and prodemocracy politicians united in their condemnation of protester violence. In fact, the article's headline began with "Condemnation from all sectors." Similarly, the headline of *Ming Pao*'s main news report on February 10 read: "Various political parties condemned violence; pan-democrats urged the government to reflect; pro-establishment issued a statement claiming that 'thugs' endanger citizens' safety." The contrasting responses from politicians on the two sides were placed under their common condemnation of violence.

The media and public reactions described above were acknowledged by the interviewed participants and observers of the incident. When asked about their impression of the society's response to the event, various interviewees evoked the term *got-jik*, which means severing of ties. The term conveys a sense of being abandoned or even betrayed. Interviewees A04 and B21 said they were deeply angry and disappointed when they saw that virtually all media and politicians condemned the violence and called for legal punishment of the protesters instead of trying to understand why violence arose.

Several interviewees (A05, A06, A11, B09, and B15) opined that they were not surprised by the society's reaction because Hong Kong has long internalized a disgust toward violence. Some interviewees acknowledged that their inclination toward localism was strengthened by what they saw as the society's lack of understanding of the protesters. Interviewee B21 stated: "Everyone was severing ties. The proestablishment, the democrats, everyone was hitting [us]. Everyone said they did not accept violence, did not support violence. [I was] angry, and it made my stance even closer to the localist. Made me feel that [the democrats] were not reliable allies. From then on nothing can be counted on them." Some interviewees noted that supporters of the protesters developed an even stronger sense of solidarity in face of public condemnation. Interviewee A06 stated: "This event consolidated the localists. It turned the localists, who were originally just a bunch of people scattering around, into a political force that the society cannot ignore." Meanwhile, some interviewees acknowledged the role played by the HKI in trying to communicate with the society and defend the protesters. Interviewee B15 stated: "The Mongkok incident might not have been caused entirely by [the HKI], but they had a big role in it. From that point onward, the Mongkok incident became tied to Edward Leung. And then, beginning from the next day, the HKI and others were the ones to defend the militant protesters." Indeed, with the voting day scheduled three weeks after the Mongkok civil unrest, the 2016 LegCo by-election would become the occasion in which Edward Leung articulated his conception of localism and defended the need of militant protest actions.

Framing Localism in the 2016 LegCo By-Election

The 2016 LegCo by-election originated from the resignation of a former prodemocracy legislator in October 2015, leading to a vacancy in the New

Territories East geographical constituency. The single-seat, single-vote system was employed. Seven candidates participated, with Alvin Yeung, a young barrister representing the prodemocracy Civic Party, being the favorite to win. Lawyer Holden Chow, a member of the Democratic Alliance for the Betterment and Progress of Hong Kong, was the main candidate from the progovernment camp. Other candidates included Wong Shing-Chi, a self-proclaimed "centrist" who was a former member of the Democratic Party, district councilor Christine Fong, two lesser-known independent candidates, and Edward Leung of the HKI.

Leung announced his candidacy in early January 2016. He explained his decision to join the election by claiming that the democrats could not represent the localists. In fact, the 2016 by-election was the first time a self-proclaimed localist candidate participated in a LegCo election. How did Leung articulate his vision and respond to criticisms surrounding the Mongkok civil unrest? Ten election forums organized by various media outlets and social groups were analyzed. Most of the forums included all candidates, but a few organized by prodemocracy online media included fewer candidates. The first forum by Commercial Radio was broadcast on January 20, 2016, and lasted for only fifteen minutes. The others were broadcast between February 15 and 25, 2016, and were longer in duration (see the methodological appendix for additional information).

There are several reasons to focus on election forums. First, they were the platforms on which the candidates elaborated their views in a relatively systematic manner. Second, analysis of election forums allows one to consider how the candidates articulated their views in response to each other. Third, since the forums differed from each other in the identity of the organizers and formats, the analysis can try to discern the discursive and performative strategies employed by Leung in various occasions.

In addition to the ten forums, the analysis also included Edward Leung's campaign rally, held on February 20, 2016. The rally provided a reference point to discern whether, how, and the extent to which Edward Leung's discourses and performance varied when he faced his own supporters as opposed to when he faced the larger public.

Conceptually, the analysis is informed by the tradition of framing analysis in social movement and communication research. Snow and Benford (1988) identified diagnostic, prognostic, and motivational framing as the three major tasks for social movement activists. That is, activists need to persuade the public by identifying a social problem and providing an analysis of its causes, offering suggestions regarding how the problem can be dealt with, and providing the rationales and messages that could move people into action (Oktavianus et al., 2023). Diagnostic and prognostic framings are more relevant to the present analysis. In addition, Gamson (1995) has emphasized the significance of constructing an opponent through framing. Social movements typically define "us" in contrast to "them." Such adversarial framing was often treated as an important aspect of diagnostic framing; that is, the identification of the causes of a social problem is often associated with the construction of the "other" who is to blame (Aslandis, 2018; Klandermans & de Weerd, 1999; Knight & Greenberg, 2011). However, in the present case, we will see that adversarial framing was also a key part of the localists' prognostic framing of the situation of Hong Kong.

Moreover, framing is a dynamic process (Benford & Snow, 2000). Chapter 2 noted how localist groups and candidates exercised self-restraints and downplayed political issues in the District Council elections in 2015. Presumably, there would be a lesser need to downplay political issues in a LegCo election. But in the following analysis, attention is still paid to whether and how Edward Leung exercised self-restraint when communicating to the wider voting public via the election forums. Aiding such an analysis is a comparison between the election forums and Leung's campaign rally.

Last but not least, in its earlier years of development, the framing perspective was sometimes criticized for having a cognitive bias. The concepts of diagnostic and prognostic framings imply a rational analysis and the presence of logical connections between causes and solutions. Later, scholars came to acknowledge the important roles emotions and affect play in various social movement processes (Gamson, 1992; Jasper, 1998). Researchers thus began to conceptualize the role of "affective framing" in social movement mobilization and persuasion (Juris, 2008; Ma, 2017; Sauer, 2019; von Scheve et al., 2016). Ruiz-Junco (2013) defined affective or emotional framing as "framing activities that social movements engage in to achieve emotional resonance" with their target audience (p. 49). The following analysis paid attention to how Edward Leung constructed not only "arguments" about social problems, but also images of the society and of the localists that carried affective appeals and addressed the moral intuitions of the public.

DIAGNOSTIC FRAMING: MAINLANDIZATION AND THE CHINESE COMMUNIST PARTY AS THE ENEMY

Edward Leung's diagnostic framing in the election forums was rather straightforward and easily identifiable. The overarching theme was the collapse of one country, two systems due to the trend of increasing influence of mainland China on the Hong Kong society, codified into the keywords of *mainlandization* and *chek-fa* (literally "reddening"). This was clearly indicated in the self-introduction by Leung in various forums. For instance, in the NOW TV forum on February 15, 2016, Leung introduced himself by saying: "[I am] a youngster who continue[s] to resist after the failure of the Umbrella Revolution, who participate[s] in politics, and who believe[s] that one can change the future of Hong Kong by one's hands. Hong Kong is our home, but the Basic Law regime has collapsed. One-country-two-systems, Hong Kong people ruling Hong Kong, and high degree of autonomy had become empty words." The overarching theme of mainlandization would be reiterated in the conversational interactions inside the forums. In the same forum, when asked by another candidate regarding when the HKI would stop their militant resistance, Leung responded: "Reopening the negotiation of political reform. Double popular elections [i.e., popular elections of the chief executive and the legislature] is the promise enshrined in the Basic Law. Those are basic human rights. We come out to resist the government only because the rights are not realized. But political reform is not our only demand. This is because the Chinese Communist Party is comprehensively reddening Hong Kong, including politics, economics, livelihood, education, etc." Notably, the idea of *chek-fa* already had a degree of prominence in public discourse in Hong Kong by the early 2010s. In the whole of 2011, the phrase *chek-fa* appeared in only 20 articles in total in *Apple Daily* and *Ming Pao*. In year 2012, the number jumped to 188. The corresponding figure stayed at above 100 for each year between 2013 and 2015. Edward Leung was drawing upon an emerging discourse in the Hong Kong society.

Edward Leung did not tie every single issue to the theme of mainlandization. In various forums, the way Leung criticized the government on a range of social policies, ranging from heritage protection and housing problems, might not differ substantially from the critiques offered by other candidates. However, there were occasions when specific issues were articulated with the theme of mainlandization, thus offering a degree of frame consistency. For instance, housing has long been an intractable problem in Hong Kong. In the forum organized by the Social Record Channel,[2] the candidates were asked how they would distribute ten pieces of land for the development of public housing, government subsidized housing, and private housing. Leung answered: "Seven will be for public housing; need to take care of people with the strongest need. Two for government subsidized housing, and one for private housing. In the current North-Eastern territory development plan, the government is not looking after the interests of Hong Kong people and the grassroots. They only care about integration between China and Hong Kong."

Leung explicitly opposed integration between mainland China and the Hong Kong society. It was particularly clearly expressed when discussing the construction of the express railway that linked Hong Kong to China's express rail system. Instead of integrating with mainland China, Hong Kong was posited as an international city. In the RTHK forum on February 21, Leung stated:

> Hong Kong has been an international city. Before 1997, Hong Kong was not a part of China, but it was already the Pearl of the Orient. This is because we paid attention to the world; we didn't focus on China. As we have to face the world, we do not need to follow the national policy agenda. [. . .] The two billion funding [on education], why don't we spend them on local students? Hong Kong students are trying hard to study their degrees, but there is a lack of educational resources.

Obviously, associated with the diagnostic framing of mainlandization is the adversarial framing of the Chinese Communist Party (CCP) and the Hong Kong government as the culprits or even the enemies of Hong Kong people. Notably, Edward Leung did not use the term *Central Government*. Rather, the names evoked were *China, the Chinese government*, and the *CCP*. Leung stopped short of urging for separating Hong Kong from China, a point to which we will return below, but he discursively refused to acknowledge the legitimacy of the Chinese government's rule over Hong Kong.

PROGNOSTIC FRAMING: MILITANT RESISTANCE AS A NECESSITY

Facing mainlandization and the loss of autonomy, Leung emphasized localism as the guiding principle of the HKI. In his explication, localism emphasizes the priority of Hong Kong people's interests, identity, and autonomy. While Leung's criticisms of existing government policies overlap significantly with those of the democrats, he indeed brought up several distinctively "localist issues," such as the need to protect the Cantonese language and the use of traditional Chinese characters (as opposed to simplified Chinese), as well as an emphasis on developing Hong Kong's "self-sufficiency." The latter was tied to more specific issues such as the building of a desalinization plant and the development of local agriculture. When questioned about how realistic it would be to render Hong Kong self-sufficient, Leung sometimes toned down his claim and suggested that the goal was to raise the "degree of self-sufficiency" of Hong Kong.

On the one hand, one might criticize Leung for not providing a more detailed and evidence-based account of how and to what degree the water and food supplies of Hong Kong can become self-sufficient. But on the other hand, lack of details for one's policy suggestions has been a common problem among all political parties in Hong Kong. In a system where political parties do not have the chance to govern (as the Basic Law stipulated that the chief executive of the Hong Kong government cannot be a party member), they do not have the incentive to invest in policy research (Lui, 2020). Therefore, despite the presence of a relatively distinctive issue agenda, Leung did not emphasize how the localists might persuade the public and then let public opinion put pressure on the government. Instead, the main part of Leung's prognostic framing focused on the notion of militant resistance. As he said in the NOW TV forum: "We will insist on the method of militant resistance. We will resist all injustices in the society [. . .] and strive for a society that belongs to Hong Kong people."

The notion of militant resistance was mainly associated with confrontational and possibly violent tactics in street protests, especially after the occurrence of the Mongkok civil unrest. Other candidates in various forums questioned Leung on the morality of militant tactics. Interestingly, rarely was there any discussion of what "militant resistance" could mean inside the legislature. An exception was an exchange between Edward Leung and Alvin Yeung of the Civic Party in the forum organized by the D100.[3] The two candidates debated about what needs to be done when unjust laws and policies supported by the progovernment legislators are to be passed. In the early 2010s, the prodemocracy legislators had started to use the tactic of filibuster inside the LegCo, but it did not succeed in stopping the policies they were objecting. Edward Leung thus asked the question of "what's next":

LEUNG: When filibuster is ineffective, would you do other things, such as to seize the rostrum?

YEUNG: I don't have as much a burden and I'm willing to try different methods. In the long run, our two camps need to cooperate more and need more mutual understanding. Perhaps we stand up together to try to stop them; perhaps more effective.

The pandemocrats need to face this issue. I'm willing to bring changes to the Civic Party.

[. . .]

YEUNG: You said you'd try all means to stop the voting [in the LegCo], but what if you stand up and are already surrounded by many others?

LEUNG: From what we see outside, very few legislators would rush to stop the voting. We are angry about this. The people send you inside, why don't you put your body there to stop the evil law from being passed? [. . .] In 2009 I opposed the express rail when I was a high school student. Today, 60 billion dollars are robbed. Nothing was achieved.

A few interrelated points can be noted from this exchange. The focus in the conversation is not on what legislators are expected to do in a well-functioning legislature deliberating about policies. The exchange is grounded in the presumed reality of a legislature in which progovernment politicians dominate and often help the government to pass bills regarded as highly problematic by the democrats. There was also a shared sense that filibuster and other previous tactics were not effective enough. Nevertheless, it does not mean that Edward Leung offered clear ideas of what could be effective. Leung's suggestion of seizing the rostrum might indeed cause a higher degree of disruption. But given the structure of the legislature, it is unclear how such tactics can achieve what filibuster cannot achieve.

This is not to dismiss Leung's argument. The point to emphasize is that Edward Leung's prognostic framing was grounded not in the expected effectiveness of the suggested actions, but in the "proven" ineffectiveness of the old tactics. In various forums, Leung emphasized that he used to be a peaceful protester. In the Commercial Radio forum on February 23, when asked if he would call upon people to participate in peaceful protests, Leung replied: "I hope I can; I joined the July 1 protest marches and June 4 vigils since I was small. I am now 24 years old and find out that these methods are completely useless in front of the government." In the forum organized by D100, when the host questioned Edward Leung about militant protests, he replied: "The Umbrella Revolution was a high-quality and peaceful civil disobedience campaign. I participated. But in the end, I only saw oppression by the police and the gangsters. Nothing was achieved. We have no chance of repeating it. [. . .] We need to think about what methods can really put pressure on the government." Putting another way, the prognosis offered is based on a sense of its necessity. In the forum organized by Television Broadcasting Ltd. on February 25, Alvin Yeung questioned Leung if militant protests would hurt innocent Hong Kong people. Leung responded: "To put real pressure onto the government, we can no longer rely on the peaceful, rational and nonviolent social movement [tactics] in the past. No one wants violence, but to use physical force to stop [the government's] violence is the only way out."

Given the emphasis on what did *not* work, Leung's prognostic framing was closely tied to a second adversarial framing, the framing of the "old democrats" as another "enemy" who were to blame for Hong Kong's current situation. For instance, in the NOW TV forum, Leung questioned Wong Shing-chi, who used to be a member of the Democratic Party but was a self-proclaimed "centrist" in the 2016 by-election: "The pan-democrats emphasized discussion-cum-confrontation for so many years, why do you say that communication and compromise represent a new way of thinking? [. . .] [C]ommunication has achieved nothing. Political parties and politicians have betrayed a whole generation of Hong Kong people. [That's why I] come out to stage a resistance, a revolution, to overthrow the government." Notably, in those forums that allowed the candidates to choose whom they would question in the interactive segment, Leung invariably picked Wong Shing-chi, the former democrat, instead of Alvin Yeung, the candidate representing the democrats. It was apparently a strategic decision to avoid directly confronting Yeung, who was a young and relatively more progressive politician from the prodemocracy camp. Leung's prognosis required the construction of a group of old-fashioned and untrustworthy politicians who failed to deliver democracy to Hong Kong people. Wong Shing-chi was the more appropriate target.

THE EXERCISE OF SELF-RESTRAINT?

As just mentioned, Edward Leung seemed to have avoided directly confronting the democrats' candidate, Alvin Yeung. This could be partly due to the need to avoid deepening the impression that his candidacy might damage the opposition forces. On the one hand, in order to win more votes, Leung would need to draw votes from citizens who were unsatisfied with the government, and that meant taking votes away from the democrats. But on the other hand, the recognition that Leung might take votes away from the democrats became a reason for some prodemocracy citizens to question his candidacy. That is, in a single-seat, single-vote election, it is unwise to have two candidates to represent the opposition. Given Leung's unlikelihood to win, some people questioned why he had to join the by-election. In the D100 forum, for instance, two citizen callers asked Leung why he did not wait for the LegCo elections in September of the same year, which adopted the proportional representation system and therefore would present a more realistic chance of winning. Leung responded by emphasizing his wish to introduce the "localist agenda" to the public.

This is an example of how participating in the LegCo by-election required Leung to face the public instead of merely the localists' supporters. Leung needed to shape his performances and discourses in a way so that they would have broader appeal and would not alienate potential voters. In fact, one can recognize from Leung's performances in the forums how he smoothened certain aspects of his views. Concerning the prognostic framing of militant resistance, Leung tried to emphasize the distinction between "violence" and "use of force," as he used the phrase *yi-mou-jai-bou*, literally meaning "using force to stop violence," to describe the HKI's approach to protests. The phrase posited the use of physical force as reactive and responsive. The localists were presented as reacting to the physical violence of the police and the institutional violence of the Hong Kong and Chinese governments.

Besides, Leung emphasized the principle of "equivalence" in the degree of violence employed. As he stated in the D100 forum: "We do not attack the police arbitrarily. We are only resisting with an equivalent amount of force when we were oppressed. We would not suddenly raise our level of force beyond that exercised by the opposite side." Certainly, one can question how degree of force can be measured, whether it is possible to constrain the use of force once violent conflicts arise, and what "equivalence" could mean when one is resisting not physical violence but institutional violence. These matters were not elaborated, but it remains notable that Leung did try to address public concerns about the use of violence by constructing the principled character of their actions.

Closely related to the question of principle was the question of "bottom line." When responding to reporters after the Mongkok civil unrest, Leung emphasized that their resistance does not have "bottom lines." The absence of bottom lines was generally taken to mean the absence of limits to the degree of violence involved in protests. It represents a refusal to consider the question of moral appropriateness of protest tactics. This stance was widely questioned by even prodemocracy commentators (e.g., Chan, 2016a). But in the election forums, Leung redefined what "no bottom line" means. For instance, in the D100 forum, the host asked Leung if "no bottom line" would mean that even assassination is acceptable when the level of force used by the police is potentially fatal. Leung replied: "No bottom line does not mean no principle. The absence of bottom line means the willingness to pay any cost according to the situation. [. . .] We are willing to give our lives. This is what we mean by no bottom lines." Through such rhetorical moves, Leung redefined the notion of "no bottom line" as referring to the absence of any limits to their sacrifices, thereby circumventing the question of whether there would be a limit to the degree of violence used by protesters.

The above also shows that there were subtle adjustments in Leung's discourses throughout the electoral process. Another example is how he responded to the incident during the Mongkok civil unrest in which a journalist was attacked by protesters. In the D100 forum on February 18, Leung claimed that it was like "sandstones" in a resistance movement; the reporter was taking close-up shots, and the protesters had the "responsibility" to protect themselves. On February 19, in the forum organized by Hong Kong University's Student Union, the host asked if Leung believed that protesters can block the camera lens of reporters. Leung first responded by reemphasizing the risks borne by protesters. But when the host followed up and asked if it means protesters can attack the Fourth Estate, Leung acknowledged that "it is difficult to answer." On February 23, in the Commercial Radio forum, the host raised the issue again. Leung replied by saying, "I would not do it [attacking reporters], and hope it would not happen, but if reporters take close-up shots, protesters need to face the risk of 10 years in prison." The hosts followed up and asked: "So you choose not to severe yourself from the other protesters, but you do not really agree with their action." Leung replied: "Can be understood this way. I would not do it, but I understand why others would." Through such adjustments, Leung straddled a line that would allow him to stand-by the protesters in the Mongkok civil unrest, while at the same time conceding to the moral judgment of the mainstream society.

In addition, Leung exercised ideological self-restraint in his discourse about *ji-ji*, which might be translated as "self-rule" or "autonomy." Since Leung announced his candidacy, he was criticized by the pro-Communist newspapers for being pro-Hong Kong independence. In the forums, however,

Leung did not mention independence at all. One might argue that he hinted at his "separatist tendency" by refusing to use the term *Central Government*. Besides, there were a few occasions when he came close to expressing a proindependence stance, such as when he used the phrase *overthrowing this government* in the NOW TV forum and when he acknowledged that *Discourse on the Hong Kong Nation*, a book published by the Hong Kong University's Student Union in September 2014, was a major influence on his view.[4] Nevertheless, other than how he called the Chinese government and the few occasions when he hinted at his political vision, he would defend his view by appealing to the existing political discourse of one country, two systems. For instance, the Registration and Electoral Office claimed that the call for *ji-ji* in his electoral pamphlet was against the Basic Law. In the forum organized by TVMost,[5] Leung responded to the controversy by saying: "The Electoral Office said *ji-ji* is against the Basic Law. But Hong Kong people ruling Hong Kong and high degree of autonomy was the solemn promise enshrined in the Basic Law. [. . .] This is another clear example of the power holders suppressing freedom of expression, freedom of thoughts, and freedom of holding political views." Similarly, in the Hong Kong University's forum, he responded to criticisms from a progovernment candidate by emphasizing that "high degree of autonomy is a form of *ji-ji*." Leung maneuvered the range of meanings captured by the phrase *ji-ji*. At one end of the spectrum, the phrase can merely refer to autonomy, which can be part of a political framework that fully acknowledges Chinese sovereignty over Hong Kong. At the other end, the phrase can point to the formation of a self-contained political community not under any higher-order sovereign. Leung employed a form of strategic ambiguity so that he could speak to his supporters without explicitly violating the dominant political framework of one country, two systems.

The self-restraint exercised by Leung became clear when the election forums were contrasted with Leung's election rally. The term *ji-ji* was mentioned much less frequently in the rally, even though Leung did not explicitly talk about Hong Kong independence either. He explained that he joined the HKI because he agreed with Wong Toi-Yeung's emphasis on fighting the Hong Kong Communist regime through militant resistance. The aim was to "build a country belonging to oneself at the end." Besides Leung, a student leader from the Hong Kong University spoke and noted that "Hong Kong independence" should not be dismissed from mainstream political discussions. A politician from Civic Passion even said: "Is localism in Hong Kong advocating radical separatism? Is supporting Edward Leung equivalent to supporting Hong Kong independence?" My answer is, "Yes, so what?" Although we cannot attribute the words of the other speakers to the HKI and Edward Leung, the separatist sentiment was much more conspicuous in the rally when compared to how Leung presented himself in the public-facing electoral forums.

AFFECTING FRAMING: THE EGG-VERSUS-WALL METAPHOR

While framing is sometimes understood as a process of constructing a cognitive account to define an existing problem and justify a way to address the problem, affective appeal is also a core element in the framing process (Jasper, 1998). How Edward Leung employed affective appeal in his discourses has already been shown in the previous sections. When facing questions and criticisms regarding the Mongkok civil unrest, Leung's approach was not to construct a "rational defense" to justify the action; rather, his approach was to appeal to the moral-affective intuition of the public by highlighting the sacrifice made by the protesters. In the D100 forum, Alvin Yeung asked Edward Leung if promoting militant resistance would be irresponsible because radicalization might put people at risks. Leung responded: "To move forward and to retreat with the people, to be arrested, to bear the consequence of possibly 10 years in jail, that shows my sense of responsibility." With this rhetorical move, Leung evaded the question of other people's safety and turned the Mongkok civil unrest from showcasing irresponsible violence to showcasing his willingness to bear personal consequences and sacrifice for the city.

The core of Leung's affective framing thus involved positioning oneself and his fellow protesters as "the weak," who might not always be "right," but nonetheless demand the support and sympathy of citizens. An influential metaphor evoked by Leung was the egg versus the wall. The metaphor was borrowed from Japanese author Haruki Murakami, who said in his speech in 2009 when he won the Jerusalem prize for the Freedom of the Individual in Society: "Between a high, solid wall and an egg that breaks against it, I will always stand on the side of the egg. Yes, no matter how right the wall may be and how wrong the egg, I will stand with the egg."[6]

Murakami was well known and respected in Hong Kong, and the egg-versus-wall metaphor was already evoked by protesters during the Umbrella Movement. In the 2016 by-election, when Leung had to "confront" Alvin Yeung, he brought up the metaphor to criticize the democrats for severing ties with the protesters, as in the TVMost forum on February 23:

LEUNG: Would like to ask both, between eggs and wall, which side do you stand by? What I don't understand is, eggs like us are putting our bodies in front of the wall, why do you condemn us for being violent? [. . .]

YEUNG: I didn't severe ties. I served as a volunteer-lawyer [for protesters . . .]. But if there are innocent citizens getting hurt, how should we respond?

LEUNG: Thanks for your help. But your Party severed ties with us. [. . .]

YEUNG: If innocent Hong Kong people are hurt, do you have moral responsibility as the person who advocated the action?

LEUNG: I am willing to bear the responsibility. I don't want to hurt the innocent. But it is because politicians and the government did not resolve the social contradictions that we regretfully have to go to the streets.

Two days later, in the forum organized by Television Broadcasting Ltd., Alvin Yeung was assigned to ask Leung questions. It resulted in another round of exchange in which the egg-versus-wall metaphor was used:

YEUNG: You told Hong Kong people: we need change; we must stand by the eggs. [. . .] But do you agree that those Hong Kong citizens who got hurt by the irresponsible behavior of the protesters are the eggs among the eggs?

LEUNG: They are eggs too, and we don't want to hurt the innocent. But in a social conflict, it is very difficult [. . .]

YEUNG: Do you agree that, in order to protect the eggs among the eggs, we need to have bottom lines?

LEUNG: Disagree. In order to fight the totalitarian power to death, there cannot be any bottom lines. The prodemocracy movement in Hong Kong had too many baggages. [. . .] [T]hat's why we still don't have democracy today.

A tone of mutual respect was maintained as the two spoke to each other. Facing Leung's evocation of the metaphor of eggs versus wall, Alvin Yeung had to emphasize that he did not severe ties with the protesters. In the Television Broadcasting Ltd. forum, Yeung appropriated the eggs-versus-wall metaphor and posited innocent Hong Kong people as the weakest party. Yeung thus presented himself as always standing by the weak even if he was not on the side of the localists. In fact, in the public discourses at the time, Alvin Yeung was not the only person trying to challenge Leung's utilization of Murakami's metaphor by problematizing the dichotomous worldview underlying its utilization. Commentator Chan King-fai (2016b), in an article published one day after the Television Broadcasting Ltd. forum, emphasized that "always standing on the side of the eggs" cannot address the situation where "some eggs may be hurting other eggs." However, these discursive moves did not challenge Leung's self-identification as "eggs." They can be considered as reinforcing the eggs-versus-wall metaphor. They attested to the strength of the moral intuition of standing by the weak and thus the appeal of the affective framing by Edward Leung.

EVALUATING EDWARD LEUNG'S FRAMING EFFORTS

Edward Leung's impressive result in the election, getting more than 66,000 and 15 percent of the votes, surprised most observers and analysts. Some postelection interpretations took Leung's results to signify people's acceptance of violence and Hong Kong independence. *Ming Pao*'s editorial on March 1, for example, said: "Violence used to be resisted by Hong Kong people, and Hong Kong independence used to be a taboo. But for Edward Leung, these were the demands that allowed him to gain political capital. [. . .] He adopted a stance that was seen as deviant, but it gained him a larger number of votes. It seems that his advocacy has changed some people, leading them to support his path of violence and Hong Kong independence." We do not have survey evidence to pinpoint why the sixty-six thousand people voted for Leung in 2016. But the framing analysis presented in the previous sections has shown that Leung was not explicit about his proindependence stance in the electoral process. Instead, he used the term *ji-ji* and remained ambiguous with regard to what he meant by it. Although he defended the use of violence in protests, he also smoothened the radical edge of his view by emphasizing the reactive and principled character of violence, redefining the definition of "bottom lines" and making concessions on specific incidents and issues such as the acceptability of attacking journalists. For members of the public who had not been closely following the words and deeds of Edward Leung and other localist activists via digital media, the image of localism and militant resistance they gained from the election campaign was a softened one. Localism went through a process of mainstreaming when it was communicated to the public.

Leung put forward a package composed of a diagnostic framing centering on the idea of mainlandization, a prognostic framing emphasizing the notions of *ji-ji* and militant resistance, a double adversarial framing in which the way of the "old democrats" was dismissed as utterly ineffective, and an affective framing positioning the localist protesters as the weak who were making huge sacrifice for Hong Kong. A voter did not have to agree with all four aspects of Leung's framing before giving him the vote. It is plausible that some voters found Leung's articulation of mainlandization deeply resonant and were willing to give him the vote even if Leung's prognosis was not entirely convincing. It is plausible that many voters were deeply dissatisfied with the performance of the democrats and would just want to have a political newcomer in the oppositional camp to "shake things up." It is plausible that some voters were convinced by the moral-affective call by Edward Leung to stand by the eggs. The framing by Leung was multifaceted, nuanced, and sometimes ambiguous, but this enhanced his appeal by broadening the range of possible reasons for supporting him.

Nonetheless, the strong showing of Edward Leung in the by-election did compel people to reconsider if the public's negative reaction toward the Mongkok civil unrest was as widespread as the unified condemnation of violence immediately after the event would suggest. As former senior government official Wong Wing-ping wrote after the by-election:

> According to a survey conducted after the civil unrest by the Third Side, less than half of the respondents condemned the unrest, while 12% "identified" with it. The same survey shows that, on the question of who should bear the responsibility for the unrest, 26.8% thought it was the government [. . .] Therefore, the voters who voted for Edward Leung would indeed disagree with Chief Executive CY Leung's claim that the civil unrest had nothing to do with the government's governance. (Wong, 2016)

As the next section will demonstrate, by March 2016, public evaluation of the Mongkok civil unrest was indeed not one-sided. People were exhibiting a substantial degree of ambivalence toward, if not support for, the idea of militant resistance.

Public Opinion toward Militant Protests by March 2016

To better understand public opinion toward the Mongkok civil unrest and militant protests at the time, data from a survey conducted by the CCPOS at the Chinese University of Hong Kong in March 2016 are analyzed (see methodological appendix). The survey contains an item asking people their attitude toward the Mongkok civil unrest. Instead of adopting a typical Likert scale ranging from oppose to support, the answering categories combined an overall attitude with a judgment of governmental responsibility. Hence the options were "condemn," "disagree but the government is partially responsible," "disagree but the government is the root of the problem," and "support." It can be regarded as an ordinal scale ranging from the least supportive to the most supportive toward the protesters.

As the first row of table 4.4 shows, only 4.5 percent of the respondents supported the protest, yet the majority did not "condemn" the protest either. Fewer than 30 percent of the respondents chose the option. A total of close to 65 percent chose one of the options that combined disagreement toward the protest action with a judgment of governmental responsibility. Between those two options, the majority chose the option that put a stronger emphasis on governmental responsibility.

Younger people showed more sympathy toward the civil unrest and/or put more emphasis on governmental responsibility. Among people between eighteen and twenty-nine, close to 15 percent supported the protest. Meanwhile, it is remarkable that better educated people were more sympathetic toward the civil unrest. While only around 2 percent of respondents without college education supported the protest, more than 7 percent of respondents with some college education did, and another 48.8 percent of these better-educated respondents found the government the root of the problem, even though they disagreed with the action. Among the youngest age group and among the highly educated citizens, more than half chose either "support" or "disagree but the government is the root of the problem."

The CCPOS survey in March 2016 was among the first surveys in Hong Kong to include "localist" as an option in the political affiliation question. Overall, only 8.3 percent of the respondents claimed to be supporters of the localists, whereas 31.9 percent claimed to be supporters of the moderate democrats, and 2.5 percent claimed to be supporters of the radical democrats (grouped together as democrats in the following analysis). Whereas 20.1 percent of the respondents claimed to be centrists, 23.2 percent did not report any political predilection. They are grouped together

Tables 4.4a–f. Public attitudes toward the Mongkok civil unrest in March 2016

Table 4.4a.

	Condemn	Disagree but the government is partially responsible	Disagree but the government is the root of the problem	Support
Whole sample	28.7	23.5	41.0	4.5

Table 4.4b. Gender (χ^2 = 5.4, p > .10)

	Condemn	Disagree but the government is partially responsible	Disagree but the government is the root of the problem	Support
Male	27.9	22.8	43.3	5.9
Female	30.9	25.1	40.7	3.3

Table 4.4c. Age (χ^2 = 92.3, p < .001)

	Condemn	Disagree but the government is partially responsible	Disagree but the government is the root of the problem	Support
18–29	10.2	20.9	54.2	14.7
30–49	31.0	20.2	46.0	2.8
50 or above	34.1	28.2	36.8	0.9

Table 4.4d. Educational level. (χ^2 = 43.7, p < .001)

	Condemn	Disagree but the government is partially responsible	Disagree but the government is the root of the problem	Support
Junior high	36.1	29.9	32.0	2.1
Senior high	34.6	26.2	37.2	2.0
Tertiary	23.7	20.2	48.8	7.3

continued on next page

Table 4.4. Continued.

Table 4.4e. Family income ($\chi^2 = 10.93$ p < .10)

	Condemn	Disagree but the government is partially responsible	Disagree but the government is the root of the problem	Support
19,999 or below	31.8	29.4	34.8	4.0
20,000 to 49,999	26.8	23.9	43.2	6.2
50,000 or above	30.5	21.5	44.3	3.6

Table 4.4f. Political orientation. ($\chi^2 = 483.9$, p < .001)

	Condemn	Disagree but the government is partially responsible	Disagree but the government is the root of the problem	Support
Localist	1.1	5.7	58.6	34.5
Democrats	9.7	23.1	64.6	2.6
Centrists	41.2	30.8	26.7	1.3
Progovernment	71.4	19.0	9.5	0.0

Note: Entries in the first row do not add to 100 percent because of the presence of "Don't know" answers. The "Don't know" answers were not included in the cross-tabulation analysis with demographic variables. N = 1012.

Source: Created by the author.

as "centrists" in the analysis. Only 13.7 percent claimed to support the progovernment faction (including the options of "pro-China," "proestablishment," and "probusiness"). Not surprisingly, political orientation related to attitude toward the Mongkok civil unrest strongly. Among the self-proclaimed localist supporters, 34.5 percent supported the protest, whereas 58.6 percent disagreed with the protest action but saw the government as the root of the problem. Other than the self-proclaimed localists, support for the Mongkok civil unrest became very rare. Among supporters of the democrats, only 2.6 percent said they supported the protest, yet 64.6 percent saw the government as the root of the problem.

Among the centrists, 41.2 percent condemned the Mongkok civil unrest. But even then, a total of 57.5 percent of these respondents saw the government either as partially responsible or as the root of the problem. Overall speaking, though outright support for the protest was very weak and restricted to a portion of a small group of self-identified localists, one-sided condemnation of the Mongkok civil unrest was far from the majority view. The relationship between education and attitude toward the protest is particularly telling as it suggests that more sympathetic attitudes came from the more politically sophisticated section of the citizenry.

In addition to attitude toward the civil unrest, the survey contained a set of statements about militant protests. Three statements presented the problematic aspects or possible negative consequences of violent protests, whereas the other three statements indicated conditional acceptance of militant actions. The design of the items was based on the premise that people are likely to support peaceful protests as a matter of abstract principle and are unlikely to support violence unless there are specified reasons to do so. Hence the issue is what kind of conditions might lead people to see militant actions as acceptable or at least understandable.

As table 4.5 shows, close to 70 percent of the respondents agreed or strongly agreed with the general statement that "the basic principle of protests is that there should not be any use of force," but there were also 14.1 percent of the respondents disagreeing with the statement. Of the respondents, 68.1 percent agreed or strongly agreed with the statement "Militant resistance would damage the moral fabric of the society even if it achieves outcomes," while 74.4 percent of the respondents agreed or strongly agreed with the statement "Militant resistance would only alienate the society, so protests should stick to the principle of nonviolence." Widespread disagreement with militant protests is not surprising. But notably, comparing a moral rationale (i.e., causing damage to the moral fabric of the society) and a strategic rationale (i.e., alienating the general public) against militant actions, a somewhat larger percentage of respondents agreed with the latter.

Reflecting the same overall support for peaceful actions, relatively more respondents disagreed than agreed with the various statements offering conditional acceptance of militant protests. Nevertheless, the proportions of Hong Kong people who agreed with those statements are not negligible: 32.0 percent agreed that "Militant resistance that is limited in degree and constrained by norms is acceptable," 28.9 percent agreed that "Militant

Table 4.5. Public attitudes toward radical actions in March 2016

	Strongly disagree	Disagree	So-so	Agree	Strongly agree	Don't know
1. The basic principle of protests is that there should not be any use of force	4.0	10.1	16.5	18.1	50.3	1.1
2. Militant resistance would only alienate the society, so protests should stick to the principle of nonviolence	4.2	6.1	14.1	21.5	52.9	1.2
3. Militant resistance would damage the moral fabric of the society even if it achieves outcomes	6.4	10.0	13.9	22.8	45.3	1.6
4. Militant resistance that is limited in degree and constrained by norms is acceptable	26.0	18.3	21.9	23.6	8.4	1.8
5. Militant resistance is understandable when all peaceful means have been employed to no avail	27.1	20.7	21.4	16.7	12.2	1.9
6. It is normal for protesters to use violence when facing violent governance	25.6	20.9	22.2	18.2	9.6	3.5

Note: Entries are percentages.

Source: Created by the author.

resistance is understandable when all peaceful means have been employed to no avail," and 27.8 percent agreed that "It is normal for protesters to use violence when facing violent governance." Notably, these percentages are larger than the percentages of respondents expressing disagreement with the statements against militant protests. That is, only between 10.3 percent and 16.4 percent of the respondents disagreed with the first three statements, but between 27.8 percent and 32.0 percent of the respondents agreed with the last three statements of the table.

What such findings suggest is the development of a degree of ambivalence toward militant protests among a portion of Hong Kong people at the time. Political psychologists had noted that people can be holding considerations both for and against an object or idea. Indeed, people can both love and hate an object (Alvarez & Brehm, 2002; Barker & Hansen, 2005; Feldman & Zaller, 1992; Lavine et al., 2001; Zaller, 1992). Overall agreement with a policy can coexist with agreement with specific considerations against the policy. In the present case, despite overall disagreement with militant protests, a significant number of Hong Kong public were also holding ideas about the conditional acceptability of militant protests.

How did attitude toward militant protests and attitude toward the Mongkok civil unrest relate to each other? A multiple regression analysis was conducted to examine how various factors combined to shape people's evaluation of the Mongkok civil unrest. The dependent variable is an item in table 4.4. For simplicity, it is treated as a linear and interval variable. The dependent variables include four demographics, three dummy variables representing people's political affiliation (localist, democrats, or progovernment, with "centrist" being the reference category), past political participation (participating in the Umbrella Movement, July 1 protests, June 4 commemoration vigils, other social protests, and voting), three media use variables, and three variables related to attitude toward militant protests.

For attitude toward protests, answers to the first three items in table 4.5 were averaged for an index on principled opposition toward militant protests. The next three items were averaged for an index on conditional acceptance of militant protests. These indices were highly negatively correlated ($r = -.66$), but they were used separately because *principled* opposition and *conditional* acceptance are conceptually distinctive.

Moreover, given the argument that people might have developed a significant degree of ambivalence toward militant actions, an index of ambivalence toward militant protests was calculated using the principled opposition and conditional acceptance variables. The construction of the

Table 4.6. Predicting public attitudes toward the Mongkok civil unrest

	Model 1	Model 2	Model 3
Demographics			
Gender	−.04	−.04	−.02
Age	−.12***	−.03	.00
Education	−.02	−.04	−.02
Family income	−.04	−.05	.01
Political affiliation			
Localist	.39***	.26***	.14***
Democrat	.37***	.28***	.22***
Pro-government	−.17***	−.16***	−.10***
Political participation			
Umbrella Movement		.23**	.14**
July 1 protests		.09**	.05*
June 4 vigils		.01	.03
Other protests		−.01	−.02
Voting		−.05*	−.05*
Media use			
News exposure		.01	.02
Social media for news		−.01	.00
Alternative media		.12**	.06
Attitude toward militant protests			
Principled opposition			−.24***
Conditional support			.17**
Ambivalence			.10*
Adjusted R^2	0.341***	0.408***	0.524***

Notes: Entries are standardized regression coefficients. N = 1012. ***p < .001; **p < .01; *p < .05.

Source: Created by the author.

ambivalence variable followed the formula of Thompson and colleagues (2005). Ambivalence might have an influence on attitude toward the Mongkok civil unrest on top of the impact of principled opposition and conditional acceptance of militant protests.

Several findings are worth highlighting. First, among the demographic factors, only age had a significant relationship with the dependent variable in model 1. No demographic has a significant relationship with the dependent variable in the full model, suggesting that the relationship between age and attitude toward the Mongkok civil unrest was completely mediated by the other factors in the model. Second, among the five political participation variables, three obtain a significant coefficient in the final model. But only participation in the Umbrella Movement has a relatively substantive relationship with the dependent variable. The finding hints at how Umbrella Movement participants might turn more sympathetic toward the Mongkok civil unrest due to their disappointment about the "failure" of the peaceful occupation campaign to pressure the government to make meaningful concessions.

Third, both news exposure and accessing the news via social media do not relate to attitude toward the Mongkok civil unrest, but in model 2, online alternative media consumption relates significantly to attitude toward the Mongkok civil unrest. Online alternative media in Hong Kong was constituted by online news outlets that adopted a more advocatory approach to the news, and some had close connections with movement groups (Leung, 2015; Yung & Leung, 2016). Nonetheless, the relationship becomes insignificant in the full model. It indicates that, if online alternative media exposure had any impact on attitude toward the Mongkok civil unrest, the impact was mediated by attitude toward militant protests. Online alternative media were probably an important source of discourses explicating militant protests. Hence consumers of such outlets were more likely to be sympathetic.

Principled opposition to and conditional acceptance of militant protests related to attitude toward the Mongkok civil unrest in the expectable manner. The former's negative relationship with the dependent variable was apparently somewhat stronger than the latter's positive relationship with the dependent variable. A possible reason is that, even if people acknowledged that militant protests could be acceptable under certain conditions, it does not mean that they saw the conditions as being satisfied when the Mongkok civil unrest occurred. Meanwhile, ambivalence has a significant positive relationship with the dependent variable. That is, in addition to whether people agree with the considerations supporting or opposing militant protests, when people agree with both types of considerations, the discomforting sense of ambivalence could drive people to become more sympathetic toward the

Mongkok protest. Attitudinal ambivalence toward violence was not only a phenomenon emerging at the time; it was a factor that could affect how people evaluate political events and actors.

Concluding Remarks

February 2016 was an eventful month for Hong Kong. Within a few weeks, the Hong Kong society was surprised twice: that a violent protest involving the throwing of bricks by protesters and the firing of warning shots by the police could happen, and an activist deeply involved in the protest could receive substantial support at the voting booth. The Mongkok civil unrest plus the LegCo by-election, as an event cluster, compelled people to alter their perceptions and judgment of reality.

The Mongkok civil unrest originally met with unified condemnation from both sides of the political spectrum as well as the mainstream media. The reaction failed to reflect the growing urge among some members of the public to search for new and more effective means to push for democracy, as well as the frustration after the Umbrella Movement. This is not to say that the democrats were entirely wrongheaded in their immediate response to the protest event. In the March 2016 survey, the overwhelming majority of the supporters of the democrats disagreed with the protest action, though they saw the government as the root of the problem. Disagreeing with the protester violence and criticizing government irresponsiveness at the same time was indeed the stance taken by the democrats. Nevertheless, by "condemning" the violence involved in the incident, the democrats had overestimated the degree to which the prodemocracy citizens objected to the Mongkok civil unrest and missed the ambivalence many people had toward the use of militant tactics. It took the results of the by-election to force the democrats and the public to face the emerging reality.

However, it would also be wrong to see the by-election result as a straightforward indication of the level of support the localists and militant protest actions enjoyed. The analysis in this chapter emphasizes the layered character of Edward Leung's framing during the by-election. Similar to the localist candidates in the 2015 District Council elections, self-restraint was exercised by Edward Leung. He put forward a somewhat softened version of militant localism when facing the voting public. There are differences between the messages circulated within the circle of hardcore localist supporters and the version of localism presented by Leung through mass media platforms during the election.

One might question if Leung's self-restrained presentation during the by-election represented his "real" opinion and/or what localism "really" referred to. However, regardless of the extent to which Edward Leung really meant what he said, if one has to understand why, over the course of the mid-2010s, the Hong Kong public seemed to have become more and more receptive toward localism, one has to pay attention to how key localist figures interacted with the broader public. Here, elections constitute an important interface in the localist-public interactions. Electoral campaigns gather the attention of the news media and the public. They offer the occasions for the articulation, communication, and contestation of meanings. The version of localism articulated and presented at this interface would be the version that most members of the public are exposed to.

The exercise of self-restraint contributed to the mainstreaming of localism. Leung's performance in the 2016 by-election shows that, when localist activists had the need to attract support from the broader public, they had to adjust their ideas in ways that make them more aligned with the norms and views of the mainstream public. This is in line with previous research on how localism evolved over time as localist activists and groups reacted to the changing political environment and to other actors (Ho, 2022).

Nevertheless, mainstreaming of localism did not proceed entirely by localist discourses and ideas moving closer to the norms of the mainstream society; it could also proceed by the mainstream society moving closer to localist discourses and ideas. To borrow from social judgment theory in social psychology, a person's attitude toward an object is marked by a center point signifying his or her most preferred position, a range of positions within the person's latitude of acceptance, and positions far beyond the range and exist in the person's latitude of rejection (Eagly & Telaak, 1982; Powell, 1966). It would be virtually impossible to persuade a person to suddenly accept something in his or her latitude of rejection. But it is possible to persuade a person to move toward a position that is closer to a certain end and yet still within his or her latitude of acceptance. When this occurs, both the most preferred position and the latitude of acceptance could shift (Petty & Cacioppo, 1996). If the process repeats itself, positions that used to be in a person's latitude of rejection might fall inside the person's latitude of acceptance. Adopting this line of thinking, when localist public figures exercise self-restraint and present a less radical version of localism to the public, more people would find localism falling inside their latitude of acceptance. The interaction between major localist figures and the public could have shifted Hong Kong people's latitude of acceptance gradually, paving the way for accepting more radical ideas in the future. This could be a way to understand the radicalization of public opinion in Hong Kong during the 2010s.

Nevertheless, the localists were not the only player in the relational field. The apparent rise of localism led to responses from the state and the democrats. Between 2016 and 2019, public opinion was responding to the reconfigurations of the political viewpoints being offered in the public arena rather than to the actions of one single faction. The relational dynamics among the localists, the democrats, and the state would be the focus of the next two chapters.

Chapter 5

Ideological Brokerage and Articulating Hong Kong's Future

After losing the LegCo by-election in February 2016, Edward Leung attempted to run in the LegCo election in September of the same year. However, Leung and five other candidates were disqualified by the Electoral Affairs Committee, who claimed that the candidates supported Hong Kong independence and did not genuinely champion the Basic Law. In late 2017, the trial of Edward Leung for his participation in the Mongkok civil unrest began. In June 2018, he was convicted and sentenced to six years in jail for rioting.

Right before Leung's trial, *Lost in the Fumes*, a documentary focusing on him, was released. The film was one of the most prominent independent documentary films about social movements appearing in Hong Kong in the 2010s (Ingham & Ng, 2022). It was not shown in any commercial cinema—a fact widely taken to signify political self-censorship (Wu, 2022)—but it aroused strong public interests. It was one of eight films recommended by the Hong Kong Film Critics Society in 2018. It won the Chinese Documentary Special Jury Mention award at the Taiwan International Documentary Festival. A brief discussion of *Lost in the Fumes* can further illustrate the continual construction and negotiation of images of localism in the public arena between 2016 and 2019.

The ninety-minute film began with a reconstruction of Leung's rise to prominence through the Mongkok civil unrest. But after introducing the protagonist in the first few minutes, the film quickly adopted a humanizing tone by portraying Leung's regret of missing his grandmother's death due to his detention at the police station. Leung also talked about his habit of smoking cigarettes and how he felt about having one of his high school classmates being charged together with him for rioting. After showing Leung's life in his student hostel, including his love of lacrosse and how injuries prevented him from continuing to play, Leung began recounting his participation in the Umbrella Movement: "After three years of hall life, I should have graduated. But I felt lost. What's next? I could neither graduate nor get a job. I started locking myself up in my room. I got mild depression and needed medication. I started taking medicine. Things got worse afterwards. I was in such a state when the September 22 class boycott happened. Suddenly it seemed I had something to do." The tone of this passage is typical of the entire film. That is, the film offers a narrative that weaves together Leung's public political participation with his private life and personal feelings and struggles. Nora Lam, the director, produced the film when she was a university student. She explained that she did not intend to produce a film on a particular political ideology.[1] She was not heavily interested in politics, but events such as the Umbrella Movement and student activism were things happening around her. She produced two short films about the Umbrella Movement with a partner. After the showing of the short films in early 2016, she was looking for a topic for her next project. Edward Leung was a good subject because he was close to her lifeworld—they were after all studying in the same faculty at the same university.

In some preparatory conversations before the shooting, Edward Leung told Nora Lam that he loved the novel *Catcher in the Rye*. Lam found the theme of the novel—loss of innocence—very appealing. Therefore, instead of a story about a political movement, Lam's idea from the beginning was to tell a story about a youngster encountering the world and experiencing growth and disillusionment. As a result, one major criticism against the film when it was released was its perceived tendency to depoliticize. One author put it as follows:

> For those people who once treated Edward Leung as the hope of social reform, who wanted to find a full explanation from him for his low profile [after 2016], or expected new articulations of his political views, they would certainly feel disappointed toward the Edward Leung who self-mockingly said at Harvard that "the Revolution of Our Time has gone to America." Another kind of criticisms surrounded the incomprehensiveness of the film. It did not sort out the political experience and thoughts of Edward

Leung, and it did not include other people's comments on and evaluation of Leung. (Lai, 2018)

For Nora Lam, such criticisms were the result of the discrepancies between what people expected and what she wanted to do. She opined that there was a stereotype of political films. Deviation from the stereotype was bound to attract criticisms. She did not intend to depoliticize Leung and localism; it was just not her intention to produce a political film. Nevertheless, despite the director's lack of intention to make a political statement, the film's approach could have its own political consequences. As another author put it, the "depoliticized" approach "had dissolved people's flattened imagination of political figures. [The film] returned to the complexities of the private self. At the same time, when [. . .] the individual is placed into the historical context of Hong Kong, the subject is enacted. Here, the subject does not refer to Edward Leung as a localist warrior [. . .]; it is a Hong Kong youth participating in politics" (Choi, 2018). Echoing Choi's (2018) interpretation, Nora Lam observed that many young leaders of the Umbrella Movement, including Joshua Wong of scholarism and Nathan Law of the Hong Kong Federation of Students, liked the film even though they did not belong to the localist faction. That is, by casting Leung into the category of "a young activist" instead of the category of "a localist," the film articulated the struggles, experiences, and feelings that were common to young movement activists of different political orientations at the time.

Moreover, Nora Lam opined that it is easy for people who did not have strong political views to like the film and its protagonist because the narrative is easy to follow. "Just like you would not hate the main character in *Catcher in the Rye*, because the author portrayed him as a very relatable person." Lam emphasized that she did not intentionally portray Leung positively in order to promote his political views; for her, creating a narrative with a likable and relatable protagonist was a matter of "common sense."

Nora Lam herself refused to speculate on whether her film had changed people's perception of Leung and localism. But following the discussion in the previous chapter, *Lost in the Fumes* could be regarded as another instance of the mainstreaming of localism, that is, the presentation of localism and localists in ways that the mainstream public could find it easier to understand and accept. In addition, in relation to the present chapter's focus, Nora Lam's film can be regarded as having deactivated the boundary between the localist camp and the democrats' camp. Instead of highlighting the distinctiveness of localist politics, the film's portrayal of Leung was recognized as capturing the common experience and sentiments of Hong Kong young people. In this sense, Lam had inadvertently acted as a bridge broker (Mayer, 2009) in the relationship between the localists and the democrats as well as the relationship between the localists and the public.

This chapter discusses the role of ideological bridge brokers in the evolution of the prodemocracy movement in Hong Kong between 2016 and 2019. Instead of examining the discourses of the major localist writers as other scholars have done (Carrico, 2022; Cheung, 2015; Ho, 2022, 2023), this chapter examines the discourses espoused by those situated between the localists and the democrats. The focus on the ideological brokers follows from the emphasis on intra-movement relational dynamics. As will be argued, the brokers problematized the boundary between the localists and the democrats through developing new frameworks and visions that both camps would find it hard to reject. These discourses thus further contribute to the mainstreaming of localism. They provide a window through which one can observe the negotiation of the relationship between the two sides within the prodemocracy movement.

The following will begin with a brief description of the discursive landscape of the prodemocracy movement in Hong Kong in the mid-2010s. It will also further explicate the concept of ideological bridge broker. It will then explain the choice of analytical focuses: the political party Demosisto and the prominent scholar-commentator Joseph Lian. Afterward, the main parts of this chapter will examine the discourses of Demosisto and Lian in turn.

From the Localists to the Bridge Brokers

Karl Marx has famously defined critical theory as the self-clarification of the struggles and wishes of the age (Fraser, 1985). When a society experiences strong sentiments related to the emergence of new struggles and wishes, one can expect "theories" to be developed for making sense of the ferments. By the mid-2010s, a range of perspectives tied to the rise of localism or the idea of the "Hong Kong nation" were developed by various authors. These perspectives are, of course, vastly different from Marxist critical theory (and many of them were regarded as "rightists" instead of "leftists"), but they could indeed be seen as attempts to clarify and direct the struggle for social and political change.

The book-length account by Carrico (2022) had outlined and discussed four streams of thought about Hong Kong nationalism developed since the early 2010s, namely, the city-state theory, self-determination, independence, and returning to British rule. The city-state theory does not promote the separation of Hong Kong from China, but it envisions Hong Kong as an autonomous polis belonging to a federation of Chinese states. To achieve this end, the Basic Law needs to be extended indefinitely. Self-determination theorists, through referencing international laws, emphasize the right of national self-determination. Their arguments centered on allowing Hong Kong people to determine their own future through a referendum. Independence thinkers emphasize the necessity of Hong Kong acquiring political independence from China. They contend that Hong Kong people should use their moral strength to gain international support for the purpose. Last, returnism refers to the return of Hong Kong to British rule. While there might not be strong moral-political principles behind the suggested arrangement, the proponents see returning to British rule through international intervention as paradoxically the most politically feasible program under existing circumstances.

The four streams do not form a coherent whole, and there can also be internal variations within each school of thinking. Each of the four streams of thought had to contend with difficult questions such as the way to define and demarcate a nation. While the development of localist thoughts was often seen as grounded in the recognition that genuine democracy under Chinese rule is impossible, for many observers, the visions articulated by the four streams of thought do not seem to be feasible either. But in any case, the four perspectives should have captured all the major ideas and positions espoused by the localists in the period.

Therefore, by the mid-2010s, what existed in Hong Kong were several streams of thought regarding Hong Kong's future that put an emphasis on Hong Kong being a distinctive nation. But these ideas arguably did not have very wide circulation in the public arena at large. Take the idea of national self-determination as the example. The February 2014 issue of *Undergrad*, the publication of Hong Kong University's Student Union, is typically credited as the place where the idea was first systematically explicated. But the publication garnered very little public attention even when it was published in book form later in the year (i.e., *Discourse on the Hong Kong Nation*). The publication came into public purview thanks to then chief executive CY Leung, who named and criticized it for promoting Hong Kong independence in his policy address in early 2015. But even after CY Leung's criticism inadvertently promoted the publication, there was a lack of prominent authors or organizations serving as the regular "spokespersons" for the notion in the public arena. Instead, the idea of self-determination would be more widely discussed later only when the political party Demosisto adopted it and developed it into the notion of democratic self-determination.

In fact, elements of the schools of localist thoughts could be appropriated and developed by nonlocalist authors and politicians into visions that integrate the localist ideas with more conventional and/or less radical ideas about democratization. For another example, as mentioned above, the city-state theory developed by Chin Wan contained a call for extending the Basic Law indefinitely. This idea was key to the document titled Resolution for Hong Kong's Future, publicly propagated by a group of democrats and prodemocracy academics in April 2016 (we will return to this document later).

In other words, in addition to the localist authors and thinkers, the discursive landscape of the prodemocracy movement in the 2010s also included people and groups who could be seen as ideological brokers. Conceptually, a broker is an agent linking two hitherto separated groups or networks together without himself or herself belonging to either group or network. It mediates the relationship between the two sides. In social movements, brokers play important roles in processes such as the diffusion of contention through information sharing and the transmission of action repertoires (Romanos, 2016; Soule & Roggeband, 2018; Walsh-Russo, 2014), frame bridging and alignment (Haydu, 2012; Vasi, 2011), and formation of linkages between grassroots actors and established organizations in networked movements (Y. Lee, 2023). Generally speaking, brokerage serves the purpose of broadening and strengthening a movement or political coalition (Young & Cross, 2002).

Von Bulow (2011) differentiated among four brokerage roles. Brokers can serve as translators who diffuse knowledge through communication activities. They can serve as coordinators who reach out to potential participants and organize the division of labor among members of a coalition. They can serve as representatives of a movement when speaking in the name of others in meetings, events, and/or media interviews. Finally, they can serve as articulators who "bridge across cleavages to bring together actors and negotiate common positions" (p. 168; also see Mische, 2008). The articulator role is particularly relevant for the present analysis. Besides, Mayer (2009) used the notion of bridge brokers to refer to brokers who primarily play the role of bridging the divide between hitherto unconnected groups. His analysis examined the role of a group of actors—ranging from individual workers who suffered from health issues to scientists—in the formation of a coalition between the labor and environmental movements through identifying health as a bridging issue.

Bridge brokers facilitate coalition formation partly through the articulation of shared frameworks that can encompass the disparate ideas and frames of various groups (e.g., Robin-D'Cruz, 2019). The work of the bridge brokers can lead to boundary deactivation, which refers to the undermining of the boundary between distinctive groups. McAdam and colleagues (2008) identified boundary deactivation as a mechanism central to an upward scale shift in many historical political movements. That is, the growth of a protest movement is often achieved by groups putting aside or crossing the boundaries hitherto separating them, thus forming a larger and stronger coalition.

The concept of ideological bridge brokers helps us understand the role played by a distinctive group of actors in the dynamic evolution of the prodemocracy movement in Hong Kong in the mid-2010s. This group of actors includes political parties such as Demosisto and the Neo Democrats, as well as prominent individual academics and commentators such as political scientist Brian Fong, economist Joseph Lian, and veteran journalist and literary figure Li Yee, among others. Notably, these political parties and individual authors may or may not see themselves as having the brokerage role. They might not have the intention to mediate the relationship between the localists and the democrats. But they are treated as ideological bridge brokers here because they did not fall squarely into either camp, and their works did bridge the localists-democrats divide in identifiable ways. If what one aims at understanding is not only localism itself but how localists related to the democrats and the public at large, the works of these ideological bridge brokers cannot be ignored.

Among the various political groups and authors who could be seen as ideological bridge brokers, the following analysis focuses mainly on the political party Demosisto and the public affairs commentator Joseph Lian. Demosisto, formed by several student leaders in the Umbrella Movement, is exemplary of how an emerging political group attempted to strategically locate itself within the evolving political space. Its leader, Nathan Law, became the youngest legislator when he won in the 2016 LegCo election, though his tenure was short-lived as he was controversially disqualified by the government (see chapter 6). For this chapter, Demosisto's discourse of democratic self-determination could be seen as a framework effectively incorporating independence as an option and democracy as a procedure as well as a basic right.

Meanwhile, Joseph Lian is an economist who was once an advisor of the Hong Kong government's Central Policy Unit in the early years after the handover. He is exemplary of prominent authors who had close ties with the elites in the prodemocracy movement (and even the political establishment), yet exhibiting sympathy toward the young localists. Writing in prestigious mainstream media outlets, his work could confer status and legitimacy to localism as a trend worthy of public attention. Lian was not merely a champion of localism. Underlying his writings was a broader concern of developing a more inclusive prodemocracy movement in Hong Kong, though his writings could attract fierce criticisms at times from not only the progovernment groups but also supporters of the moderate democrats.

Demosisto and Democratic Self-Determination

Demosisto was formed in April 2016. Nathan Law, a leader of the Hong Kong Federation of Students during the Umbrella Movement, served as the founding chairperson. Among the other leaders was Joshua Wong of Scholarism. The party had around thirty founding members, many of whom came from civil society groups active during the Anti-National Education campaign in 2012 and the student groups active in the Umbrella Movement. Nathan Law recalled that they established the party because "the Umbrella Movement needed to be represented."[2] Derek, a founding member of Demosisto, also recalled that the establishment of the party was motivated by the wish to sustain the influence of the Hong Kong Federation of Students and Scholarism.[3]

POSITIONING OF DEMOSISTO: BETWEEN THE DEMOCRATS AND THE LOCALISTS

Law's statement quoted above implies a judgment that neither the existing prodemocracy political parties nor the emerging localists could represent the Umbrella Movement. Otherwise, the student leaders could have joined the existing parties instead of setting up their own. Therefore, putting aside whether there were individual ambitions involved, the formation of Demosisto was grounded in a perception of a "gap" between the emerging localists and the conventional democrats. Demosisto positioned itself within this gap. This was clearly reflected in the public speeches and writings of the leaders. In a Facebook post in July 2016, Joshua Wong wrote: "Beyond the traditional democrats and the localists, we believe Hong Kong need[s] a new political path. [We] need proactive organization and actions in order to overcome the passivity and accumulated weakness of the pan-democrats, and we need the determined insistence on the value of democracy in order to respond to the xenophobic anxiety of localism."[4] Understandably, as a political party led mainly by young activists, the mainstream media and the public were more interested in comparing Demosisto to the emerging localist groups. As a result, more efforts were spent by the Demosisto leaders on distinguishing themselves from the localist label. For instance, when responding to journalists' questions in the press conference for the founding of the party, the leaders stated: "Demosisto does not belong to the localist faction, so the question of whether we are 'middle-of-the-road localists' does not arise. Our stance in unequivocal. We support Hong Kong people's self-initiated and self-driven social movement that fights for the right to autonomy and self-determination. But we refuse to promote democracy through creating enemies and encouraging xenophobia."[5] Whether localism must be equated with xenophobia is a moot point. Leaders of Demosisto were responding to public perceptions of localism. Certainly, differentiating oneself from others requires not only the adoption or rejection of labels. It also requires the articulation of positions on key issues of contention. For instance, on militant protests, Demosisto claimed in a response posed on its Facebook page on June 23, 2016: "Demosisto supported non-violent direct action with principles and bottom lines. [. . .] Non-violence is defined as actions that do not target at hurting other people."[6] The statement, on the one hand, adopted the democrats' emphasis on nonviolence, and it rejected Edward Leung's claim of "no bottom lines" in protests. But on the other hand, Demosisto signified its "will to fight" through the notion of direct action and restricting the meaning of "violence" to "hurting other people." By the latter definition, vandalizing shops or public properties is not ruled out (though it is not to say that Demosisto would necessarily support or engage in vandalism).

For another example, commemoration of the Tiananmen crackdown in Beijing in 1989 was an annual political event in Hong Kong. For the older generation of democrats, striving for democratization in China and striving for democratization in Hong Kong are closely linked to each other. But with the rise of localism, a new generation of young people started to question the relevance of Tiananmen commemoration to the prodemocracy movement in Hong Kong. As Lee and Chan (2021) explained, this led to a process of memory repair in which memory entrepreneurs had to rearticulate the significance of the historical event under the new political context. Demosisto was a participant in this memory repair process. The political party published ten Q&As via its Facebook page between May 27 and 31,

2016. They explained the party's stance on the matter: it supported the call for rehabilitating the student movement in 1989; it saw promoting a democratic China not so much a responsibility of Hong Kong people as a strategy in the struggle for Hong Kong's democratization; and it announced the party's participation in the annual vigil held by the Alliance in Support for Patriotic Democracy Movement in China.[7] Yet it also supported other groups to commemorate the event in other ways. On the overall significance of June 4, Demosisto wrote:

> The June 4 massacre was a part of the 1989 pro-democracy movement; it was hard evidence of the CCP's violent rule. It was a very important historical event for Hong Kong. On June 5, 1989, 70 "secretive men" entered Hong Kong, claiming to visit their relatives. In the early morning of June 7, 15 of them initiated an incident in Mongkok, leading the Alliance to cancel their planned protest march, originally estimated to be participated by 1.5 million people. [. . .] Demosisto call for a rigorous examination of Hong Kong history. We believe we should not hold the biased view that people who commemorate June 4 are "poisoned by the pan-Chinese passion flower" and let such biases lead us to ignore events that indeed influenced Hong Kong's democratization.[8]

Demosisto thus insisted on the significance of Tiananmen commemoration, but it looked at the events in 1989 from the perspective of Hong Kong history, instead of contemporary Chinese history. Demosisto was certainly not the only group that attempted to localize Tiananmen commemoration in face of the challenge of localism (Lee & Chan, 2021). For the present discussion, it illustrates the careful positioning of Demosisto as in between the localists and the democrats.

Locating oneself in-between two political factions does not automatically make one a bridge broker. Instead, the construction of in-betweenness inevitably requires effort to differentiate oneself from both sides, as the above passages had illustrated with regard to action repertoire and attitude toward June 4. Therefore, theoretically speaking, positing oneself as between two sides could mean an effort to remap the political space; it could even mean turning both sides into one's antagonists. However, Nathan Law recalled that the party maintained good relationships with both the localists and the democrats. It was partly because of the lack of huge political controversies and events between mid-2016 and mid-2019 that would divide the various factions of the political opposition. He opined that hostility often existed mainly among supporters of different factions instead of the leaders.

Demosisto also did not try to establish its own position through attacking the democrats. The latter was recognized by Fermi Wong, a social worker famous for her work on ethnic minorities in Hong Kong. Wong joined the founding press conference of the political party. She noted that Demosisto criticized movement activists of the earlier generation relatively infrequently. "When the localists criticized the older generation and the democrats as rubbish middle-aged people, Demosisto did not."[9] The maintenance of mutual respect between Demosisto and other political actors could be seen as a condition for its bridge broker role.

THE DISCOURSE OF DEMOCRATIC SELF-DETERMINATION

Central to Demosisto's ideological bridge broker role was its articulation of democratic self-determination as a new political project. As pointed out earlier, Demosisto was not the only or the first one to employ the notion of self-determination. A discussion of national self-determination was offered by the Hong Kong University Student Union in 2014. Besides, in late April 2016, about two weeks after the establishment of Demosisto, thirty-two prodemocracy politicians and academics cosigned the statement Resolution for Hong Kong's Future (Resolution hereafter) via social media. A brief discussion of the Resolution can serve as a point of comparison to shed light on the specific characteristics of Demosisto's discourse.

The Resolution began by recounting the history of the democrats' desire for "reunion in democracy" in the 1980s. The hope was to bring about democratization in China and Hong Kong through positive interaction between the two places. The hope was dashed by subsequent developments over the years. It was finally crushed by the NPC decision on August 31, 2014, which set up a highly restrictive framework for popular election of the chief executive of the Hong Kong government. Under such circumstances,

> Hong Kong people must defend the city's various rights under the Basic Law and strive for changing the unreasonable stipulations, so as to fully establish and protect Hong Kong's autonomy. [. . .] We believe that the political position of Hong Kong after 2047 must be determined by Hong Kong people via a fully democratic and legally binding mechanism. As long as Hong Kong people

can exercise the right to self-determination according to the principle of "internal self-determination," "permanent continuation of autonomous governance" should be the appropriate choice for resolving the question of Hong Kong's future for a second time.[10]

The Resolution thus put forward the idea of self-determination as a procedure, but it simultaneously proclaimed "permanent continuation of autonomous governance" as the substantive position that would be most suitable for Hong Kong. The Resolution is grounded on a critique of the contemporary practice of one country, two systems, but "permanent continuation of autonomous governance" does not involve a call for the end of the formula. It was essentially a call for practicing one country, two systems as the prodemocracy citizens in Hong Kong would conceive it, that is, a social contract that guarantees the rights and liberties of Hong Kong people (Scott, 2017).

No matter whether "permanent continuation of autonomous governance" was indeed a plausible and attractive option for Hong Kong people, one could question the Resolution for its internal tension: If self-determination was to be realized by a legally binding vote, how could one be certain that permanent continuation of autonomous governance would be chosen by the public? Since the Resolution was put forward only by a group of individuals, there was no systematic and organized effort to further elaborate the text and resolve the issues involved.

In comparison, Demosistō's articulation of democratic self-determination offered a more coherent, if also more radical, vision for the future of Hong Kong. Similar to the Resolution, Demosistō highlighted the political future of Hong Kong after 2047 as the question to be addressed. Even before the formation of the party, Joshua Wong (2015) had already argued that the core question for Hong Kong's future is no longer political reform; rather, the question is: what's next after "no change for 50 years"? What Hong Kong people needed to strive for is not only popular election, but also the right to self-determination. Derek recalled that, back in 2016, leaders of Demosistō had a vague timeline in mind. The 1997 question was dealt with in the 1980s, so the 2047 question might also be dealt with in the early 2030s. Situated in 2016, there would be about fifteen years to develop the ground and mechanisms, such as legalized public referendum, for realizing self-determination in 2047.

On June 27, 2016, Demosistō (2016) published its declarative article "Self-Determination Sets Sail: The Road Map of Our Self-Determination Movement" on the newspaper *Ming Pao*. The article presented a broad framework for moving toward self-determination, emphasizing the need to transcend the discourse of "political reform" and focus on the question of Hong Kong's future, to realize the notion of popular sovereignty through a public vote on the future of the city, and to achieve socioeconomic autonomy through an integration of political and community movements. The article then outlined five main directions for the movement for self-determination: (1) to establish self-determination on Hong Kong people's political agenda through a nonlegally binding public vote, (2) to strive for the legal recognition of people's right to self-determination through a public referendum law, (3) to draft a Hong Kong charter to outline the vision of the various aspects of the future of Hong Kong, (4) to initiate international lobbying and gain international support, and (5) to carry out the public referendum on the future of Hong Kong, including its sovereignty and right to govern. The article specifically mentioned the notion of independence:

> Although Demosisto does not advocate for independence, in order to realize the ideal of "popular sovereignty," we agree that the public referendum should include the options of independence and local self-government. No matter whether and how sovereignty and the constitutional framework will change, the premise must be allowing Hong Kong people to exercise democratic self-government. If independence is not included as an option in the public referendum, it will not be able to resolve the legitimacy problem of Hong Kong's political system.

Demosisto carefully positioned itself in relation to independence. The verb *advocate* instead of *support* is used in the quoted passage. That is, Demosisto would not promote Hong Kong independence, but the passage does not rule out the possibility that the party or its leaders might hold positive views toward it. When asked about how the group thought about Hong Kong independence in the press conference for the founding of the party, the leaders responded: "Having an independent sovereignty is a very ideal status for Hong Kong. If we put aside the reality constraints, probably no supporter of democracy would be against Hong Kong independence. But if we look around the world, many places are still influenced heavily by their former sovereign countries or international powers even after formal independence. [. . .] This kind of independence is meaningless."[11] This answer expressed a positive view toward Hong Kong independence, even calling it an ideal status for the city. Nevertheless, after publicizing the notion of self-determination, the party and its leaders refrained from further expressing any predilection on the idea of Hong Kong independence. Instead, efforts were spent on differentiating between self-determination and independence. For instance, in an article published in May 2016, Nathan Law rejected the idea that self-determination is "euphemism for Hong Kong independence": "A democratic public referendum must not rule out a political vision supported by a significant portion of the public. [. . .] We must point out that self-determination through public referendum does not necessarily take Hong Kong toward independence" (2016).

Overall, in Demosisto's scheme, Hong Kong independence is only an option. Demosisto thus treated Hong Kong independence as within the boundary of what Hallin (1986) called the "sphere of legitimate controversy." It is something that people have the right to discuss and even advocate, but the party would maintain its distance from and neutrality toward the idea.

DEMOCRATIC SELF-DETERMINATION AS A BROKER FRAME

The notion of democratic self-determination articulated by Demosisto has the quality of a broker frame. On one side, the discourse incorporated Hong Kong independence as an option in the proposed public referendum. Some localists might not be fully satisfied, but it would be difficult to argue against putting independence forward as an option among others for people to choose. This can be contrasted with the idea of internal self-determination in the Resolution. The Resolution did not specify whether independence would be included as an option, and Tanya Chan, a Civic Party politician who co-signed the Resolution, publicly said that Hong Kong independence should not be an option.[12]

On the other side, it would also be difficult for the democrats to argue against the idea of a public referendum because it is indeed a democratic procedure in place in many countries. Pro-democracy citizens in Hong Kong were familiar with the fact that, at least in some democratic countries, public referendum on independence of part of the country (e.g., Scotland in the UK) was allowed to be held. Hence it would be hard for supporters of democracy to come up with a justification for ruling out Hong Kong independence as an option if a public referendum on Hong Kong's future is to be held. Notably, by focusing on the year 2047, Demosisto had already rendered its proposal less radical than it would have been if a different timeline or no specific timeline is provided. As Derek opined: "There were concerns about the 'red lines.' [By sticking to 2047] I am only trying to argue for something you haven't said or haven't confirmed." Demosistō could claim that its proposal does not violate the Basic Law because the miniconstitutional document said nothing about the political arrangement after 2047.

Certainly, for China, Hong Kong independence is a cardinal sin and should not even be an option. Hence China was unlikely to see democratic self-determination as distinctive from Hong Kong independence. In fact, the pro-Communist newspapers heavily criticized Demosistō for fanning the flame of independence. Nathan Law noted that Demosistō was fully aware of how the state would interpret its proposal. But there was no National Security Law in 2016. Hence there were fewer concerns about the political risks involved. More importantly, as a political party aiming at participating in elections, they had to appeal to the local public, and "you just needed to explain the idea to Hong Kong people." Similarly, Derek recalled:

> Of course, you knew that Beijing would equate you with the localists and the proindependence faction, though we did not expect things to happen so quickly. Our thought was that, through packaging the idea in a way to make it so-called milder, it would allow us to enter the prodemocracy mainstream. When the whole thing becomes what the democrats also agree with, then it is more difficult for [the state] to isolate you from other oppositional forces and close you down.

Derek's comment illustrated the strategic thinking of how the construction of a broker frame can tie Demosistō and the democrats together and make it more difficult for the state to divide and rule, an issue to be further discussed in the next chapter. Here, suffice to remark that the core members of Demosistō did not perceive any significant objection to their discourse from other parties in the prodemocracy movement. Derek recalled that the democrats did not object to self-determination. In fact, the Democratic Party adopted the term in subsequent years. Nathan Law noted that he did not hear any major objections from the localists either. "At most there were some localists who asked if new immigrants would be allowed to vote in the public referendum. If yes, they would not support the referendum. But this is not an objection to the basic ideas [of public referendum and self-determination]."

There were other politicians and activists putting forward other articulations into the political marketplace of ideas at the time. For example, Terence was a young activist who established a new political group in 2017. He described both Hong Kong independence and democratic self-determination as "just slogans." He emphasized that one should work on enhancing Hong Kong's capability of self-government. Only when the relevant capability is in place can people make a meaningful choice regarding Hong Kong's future.[13]

Terence's idea of building the conditions for Hong Kong's autonomy does not contradict the idea of independence or self-determination, but if Demosisto's "roadmap" emphasizes establishing the right to self-determination through enacting a public referendum law, Terence's emphasis was more on building the social and economic capacities pertinent to self-sustainability of Hong Kong. Another way to understand Terence's critique of democratic self-determination is to note that, by putting the emphasis on establishing the right and the procedure for Hong Kong people to determine the city's future, Demosisto actually refrained from outlining its own vision for the future of the city. Nathan Law acknowledged that there was a degree of strategic ambiguity in the discourse of democratic self-determination—strategic both in the sense of not provoking the Chinese government too directly and in the sense of facilitating participation by people with different visions of Hong Kong's future.

The first test of the popularity of Demosisto came in the 2016 LegCo elections. The party originally planned to put forward two candidates, though one of them pulled out due to lack of funding, leaving chairperson Nathan Law as the only representative. Throughout the elections, Law joined hands with activist Eddie Chu and Lau Siu-lai to form a "self-determination faction." All three candidates won in their respective geographical constituencies. Nathan Law, in particular, won one of the six seats in the Hong Kong Island constituencies with 50,818 votes. He won more votes than the candidate list of the Democratic Party (42,499 votes) as well as the candidate list of the Civic Party (35,404 votes). Interestingly, preelection polls showed that level of support for Law was very low two months before election day. But his support grew gradually, forming a momentum that propelled him to victory (Tang & Lee, 2019).

However, similar to the case of Edward Leung in the 2016 LegCo by-election, one cannot jump to the conclusion that the electoral performance of Nathan Law affirmed the appeal of democratic self-determination. Nathan Law saw himself as the beneficiary of the vote coordination campaign carried out by the democrats.[14] He also identified a number of other factors behind his victory, including the lack of effort on the part of certain progovernment candidates toward the end of the electoral campaign period. Derek noted that Law was competing in the Hong Kong Island constituency, which was very much a middle-class-dominated area. The campaign thus emphasized Law's image as a "good boy": "the whole thing was really about being young and fresh; that's the nature of the Hong Kong Island."

Nevertheless, even though the victory of the self-determination camp in the 2016 election could not be simplistically equated with the appeal of self-determination, it did confirm the idea that many prodemocracy citizens were looking for alternatives. Law believed that he captured many voters who neither accepted the localists nor wanted to vote for the existing democrats. His campaign captured those people in the middle. Derek believed that many supporters of democracy wanted something fresher, but they could not jump to localism all at once. In comparison to the localists, "Nathan's or Eddie Chu's image can appeal to these so-called reform-minded democrats."

This reading of public opinion is consistent with the idea that, to understand the political dynamics in Hong Kong in the period, one needs to examine not only the localists and the democrats, but also what exists in between. In any case, although there were no opinion surveys directly show-casing Hong Kong citizens' attitude toward democratic self-determination, it will be argued later in this chapter that democratic self-determination did resonate with the basic attitudes of Hong Kong people toward the ideas of democracy and Hong Kong independence. But before we turn to survey data, the next section will discuss an exemplary case of another type of ideological bridge brokers in the public arena.

Political Commentators as Articulators

News and public affairs commentators play important roles in interpreting the significance of political events and phenomena. Earlier chapters have discussed how election results and the Mongkok civil unrest were interpreted in the news pages, which could potentially shape the understanding of the public and the elites. Beyond specific incidents and controversies, we could expect the rise of localism to have been the subject of continual articulation and interpretations by commentators.

The localists had their own prominent authors, typically active in the online environment and often described as KOLs (key opinion leaders) in local parlance. One example is Lewis Loud, whose writings were treated by the more left-leaning progressives in Hong Kong as exemplary of a kind of toxic right-wing localism (P. S. Y. Ho, 2021). However, given the focus on ideological brokerage, more pertinent to the present analysis are a few prominent authors who had deep connections with the democrats but became localist sympathizers in the 2010s. Li Yee and Joseph Lian are two prime examples. Li was a journalist and a literary figure who established a public affairs magazine and started commenting on politics in the 1970s. Originally a supporter of the Communist vision, he became disillusioned and turned himself into a fierce critic of the CCP by the end of the 1970s (Li, 2022). Lian is an economist, former faculty member at the business school of the Hong Kong University of Science and Technology, former chief writer at the *Hong Kong Economic Journal*, and former full-time consultant for the Hong Kong government's Central Policy Unit in the early years after the handover. Both had regular columns in mainstream newspapers in the 2010s. Both regularly commented on localism with a recognizably sympathetic, if not outright supportive tone.

The fact that localism could attract sympathy from such authors as Li and Lian is illustrative of the appeal of the rising political current. Besides, having such prominent sympathizers can confer status to localism. The writings by such authors helped established localism as something worthy of attention and serious interrogation. While the writings of localist KOLs might have reached mainly their own supporters and political junkies attending closely to online discourses, the writings by Lian and Li had better potential to reach a wider readership. Moreover, given their background, one can expect authors such as Lian and Li to articulate localism in ways that would render it relatively more acceptable to the prodemocracy mainstream. That is, one can expect them to—intentionally or not—play the role of ideological bridge brokers through their writings.

This section examines the writings of Joseph Lian (see methodological appendix for information about material collection). According to Lian,[15] when he started writing for newspapers in the 1990s, his original goal was to apply academic knowledge to the commentary of public affairs. But by the 2010s, he developed the idea that he should stand by the weaker side within the prodemocracy movement. At that time, the localists apparently constituted the group being ostracized from within the prodemocracy movement. He therefore started writing about localism with a more sympathetic tone. Once he started, he discovered that localism indeed had its potential as a way of thinking. On the one hand, he aimed primarily to explicate and develop the ideas of localism. That is, he might not have the conscious goal of establishing a broker frame. But on the other hand, Lian acknowledged that he would like to encourage prodemocracy citizens to read localism more sympathetically. Hence one may expect his writings to involve, to a certain degree, the mainstreaming of localism.

The first thing to note about Lian's explication is his identification of localism as the future direction for the prodemocracy movement. Even before the Umbrella Movement started, Lian had predicted a shift from "resisting the communists by democracy" to "resisting reddening through localism." He explicated in an article on September 1, 2014, the day after NPC's decision on the electoral framework for the chief executive of Hong Kong:

> Because Beijing's interference into Hong Kong affairs is comprehensive and not restricted to political reform, the reaction would also be all-rounded. These two factors together would lead social movement to shift its path from the long-held theme of "resisting the communists by democracy" to "resisting reddening through localism." The former is about abstract values and political rationality. It focuses on fighting for the future. The latter is about concrete matters and cultural sensitivities. It cares about protecting the here and now. (Lian, 2014a)

In another article published about ten days before the above-quoted piece, Lian even predicted that "the term 'pan-democrats' will gradually fade out and changed into 'pan-localists'" (Lian, 2014b). Certainly, predictions may not be materialized. The term *pan-democrats*[16] would not fade out in Hong Kong for years to come. And as the political reality evolved, Lian could change his judgment. By the end of February 2016, after the Mongkok civil unrest and the LegCo by-election, Lian argued that the internal split within the opposition had reached a new equilibrium. He described the internal split as not only inevitable but also good for the prodemocracy movement. "The internal split among the democrats under the state's repression is a systemic reaction and an improvement" (Lian, 2016a). This is because governmental repression inevitably leads to radicalization of part of the public, whereas others would remain moderate. The democrats must exhibit an internal split to respond to both groups of supporters. The emergence of a radical faction is therefore natural and beneficial.

Lian treated localists as part of the prodemocracy movement (as this book does). The rise of localism was not so much the emergence of a "third force"—as some localist commentators might prefer to characterize it—than the emergence of an internal split within the prodemocracy camp. This characterization thus emphasizes that the localists and the democrats are on the same side. Besides, underlying Lian's writings is the value of diversity. The emergence of an internal split can be an improvement because a more diversified prodemocracy camp can better respond to a more diversified prodemocracy public. Moreover, Lian acknowledged the radical character of the localists, but he posited radicalism as a response to state repression. The implication is that if people saw the rise of radical protests as problematic, they should primarily blame the state instead of the protesters.

In addition to the above characterization of the rise of localism, Lian developed distinctive ways to both describe and prescribe the radical tactics and ideologies of the localists. Regarding protest tactics, Lian appropriated the notion of "violence on the edge" to make sense of militant protests. In a public forum held in September 2015, Lian explained: "The 'theory of violence on the edge' posits that movement activists would not use violence; but they would push their non-violent actions to the limit of what the power holders can tolerate. It not only attracts widespread attention in the process, but also provokes the regime to employ unjustified violence, which would lead people to condemn the power holders and turn to support the movement."[17] The "theory" offers a justification for adopting militant actions, but it retains the notion of nonviolence and adds the constraint that the militant actions should aim at being just enough for provoking the state into unjustified actions. In an article published right after the incident, Lian framed the question of protest violence as follows:

> After the [Umbrella Movement], the Special Administrative Region Government threw away the restraint on violent repression. [. . .] Young resisters, after gaining the experience of violence, will turn even more to militant actions. There will be more "violence on the edge." [. . .] After failing to achieve democracy through peaceful means, [. . .] is it true that [the democrats] still cannot accept "using force against violence" [. . .]? Of course, this is not to say that social movements always have to be violent. The question is: in principle, can non-peaceful and violent strategies be included in future protests? (Lian, 2016b)

The article does not justify the actions in the Mongkok civil unrest in particular. In fact, one could question if the localists' actions in the Mongkok civil unrest fitted the theory of "violence on the edge." Nonetheless, in the above passage, after positing the government as the culprit of radicalization, the article puts forward the generalized question of whether the principle of nonviolence remains necessary. Meanwhile, the article still uses the phrase "violence on the edge." That is, it retains the idea that the reasonableness of the use of violence is tied to the degree of violence involved.

Regarding ideology, Lian's writings did note the nonequivalence between localism and Hong Kong independence as well as the nonequivalence between self-determination and independence. In 2014, Lian stated: "It should be noted that talking about the nation and thinking about whether 'Hongkonger' can be called a nation on its own does not necessarily imply a discussion of 'Hong Kong independence'" (Lian, 2014c). In an article published in April 2016, Lian criticized Beijing for equating self-determination with independence. He warned that if the Chinese government branded opponents as betrayers of the country too easily, the result would only be the creation of more enemies. "Now [Beijing] treats all those who advocate for self-determination as pro-independence, the result is that those who are framed as such would 'smash the bowl,' and everyone would gradually become 'reluctantly pro-independence'" (Lian, 2016c).

However, it does not mean that Lian had refrained from talking about Hong Kong independence himself. Instead, he proposed the concept of "legalistic Hong Kong independence" as a framework within which the search for independence of Hong Kong can be articulated. Lian acknowledged that Hong Kong independence has no chance to be materialized when the Basic Law is in place: "Even without the action by the People's Liberation Army, the majority of Hong Kong people who value the rule of law would not support independence because of the lack of legal ground" (2016d). He noted that all articulations of separatism of Hong Kong from China were either premised on amending the Basic Law or focusing on the political arrangement after 2047. These ideas can be described as "legalistic independence" because they did not violate the Basic Law. Besides, these ideas did not pose immediate threats and challenges to the state.

The article then put forward four other examples of legalistic independence. The first referred to articulations of how Hong Kong may try to attain independence when the current regime comes to an end. The second refers to the possibility of articulating an arrangement for Hong Kong independence that would be considered as constituting a win-win situation by Beijing. The third refers to academic analyses and discourses about Hong Kong independence. The fourth refers to efforts to justify independence when Beijing violates its social contract with Hong Kong. The value of the generalized concept of legalistic independence is that it could open up the space of imagination, while supposedly not directly violating existing laws or the existing constitutional arrangement of the Special Administrative Region.

Instead of putting forward one specific "theory" of Hong Kong independence, Lian created the discursive resources that would facilitate the discussion of the topic. On the whole, on both protest tactics and movement ideologies, Lian offered support to the localists by developing plausible ways to justify militant actions and the pursuit of independence. However, Lian's writings also smoothed the most radical aspects of localism: the notion of "violence on the edge" would constrain the degree of violence involved in protest actions, whereas the idea of legalistic independence would confine the pursuit of Hong Kong independence to conceptions that do not violate the existing constitutional arrangement.

Mainstreaming of localism could also be seen in how Lian dealt with other controversial issues, such as new immigrants from the mainland. In an article published in December 2015, Lian urged the localists to see immigrants from mainland China as "potential localists" who might become "'Hongkongers' in the next election or occupation campaign" (2015a). Hence, it is unnecessary to be overly suspicious or harbor a priori hostility toward the new immigrants.

Ultimately, Lian did not try to establish the localists as a force that would defeat the traditional democrats. The underlying goal of his writings was to promote a stronger prodemocracy movement, and helping the localists to better develop their ideas was a means to achieve the goal. It is therefore not surprising that his writings would regularly involve efforts to find common ground for the localists and the democrats. There were also calls for the localists and the democrats to put aside their resentment against each other. Lian found the tendency on the part of some movement activists to criticize others as *ghosts*—a term used by activists and supporters to refer to covert agents of the state—particularly problematic and has written against it. In various articles, he called upon the democrats to try to accept the rise of localism and even incorporate elements of it into their own platform: "After the Occupy Movement, the two major pro-democracy parties need to show positive reactions toward these new [localist] discourses that had gained widespread support among young people. They needed to absorb the acceptable elements and incorporated them into part of their platforms. Ignore the powerholders who want to ridicule the mutually beneficial interactions between different generations as 'the pan-democrats being dragged or hijacked by young people'" (Lian, 2015b). Lian thus played the role of an ideological bridge broker between the localists and the democrats in a distinctive way.

He did not construct a broker frame that could incorporate the key ideas from both sides. He tried to, as stated earlier, encourage the prodemocracy mainstream to adopt a more sympathetic attitude toward localism, and he did that partly by creating the discursive resources for developing less radical and more coherent forms of localism. He tried to help the localists to grow into a respectable faction within the broader prodemocracy movement and call upon the two sides to maintain mutual respect.

It is difficult to assess the influence of Lian's writings. Lian himself recognized that there were localists who liked him, thinking, "This old guy is supporting us," and there were localists who disliked him, still classifying him as one of the "old democrats." For the present chapter, the analysis is not grounded in assumptions about the actual influence of one specific author. The analysis highlights the presence of prominent authors such as Lian who, like Demosisto, were in between the localists and the democrats and discursively negotiating a less antagonistic relationship between the two sides.

Public Attitude toward Hong Kong's Future in the Mid-2010s

If the bridging efforts of the ideological brokers were effective, one could expect the localists and the democrats to have become less hostile toward each other over time. We will look into survey data addressing the question of (de)polarization within the prodemocracy movement at the end of chapter 6, after state-movement interaction is also examined. Here, it would be meaningful to examine public opinion in the mid-2010s on the question of Hong Kong's future. Specifically, Demosisto's concept of democratic self-determination treats Hong Kong independence as one option among others, while one might see Joseph Lian's writings as promoting *the discussion of* Hong Kong independence (within legalistic boundary). How did such treatments of Hong Kong independence correspond to public opinion at the time?

Between 2014 and 2020, the CCPOS at the Chinese University of Hong Kong conducted a series of surveys under its Hong Kong Public Opinion and Political Development program (see methodological appendix for information about methods). The surveys conducted in 2016 and 2017 included questions asking respondents whether they would support maintaining one country, two systems, complete integration with mainland China, and Hong Kong independence, respectively, after 2047. The three possibilities were not listed as mutually exclusive options. Instead, there were three questions asking the respondents about the desirability of each of them. As table 5.1 shows, in 2016 and 2017, the majority of the public—about 70 percent—supported the maintenance of one country, two-systems. Only about 4 percent to 6 percent of the respondents were against continuing it. In contrast, only 17 percent and 11 percent in the two surveys, respectively, supported Hong Kong independence. These figures were similar to the percentages supporting complete integration with mainland China.

These figures suggest that supporters of Hong Kong independence constituted only a minority. However, although Hong Kong people did not support independence, they treated independence as an idea up for discussion. In a survey conducted by CCPOS in March 2016 (the same survey examined in chapter 4), the respondents were asked if they would agree with a series of statements related to Hong Kong independence (also see Lee, 2018a). The statements can be treated as indicators of three concepts: principled objection against independence, pragmatic objection against independence, and acknowledgment of independence as a legitimate option. The first refers to objection to Hong Kong independence due to the principle of national unity. As table 5.2 shows, 46.5 percent of the respondents agreed with the statement "Hong Kong is part of China; Hong Kong independence is an act of splitting the mother country." More people agreed than disagreed with the statement.

Table 5.1. Support for possible post-2047 arrangements for Hong Kong (surveys in 2016 and 2017)

		Maintain one country, two systems	Complete integration with mainland China	HK independence
2016 / 7	Support	69.6	13.8	17.4
	Against	6.0	59.2	57.6
2017 / 5	Support	71.2	14.7	11.4
	Against	4.9	58.6	60.2

Note: Sample sizes for the two surveys were 1,010 and 1,028, respectively.
Source: Created by the author.

Table 5.2. Public attitudes regarding Hong Kong independence (survey in March 2016)

	Strongly disagree/ Disagree	Strongly agree / Agree	Mean
Principled objection: Hong Kong is part of China; Hong Kong independence is an act of splitting the mother country	27.3	46.5	3.34
Pragmatic objection 1: Hong Kong is too small and has too few resources; independence is not advantageous	22.8	56.3	3.61
Pragmatic objection 2: Promoting independence is only going to bring negative consequences because the Central Government would not allow it	15.6	60.0	3.76
Pragmatic objection 3: One country, two systems is better than independence as long as the Central Government is willing to maintain it	7.6	69.8	4.00
Legitimate option 1: If Hong Kong's democracy and freedom do not improve or even get worse, independence is something that needs to be considered	44.2	26.6	2.64
Legitimate option 2: Although it does not necessarily deserve support, publicly discussing Hong Kong independence is fine	28.0	43.2	3.19

Note: Answers were given by a five-point Likert scale (from 1 = strongly disagree to 5 = strongly agree). N = 1,012.

Source: Created by the author.

In comparison, 56.3 percent of the respondents agreed with the statement "Hong Kong is too small and has too few resources; independence is not advantageous," 60.0 percent agreed that "the Central Government would not allow independence; so promoting independence is only going to bring negative consequences," and close to 70 percent agreed that "one country, two systems is better than independence as long as the Central Government is willing to maintain it." In other words, more Hong Kong people objected to independence because of pragmatic considerations.

Since objection to independence was primarily grounded in pragmatic considerations, it is not surprising to see many people treating independence as an idea that can be publicly discussed: 43.2 percent of the respondents agreed that "although it does not necessarily deserve support, publicly discussing Hong Kong independence is fine." Only 26.6 percent of the respondents agreed that "if Hong Kong's democracy and freedom do not improve or even get worse, independence is something that needs to be considered." The low percentage is possibly due to the fact that it conveys a relatively more supportive attitude toward independence, though the attitude is conditioned by future happenings. Here, we can see how Demosisto's articulation of democratic self-determination was consistent with public opinion: independence was not something many Hong Kong people embraced explicitly and unconditionally at the time, but it is an option that should not be ruled out in advance.

Table 5.3a to 5.3c illustrates the bivariate relationships between attitudes toward Hong Kong independence and several other factors. First, people with higher educational levels were less likely to oppose to Hong Kong independence on both principled and pragmatic grounds, and they were more likely to acknowledge independence as a legitimate option. Younger citizens were less likely to object to independence on both principled and pragmatic grounds, and they were substantially more likely to see independence as a legitimate option. Obviously, supporters of the localists were most likely to treat independence as a legitimate option and least likely to object to independence on both principled and pragmatic grounds. Centrists and proestablishment citizens were at the other end, with democrats being in between.

Tables 5.3e to 5.3g show that participants in the annual July 1 protests, June 4 vigils, and the Umbrella Movement were less likely than nonparticipants to object to independence and more likely to see independence as a legitimate option. Besides, citizens who expressed support for the Mongkok civil unrest were least likely to object to independence on either principled or pragmatic grounds, and they were most likely to see independence as a legitimate option. People who condemned the civil unrest were located on the

Tables 5.3a–g. Attitudes toward independence by age, education, and attitudes toward the Mongkok civil unrest (survey in March 2016)

Table 5.3a. Education

	Principled objection	Pragmatic objection	Legitimate option
Not tertiary	3.41	3.92	2.75
Tertiary	3.19	3.53	3.26
F	4.9*	32.8***	43.9***

Table 5.3b. Age

	Principled objection	Pragmatic objection	Legitimate option
18–29	2.65	3.16	3.64
30–39	3.23	3.66	3.13
40–49	3.64	3.94	2.65
50 or above	3.60	4.20	2.49
F	22.6***	47.1***	48.7***

Table 5.3c. Political faction

	Principled objection	Pragmatic objection	Legitimate option
Localists	2.05	2.65	4.07
Democrats	3.07	3.61	3.24
Centrists / Progovernment	3.69	4.07	2.55
F	36.8***	56.4***	60.1***

Table 5.3d. Attitude toward Mongkok civil unrest

	Principled objection	Pragmatic objection	Legitimate option
Condemn	4.22	4.44	2.25
Disagree but government has responsibility	3.33	3.89	2.85
Disagree but government is the root cause	2.85	3.40	3.33
Support	2.00	2.39	4.44
F	80.0***	117.6***	91.1***

continued on next page

Table 5.3e. Participated in July 1 protests

	Principled objection	Pragmatic objection	Legitimate option
No	3.42	3.86	2.84
Yes	2.66	3.27	3.54
F	26.9***	34.7***	37.8***

Table 5.3f. Participated in June 4 vigils

	Principled objection	Pragmatic objection	Legitimate option
No	3.39	3.84	2.86
Yes	2.74	3.30	3.54
F	14.3***	20.3***	24.7***

Table 5.3g. Participated in the UM

	Principled objection	Pragmatic objection	Legitimate option
No	3.55	3.98	2.70
Yes	2.54	3.08	3.73
F	89.0***	152.5***	146.6***

Note: Entries are mean scores on a five-point Likert scale. F-values are derived from one-way ANOVA. N = 1,012. ***p < .001; **p < .01; *p < .05.

Source: Created by the author.

opposite side. Nevertheless, these findings should not lead one to conclude that protest events such as the June 4 vigils or the Umbrella Movement were themselves proindependence. To the extent that people who supported Hong Kong independence were primarily those who disliked the Chinese and Hong Kong governments most strongly, and the various protest events were primarily participated by citizens who strongly disliked the government, it is natural that protest participants or sympathizers would, on average, have more positive views toward Hong Kong independence.

The findings in table 5.3 do not show much difference between principled and pragmatic objection toward independence, in the sense that whoever more likely to object to Hong Kong independence as a matter of principle were also more likely to object to independence due to pragmatic reasons. These people would also be more likely to see independence as a legitimate option. Somewhat more differentiating findings could be derived in multivariate analyses predicting people's scores on the three indicators. Specifically, table 5.4 summarizes the findings of multiple regression analyses using principled objection, pragmatic objection, and legitimate option as the dependent variables. The independent variables include four demographics, three indicators for political efficacy, three variables for political affiliation (support for the localists, support for the democrats, and support for the progovernment faction, with centrists or no inclination being the reference category), four political communication variables, and three political participation variables.

Table 5.4. Predicting attitudes toward Hong Kong independence (survey in March 2016)

	Principled objection	Pragmatic objection	Legitimate option
Gender	−.04	−.05	.05
Age	.06	.15***	−.17***
Education	.10**	.04	−.02
Family income	.12***	.06*	−.09**
Internal efficacy	.04	.06*	−.02
Collective efficacy	−.09**	.03	.03
External efficacy	.34***	.30***	−.27***
Localist	−.15***	−.20***	.15***
Democrats	−.03	−.03	.07*
Progovernment	.12***	.13***	−.17***
News attention	.10**	.11**	.04
Discussion	.04	.01	−.05
Use social media for info.	−.06	−.02	−.02
Alternative media	−.06	−.07	.09*
Umbrella Movement	−.10**	−.13***	.08*
June 4 rally	−.00	−.00	.00
July 1 protest	.02	.01	−.01
Adjusted R²	0.284***	0.349***	0.332***

Note: Entries are standardized regression coefficients. Missing values were replaced by mean scores. N = 1,012. ***p < .001; **p < .01; *p < .05.

Source: Created by the author.

Several findings are worth highlighting. First, older respondents were much more likely to object to Hong Kong independence due to pragmatic considerations, and they were much less likely to see independence as a legitimate option. But when all other factors are controlled, age does not relate significantly to principled objection. That is, people of different age groups did not differ from each other in terms of the extent to which they would object to Hong Kong independence because Hong Kong belongs to China as a matter of principle.

Second, education relates positively to principled objection in multiple regression. This reverses the relationship between the two variables in table 5.3. At the same time, education does not relate to pragmatic objection and legitimate option significantly. These findings show that the relationship between education and the dependent variables was largely mediated by political attitudes, communication, and participation. That is, more educated people exhibited more positive attitudes toward independence at the bivariate level because they were more supportive toward democracy and more likely to have participated in protests. Once all other factors were controlled, the relationships largely disappeared. More educated people were even found to be more likely to object to independence from the principled point of view.

Third, attention to the mainstream news media was positively related to both principled objection and pragmatic objection. That is, those who paid close attention to the news in the mainstream media were more negative toward independence. This is in line with survey research findings from the Umbrella Movement (Lee & Chan, 2018). The mainstream media in Hong Kong were deeply embedded in the society's dominant political economic structure. Self-censorship was widespread (Au, 2017). Hence, either due to media effects or audience selectivity, the audience of the mainstream media tended to be more politically conservative.

Fourth and in contrast to the mainstream news media, consumers of alternative media were more likely to see independence as a legitimate option. Notably, although the variable also obtains negative coefficients in the first two columns of table 5.4, the coefficients were not statistically significant. This suggests that the independence-related discourses on the prodemocracy alternative media were likely to be similar to the writings of Joseph Lian analyzed in the previous section; that is, the discourses legitimized and promoted *the discussion* of independence more than legitimized and promoted independence itself. Hence, exposure to such discourses could primarily lead people to recognize the legitimacy of discussing Hong Kong independence, but not necessarily to support Hong Kong independence.

Last but not least, support for the democrats related to the three dependent variables in exactly the same way as exposure to alternative media did. That is, after controlling for all other factors, supporters of the democrats were as likely as the centrists to object to Hong Kong independence based on principled or pragmatic grounds, but they were more likely than the centrists to see independence as an idea up for discussion. Among Hong Kong people, support for democracy implies the embracing of a set of liberal values, including freedom of expression and political tolerance. Hence, supporters of democracy are more likely to adopt the view that one should defend the right of others to express their opinions even if one finds the opinions disagreeable. In one sense, this reconfirms the point already made in table 5.2: many prodemocracy citizens would think that, even if independence is a highly controversial idea, the society should allow relevant public expressions and discussions. This is arguably the crux of public opinion toward independence in Hong Kong in the mid-2010s, and this is also the main reason why Demosisto's democratic self-determination and Joseph Lian's efforts to promote the discussion of independence could be considered as rhyming with public sentiments.

Concluding Remarks

This chapter discusses the evolution of the prodemocracy movement in Hong Kong between 2016 and 2018 by focusing on the role of two types of ideological brokers who were situated between the localists and the democrats. The premise behind the discussion is that, in order to understand how actors on two sides within a movement relate to each other, the role of actors who mediate between the two sides cannot be ignored. In Hong Kong, the conflicts between the localists and the democrats during and after the Umbrella Movement, including the localists' fierce criticisms of the democrats and the democrats' condemnation of the Mongkok civil unrest, had fueled antagonism between the two camps. However, as this chapter illustrates, there were actors who worked to alleviate the antagonism, thus sowing the seeds of reconciliation.

This chapter employs the notion of brokerage to understand the role of Demosisto and authors such as Joseph Lian, but they were not brokers in the sense of being the in-between coordinators of actions or channels of communication and information. They were mainly articulators (Mische, 2008; von Bulow, 2011) who produced bridging discourses that either incorporate ideas from both sides and integrate them into a relatively coherent framework (i.e., Demosisto's democratic self-determination) or generate symbolic resources for the two sides to develop their own discourses in ways that would make their positions coming closer to each other (e.g., Lian's notions of violence on the edge and legalistic independence). Besides, one can argue that their discursive efforts had—similar to Edward Leung's self-presentation during the 2016 by-election—the impact on mainstreaming localism for the general public. In this sense, Demosisto and authors such as Joseph Lian could also be seen as ideological brokers in the relationship between the localist faction and the prodemocracy citizens.

Demosisto or Joseph Lian might not consciously consider themselves as brokers. Demosisto, after all, is a political party on its own. Given the proportional representation system in place in LegCo elections during the 2000s and 2010s, they could be competing with both the localists or the democrats for seats. According to Lian, his primary aim was to help the localists to articulate their views. But the actions and discourses of Demosisto and Lian tended to bring the two camps closer to each other instead of further polarizing the prodemocracy movement. If Demosisto's idea of democratic self-determination and/or some of Lian's suggestions for the two sides were adopted, the boundary between the localists and the democrats would be deactivated (McAdam et al., 2008). They were therefore treated as brokers due to the significance and plausible consequences of their work.

A shift of focus from the dichotomy of the radical versus the moderates to the actors in-between the two sides led to a shift of identification of the key actors for academic analysis. An interesting phenomenon in the literature on localism in Hong Kong is that, despite Demosisto's public rejection of the label, quite a few academic studies treated Demosisto as a localist group (e.g., Ng & Kennedy, 2019). But because Demosisto was obviously not the prototypical localist group, it tended to receive less analytical attention when compared to the HKI and Youngspiration. Indeed, if we adopt the dichotomy of the localists versus the democrats, we would be forced to classify Demosisto as belonging to one of the two camps. In either case, Demosisto would be pushed to the periphery—treated as a localist group, it is not as important as the HKI or Youngspiration; treated as part of the democrats, it is not as influential, resourceful, and powerful as the Democratic Party and the Civic Party.

Nevertheless, the dichotomous view is unnecessary. In a somewhat different classification scheme, Cheng and Yuen (2024) put Demosisto together with the Civic Party as the "neo democrats" situated between the old democrats and the localists. Their approach and this book concur in seeing Demosisto as located between two camps. The difference is that, by identifying Demosisto as a broker, this book pinpoints a specific role played by the group (as well as other actors) in the political dynamics in Hong Kong during the period.

Nevertheless, the presence of brokers such as Demosisto was not the only factor facilitating the gradual reconciliation between the democrats and the localists between 2016 and 2019. As already mentioned in this chapter when discussing the writings of Joseph Lian, state repression had also played a role in encouraging solidarity within the prodemocracy movement. The state is a key actor in the relational dynamics in the political field. The triangular interaction between the state and the various players inside the prodemocracy movement will be the subject of the next chapter.

Chapter 6

State Repression and Affective Depolarization

The previous chapter discussed the relationship between the moderate and the radical flanks of the prodemocracy movement, with particular attention paid to the ideological brokers situated between the two sides. The ideological brokers developed positions and discursive resources that could potentially serve as the common ground for the whole prodemocracy movement. However, the dynamic within the prodemocracy movement was shaped also by external forces, especially the strategies and actions of the state.

A distinctive body of social movement research has focused on the notion of the radical flank effects. What could happen to the moderates when radicals appear on the scene? The classic study by Haines (1984) differentiated the negative radical flank effects from the positive radical flank effects. Negatively, the transgressive actions of the radical flank might undermine the legitimacy of a movement. It could arouse public opposition and cost a movement its public support. Positively, the radical flank could create incentives for the powerholders to collaborate with the seemingly more reasonable moderates. Haines (1984) showed that donations received by moderate groups in the American civil rights movement increased when radical groups gained prominence, signifying the presence of a positive radical flank effect. Other scholars noted how moderate activists might deliberately distance themselves from the radicals in order to attract elite support (McCammon et al., 2015). Yet other studies have shown the possibility of the radicals and the moderates working together to maximize the pressure on the powerholders to make concessions (Ellefsen, 2018; Robnett et al., 2015).

In 2010s Hong Kong, neither the typical positive radical flank effects nor the typical negative radical flank effects seem to have emerged. For a period of time, the moderates in the prodemocracy movement did to a certain extent distance themselves from the radicals. The distancing was indicated by the internal conflicts during the Umbrella Movement (chapter 2) as well as the moderates' immediate reactions to the Mongkok civil unrest (chapter 4). However, such developments did not lead the state to try to collaborate more closely with the moderates. The typical positive radical flank effect did not materialize. At the same time, although there were many Hong Kong citizens who rejected the localists' actions, the prodemocracy movement did not seem to lose much public support over time. While there was a decline in social mobilization between 2016 and early 2019, it was primarily a result of citizens' sense of inefficacy and frustration, instead of perceived illegitimacy of the prodemocracy movement. The typical negative radical flank effect also did not materialize. Instead, the moderate camp itself as well as the supporters of the prodemocracy movement in general were radicalizing. Even the Democratic Party, the main moderate prodemocracy party, saw the emergence of a new generation of politicians who were more adaptive to confrontational actions.

State actions hold one of the keys to understand this development. Studies on positive radical flank effects were conducted mostly in democracies, where the political elites are usually more pluralistic. In face of the rise of radicalism, it is likely that at least part of the elites would be willing to collaborate with the moderates. But what if the ruling elite does not prefer collaboration? What if, instead of collaboration, the state represses both the moderates and the radicals indiscriminately?

Earl and Braithwaite (2022) defined social movement repression as "state or private actions focused on preventing, limiting, or constraining protest or social movements" (p. 228), whereas political repression refers to "state or private actions that affect any form of political participation, including both institutional and extra-institutional participation" (p. 228). A significant part of the literature on social movement repression has focused on deterrence versus backfiring effects (Lewis, 2023; Lichbach, 1987). On the one hand, repression can undermine social mobilization by raising the costs of participation (e.g., personal safety and legal repercussions). On the other hand, repression may mobilize even more people to protest because of the moral outrage it generates. Scholars have found numerous cases of backfiring effects, especially when other political opportunities are present (Aytac et al., 2018; Demirel-Pegg & Rasler, 2021; Martin, 2007; O'Brien & Deng, 2015; Schock, 1999).

In addition to political opportunities, one factor that could influence whether backfiring occurs or not is whether the repression exercised is selective or indiscriminate, that is, whether the repression targets a selected group of the more radical protesters or simply everyone. Selective repression may create incentives for the moderates to differentiate themselves from the radicals (Jamte & Ellefsen, 2020). In contrast, indiscriminate repression could change the calculus of activists and movement supporters. Ives and Lewis (2020) argued that movement radicalization was more likely to occur when nonviolent protests were also repressed by the state. This is because when even peaceful protests are repressed, the costs for engaging in peaceful and nonpeaceful protests become more similar to each other. In other words, the marginal costs for engaging in violent protests decreases, leading more people to adopt violent tactics.

Besides, indiscriminate repression by the state can solidify the relationships among protest groups. For example, Over and Taraktas (2017) argued that in the 2013 Gezi protests in Turkey, state repression triggered mass protests because people perceived the target of repression as innocent. State repression led to boundary deactivation and the subsequent formation of a broad coalition of protesters. Moreover, indiscriminate repression can undermine the moderates' role as the "buffer" between the radicals and the state. For instance, Thompson and Cheng (2023) noted three commonalities between the waves of protests in 2019 and 2020 in Hong Kong and Thailand. One of the commonalities is the marginalization of the moderates in the years preceding the protests. The conflict between the state and the radical camp became more direct. This furthered the trend of radicalization.

Studies about backfiring effects mostly concentrated on how people react to the actions of the police at the peak moments of social mobilization (e.g., Anisin, 2016; Li et al., 2024). Backfiring is typically indicated by an enlarged protest crowd or the adoption of more confrontational actions. However, backfiring may also exist outside the peak of mobilization. Even if repression does not generate immediate protest actions, it could lead to outcomes such as the accumulation of grievances, persistence or deepening of perceived injustice, or increased solidarity among the oppositional forces.

This chapter illustrates such a process in Hong Kong between 2016 and mid-2019. Here, it is useful to first recall the analysis of movement-state interactions between the Umbrella Movement at the beginning of chapter 2. The moderate democrats, represented by the Democratic Party, tried to engage the state through supporting the political reform proposal put forward by the Hong Kong government in 2010. The Democratic Party suffered from an electoral setback as a result. They also felt "cheated" by the state, as there were few further opportunities to communicate with the Chinese government after the passing of the political reform proposal. The engagement approach became unsustainable, paving the way for the occurrence of the Umbrella Movement.

According to sociologist Chan Kinman, leader of the Occupy Central campaign, there were still representatives from Beijing coming to Hong Kong to talk to the movement leaders after the Umbrella Movement began, but the representatives emphasized that the NPC decision on August 31, 2014, cannot be reversed. That is, China would insist on institutionalizing a tight pre-selection mechanism before a popular vote for the chief executive of the Hong Kong government. Chan realized by that time that, in the eyes of the Chinese government, attempts to set up a political system with significant power of self-government would be equivalent to Hong Kong independence. There was no longer any façade over China's intention. After 2014, the Chinese government still sent representatives to Hong Kong to talk to members of the prodemocracy parties. But, according to former Democratic Party chairperson Lee Wing-tat, it was more a part of China's "united front work" (Cheng, 2020) than a genuine attempt to communicate with the prodemocracy camp. He noted that those representatives talked not only to the influential figures inside the Democratic Party, but also to other members, such as district councilors or even their assistants. The aim was to find out those individuals who could be coopted.

In Chan Kinman's judgment, in the 2010s, the Chinese government had already shown its intention to suppress the whole prodemocracy movement. Chan opined that, for China, the moderate parties had longer histories and stronger support bases. If the Chinese government did not want to give genuine democracy to Hong Kong, then in the long run, the moderates—rather than the radicals—could present a bigger challenge to the state. This is because the radicals had relatively weaker public support, whereas the moderates had stronger legitimacy. Therefore, state repression did not target only the radicals (that is, the localists). On the one hand, the radicals' actions, being more disruptive and even at times violent, subjected them to quicker and harsher repression. But on the other hand, repression did not stop at the boundary between the localists and the democrats.

Specifically, this chapter will recount the indiscriminate state repression in the electoral and the legal arenas between 2016 and early 2019. Afterward, the chapter will present an analysis of affective depolarization, understood as an outcome of indiscriminate repression, between supporters of the localists and supporters of the democrats by early 2019. The concluding section of this chapter will discuss the possible reasons behind the Chinese state's approach to the prodemocracy movement in Hong Kong.

Electoral Repression through Disqualification

Since their institutionalization in the early 1990s, direct elections of the District Council and the LegCo in Hong Kong were largely fair and corruption free. Challenges to electoral integrity arose since the 2010s, however. The period saw more media reports of suspected electoral fraud such as vote packing, that is, illegal registration of voters using "fake addresses" in order to affect election results (Ma, 2017). There were suspicions about gerrymandering by the government-appointed Electoral Affairs Commission. Using a data set about changes in constituency boundaries, Stanley Wong (2019) showed that constituencies won by prodemocracy candidates were more likely to have their boundaries adjusted, and boundary adjustment did reduce the prodemocracy incumbents' overall chances of reelection.

Perceived electoral integrity was further damaged in the 2016 LegCo elections when the Electoral Affairs Commission set up a new rule and required all candidates to sign a declaration form to proclaim their acceptance of Hong Kong being an inalienable part of China. This was in addition to the existing requirement for candidates to sign a declaration in the nomination form to uphold the Basic Law. The new rule was largely seen as a move to bar Edward Leung of the HKI from running in the election.

Facing the threat of disqualification, Edward Leung changed his public stance, altered the contents of his Facebook page, and signed the confirmation form. Yet he also publicly suggested that his move was a matter of "wearing a helmet." That is, it was a means of self-protection that might or might not reflect his true views. In early August, the returning officer in charge of determining the validity of candidacy decided to disqualify Edward Leung. The officer provided a twelve-page reply, which included a transcript of Leung's remarks made at a press conference after submitting the signed confirmation form. Based on Leung's remarks, the officer wrote that Leung intended to enter the LegCo with "whatever means," and "once he becomes a lawmaker, he would continue to advocate independence" (Ng et al., 2016).

In addition to Edward Leung, four other candidates were barred from entering the election due to their "failure" to meet the new requirement.

Three of them refused to sign the confirmation form, and the fourth was barred because the returning officer did not accept the sincerity of the confirmation based on the candidate's public statements.

The new rule and its implementation were highly controversial not only because it allowed government officers to determine the validity of a candidacy based on perceived sincerity of the confirmation, but also because forty-two candidate lists belonging to the prodemocracy camp were allowed to join the election despite their refusal to sign the form. Meanwhile, Youngspiration, another localist group that had expressed its proindependence stance previously, and Demosisto, which advocated democratic self-determination, were allowed to enter the election.

It is difficult to ascertain the actual impact of Leung's disqualification on the electoral outcome. Youngspiration, seen as the flagship of the proindependence localists in the absence of the HKI, won two seats in the geographical constituencies. Yau Wai-ching got 20,643 votes and won narrowly in the Kowloon West constituency, beating veteran radical democrat Wong Yuk-man by 400 votes. In New Territories East, where Edward Leung would have run if he had not been disqualified, Baggio Leung of Youngspiration won with 37,997 votes, which was lower than the 66,524 votes won by Edward Leung in the by-election in February 2016. However, the by-election was a single-seat, single-vote contest with seven candidates, whereas the New Territories East election in September 2016 had twenty-two candidate lists competing against each other in a proportional representation system. Votes understandably spread much more thinly across the candidate lists.[1]

If the controversy stopped at the point of disqualification of candidacy, it could have been a case of discriminate repression because only a few of the most prominent or explicitly proindependence figures were barred. However, disqualification of Edward Leung turned out to be only the backdrop of the events that followed. On October 12, 2016, the newly elected legislators were scheduled to take an oath and assume their office. Instead of solemnly reading out the seventy-seven-word oath, several legislators staged different kinds of symbolic protests in the oath-taking ceremony. Nathan Law of Demosisto, for instance, gave a one-minute speech before taking the oath. He criticized the oath-taking ceremony as having become a tool used by the authority to suppress public opinion. When reading the oath, he raised his tone at the end of the sentence expressing allegiance to the People's Republic of China, thus sounding like asking a question. Lau Siu-lai, who ran as a member of the "self-determinist camp" during the election, read the oath in slow motion.

The most controversial were the actions undertaken by the two Young-spiration legislators. When reading the oath, Yau Wai-ching changed the wordings and said: "I will be faithful and bear true allegiance to the Hong Kong nation and will to the best protect and defend the values of Hong Kong." She then unveiled a banner reading "Hong Kong is not China." When told to repeat the oath and read it correctly, Yau read the original oath but changed all references to People's Republic of China into "the People's Refucking of Shina" (with Shina understood as a derogatory reference to China used by the Japanese in the early twentieth century).[2] Baggio Leung carried out virtually the same act when he took his oath.

There had been symbolic protests during oath-taking ceremonies in the past, but that in October 2016 was the first time pro-Hong Kong independence sentiments were explicitly expressed inside the LegCo chamber by elected legislators. While the LegCo chairperson was inclined to allow the two legislators to retake the oath, the Chinese government took swift action. On November 7, the NPC interpreted Article 104 of the Basic Law, according to which legislators "must, in accordance with law, swear to uphold the Basic Law of the Hong Kong Special Administrative Region (SAR) of the People's Republic of China and swear allegiance to the Hong Kong SAR of the People's Republic of China" when assuming office. The NPC issued a thousand-word "interpretation," which stated that oath taking "must comply with the legal requirements in respect of its form and content." Besides,

> An oath taker is disqualified forthwith from assuming the public office specified in the Article if he or she declines to take the oath. An oath taker who intentionally reads out words which do not accord with the wording of the oath prescribed by law, or takes the oath in a manner which is not sincere or not solemn, shall be treated as declining to take the oath. The oath so taken is invalid and the oath taker is disqualified forthwith from assuming the public office specified in the Article.[3]

It was the fifth time since the transfer of sovereignty in 1997 that the NPC exercised its power to interpret the Basic Law. Interpretation of the Basic Law by the NPC had long been seen by critics as damaging the rule of law in Hong Kong (Jones, 2015). The interpretation discussed here illustrates two problems. First, according to Article 158 of the Basic Law, interpretation by the NPC shall be restricted to matters that are the responsibility of the Central Government (e.g., foreign affairs) or concerning the relationship between the Central Government and Hong Kong. Procedurally, the SAR court shall initiate and seek interpretation of relevant provisions by the NPC. The above-discussed interpretation deviated from the procedure, and it is questionable if oath-taking in the LegCo constitutes affairs that are the responsibility of the Central Government or concerning the relationship between the Central Government and Hong Kong.[4] Second, instead of interpretation, the NPC decision ostensibly added new requirements and stipulations regarding oath taking in the LegCo. It was, as Fong (2021: 208) put it, effectively an act of legislation rather than interpretation.

The NPC interpretation allowed the high court to quickly disqualify Baggio Leung and Yau Wai-ching on November 15, 2016. The Court of Appeal confirmed the high court's ruling in January 2017, stating that the NPC interpretation of the Basic Law had automatically disqualified the two from assuming their offices. Notably, even with the NPC interpretation, the Hong Kong court's ruling could still be questioned on legal grounds. Yap and Chan (2017) offered three criticisms of the court ruling. First, nothing in the NPC interpretation explicitly stated that legislators would be "automatically" disqualified for failing to take the oath properly. Second, the NPC interpretation did not give the court the power to decide if a legislator should be disqualified. The case should be returned to the chair of the legislature for decision making. Third, the NPC interpretation was unclear on whether the interpretation should be retrospectively applied. For Yap and Chan (2017), the court had unnecessarily participated in the removal of the two Youngspiration legislators, thus subjecting itself to the criticism that "it had now become an enabler of the executive government's political agenda" (p. 15). The court's ruling had seemingly encouraged the Hong Kong government to go a step further to seek disqualification of four other legislators involved in the oath-taking controversy. In July 2017, the court handed down the judgment to disqualify Nathan Law, Lau Siu-lai, Edward Yiu, and Leung Kwok-hung.

For this chapter, the most important point to note is that the Hong Kong and Chinese governments attempted to disqualify all six legislators, instead of drawing a line between the acceptable ones and the outcasts. Theoretically, the state could have disqualified only the two Youngspiration legislators, signifying the unacceptability of explicit expression of proinde-pendence sentiments inside the LegCo. It could have disqualified the two Youngspiration legislators plus Demosisto's Nathan Law, thus including the leading advocates of democratic self-determination into the pool of people to be barred from the LegCo. In contrast, the state disqualified even Edward

Yiu, a university professor and a specialist in surveying. Yiu's antics in the oath-taking ceremony were restricted to adding the statement that he would definitely "defend institutional justice, strive for genuine popular election, and serve the sustainable development of Hong Kong." The judge wrote in the verdict that Yiu undoubtedly intended to add the extra words and thus plainly breached the exact form and content requirement of the oath (Zhao, 2017). Yiu's disqualification signified the state's refusal to tolerate even a relatively "soft" symbolic challenge to its power inside the LegCo chamber.

Once the floodgate was opened, the ghost of disqualification would continue to haunt the prodemocracy camp, and the boundary of acceptability would move further in subsequent elections. In order to allow its member Agnes Chow to participate in the LegCo by-election in March 2018, Demosisto removed the call for democratic self-determination from its website. Despite the concession, Chow was disqualified on the ground that she belonged to Demosisto, and the political party had been calling for self-determination for the city. The decision effectively barred Demosisto from participating in elections in the future. Demosisto announced in May 2018 that the group would change from being a political party to being a civic political association. Then, in December 2018, legislator Eddie Chu was banned from a village election after being questioned on his view toward Hong Kong independence and self-determination. The disqualification of Eddie Chu came even though he was sworn into the legislature in 2016.

Such developments showed the willingness of the Hong Kong government to continue to raise the bar of entrance to the formal political arena. Certainly, in 2018, prodemocracy politicians still had a substantial presence within the LegCo. The earlier disqualified Edward Yiu was allowed to run in the March 2018 LegCo by-election after Agnes Chow's disqualification (though he lost). But overall speaking, once the mechanism of disqualification was established, the "red lines" could be further extended. As Joshua Wong of Demosisto said when responding to the disqualification of Agnes Chow: "Two years ago, only nominees promoting independence were banned. Now, people advocating 'self-determination' are permanently banned from running. No one knows if Beijing will redraw the red line so that all democrats who oppose the legislation of Article 23 will be banned as well" (Chung & Cheung, 2018). Joshua Wong's worry would materialize in July 2020, when the government disqualified twelve prodemocracy candidates from the LegCo election, originally scheduled to be held in September of the year, because they opposed the newly enacted national security law. After the election was postponed due to the COVID-19 pandemic, the Hong Kong government disqualified four current legislators, including three from the Civic Party, after the NPC passed a resolution to expel legislators who supported Hong Kong independence, appeal to foreign governments to interfere with Hong Kong affairs, or refuse to accept China's rule over the city.

A year later, the Chinese government reformed the electoral system of the Hong Kong legislature, reducing the proportion of directly elected seats from 50 percent to only 22.2 percent. In July 2023, the LegCo passed the government's proposal to reform the District Council elections. The proportion of directly elected seats would be drastically reduced from 94.4 percent (452 out of 479 seats) to only 18.7 percent (88 out of 470 seats). The reform also set up new rules requiring people who want to run in the District Council elections to obtain nominations from three district-level consultation bodies. In the 2023 District Council elections, candidates from the Democratic Party failed to obtain enough nominations to enter the race.[5] This completed the process of indiscriminate electoral repression. But for the present chapter, the important point to note is that the process of discriminate electoral repression had already started in 2016.

Legal Repression of Protests

The relationship between the legal system and social mobilization does not have to be a repressive one. Instead, social movements can utilize legal means to advance their causes (Burstein, 1991). In the final years of colonial rule, Hong Kong has developed an independent and competent judiciary, a legal profession trained in the common law tradition, and a government-funded legal aid system. Together with the enactment of the Bill of Rights Ordinance in 1991, the establishment of a final appellate court within Hong Kong, and the growth of cause lawyering, political opportunities were shifted toward the legal system. The immediate posthandover years witnessed the rise of legal mobilization (Tam, 2013). It was not uncommon for social movement actors to pursue their goals through legal means, especially judicial review.

Nonetheless, Beijing also had the strategy of "legalization without democratization" in its governance over Hong Kong (Hiroko, 2020; Zhu, 2019). Immediately after the handover, the provisional legislature reversed earlier amendments to the Public Order Ordinance and restored police power to curtail public gatherings. Demonstrations with more than fifty people or marches with more than thirty people had to obtain a letter of no objection from the police (Jones, 2015: 146). Into the 2010s, as protests radicalized, the government and its supporters increasingly turned to legal means to undermine social mobilization. During the Umbrella Movement, government supporters applied for legal injunctions to facilitate the government's attempt to clear the occupied sites (Lee & Chan, 2018; Shen, 2019). Nine movement leaders were later charged. All were convicted, and four had to serve prison sentences of eight to sixteen months. In a separate court case, three young activists—Nathan Law, Joshua Wong, and Alex Chow of the Hong Kong Federation of Students—were convicted for charges related to the protest actions in the evening of September 26, 2014. Regarding the Mongkok civil unrest, ninety-one individuals were arrested. Charges included rioting, arson, assaulting the police, and illegal assembly. The charge of rioting carries a sentence of up to ten years in prison. In the end, twenty-three individuals—including Edward Leung—were convicted for rioting, with the heaviest sentence being seven years in jail.

From the perspective of the state, the use of legal means can make protest control apparently more legitimate. As noted in chapter 2, the Hong Kong government repeatedly emphasized how the Umbrella Movement violated the rule of law, though the latter was defined merely in terms of rule following and willingness to bear legal consequences. From the critics' perspective, however, the above court cases and developments constituted legal repression of social protests, which can be defined as "a process whereby the state and/or non-state elites attempt to diminish dissident action, collective organization, and the mobilization of dissenting opinion by inhibiting collective actions through raising the costs and/or minimizing the benefits of such actions, by way of law and criminal justice" (Ellefsen, 2016: 445).

Certainly, to establish the presence of legal repression, one has to demonstrate in what sense the court cases and their decisions were unjust or at least questionable. The following pages would examine the riot cases associated with the Mongkok civil unrest and the trial of the Umbrella Movement leaders.

The analysis is grounded in a view that sees a court decision as constituted by a combination of three elements. First, the court has to make its judgment based on the legal principles associated with the law being applied, whereas observers might question why a certain law is chosen in the first place and whether the law and its associated principles are reasonable. Second, the court has to consider the facts of a case, and the facts have to be interpreted in relation to the legal principles. Third, the facts of a case may also need to be interpreted within an appropriate social framework (Burns, 2016, 2018). Common sense, understood as knowledge about the world and about human actions that are taken for granted by members of a community, plays an important role in rendering a court judgment sensible and coherent (Cochran, 2017; Jasanoff, 2018; Laugerud, 2020). The following analysis pays particular attention to the characteristics of the law being utilized and the characteristics of the commonsense assumptions involved in the court verdicts.

In an earlier article, F. Lee (2023b) has uncovered, through a close reading of the court verdicts, the hegemonic commonsense assumptions underlying the judgments given by Hong Kong courts in cases related to the Umbrella Movement, the Mongkok civil unrest, and the Anti-ELAB protests. The following draws upon the analysis presented in that article. But given the focus of this chapter, it examines the cases associated with the Umbrella Movement and the Mongkok civil unrest only (see methodological appendix for more information about the materials analyzed). Besides, the analysis below also draws upon media materials and legal scholars' analysis of the laws involved. Although the Umbrella Movement occurred before the Mongkok civil unrest, many of the trials related to the Mongkok civil unrest were completed before the trial of the Umbrella Movement leaders. The following discussion thus begins with the rioting cases associated with the Mongkok clash.

RIOTING IN THE MONGKOK CIVIL UNREST

The riot law in Hong Kong was part of the Public Order Ordinance enacted in 1967, before then, the common law was followed. The riot law was used only sparingly since its enactment. Relevant cases include a riot in 1983 in association with a squatter-clearance operation, the Whitehead Detention Center riot in 1989, and a riot at the Hei Ling Chau Drug Detention Center in 2000 (Ng et al., 2020). Section 18 of the Public Order Ordinance stipulated that there is an unlawful assembly "when 3 or more persons, assembled together, conduct themselves in a disorderly, intimidating, insulting or provocative manner intended or likely to cause any person reasonably to fear that the persons so assembled will commit a breach of the peace, or will by such conduct provoke other persons to commit a breach of the peace." Section 19 of the ordinance further stated that "when any person taking part in an assembly which is an unlawful assembly [. . .] commits a breach of the peace, the assembly is a riot and the persons assembled are riotously assembled."[6]

For the present purpose, a key question is whether the riot law was reasonably construed by the Hong Kong court in its application. On this question, Ng and colleagues (2020) provided a thorough critique from a legal perspective. They compared the Public Order Ordinance's stipulation with the British common law. The latter identified five elements as necessary to constitute a riot:

> (1) a number of persons not less than three; (2) a common purpose; (3) execution or inception of the common purpose; (4) an intent on the part of the number of persons to help one another, by force if necessary, against any person who may oppose them in the execution of the common purpose; and (5) force or violence, not merely used in and about the common purpose but displayed in such a manner as to alarm at least one person of reasonable firmness and courage. (Ng et al., 2020 938)

Apparently, one key difference between the Hong Kong law and the common law is that the Hong Kong law does not explicitly require the element of "common purpose." Yet Ng and colleagues noted that, when the court adjudicates on any case of rioting, "there must be a sufficient nexus between the conduct of the defendants to justify considering them together" (2020, 939). Therefore, practically speaking, the Hong Kong court still had to consider whether a common purpose existed. The question thus becomes how the court understands "common purpose" in the riot cases.

In *Hong Kong SAR v Mok Ka To*, one of the cases associated with the Mongkok civil unrest, the judge ruled that "as long as other evidence can prove that these people who carried out the conduct intended to carry out the same conduct with other people present, they were having the common purpose of carrying out the conduct."[7] This understanding of common purpose was reconfirmed in the case against Edward Leung. Nonetheless, Ng and colleagues (2020) criticized this judgment for mixing up "purpose" and "manner." In common law, *common purpose* refers to something beyond the common action at present. That is, the pertinent question should be whether people are carrying out the same action for a common purpose, such as expressing discontent against the government or attacking a social group. But in the Hong Kong court, "carrying out the same action" *becomes the common purpose.* This move broadens the scope of rioting substantially.

In addition, the court also needed to consider what it means for a person to have participated in a riot. In *Hong Kong SAR v. Mok Ka To*, the court stated: "On the other hand, the defendant can, by virtue of his/her presence at the site of rioting, support and/or encourage and actually support and/or encourage other people to participate in rioting. In this case the defendant can also be seen as participating in a riot."[8] Ng and colleagues criticized this judgment for allowing the prosecution to allege that "once a defendant knew there was a riot, and persisted to stay at the scene, his continued presence was furthering the riot by lending support in numbers and encouraging others to commit breach of the peace" (2020: 951). The burden of proof is shifted to the defendant, who needs to explain his/her continual presence at the protest site.

In other words, the Hong Kong court understood both "common purpose" and "taking part" in such broad terms that the scope of application of rioting was expanded significantly. Ng and colleagues criticized the court's construal for encroaching upon the right to freedom of assembly. Following the court's ruling, "whenever a breach of the peace threatens to occur in a public assembly, one has to leave the scene at once to avoid arrest and prosecution" (2020: 959).

Nonetheless, the court could not arrive at a judgment merely by considering legal principles. Judges have to consider the facts associated with a case as well as the arguments put forward by both the prosecution and the defense, and they often have to rely on "common sense"—explicit statements or unstated assumptions taken as self-evident—when judging the validity or relevance of the facts and arguments presented. Specifically, Ng and colleagues (2020) have noted that the court could take sheer presence at the site of rioting as evidence of participation. The defendants thus need to explain their presence. The judge, then, has to decide if the defendants' explanations are acceptable or not, often based on their own assumptions about human behavior and motivations. For example, in *Hong Kong SAR v. Tam Pak-hei* and others, one defendant claimed that, although he was facing the police, he did not intend to participate and did not think of the danger involved in staying there. The judge disagreed: "I found the second defendant's explanation and understanding to be as unreasonable as those from a sleepwalker or mentally disabled. Merely watching the video could allow one to see how dangerous the condition was. [. . .] If the police decided to press ahead, the second defendant and others would bear the brunt."[9]

This passage contains two interrelated assumptions. The first can be called the "assumption of perceptiveness": that any person at the protest site can perceive the environment clearly and identify the "danger." The second can be called the "assumption of risk aversion": that normal people are highly sensitive toward danger and tend to avoid risk. This second assumption was explicitly stated in an earlier paragraph in the same verdict. The judge wrote that, according to common reasons, "anyone at the site should know that he could be seen as one of the protesters. Given how the crowd was throwing things, one should know that there is a chance of oneself being hurt. A normal person should know that he is in a dangerous place, and the normal reaction is to leave as soon as possible."[10] According to F. Lee (2023b), such assumptions regarding how a normal and reasonable person would behave appeared in several other cases. The idea that people should leave the site of rioting immediately is grounded not so much in legal reasoning than in assumptions about human behavior treated as self-evident by the judges.

In addition, the court typically treated the police as the guardians of social order. Challenging the police by itself would constitute an act of disruption. In *Hong Kong SAR v. Sin Ka Ho*, the judge stated: "There were several attempts to charge the police checkline. [. . .] Charging a police checkline lawfully formed to prevent people from moving beyond it *must be* disorderly conduct and a breach of the peace" (emphasis added).[11] Given the status conferred to the police, in the cases being examined, the Hong Kong court almost never considered if the police's strategies were appropriate. Specifically, in the Mongkok civil unrest, the arrival of 250 police officers with an elevated platform heightened the tension at the site. After conflicts broke out, a police officer fired two warning gunshots into the sky, which aroused strong public concern (see chapter 3). But the court cases contained no discussion of whether the police had acted appropriately and whether police actions had shaped the dynamics of the protest.

As the judges ignored the possible impact of police-protester interactions, protest behavior was largely understood in terms of how the protesters influenced each other. In several verdicts, judges brought up the theme of emotional contagion. For example, in *Hong Kong SAR v. Sin Ka Ho*, the judge argued that the defendants' violent actions "would undoubtedly provoke others to commit a breach of the peace."[12] In a later paragraph, the judge wrote: "It is a common feature of mass disorder that if individuals within the crowd act violently, this will in turn inflame and encourage others to behave similarly."[13] In *Hong Kong SAR v. Wong Yam Choi* and another, the judge wrote about the first defendant: "Under the influence of alcohol as well as the volatile and emotional crowd surrounding X [the defendant] lost all self-control as seen in the news footage."[14]

Such portrayals of protester psychology are similar to classic theorization of collective behavior by social psychologists in the early twentieth century (e.g., Le Bon, 2001/1895). Such theories emphasized that the energy generated by the presence of others can erode individual judgment and rational thinking (Buechler, 2011: 52–53). In this portrayal, "crowds are inherently irrational, unavoidably malleable, driven by impulse and emotion with a natural tendency towards violence and disorder" (Stott et al., 2020: 815).

F. Lee (2023b) argued that, once the commonsense assumptions were adopted, they tended to appear across the cases relatively consistently. In some individual cases associated with the Anti-ELAB protests, the commonsense assumptions may combine with the facts of the case to generate an outcome favorable to the defendants. But overall, the assumptions tended to limit the range of defenses and arguments that would be accepted as reasonable by the court. Together with the way the legal principles were interpreted, the law in Hong Kong could be criticized for casting an unreasonably wide net on what constitutes rioting.

INCITEMENT IN THE UMBRELLA MOVEMENT

When the proponents of Occupy Central kickstarted their campaign, they emphasized their willingness to bear the legal consequences of their acts of civil disobedience. Toward the end of the Umbrella Movement, the three original initiators of the Occupy campaign—legal scholar Benny Tai, sociologist Chan Kinman, and Reverend Chu Yiu-ming—surrendered themselves to the police. Legal prosecution came only in 2018. What the Umbrella Movement leaders did not foresee was the charge evoked by the government. The case could have been treated as a matter of unauthorized assembly, which can result in imprisonment for up to twelve months. Instead, the three leaders were charged for conspiring to create a public nuisance. The trio plus six other activists were charged for the common law offence of inciting others to create a public nuisance as well as inciting others to incite more people to create a public nuisance. Each of the charges carries a maximum penalty of seven years in jail. The defense counsel challenged the prosecution's choice of charges, calling them "unprecedented" and "most exotic and extraordinary." He stated that there is no rationale for the government to use those charges "unless they are seeking to maximize the punishment to be inflicted" (Ng, 2018).

Since there was only one single major case directly related to the act of prolonged occupation in the Umbrella Movement, we can attempt a closer reading of the judgment. According to the law and as set out in the court's verdict, to prove a case of incitement, it is necessary to show that: (1) the defendant incited a person (that is, the incitee) to do an act that would involve the commission of the offence of "public nuisance," and (2) the defendant intended or believed that the incitee would do the act with the mens rea required for the offence of "public nuisance."[15] As long as the intention existed and the act of incitement was carried out, whether the incitement was successful or not is irrelevant.

In the trial, the defense tried to argue that the defendants did not intend to have a large-scale occupation. The original intention of the leaders was a relatively small-scale occupation that would last only for a few days. The seventy-nine-day Umbrella Movement arose only due to the tear gas fired by the police on September 28. The defense offered evidence through an expert witness, showing that most Umbrella Movement participants did not see themselves as reacting to the call to action issued by the initiators of Occupy Central; instead, many protesters acknowledged that they were driven to act because of the police's firing of tear gas. The judge ultimately saw the expert evidence as irrelevant because, as mentioned above, effectiveness is not a required element for a person to be found guilty of incitement. However, from the defense's perspective, the evidence from the expert witness was supposed to support the argument that the police's firing of tear gas was the main driving force behind the prolonged occupation. The defendants could not have intended the police to fire tear gas into the crowd.

In addition to putting aside the expert evidence, the judge rejected the defense's argument based on three grounds. An interrogation into these arguments could illustrate the (questionable) understanding of protests underlying the verdict. First, the judge argued that the defendants had indeed thought of the possibility that the police would use tear gas. The verdict quoted what Chan Kinman said on September 28, 2014: "If the police disperse us with tear gas, we, the rally, will make an announcement about the location where everyone, citizens who got scattered, can gather afterwards. We will tell everyone about these measures very soon." Based on this statement, the judge argued that the police's use of tear gas "was something that the [Occupy leaders] clearly had in mind" when they announced the beginning of occupation.[16] Nonetheless, from the statement, there was no sign that Chan Kinman expected the police's tear gas to lead to the immediate and quick upscaling of the occupation. Chan's focus was only on how the occupiers could gather again in case the police used tear gas. More fundamentally, the judge had seemingly mixed up "planning for something" and "getting oneself prepared for certain contingencies." To reiterate the conceptual distinction made in chapter 3, to plan a protest event is to systematically work out a course of action to follow, whereas to prepare for contingencies is to equip oneself with the resources, capabilities, and/or ideas that would help one handle emerging situations, often through improvisation. When a group of people plan a collective action, they naturally need to consider how they should react to a wide range of possible scenarios. Having considered a possible scenario does not entail expecting or intending it to happen.

Second, the judge contended that there was evidence about the intention of the defendants to carry out a large-scale and prolonged occupation. The evidence cited, however, was largely constituted by the words and slogans shouted by the defendants on the first day of the occupation campaign. For instance, after quoting the statements made by various defendants in different locations, the judge summarized:

> In my judgment, the fact that D5 asked for the over-cramming of places beyond Tim Mei Avenue [. . .], taken together with what D5 said in Exhibit P61, i.e., that the demonstration at Tim Mei Avenue was "a fight in relays," and what he said in Exhibit P35, i.e., he challenged the Police to clear and lock up a turnout of 50,000 people. I am sure that D5 intended that the occupation he incited would be a continued occupation for an indefinite period.[17]

This paragraph could be criticized for ignoring the typical character of movement-related speeches. On the site of a collective action, activists would normally speak in a hyperbolic manner. "Overcram" and other word choices were indeed adopted to encourage the participants, but it does not entail that the leaders believed, at the point when the speeches were made, that a long-lasting occupation would arise.

Third, the judge questioned why the three leaders of the Occupy Central campaign did not withdraw or call for the cessation of the movement when it became a large-scale occupation. The judge argued that "the [leaders] wanted to ride with the tide of events, *i.e.*, with a large number coming out to occupy public roads, the [leaders] wanted to make the best use of the circumstances to the advantage of the movement."[18]

What the judge ignored is that, when the movement evolved into a large-scale protest, it might no longer be possible for the leaders of the Occupy Central campaign to control the movement. The judgment had seemingly assumed the effectiveness of movement leadership, that is, as long as the leaders were willing to call for the end of occupation, participants would listen and go home. It ignored the point that, after the announcement of its beginning, the Occupy Central campaign quickly evolved into a decentralized Umbrella Movement without effective leadership (see chapter 2; A. Chow, 2019; Lee & Chan, 2018). Even if the leaders had called for the cessation of occupation, the chance was that the occupiers would not follow. Certainly, it might be argued that the point is not whether the leaders' call for retreat would have been successful; it is only a matter of whether the leaders had tried to ask people to leave. However, given the unlikelihood of people leaving the occupied site, one might argue that remaining at the site and trying to maintain order and continue to steer the movement was the most responsible thing the leaders could do at that time.

Tellingly, the defense actually questioned why the police did not evict the occupied site and start arresting people immediately after September 28. That is, while the prosecution made an argument based on the apparent nonaction of the leaders, the defense made a similar argument against the apparent nonaction of the police. On this point, the judge wrote: "If the Police were to arrest D2 the day after the firing of tear gas, when emotions of protesters still went high, as evidenced by the increase in the numbers of protestors on Harcourt Road, such arrest action might just stir up further reaction that the Police did not want to see."[19]

The judge evoked the "evidence" of an increase in number of protesters to sustain the statement that the emotions of protesters were going high and then made the point that arrest action could stir up further reaction from the protesters. The latter argument was put forward without referring to any arguments made or evidence provided by the police or the prosecution. It was evoked by the judge as self-evident and used to construct a plausible justification of the police's nonaction. This is in line with the point made earlier that the judges rarely questioned the strategies and actions of the police. Nonetheless, juxtaposing the judge's perspective on the defendants and the police against each other, one could criticize the judge for applying a double standard when making sense of the actions of the defendants and the actions of the police. While neither side took immediate action, the police were assumed to be professional and adopting the correct strategy given the context, whereas the defendants were assumed to be aiming at taking advantage of the evolving situation.

On the whole, the verdict against the Umbrella Movement leaders was based on the court's adoption of certain argumentative moves and assumptions about protests. The verdict equated preparation for contingencies with planning, read protest slogans and speeches literally, assumed the effectiveness of movement leadership, and refused to question police actions. These assumptions are highly questionable for people familiar with the character of social protests.

REMARKS ON INDISCRIMINATE LEGAL REPRESSION OF PROTESTS

The analyses in the previous sections aimed at illustrating how the punishment against the participants in the Mongkok civil unrest and the Umbrella Movement leaders constituted legal repression. This is not to say that it would be wrong to punish protesters by law in any case or in any way. The Umbrella Movement leaders, in particular, were prepared to bear the legal consequences of their actions. However, in both the Mongkok civil unrest and the Umbrella Movement, the state evoked harsh laws against the defendants. In addition, the court interpreted legal principles in ways that expand the coverage of the laws, and the judges invoked commonsense assumptions about protest actions that are questionable and tend to lead to relatively easy conviction.

The analysis emphasizes the presence of commonsense assumptions in the court judgments. It should be reiterated that those ideas—for example, the assumption that normal and reasonable people are against taking risks—were treated as "common sense" in that they were not supported by specific evidence, elaborate arguments, or legal principles. They existed in the court judgments as implicit assumptions or explicit statements that are presumed to be self-evident. These ideas and assumptions provided the ground upon which facts and claims were evaluated. Some of them were intertwined with the court's interpretation of legal principles.

In the context of this chapter, the analysis in the two previous sections showed that legal repression of protesters was indiscriminate. Of course, the participants in the Mongkok civil unrest had carried out more confrontational and violent actions. Hence, they were subjected to the more serious charge of rioting and heavier punishment in the form of longer prison sentences. Yet the state was also criticized for trying to maximize the penalty against the Umbrella Movement leaders. There was no sign of the state adopting a more conciliatory approach toward the defendants in the Umbrella Movement trial.

A possible outcome of indiscriminate legal (and electoral) repression is the reduction of animosity between the moderate and the radical camps. As people on the two sides saw that the other side was also targeted by the state, boundary deactivation could occur. Both Lee Wing-tat and Chan

Kinman, two of the nine defendants in the Umbrella Movement case, acknowledged such an impact of their trial. According to Lee Wing-tat, veteran members of the Democratic Party saw his inclusion as a defendant in the trial as helping to prevent the party from being criticized. "If we have a relatively famous person there [among the defendants], then we can avoid certain criticisms, like people saying that you are not a part of even such a big movement."

For Chan Kinman, the trial of the Umbrella Movement leaders offered a chance for the ideals associated with the movement to be expressed and heard again. He recalled that there were more and more people coming to observe the trial as it went on. Regarding whether his imprisonment had influenced how others perceived him, he acknowledged that even some pro-government officers within the Correctional Services Department expressed their "respect" for him because of his willingness to "pay the bill" (that is, keeping one's promise). After he finished his prison term in 2020, he received letters from some young militant protesters who were detained because of their actions in the 2019 Anti-ELAB protests. The militant protesters told him that the trial of the Umbrella Movement leaders had influenced their way of thinking. Chan believed that his imprisonment was "meaningful" to some prodemocracy supporters, no matter whether they were on the moderate or the radical flank.

Beyond the individual experiences and observations from Lee Wing-tat and Chan Kinman, the next section will draw upon representative survey data to examine depolarization within the prodemocracy movement between 2016 and 2019.

Affective (De)polarization in Public Opinion between 2016 and 2019

Political polarization has been a concern in public opinion studies in the United States and many European countries in the past two decades (Benson, 2023; Schedler, 2023). Conceptually, political or public-opinion polarization can refer to people taking more and more extreme attitudes on various policy and political matters. It can also refer to ideological sorting, that is, people holding more and more ideologically consistent sets of policy beliefs (DiMaggio et al., 1996). Nonetheless, more pertinent to the analysis in this book is the notion of affective polarization, which refers to the extent to which people feel positively about the political in-group and negatively toward the political out-group (Iyengar et al., 2012; Wagner, 2012). The concept highlights polarization as a matter of affect rooted in people's identification with their political in-groups. Comparative research shows that increasing affective polarization was by no means a worldwide trend (Boxell et al., 2024). Nevertheless, researchers are still concerned with affective polarization because it could undermine trust, make cross-party collaboration more difficult, and thus renders governance less effective (Hetherington & Rudolph, 2015).

Affective polarization has also been a concern among Hong Kong researchers. For instance, Kobayashi (2020) found that social media use was related to affective polarization positively among people who identified themselves as Hongkongers or Chinese, but negatively among "dual identifiers," that is, people who identified themselves as both Hongkongers and Chinese. Liang and Zhang (2021) showed that online incivility mediated the relationship between exposure to disagreement and affective polarization.

In these Hong Kong studies, polarization was typically conceptualized and measured in terms of the animosity between supporters of the prodemocracy camp and supporters of the progovernment camp. The present analysis, in contrast, is interested in what may be called "internal" and "external" affective polarization for the supporters of the prodemocracy movement. Internal affective polarization is polarization internal to the prodemocracy movement. It is the extent to which supporters of the moderate and radical flanks within the prodemocracy movement harbor negative views toward each other. In contrast, external affective polarization is the degree to which supporters of the prodemocracy movement—encompassing both the supporters of the moderate democrats and the militant localists—and supporters of the government harbor negative views toward each other.

The following analysis draws upon two representative surveys conducted in July 2016 and March 2019, respectively (see methodological appendix for more information). Both surveys contained three items asking the respondents to rate "the democrats," "the localists," and the "progovernment camp." Table 6.1 summarizes the respondents' ratings of the different political factions. The first row shows that, in year 2016, the localists received the lowest rating at 3.38 on a 0-to-10 scale, whereas the progovernment faction and the democrats obtained ratings of 3.98 and 4.50 respectively. The overall ratings did not change substantially between the two surveys. In March 2019, the rating of the localist faction remained virtually unchanged at 3.42, while the ratings for the democrats and the progovernment faction declined somewhat to 4.26 and 3.59 respectively.

Table 6.1a–c. Citizens' ratings of political factions in 2016 and 2019

Table 6.1a. 2016

	Localists	Democrats	Opposition	Progovernment
Overall	3.38	4.50	3.96	3.98
Localists	6.78	4.28	5.53	1.69
Democrats	4.04	5.78	4.94	3.14
Opposition (democrats and localists combined)	4.53	5.52	5.05	2.88
Centrists	2.94	3.96	3.47	4.15
The progovernment camp	1.21	3.02	2.20	6.82

Table 6.1b. 2019

	Localists	Democrats	Opposition	Progovernment
Overall	3.42	4.26	3.88	3.59
Localists	6.08	5.01	5.54	1.99
Democrats	4.54	5.83	5.20	2.53
Opposition (democrats and localists combined)	4.81	5.69	5.26	2.44
Centrists	2.91	3.67	3.35	3.62
The progovernment camp	1.67	2.67	2.19	6.47

Table 6.1c. Differences

	2016	2019	2019 minus 2016
Localists over democrats	2.50	1.07	−1.43
Democrats over localists	1.74	1.29	−0.45
Opposition over progovernment	2.17	2.82	0.65
Progovernment over opposition	4.62	4.28	−0.34

Note: Opposition refers to the combination of supporters of the localists and supporters of the democrats. Rating of opposition is therefore the average of rating of localists and rating of democrats. Rating by opposition refers to rating by people who considered themselves democrats and people who considered themselves localists combined together.

Source: Created by the author.

More important for the present discussion is how supporters of different political orientations rated the various factions. Table 6.1a shows that, in the 2016 survey, supporters of the localists gave an average rating of 6.78 to their own faction. Predictably, people tend to rate their own faction most positively. The localists' ratings of the other factions were therefore lower: the average rating given to the democrats was 4.28. The difference between the localist supporters' rating of their own faction and of the democrats was 2.50 (6.78—4.28). Meanwhile, supporters of the democrats gave an average rating of 5.78 to their own faction, and the ratings given to the localists was 4.04. The difference was 1.74.

Table 6.1b shows the results obtained from the 2019 survey. In March 2019, supporters of the localists gave an average rating of 6.08 and 5.01, respectively, to the localists and the democrats. The difference between the localist supporters' rating of their own faction and of the democrats was only 1.07. This is substantially smaller than the difference of 2.50 registered in the 2016 survey. Meanwhile, supporters of the democrats gave an average rating of 5.83 and 4.54, respectively, to the democrats and the localists. The difference between the two ratings was only 1.29. This is also significantly smaller than the difference of 1.74 registered in the 2016 survey. In other words, both the democrats' and the localists' supporters exhibited lower levels of affective polarization against the other side. We see clear evidence of internal affective depolarization between the two surveys.

Notably, there was no similar trend of depolarization between supporters of the opposition (democrats and localists combined) and supporters of the progovernment faction. As table 6.1 shows, supporters of the democrats and localists, when combined, rated the opposition faction and the progovernment faction at 5.05 and 2.88, respectively, in the 2016 survey. The difference between the two ratings is 2.17. In March 2019, their rating of the opposition faction increased slightly to 5.26, while their rating of the progovernment camp declined further to 2.44. The difference between the ratings of the opposition and of the progovernment faction thus increased to 2.82.

Nonetheless, a similar trend toward more polarized ratings of the opposition and of the progovernment faction did not appear among the government supporters. In 2016, government supporters rated the progovernment faction and the opposition at 6.82 and 2.20, respectively. The corresponding figures in March 2019 were 6.47 and 2.19, the government supporters' rating of the opposition remained virtually the same, but their rating of the progovernment faction decreased somewhat. The result is that the difference between the two ratings also declined somewhat from 4.62 to 4.28.

Nevertheless, if we focus only on how supporters of the localists and the democrats evaluated the various political factions, we can indeed argue that there was a combination of internal depolarization and external polarization between 2016 and early 2019: supporters of the two camps within the prodemocracy movement had become relatively less antagonistic toward each other, and they have become more antagonistic toward the progovernment camp.

While table 6.1 shows the degree of internal and external affective polarization at the collective level, we can further examine affective polarization at the individual level. For simplicity, the analysis focuses on the 2019 data and is restricted to supporters of the localists and the democrats. Internal polarization is a respondent's rating of his/her own side minus his/her rating of the other side within the prodemocracy movement, whereas external polarization is a respondent's rating of his/her own specific side within the prodemocracy movement (e.g., only "localists" for localist supporters) minus his/her rating of the progovernment side. Calculated as such, the two indices are positively correlated at $r = .45$ ($p < .001$) because both indices depend on how the respondents rated their own camp.

Table 6.2 summarizes the results of a regression analysis predicting external polarization, internal polarization, and ratings of the three camps among supporters of the localists and the democrats. The first two columns show that older people and people with higher levels of internal efficacy exhibited higher levels of both external and internal polarization. It seems that the self-confidence regarding one's ability to understand politics and participate in public affairs could translate into confidence about the superiority of one's own faction over the others. Predictably, people with lower levels of external efficacy, that is, people who saw the government as irresponsive to public opinion, exhibited higher levels of external polarization because they rated the progovernment camp lower.

Acceptance of radical actions—operationalized by the respondents' acceptance of "charging the police line" and "occupying public roads," each registered through a five-point Likert scale—related positively to both external and internal affective polarization. The positive relationship between external polarization and acceptance of radical actions is easy to understand. As the last three columns of table 6.2 show, people who accepted radical protest actions to larger extents rated the progovernment camp more negatively. Meanwhile, these respondents rated both the democrats and the localists more

Table 6.2. Regression analysis of ratings of factions and polarization

	External polarization	Internal polarization	Rating democrats	Rating localists	Rating progovernment
Gender	.04	.01	.15**	.15*	.10*
Age	.30***	.31***	.22***	–.05	–.22***
Education	.02	.32	.09	–.20***	.05**
Income	–.02	–.04	–.07	–.03	–.04
Localist	.12	.33*	–.03	.02	–.04
Internal efficacy	.18***	.13*	.15*	.07	–.11*
External efficacy	–.19***	.06	.05	–.00	.32***
Accept radical action	.43***	.14*	.31***	.20**	–.33***
Adjusted R^2	0.329***	0.086***	0.132**	0.119***	0.358***

Note: Only supporters of the democrats and the localists are included. Entries are standardized regression coefficients. N = 339. ***p < .001; **p < .01; *p < .05.

Source: Created by the author.

positively. These contribute to the relationship between external polarization and acceptance of radical actions.

Comparatively, the positive relationship between internal polarization and acceptance of radical actions is more surprising. One might have expected acceptance of radical actions to relate positively to rating of the localists because of the localists' advocacy for militant protests, and negatively to rating of the democrats if people generally perceive the democrats as rejecting militant protests. But as just noted, acceptance of radical actions actually related to the rating of the democrats positively and particularly strongly. This contributed to the positive relationship between acceptance of radical actions and internal polarization in the second column of table 6.2. On the whole, the key finding here is that, by March 2019, support for radical actions no longer drove people to evaluate the localists and the Democrats in contrasting manner. This can be taken as an indicator of the prodemocracy citizens' recognition of the radicalization of the moderate flank of the prodemocracy movement.

Concluding Remarks

This chapter examines state repression of the Hong Kong prodemocracy movement in the 2010s. The analysis focuses on indiscriminate repression of both the moderate and radical flanks of the prodemocracy movement in the electoral and legal arenas. The repression was indiscriminate not because the same punishments were executed on the localists and the democrats. The two Youngspiration legislators were disqualified before the other four prodemocracy legislators were, and the Mongkok protesters received longer prison sentences when compared to the Umbrella Movement leaders. But these "differential treatments" were grounded in the fact that the localists' actions were indeed more transgressive. The repression was indiscriminate in the sense that, when handling the localists and the democrats, the state adopted the same approach of pushing the limits of possible punishment.

Why did the Chinese state choose to exercise indiscriminate repression instead of coopting and collaborating with the moderate democrats? It is beyond the scope of the present analysis to give a full and documented explanatory account of the state's strategic considerations. But three relevant points can be briefly discussed.

First, although this chapter emphasizes the presence of indiscriminate repression, it does not entail that the Chinese state had never tried to divide and rule. China's united front work in Hong Kong partly involved the development of grassroots associations to consolidate social support to the government (Cheng, 2020; E. W. Y. Lee, 2020a, 2020b); it also partly involved the cooptation of opposition elites. However, there was ultimately no common ground for the state and the moderate democrats on the question of democratization. Notably, the Democratic Party was "moderate" in the Hong Kong context in the sense that, for a long period of time, it was willing to recognize the legitimacy of the one-country-two-systems framework, accept gradual political reform, communicate with the Chinese government, and cling onto the principle of nonviolent actions. But even the Democratic Party would insist on the institutionalization of unfiltered popular elections for the chief executive of the Hong Kong government. Throughout the 2010s, this insistence was further consolidated by the relational dynamics within the prodemocracy movement, citizens' choices expressed through electoral votes, and development inside the Democratic Party (e.g., the emergence of younger politicians who were more sympathetic toward a more confrontational approach). On the other side, the Chinese government insisted on setting up a mechanism to control the candidacy of elections of government leaders in Hong Kong. The ideological gap between the state and the moderate democrats was too big to be bridged.

Second, the Chinese state's approach to governing Hong Kong cannot be dissociated from the situation within the mainland. From the 1990s to the first decade of the new millenium, China had undergone a period of (limited) liberalization. The country witnessed the growth of investigative reporting and other forms of critical journalism (Tong, 2011), civil society organizations (Tweets, 2014), human rights lawyering (Lei, 2018), and contentious politics both online and offline (Chen, 2012; Yang, 2009). Lei (2018) argued that there was the emergence of a contentious public sphere in China by the early 2010s. However, such developments also aroused concerns among the party leadership. Meanwhile, the global financial tsunami in 2008 altered China's status and role in the international political economy, and the Chinese government gained new "institutional self-confidence." The trend of liberalization was therefore reversed in the last years of Hu Jintao's governance, as the party state placed much more emphasis and resources on "preserving stability" (Beja, 2019). The trend was exacerbated after Xi Jinping came to power. Xi reinvigorated the party leadership system in order to make the CCP a tightly disciplined instrument to govern China (Tsang & Cheung, 2022). Control of the news media, online communication, and civil society was severely tightened (Dirks & Fu, 2023; Repnikova, 2018).

The Chinese government was particularly concerned with preventing the diffusion of political contention from Hong Kong into the mainland (Huang & Li, 2024). More broadly speaking, China's increasing autocratic influence over Hong Kong in the 2010s (Fong, 2021), was part of a nation-wide trend of autocratization.

Third, when the Hong Kong-mainland relationship is concerned, the city has historically been treated as an "exceptional space" by the Chinese government. It was the window that allowed China to maintain indirect contact with the Western world during the Cold War decades. By the time of the transfer of sovereignty, Hong Kong was an international financial hub that had a crucial role to play in aiding China's economic development. Hong Kong's GDP was more than a quarter of China's GDP in 1994, and the corresponding figure still stood at 18.9 percent in 1997 (Hung, 2022: 47). There were strong reasons for China to keep Hong Kong as an exceptional space. In fact, creating and maintaining spaces with relatively larger degrees of flexibility and freedom—the Special Administrative Regions and the Special Economic Zones—was the main approach adopted by the Chinese government to engage with the global economy (Ong, 2006). However, with China's rapid economic growth throughout the 1990s and into the 2000s, by 2016, Hong Kong's GDP was only 2.9 percent of China's GDP. Although Hong Kong still had important roles to play to the Chinese economy, such as by providing an offshore market for Renminbi (Hung, 2022), the city's importance to the Chinese economy had undeniably declined over the years. This implies the declining need for China to maintain Hong Kong's exceptional status (Cheng, 2023).

In sum, the width of the ideological gap between the state and the democrats, the trend of autocratization inside mainland China itself, and the declining significance of Hong Kong to the national economy offered the background against which the Chinese state's increasingly hardline approach toward Hong Kong can be understood.

Notably, this chapter focused on electoral and legal repression because the two were conspicuous examples happening in distinctive institutional contexts, where a relatively clear parallel regarding the repression suffered by the localists and the democrats could be reconstructed. This does not mean that repression was restricted to these two arenas. To give one further example, in August 2018, the Foreign Correspondents Club (FCC) in Hong Kong invited then chairperson of the Hong Kong National Party Chan Ho-tin to speak at the club. The invitation came at a time when the Hong Kong government was considering banning the Hong Kong National Party.

Progovernment politicians heavily criticized the FCC's decision to invite Chan to speak. The FCC stood firm. One month later, the Hong Kong government officially outlawed the political party. The controversy did not end there. In early November, the Hong Kong government refused to renew the working visa for *Financial Times* editor Victor Mallet. The government did not explain the decision, but it was widely believed to be related to Mallet's role as FCC vice president and the host of Chan's speech in August.

The FCC was not part of the prodemocracy movement in Hong Kong, but it is part of the liberal institution of the "free press" in the city. From the perspective of professional journalism in the liberal tradition, interviewing someone (or hosting the talk of someone) does not mean endorsing the views of the person. It is just a part of an effort to allow the public to have access to a diverse range of viewpoints. But even holding such a stance was enough to subject oneself to the state's punishment as the Chinese state refused to see Hong Kong independence as within the realm of legitimate controversy.

This chapter shows that a trend of affective depolarization among supporters of the democrats and the localists had already started between 2016 and early 2019. It should be noted that the process was far from complete. That is, the current analysis does not suggest that the localists and the democrats no longer held any negative views or feelings toward each other by early 2019. What the survey data shows can be only the beginning of a trend of depolarization, but this development was crucial for understanding the character of and dynamics in the Anti-ELAB Movement. Meanwhile, affective depolarization should be understood as a combined result of the dynamics discussed in chapter 5 and the present chapter. The work of the ideological brokers helped maintain the linkage between the moderates and the radicals and tie the two sides together, whereas indiscriminate state repression could have made the work of the brokers more effective. In other words, efforts of ideological brokering within the prodemocracy movement and indiscriminate repression by the state reinforced each other.

With both the radical and the moderate camps of the prodemocracy movement undergoing a process of radicalization, and as the state continued to adopt a hardline and indiscriminate approach to the prodemocracy movement in Hong Kong, a more severe clash would seem to be inevitable—at least when one looks at it with the benefit of hindsight. The clash arrived in 2019 with the Anti-ELAB movement.

Chapter 7

The Anti-ELAB Protests

In February 2019, in order to address a murder case in which a Hong-konger killed his girlfriend in Taiwan, the Hong Kong SAR government proposed to amend the Fugitive Ordinance to allow extradition of criminal suspects to Taiwan and mainland China. Although the amendment aroused immediate concerns, the level of social mobilization was originally low when political parties and movement groups started organizing protests in March. Yet public worries about political abuse of the amendment grew. Even the usually progovernment business sector expressed concerns. A protest march held on April 28, 2019, was attended by 130,000 citizens, according to the organizer Civil Human Rights Front (CHRF). In May, meetings inside the LegCo turned confrontational. A wave of online petitions emerged, with citizens organizing themselves based primarily on their alma maters (Yuen & Tong, 2021). The social ferment coincided with the thirtieth anniversary of the Tiananmen incident in early June. Social mobilization culminated in the 1 million-strong protest march on June 9.

The Hong Kong government did not back down immediately. On June 12, when the LegCo was scheduled to have the second reading of the bill, tens of thousands of protesters surrounded the LegCo Building and forced the cancelation of the meeting. Police-protester clashes occurred. Protesters threw bricks at the police, while the police fired tear gas and bean bag bullets. The police chief subsequently branded the protest a "riot." The government "suspended" the amendment bill on June 15. Protesters were not satisfied: they demanded the formal withdrawal of the bill, the retraction of the riot definition of the June 12 protests, and the release of the arrested protesters. The government finally withdrew the bill in early September, but it would not make any concessions on other demands.

Between June 2019 and January 2020, hundreds of protest events were held across the city. Without organizational leaders capable of steering the movement as a whole, existing social and political groups, activist networks, and ordinary citizens self-coordinated and conducted a wide range of activities. Protest repertoire diversified, including the erection of "Lennon Walls" for posting promovement messages (Li & Whitworth, 2023a), Baltic-inspired human chains, airport rallies, political consumerism (Chan, 2022; Fong & Lee, 2023), labor unionization (Chan & Pun, 2020; A. Chan, 2020), collective singing in shopping malls, international lobbying (F. Lee, 2023c; Ho, 2024), and lunch-time flash mobs. At the same time, protest tactics radicalized quickly. By end of August, militant protesters were throwing molotov cocktails. There were other controversial tactics such as vandalism, vigilantism, and doxing (Li & Whitworth, 2023b). Of course, the protesters were not the only ones raising the level of physical force. Police use of force evolved from tear gas and bean bag rounds to crowd control vehicles and, in a couple of occasions, real bullets. More generally, the police increasingly relied on paramilitary tactics to handle the protests (Pubrick, 2019; Stott et al., 2020), which inadvertently added fuel to the fire.

Remarkably, the increasing level of violence did not lead to a substantial loss of public support for the movement. In November 2019, the democrats and movement activists won a landslide victory in the District Council elections, capturing 388 out of 479 seats (Shum, 2021). There were certainly debates among movement supporters regarding whether specific actions, such as vigilantism, had gone too far. But overall, the moderate and militant protesters continued to exhibit a high degree of solidarity (Lee, 2020).

The Anti-ELAB Movement did not have a definite end point. Protest activities were suppressed first by the outbreak of COVID-19 in late January 2020 and then by the National Security Law enacted on June 30 of the same year. In a survey conducted in June, 2020, 45 percent of Hong Kong people reported that they had participated in the movement in some ways (Cheng & Yuen, 2024: 5). The Anti-ELAB Movement was the largest protest movement in the city's history, a case of "total mobilization" (Cheng et al., 2022).

This chapter does not offer a comprehensive description, evaluation, and explanation of the highly complex Anti-ELAB Movement. As explicated in the introductory chapter, this book aims to examine the relational dynamics in the period between the Umbrella Movement and the Anti-ELAB protests in order to explain both the continuity and transformation of the prodemocracy movement in Hong Kong. Given this focus, several distinctive features of the 2019 protests constitute the focus of this chapter. These features include high levels of internal solidarity, rapid tactical radicalization, high levels of public tolerance toward the radicalizing actions, and ideological radicalization and its limits.

The previous chapters have already provided part of the explanation of these features of the Anti-ELAB protests: public ambivalence toward militant protests was already present by the time of the Mongkok civil unrest; prominent localist activists articulated a softened version of localism when facing the public; the work of ideological brokers and indiscriminate repression by the state contributed to the beginning of a trend of affective depolarization within the prodemocracy movement. Such events and dynamics between 2015 and 2019 sowed the seeds of the aforementioned features observed during the 2019 protests.

Nevertheless, consistent with the relational approach emphasized in this book, the dynamics and events recounted in the previous chapters were not mechanical causes of the features of the Anti-ELAB Movement. They could be considered as background conditions and initial input. The development of solidarity and the trend of radicalization were also driven or sustained by the dynamics within the Anti-ELAB Movement itself. Ultimately, an important part of the relational dynamics within the Anti-ELAB Movement could be considered as a condensed replication of the relational dynamics that the prodemocracy movement experienced between 2015 and 2019.

This does not mean that the dynamics within the Anti-ELAB Movement are completely the same as those within the prodemocracy movement between 2015 and 2019. Most fundamentally, the range of key actors involved in the Anti-ELAB protests was somewhat reconfigured. First of all, given the decentralized character of the movement, the interaction between established activists and groups belonging to the moderate and radical camps of the prodemocracy movement was less important than the interaction between the moderate and militant protesters. Besides, another important feature of the Anti-ELAB movement that is worth highlighting up front is the role of "the international society" as an actor (F. Lee, 2023c; Ho, 2024). Prodemocracy politicians and activists in Hong Kong had a long history of connecting with activists and movement groups overseas, and the Chinese government had always been highly wary of "foreign intervention." Foreign manipulation was one of the three major counterframes promoted by the state against the Umbrella Movement (Lee & Chan, 2018). Nonetheless, before 2019, foreign governments were not particularly attentive to the prodemocracy movement in Hong Kong. In contrast, Hong Kong activists found a much more receptive international environment in 2019 as a result of changes in international relations in the late 2010s, especially the development of a more antagonistic relationship between China and the United States (F. Lee, 2023c). International actors, including foreign media and governments, had more prominent roles to play in the Anti-ELAB protests, most conspicuously signified by the passing of the Hong Kong Human Rights and Democracy Act by the US Congress in November 2019.

However, for the purpose of this book and chapter, the slight reconfiguration of the key actors involved would not alter how a set of mechanisms already discussed in the previous chapters—for example, ideological brokerage, indiscriminate state repression, the impact of contingent events, and the mainstreaming of localism—could help explain the evolution of the Anti-ELAB Movement and several of its core features. To substantiate this contention, this chapter will recount the processes of solidarity maintenance, tactical radicalization, and ideological radicalization during the movement. The discussion will highlight phenomena such as the continual negotiation of movement solidarity, emergence of Liberate Hong Kong, Revolution of Our Time as a broker frame, the moderate protesters' experience of "indiscriminate state repression," protesters' uptake of political identity labels, and the exercise and limitations of collective self-restraint. The concluding section will summarize how the various relational dynamics could help us make sense of the movement.

Solidarity amidst Radicalization

DISCURSIVE CONSTRUCTION OF THE ETHICS OF SOLIDARITY

As a highly decentralized movement, established political groups did not play a central leadership role. The distinction between the democrats and the localists was therefore less pertinent than that between the moderate and militant protesters. (The former refers to citizens who joined only the peaceful actions, whereas the latter refers to protesters who were willing to engage in confrontational actions, including physical conflicts with the police.) The militant protesters were more likely to be supporters of the localists, though the correlation between the democrats/localists divide and the moderates/militants divide is not perfect. For clarity, this chapter mainly adopts the notions of moderates and militants when describing the protesters.

On the surface, solidarity between the moderates and the militants in the Anti-ELAB Movement was first and foremost signified by the general absence of criticisms against militant actions. During the surrounding of the LegCo Building on June 12, images of protesters throwing bricks were already captured by television. But different from the Mongkok civil unrest, the act was not met with conspicuous and fierce criticisms from the moderate activists and movement supporters.

Of course, this does not mean that all movement supporters favored radical action. In fact, throughout June, one could see groups of Christian pastors and social workers in the protest "frontline" trying to act as buffers between the protesters and the police. Most tellingly, moderate protesters would follow the onsite pastors to try standing in front of the police and singing "Sing Alleluia to the Lord." The action signified the moderate protesters' attempt to calm down the situation and prevent violent conflicts by using creative means. The pastors and social workers represented the moderates' preference for nonviolence, but they also exhibited a willingness to stand together with the militants.

More important, solidarity was not only a "fact." From the early days of the Anti-ELAB Movement, protesters had articulated discursively an ethics of solidarity. This ethics of solidarity was promulgated and utilized in online discussions among movement supporters and participants. Lee (2020) highlighted three elements of the discourse of solidarity. The most basic element is a set of solidarity slogans. One prominent example is "Brothers climbing mountains, each offering one's own efforts." The slogan promoted the idea that the moderates and militants are using different means to achieve the same goal. They should continue to do what they prefer without interfering with each other. The slogan preached tolerance, and it aligned with the emphasis on the rejection of centralized leadership.

Another frequently used solidarity slogan was "no severing of ties." It served as a moral command: one should not sever ties with fellow protesters no matter what happened, even if some fellow protesters had engaged in controversial acts. The solidarity slogans could become particularly prominent when internal debates about the justifiability of specific actions inevitably arose as radicalization continued. Figure 7.1 shows the number of posts mentioning "no severing of ties" in the online forum LIHKG, which was a highly important communication platform for movement supporters (Lee, Liang, et al., 2022).[1] Most notably, usage of the phrase reached a peak on August 13 and 14. This is readily understandable in relation to the

Figure 7.1. No. of posts on LIHKG mentioning "no severing of ties." *Source:* Created by the author.

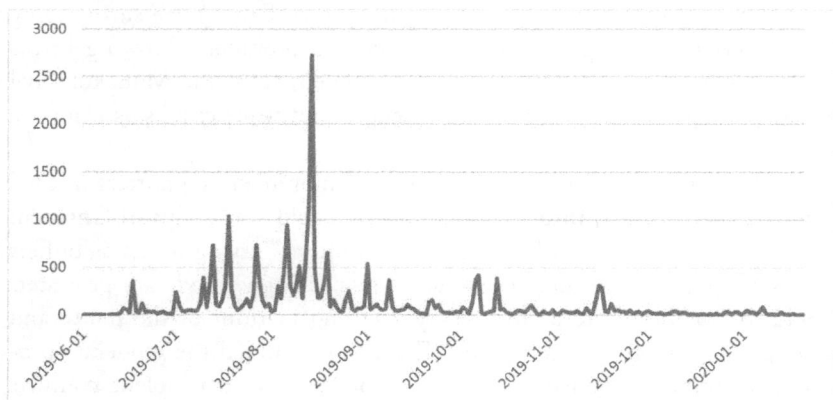

occurrence of protest events. On August 13, protesters occupied the Hong Kong International Airport. Some protesters stopped tourists from taking their flights. A group of protesters detained a person who turned out to be a state media journalist from the mainland. The action created huge controversies, leading many movement supporters to evoke the command of no severing of ties.[2]

In addition to the online data, the popularity and utility of the solidarity slogans could be discerned in a series of protest onsite surveys conducted in various protests in August 2019 (see methodological appendix for information about the surveys), in which the protesters were asked if they saw a set of slogans as representative of the Anti-ELAB Movement. Table 7.1 summarizes the results. The most representative slogans were those expressing the protesters' anger toward the power holders. But the set of solidarity slogans, including "brothers climbing mountains," "going up and down together," and "no severing of ties," were also treated as highly representative by a substantial majority of the protesters. Moreover, consistent with the LIHKG data, the percentages of protesters seeing "no severing of ties" as representative of the movement jumped significantly on August 16, right after the August 13 airport protest.

Besides solidarity slogans, derogatory speech against forces opposing the movement constituted another key element of the discourse of solidarity. Throughout the 2019 protests, many movement supporters called

Table 7.1. Protest participants' perceptions of representativeness of movement slogans

	Date of protest onsite survey					
	8/4	**8/10**	**8/11**	**8/13**	**8/16**
Slogan expressing criticisms: No rioters, only tyranny	92.1	92.2	89.3	91.8	88.8
Slogan expressing criticisms: Hong Kong police consciously violating the law	90.4	87.4	85.4	90.9	86.4
Solidarity slogan: No snitching, no severing of ties	65.3	70.0	70.7	69.1	82.0
Solidarity slogan: Brothers climbing mountains, each offering one's own effort	65.4	67.3	69.7	60.8	78.8
Solidarity slogan: Going up and down together	75.1	74.8	79.3	73.8	78.0
Solidarity slogan: Hong Kong people, add oil	78.4	77.0	73.8	70.7	63.8
Slogan expressing demands: Liberate Hong Kong, revolution of our time	69.1	67.0	66.4	73.6	81.5
Slogan expressing demands: I want genuine universal suffrage	51.3	50.7	56.9	45.8	51.3
N	1272	2309	412	485	632

Note: Entries are percentages indicating the slogan as "quite representative" or "very representative" in a five-point scale.

Source: Created by the author.

police officers "dogs" and/or "black police" (connoting a linkage between the police and gangsters). Some protesters used sexist descriptions of the female family members of police officers. Some called senior citizens who supported the government "rubbish elderly." Hatred toward the out-group could consolidate the in-group. While the use of derogatory speech can be seen as problematic, negative labeling and even dehumanizing depictions of "the other" could contribute to intramovement solidarity.[3]

Figure 7.2 shows the number of posts on LIHKG mentioning "black police" on each day between June 1, 2019, and July 10, 2020. The peak was on August 12, 2019, the day after the August 11 protests, during which a young female protester's right eye was seriously injured, with protesters generally believing that the police's bean bag rounds were the culprit. At night, police officers were filmed chasing and pushing protesters who were leaving a protest site and running down the stairs of a metro station, creating danger in the process. These actions, and similarly controversial actions during other protest events on other days, aroused public outrage and solidified the use of derogatory speech against the police.

A third element of the discourse of solidarity was constituted by disciplinary tropes utilized by protesters to dismiss dissent. Figure 7.3 shows the growing use of two disciplinary tropes between June and August 2019. "Leading the wind" refers to attempts to channel public sentiments into a direction not conducive to the movement, whereas "air-conditioned strategist"

Figure 7.2. No. of posts on LIHKG mentioning "black police." *Source:* Created by the author.

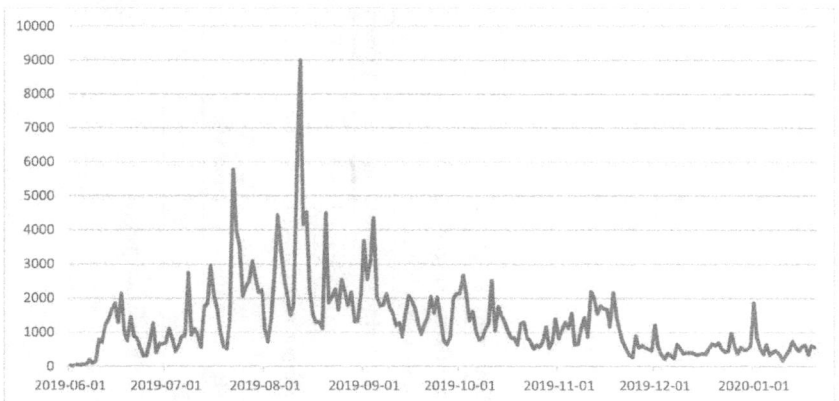

was used to describe people who did not go to the protest frontline, but stayed in comfortable places to comment on movement strategies. The former was often used to dismiss an argument by imputing suspicious motivations behind it, whereas the latter was used to dismiss a person's credibility and the relevance of his/her arguments through pointing toward his/her lack of experience of frontline actions. Obviously, the notion of air-conditioned strategists was particularly likely to be used by the militants against the moderates. The appearance of disciplinary tropes resulted from the growth of debates among the protesters as movement tactics radicalized, while their usage restricted the range of legitimate opinions and speakers.

It is beyond the scope of the present discussion to illustrate in detail how the solidarity slogans, derogatory speech, and disciplinary tropes were used simultaneously to manage internal debates. With the use of derogatory speech and disciplinary tropes, the maintenance of movement solidarity can be at the cost of heightened affective polarization in the society at large and the possible suppression of dissent within the movement. In fact, various authors have reflected upon these problematic aspects of the movement (e.g., Anonymous, 2021; Gube & Halse, 2023; P. S. Y. Ho, 2020; Lai, 2021). What the discussion here illustrates is the point that, although the dynamics in the years before the Anti-ELAB protests had made movement solidarity more plausible, solidarity was continually and actively constructed, promoted, and negotiated through discursive innovations during the movement.

Figure 7.3. No. of posts on LIHKG mentioning "leading the wind" and "air-conditioned strategist." *Source:* Created by the author.

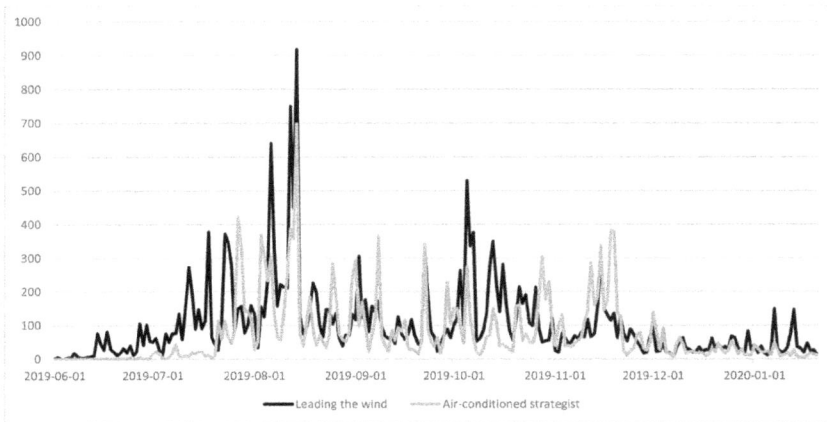

REASONING ABOUT RADICALIZATION

Throughout the movement, the presence of solidarity captured many observers' attention because of its maintenance in spite of continual tactical radicalization. Drawing upon the relational framework by Alimi and colleagues (2012), Lee, Yuen and colleagues (2022) explained the trend of tactical radicalization in the Anti-ELAB Movement by referring to interactions in four arenas. First, radicalization was driven by evolving perceptions of threats. The initial threat of the extradition bill was articulated by the protesters as an "end game." The protesters responded with the idea of mutual destruction (S. C. K. Chan, 2020), which posited that Hongkongers had little to lose if China adopted extreme measures to suppress the city. The discourse of mutual destruction urged the protesters not to be afraid of raising the stakes. Second, regarding movement-state interaction, radicalization was driven by the cycle of violence outbidding between the police and the protesters. The police's paramilitary tactics led the protesters to act even more disruptively, which in turn led the police to upgrade the use of force.

Third, radicalization was partly driven by the interaction between the protesters and the counterprotesters. More specifically, countermobilization became a driving force behind movement radicalization through the "Yuen Long Attack" on July 21, 2019, in which a group of suspected gangsters attacked protesters and citizens indiscriminately at the Yuen Long metro station. There was evidence that the police were aware of the possibility of an upcoming attack yet did nothing to prevent it. The specters of counterprotester violence and perceived police bias were directly responsible for the emergence of vigilantism in the movement. Finally, regarding the internal interaction within the movement, the condition and construction of solidarity between the moderates and the militant protesters also facilitated the adoption of increasingly militant tactics by the frontline protesters.

Nonetheless, for the present discussion, the more important thing to explain is not radicalization per se, but the significant level of public acceptance of radical protests. Table 7.2 summarizes the findings based on several relevant items included in the protest onsite surveys between July and December, 2019. Notably, the protesters did not necessarily see radical protests as highly effective. On July 1, when asked to respond by using a five-point Likert scale, only 11.5 percent of the protesters strongly agreed with the statement "Radical protests can make the government listen to the public." The item had a mean score of 3.17. Perceived effectiveness of radical protests increased over time. By December 8, the item would obtain

Table 7.2. Agreement with statements related to radical protests

	Date of protest onsite survey						
	7/1	7/21	8/4	9/15	10/14	12/8
Radical protests can make the government listen to the public	11.5 (3.17)	18.0 (3.57)	15.7 (3.48)	22.2 (3.74)	24.0 (3.87)	23.8 (3.82)
Radical protests will lead to negative reactions from others in the society	12.3 (3.52)	4.8 (3.11)	7.4 (3.18)	3.8 (2.98)	6.8 (3.22)	4.1 (2.91)
Combination of peaceful rallies and confrontations can maximize effectiveness	43.7 (4.04)	52.4 (4.32)	64.3 (4.50)	64.0 (4.55)	70.8 (4.60)	65.5 (4.54)
When the government doesn't listen, radical actions are understandable	54.7 (4.33)	68.9 (4.64)	79.1 (4.73)	77.3 (4.75)	86.7 (4.85)	85.2 (4.83)
N	1169	680	1272	911	662	902

Notes: Entries are percentages "strongly agree" with the statements in a five-point Likert scale. Figures in parentheses are mean scores.

Source: Created by the author.

a mean score of 3.82. Nonetheless, only 23.8 percent of the respondents strongly agreed with the statement.

In comparison, the majority of the protesters strongly agreed with the statement "When the government doesn't listen, radical actions are understandable." In the protest on July 1, 54.7 percent of the respondents strongly agreed with the statement. The percentage rose to 79.1 percent one month later, and it stood at 85.2 percent in the protest on December 8. It should be noted that the protest onsite surveys were conducted during peaceful protest marches and rallies. The respondents, therefore, were supposedly constituted mainly by those who would not engage in radical actions. Yet the findings in table 7.2 show that, especially into August and September, movement participants had a strong consensus of the "understandability" of radical protests. Most participants held a belief in the power of the combination of peaceful rallies and confrontations, and they were not particularly worried about the possible negative effect of radical protests on public opinion.

The moderate protesters exhibited an increasing degree of "understanding" toward militant protests despite the increasingly controversial character of some of the militant actions. Here, the sustenance of sympathetic attitudes toward militant protests had to be understood in relation to how protesters had tried to exercise collective restraint. At different stages and moments, movement supporters tried to articulate the norms and rules that should be applied to militant actions. For instance, immediately after the airport protest on August 13 mentioned in the previous section, a post on LIHKG tried to propose a set of "military rules":

> After tonight, does anyone feel that the frontline brothers need a set of military rules? For examples: 1. No beating of journalists; 2. No beating of medical workers; 3. No use of laser pointers or flashlights in the absence of black police; 4. No abuse or torture; 5. No attack on ordinary citizens.
>
> Even if this is a war, discipline is of utmost importance to any army. Otherwise, one or two stupid things can destroy [the movement]. When it is a round of peaceful and rational protest, be peaceful and rational. When it is time for militant protests, then be militant thoroughly.[4]

The post received 5778 likes and only 278 dislikes. It is highly illustrative of the negotiation of protest norms. The author used the solidarity signifier *brothers* to refer to the frontline protesters. The post thus followed the command of "no severing of ties." The author acknowledged that the situation was comparable to a "war," implying that the author did not dismiss the use of violence. S/he was only proposing a set of "military rules" because an army needs discipline, and there are moral norms that even soldiers have to abide by.

Discussions and constructions of such norms for militant actions appeared repeatedly in relation to other events and tactics. For vigilantism, many movement supporters held beliefs about the importance of proportionality. For instance, in a focus group study conducted in 2020 to understand public attitudes toward violent protests (see methodological appendix for the focus group method), one participant said: "I agree to fight back when the counterprotesters are holding knives and intending to hurt the protesters. But it would be excessive if the counterprotesters only expressed their opposition verbally. Level of force should be proportionate. I accept subduing or pushing the counterprotesters away if they obstruct the progress of the protest, but I would have concerns if the use of force leads to death and injuries." Similarly, when vandalism emerged in September 2019, many movement supporters articulated the following rule: renovating shops that are black (i.e., owned and run by gangsters); decorating shops that are red (i.e., owned by Chinese capital); boycotting shops that are blue (i.e., supporting the government); and buycotting shops that are yellow (i.e., supporting the movement). *Renovation* was the euphemism for vandalism, whereas *decoration* refers to the use of memo papers to build Lennon Walls outside a shop for movement supporters to post messages. Figure 7.4 shows three posters circulating online during the protest movement promoting the same code of shop-targeting actions.

Admittedly, these efforts of norm construction and collective restraint had two limitations. First, it was very difficult to achieve consensus among all protesters on the details of the norms for specific types of actions. Different sets of norms could have been promoted and generated without the movement supporters ever making a collective decision on which set to adopt. Second, frontline militant protesters did not necessarily follow the rules and norms. In fact, some militant protesters might see the moderates and those who proposed these norms and rules as air-conditioned strategists. And there were many cases in which militant protesters violated the norms widely circulated online (e.g., many "red shops," such as Chinese banks, were vandalized instead of merely "decorated"). However, the presence of efforts to construct the norms of militant protests remains significant. With these efforts, movement supporters did not have to choose between simply

Figures 7.4a–7.4c. Posters promoting the code of conduct for actions toward different types of shops. *Source:* Public domain.

accepting or rejecting all militant protests. They could try to develop more nuanced and complex views toward the justifiability of radical protests. This, in turn, helped the maintenance of solidarity.

EXPERIENTIAL BASIS OF AFFECTIVE SOLIDARITY

The common experiences of police repression also contributed to the maintenance of solidarity (Li et al., 2024). The large-scale protest marches in July and August, 2019, typically involved a peaceful and approved protest march in the afternoon hours, followed by confrontations and clashes between the militant protesters and the police in the evening hours, sometimes extending into late night. By the time the confrontations began, most of the moderate protesters had left the scene. The militant protesters who confronted the police were much more likely to have been subjected to police violence or arrested.

However, the moderate protesters could have four types of surrogate experiences of police violence. First, many major protest events were live broadcasts by television stations, online media, and citizen or student journalists via social media. Such live broadcasts constituted a type of affective news (Fang & Cheng, 2022; Luqiu, 2021) for movement supporters, and numerous controversial cases of police violence were shown. Past research about the Umbrella Movement has suggested that televised images of police violence could have led to mediated instant grievances (Tang, 2015) that drove more people to protest. How live media images of police violence could have enraged the bystanding public cannot be underestimated. In one particularly prominent case, live media images captured the police raiding the Prince Edward metro station, beating protesters who were returning home on a train. The event would later generate the rumor that the police had beaten protesters to death inside the station that night.[5]

Second, in some originally peaceful protest events, the arrival of the police might have triggered the "evacuation" of the moderate protesters. One example from the author's field observation can be given here. Toward the end of a peaceful rally in late September 2019, in the Admiralty district, protesters were led to "evacuate" and rush toward the Central District. Along the route, a few protesters acted as "guides" to inform the evacuating protesters about the location of the police officers. In fact, these "guides"[6] might have exaggerated the threats from the police,[6] but they created a very tense and fearful atmosphere. It was not the only time the author joined or witnessed an "evacuation." Although the evacuating protesters did not really suffer from any actual police violence, the shared experience could have strengthened the impression of a repressive police force and the sense of solidarity with fellow protesters.

Third, many moderate protesters had friends and acquaintances who had experienced police violence. In the protest onsite survey conducted on December 8, 2019, as many as 40.9 percent of the respondents said that they had friends or acquaintances having been arrested, while 23.5 percent reported having friends or acquaintances subjected to police violence. 26.0 percent of the respondents had witnessed police arrests on protest sites, whereas 35.4 percent had the experience of escaping from the police. (The high percentage of respondents having the experience of "escaping from the police" could be understood in relation to the evacuation experience described in the previous paragraph.)

Fourth, since protest events spread throughout the city, police-protester clashes occurred in many residential areas in Hong Kong. In the December 8 onsite survey, 52.2 percent of the respondents reported that the police had used tear gas in their neighborhood. While progovernment citizens might blame the protesters for bringing conflicts into their residential areas, movement supporters were likely to treat the police's use of tear gas in residential districts as a serious intrusion of state violence into their everyday lifeworld.

The above can be considered as the experiential bases of affective solidarity. The evacuation experience and the police's use of force in residential areas, in particular, could have contributed to the perception of indiscriminate police repression. Moreover, since the moderates were aware of how the militant protesters were being treated, they could have developed a kind of survivor guilt. The phenomenon of guilt became more obvious as the number of arrests continued to rise. As table 7.3 shows, by early December, 80.4

Table 7.3. Solidarity with and guilt feelings toward militant protesters

	December 8	January 1
I feel that they are sacrificing for the peaceful protesters	80.4 (4.77)	74.0 (4.67)
I feel that peaceful protesters are indebted to them	55.8 (4.28)	50.2 (4.20)
They make me feel that I am paying too little for the movement	57.5 (4.37)	47.7 (4.23)
I feel guilty when I see them being arrested	68.7 (4.59)	62.6 (4.51)
I cannot agree with their radical protest actions	4.1 (1.97)	6.1 (2.25)
I feel that they are voicing out on behalf of me	74.0 (4.69)	60.8 (4.51)
I feel that we are in the same boat	79.9 (4.77)	70.7 (4.66)
I feel that I am one of them	57.2 (4.41)	46.6 (4.24)
N	902	1306

Notes: Entries are percentages of "strongly agree" with the statements in a five-point Likert scale. Figures in parentheses are mean scores.

Source: Created by the author.

percent of protest participants strongly agreed that the militant protesters were sacrificing for the peaceful protesters. The five-point Likert-scaled item had a mean score of 4.77. Besides, 55.8 percent strongly agreed that the peaceful protesters were indebted to the militants, 57.5 percent strongly agreed that the militants made them feel that they were paying too little for the movement, and 68.7 percent strongly agreed that they felt guilty when they saw the militant protesters being arrested.

Meanwhile, in the December 8 survey, 74.0 percent of the respondents strongly agreed that the militant protesters were voicing out on behalf of them, 79.9 percent strongly agreed that the moderates and the militants were on the same boat, and 57.2 percent strongly agreed that they were "one of them." The figures dropped somewhat in the January 1 survey. Yet the overall level of solidarity with the militant protesters remained high. Indeed, analyzing the same set of data, Tang and Cheng (2021) showed that the feelings of guilt toward the militant protesters could explain people's acceptance of radical protest tactics as well as feelings of solidarity.

In sum, while the relational dynamics in the few years before the 2019 protests had facilitated the beginning of affective depolarization between the moderate and the radical flanks of the prodemocracy movement, thus setting the stage for a more cohesive movement to arise, the maintenance of solidarity in a rapidly radicalizing movement was made possible by the discursive construction and employment of an ethics of solidarity, the negotiation of norms and rules to be associated with militant actions, the perception and experience of indiscriminate police repression, and the development of feelings of guilt.

Claim Radicalization and the Rise of a Broker Frame

CLAIM MAKING AND TRANSFORMATION IN THE ANTI-ELAB PROTESTS

Social movement research has differentiated between tactical and ideological radicalization. The two can be related to each other—groups pursuing radical goals and adopting radical ideologies are more likely to adopt radical tactics. The two can feed into each other, as the turn toward more radical ideologies and goals can be a reason for people to take up more disruptive and violent tactics (Bosi & della Porta, 2012). However, not all groups pursuing fundamental changes in social and political structures adopt highly disruptive and violent tactics, and not all groups adopting highly disruptive and violent tactics pursue fundamental changes (Yaziji & Doh, 2013). Therefore, ideological radicalization is a distinctive dimension of the Anti-ELAB protests that needs to be discussed separately.

The concern with ideological radicalization leads to the consideration of claim making and claim transformation, that is, the articulation, expression, and transformation of movement demands (Almeida, 2009: 9–10). Hong Kong scholars have noted that, after the transfer of sovereignty, the civil society has been more capable of defending existing freedoms than striving for new rights (Ma, 2005). Social mobilization had stopped national security legislation in 2003 and the turning of national education into a secondary school core subject in 2012. The Anti-ELAB protests also began with the defensive goal of rejecting the extradition bill.

However, demands expanded as protests unfolded. After the police-protester clashes on June 12, the police described the protests as a "riot." This implied that the arrested protesters could face punishment of up to ten years in jail. Protesters began to demand the retraction of the "riot definition" and the release of the arrested. Nevertheless, the range of demands did not expand substantially afterwards. Instead, in mid-June, the notion of "five demands" emerged. The notion can be traced to the suicide of protester Leung Ling-kit on June 15. When committing the suicide outside a shopping mall, Leung unfurled a banner that read "complete withdrawal of the bill; we are not rioting; release the students and the injured; Carrie Lam steps down; help Hong Kong." This could be considered the first version of "five demands."

Given the decentralized character of the movement, it is impossible to give a comprehensive account of the various versions of five demands put forward by different groups and individuals. The following are some of the more prominent versions of "five demands" proposed between mid-June and mid-July that were registered in news media reports:

1. June 16, CHRF: Withdraw the bill; call the police to account for firing guns; release the arrested and stop prosecution; retract the riot definition of the June 12 clash; [Chief Executive] Carrie Lam steps down.

2. July 1, a group of protesters who broke into the LegCo building: Withdraw the bill; retract the riot definition; withdraw all charges against protesters; investigate police abuse of power thoroughly; disband the LegCo and immediately institutionalize genuine popular elections.

3. July 9, prodemocracy legislators (as a collective): Withdraw the bill, retract the riot definition, establish an independent commission of inquiry (COI) to investigate police violence; no arrest and prosecution of protesters; [Chief Executive] Carrie Lam steps down.

4. July 9, CHRF: Withdraw the bill; retract the riot definition; establish an independent COI to investigate police violence; no arrest and prosecution of protesters; institutionalize genuine popular elections.

CHRF's list on July 9 would go on to be the overwhelmingly most prominent version of five demands in later months. But this does not mean that CHRF was the organization most capable of imposing its version of five demands onto the movement. CHRF itself changed the list between June 16 and July 9, mainly by replacing "Carrie Lam steps down" with "institutionalization of genuine popular elections." In fact, on June 26, CHRF organized a rally on the eve of the G20 Summit in Osaka to appeal to the international community for support. "I Want Genuine Popular Elections," a slogan of the Umbrella Movement, was shouted on stage. Yet the slogan was booed by many young participants. The negative response was partly driven by a refusal to shift the focus of the movement before the arrested were rescued. It was partly driven by a distrust of central leaders and established groups, a prominent sentiment among young people since the Umbrella Movement (Ku, 2019; Lee & Chan, 2018).

The inclusion of genuine popular elections into the five demands gained more support only after the protests on July 1. After a large-scale protest march organized by CHRF in the afternoon, protesters surrounded the LegCo Building in the evening. A small group of protesters broke into the building to stage a protest. Leung Kai-ping, a young PhD student without formal political affiliation, took down his mask and read a declaration. The declaration posited democratization as the movement's ultimate goal. This militant performance helped consolidate the place of "democratic reform" in the list of major movement demands.

The significance of the July 1 action is illustrated by figure 7.5, which shows the number of posts on LIHKG mentioning the phrase *five demands*. Although the phrase appeared in mid-June, it rose to prominence only after July 1. The first small peak of the use of the phrase appeared on July 5. The phrase was used even more prominently later, with the sharpest peak

Figure 7.5. No. of posts containing the phrase *five demands* on LIHKG. *Source:* Created by the author.

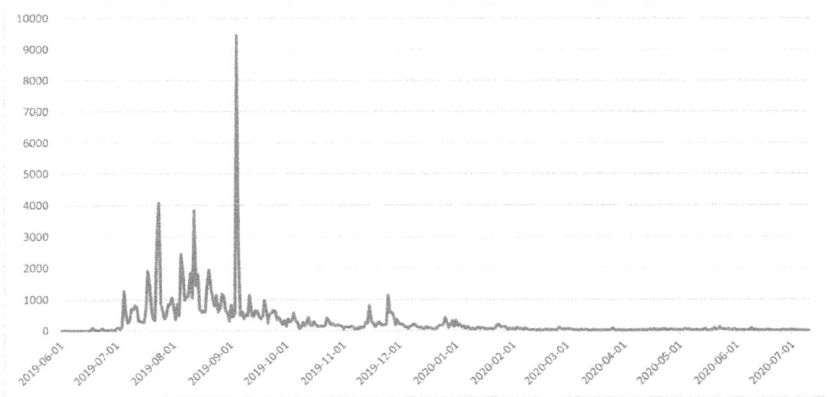

appearing on September 4, the day the government announced the withdrawal of the bill.

In any case, the emergence of the five-demands formula and the articulation of its contents involved both the work of established movement organizations and a bottom-up process in which individual protesters and contingent events mattered. CHRF was the first organization to put forward the notion of five demands to the mainstream news media. The consolidation of a common understanding of what the five demands include required recognition by movement organizations and politicians. But in the interim, the performance of individual protesters and movement supporters' approval expressed online were crucial.

In terms of content, several characteristics of the five demands can be noted. First, many possibly relevant demands were excluded. Consider the demand for the resignation of top officials. Even if one accepts the argument that systemic reform is more important than leadership change, democratic reform could have been added as a sixth demand instead of replacing resignation by officials. There was seemingly an urge to limit the number of demands to five. Second, the five demands are all politically moderate. The establishing of a COI to investigate the police, for instance, follows a long-established convention of COIs in Hong Kong. In subsequent public discussions, movement supporters even acknowledged that the COI could look at the protests holistically instead of focusing only on police violence.

Meanwhile, democratic reform was enshrined in the Basic Law and was taken by the Hong Kong society as the Chinese government's promise under one country, two systems. The demands do not challenge the basic rules and constitution of the regime.

Third, there was a general refusal to radicalize the five demands. For instance, beginning in mid-August, with the intensification and accumulation of police violence and misconduct, many protesters started shouting for the disbanding of the police force. Disbanding the police force could have been incorporated as a sixth demand or used to replace the call for a COI. In the online arena, one could indeed find versions of five demands produced by individual citizens that incorporated such a change. But the version of five demands consolidated in mid-July remained overwhelmingly the most dominant one.

The stability of the five demands signifies the movement's ideological restraint. But what explains this restraint? One plausible interpretation can focus on the supposed strategic considerations behind the claim-making process. In the Anti-ELAB Movement, there were no leaders capable of devising movement strategies holistically. Instead, civil society groups, activists, and citizen participants responded to each other as the movement evolved. The sheer size of the movement and the movement's attempt to seek both local and international support strengthen the need to appeal to the largest common denominator. Inevitably, movement participants held varying views regarding the relationship between Hong Kong and China. To maintain unity, the movement needed to phrase its claims in ways that would be acceptable to all. For example, some protesters may have regarded the demand of setting up a COI as too moderate, but it was the demand that received the strongest public support in polls.[7] Meanwhile, genuine popular election is a basic demand that would be readily understandable by the international society and foreign publics. The formula of five demands and the set of demands consolidated since mid-July thus suited the movement's purpose because of their concreteness and moderation.

However, alongside the intensification of protester-police conflicts, protesters did develop more antagonistic rhetoric and claims. In addition to the aforementioned "disbanding the police force," protesters shifted the early slogan Hongkongers, Add Oil to Hongkongers, Resist, and then to Hongkongers, Revenge. These slogans and demands did not displace the five demands. They could be heard simultaneously in protest events. Among the emerging radical slogans, the notion of Liberate Hong Kong, Revolution of Our Time was particularly important, not least because it was adopted from the localist leader Edward Leung.[8]

Notably, the Chinese phrase used in the slogan is *kwong-fuk*, which was the phrase used by the localists for their "reclaim actions" (chapter 4). Hence, the first part of the slogan can either be translated as "liberate Hong Kong" or "reclaim Hong Kong." In any case, as figure 7.6 shows, the slogan gained huge prominence in LIHKG in the second half of July. As table 7.1 has already shown, 69.1 percent of the participants in the protest marches on August 4 saw the slogan as representative. The percentage grew further to 81.5 percent by the end of August.

Liberate Hong Kong, Revolution of Our Time did not displace the notion of five demands on protest sites. Table 7.4 presents data derived from a compilation of protest-event-related materials derived from two Telegram channels: CHRF and a channel created by movement participants that was widely use by protesters to share mobilizing information.[9] All posts related to specific protest activities were screened. Table 7.4 shows that, between late July and late September, *five demands* was the dominant phrase used in the promotional materials of protest events. In the later stages of the movement, the gap between the use of *five demands* and *revolution of our time* closed. But overall speaking, *five demands* still appeared in the promotional materials of a larger number of protest events.

Figure 7.6. No. of posts containing *Liberate Hong Kong* and *Revolution of Our Time* on LIHKG. Note that the two lines almost overlap with each other completely. *Source:* Created by the author.

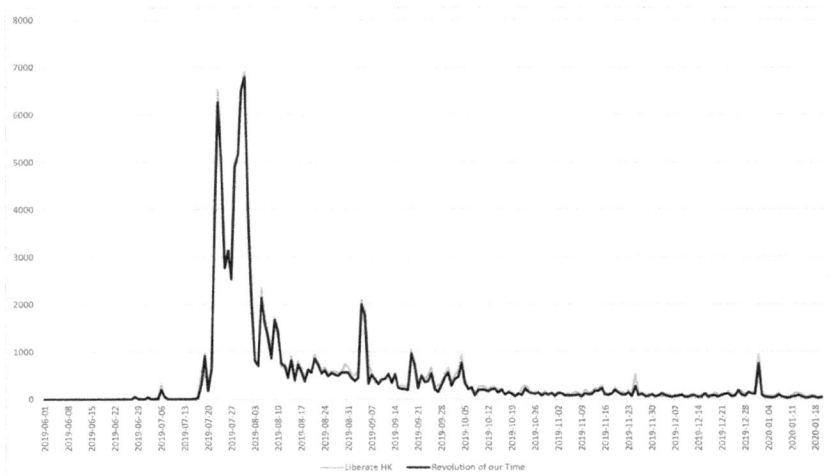

Table 7.4. Demands indicated in posters associated with protest events, July 28, 2019, to January 19, 2020

	Total	Five Demands	Revolution of Our Time	Other Police-related
July 28 to September 30	27	24	7	4
October 1 to November 30	45	18	12	16
December 1 to January 19	30	13	8	5

Note: Entries are number of posters.
Source: Created by the author.

Certainly, when compared to five demands, the slogan Liberate Hong Kong, Revolution of Our Time does not point to concrete actions that the protesters requested the government to do. How should we understand the meanings and role of this slogan in the 2019 protests?

Liberate Hong Kong, Revolution of Our Time as a Broker Frame

On July 21, 2019, after the protest march in the afternoon, thousands of protesters continued their action and gathered in front of the Chinese Liaison Office (CLO) at night. Protesters painted insulting and provocative slogans onto the outside walls of the building, and the national emblem outside the building was defaced. It was the first time during the Anti-ELAB Movement that an institutional representative of the Chinese government was targeted.

Coincidentally, the protest in front of the CLO was upstaged by the Yuen Long attack happening later in the same night. Media and public attention in the subsequent weeks focused largely on the much more shocking Yuen Long attack instead of the protest in front of the CLO. Nevertheless, from the perspective of the Chinese government, the CLO protest occurred at a time when the slogan Liberate Hong Kong, Revolution of Our Time became increasingly prominent on protest sites. This development had ruffled the Chinese government's feathers. On August 5, Chief Executive Carrie Lam criticized protesters for chanting the Liberate Hong Kong slogan. She claimed that the protesters' actions challenged national sovereignty, threatened one country, two systems, and would destroy the city's prosperity and stability (Lam,

2019). In the same week, a major Chinese official said that the Anti-ELAB protests had shown features of "color revolution" (Chung & Cheung, 2019), though he did not single out the Liberate Hong Kong slogan for criticism.

Facing the government's attempt to impose a highly charged reading of the slogan and impute a seditious intention behind the protesters' actions, various commentators and public figures responded by looking into the popular, current usage of the keywords and offer more moderate interpretations of the slogan. For example, in an article published on August 8 in a local Chinese newspaper, a senior academic and an exgovernment official reported what they heard at a forum organized by student representatives from eight universities:

> Almost all [. . .] pointed toward the same question asked by many Hong Kong people now: Why the Hong Kong we are familiar with had changed into something unrecognizable? The meaning of liberate Hong Kong is to let Hong Kong regain its "glamor." [. . .] One has to "reform the home, improve the home." [. . .] The meaning of revolution of our time is that they are a generation no longer focusing on "eating, playing, and sleeping," but pursuing non-material values. In the political arena, that means democracy, freedom, and human rights. (Chan & Yau, 2019)

For another example, on August 13, US-based sociologist Hung Ho-fung offered his own analysis in an audio commentary published through Radio Free Asia:

> The slogan "Reclaim Hong Kong Revolution of Our Time" is very broad and ambiguous. You can understand it in whichever way you want. The term "reclaim" came from the anti-parallel trading protests such as "reclaim Sheung Shui" and "reclaim Yuen Long" several years ago. Those were about livelihood issues. [. . .] And Hong Kong is a place where the term "revolution" was so widely used to the extent that food adverts could also say "food revolution." "Revolution of Our Times" of course does not necessarily relate to Hong Kong independence.[10]

One does not have to agree with the interpretations offered by these commentators. The point here is that, in response to the government, commentators supportive or sympathetic toward the movement offered their interpretations of the slogan and dissociated it from the idea of Hong Kong independence. However, they did not reject the slogan. Instead, they tried to make use of its ambiguity to produce other possible readings of it.

What ensued, in other words, was a public and discursive contestation of the meanings of the slogan. On the one hand, government officials and progovernment media continued to tie the slogan to separatism. For instance, on October 21, the Communist-sponsored newspaper *Ta Kung Pao* ran a commentary titled " 'Five Demands' aims at seizing power, 'Revolution of Our Time' aims at subversion," whereas another article was titled "The essence of 'Liberate Hong Kong, Revolution of Our Time' is Hong Kong independence." But on the other hand, the multivocality of the slogan was repeatedly emphasized in many media materials. For instance, one episode of RTHK's *Hong Kong Connection*, aired in early August and titled "Revolution of Our Time?," tried to investigate the meanings associated with the slogan. Most of the interviewees in the episode denounced the idea that the slogan had the implication of Hong Kong independence when being used in the ongoing protests.

Amidst such contestation in public discourses, movement supporters were developing and negotiating their understandings of the slogan. Table 7.1 shows the increasing level of acceptance of the slogan by the protesters over time. The increasing level of acceptance was grounded partly in how various protesters constructed the meanings of the slogan in ways that they would find acceptable. In the aforementioned focus group study conducted in 2020, discussants were asked to comment on various protest slogans. Regarding Liberate Hong Kong, Revolution of Our Time, one discussant opined:

> At first, I felt I couldn't shout the slogan, because at first I saw it as related to Hong Kong independence. Even today, I use the term *Umbrella Movement*, not *revolution* because *revolution* connotes overthrowing the government, and that was not my aim. I'm not pro-Hong Kong independence. [. . .] But the movement changed gradually; now it's about striving for genuine popular election, making Hong Kong a place with peace, democracy, and freedom; it's about striving for justice. So, I gradually can shout this slogan. In addition, I think the slogan represents our spirit; it unites Hong Kong people. [. . .] [W]hen I shout, I feel connected with other Hong Kong people.

The participant's self-reflection illustrated how people's understanding of a slogan can shift and how the slogan could take up not only cognitive meanings but also affective content. Other focus group participants expressed varying views on what *liberate* and/or *revolution* referred to. Certainly, individuals could indeed aim for Hong Kong independence, as shall be discussed later. But here, what is noteworthy are the varieties of interpretations offered. The following are excerpts of the views expressed by three participants in the focus group study:

> It's easy to understand Liberate Hong Kong. You claim this place back. Because our generation has an imagination of this place's future. [. . .] And Revolution of Our Time [. . .] for us, this revolution is about our insistence on democracy.

> Why Liberate Hong Kong? Because it is very bad now; the system is collapsing, so I have to liberate. For Revolution of Our Time [. . .] revolution in the general sense is to create changes. So facing such an ambiguous slogan, you shout if you like.

> My "liberation" is about one country, two systems. There is a boundary. You don't mess with me, and I don't mess with you. In fact, I am not interested in messing with you. I have trouble just taking care of myself.

These statements illustrate that different goals can be subsumed under the slogan, and they also illustrate that the movement participants were conscious of the slogan's ambiguity. It is not just that people interpreted the slogan differently; people were aware of how others could be interpreting it differently, and they were willing to accept its multivocality. In addition, many participants were aware of the government's attempt to impute a radical meaning to the slogan. But instead of abandoning it, movement participants insisted on defying the government and exercising their agency to (re)define what the slogan could mean. This latter sentiment was expressed by another focus group participant: "For me, we are recovering certain values of our society. I think we can redefine [the slogan], that is, how we understand Liberate Hong Kong, Revolution of Our Time. I shouldn't stop speaking just because you label me. [. . .] I think I need to redefine those words, that is, in this movement, in 2019, what it means."

In their theorization of the logic of connective action, Bennett and Segerberg (2013) emphasized the role of symbolically open and inclusive "personal action frames" in networked mobilization. Instead of a classic collective action frame that contains a coherent account of an issue, a personal action frame is very often a phrase that can capture people's imagination yet does not require them to come to the exact same understanding of its meanings. Liberate Hong Kong, Revolution of Our Time had this key characteristic of a personal action frame.

In addition, given the background of tactical and ideological radicalization in the Anti-ELAB Movement, the slogan can also be understood as a broker frame. It is a statement commonly adopted by both the moderates and the militants. The rhetoric of liberation and revolution allowed the more radical protesters to express their strong sentiments, which for some might indeed contain a desire of independence. But as long as the slogan remains ambiguous, it allows the moderates to appropriate and redefine it to refer to other goals.

In sum, similar to tactical radicalization, ideological radicalization can pose a challenge to the maintenance of solidarity. The previous pages have shown that this challenge was handled in the Anti-ELAB Movement by two means: to retain the moderate "five demands" as the major representation of the movement's goals, and to turn Liberate Hong Kong, Revolution of Our Time into a broker frame that both the moderates and the militants could use, with everyone having the liberty of defining the slogan in one's own preferred way.

Proindependence Sentiments and Localism in the Protests

EVOLUTION AND LIMITS OF PROINDEPENDENCE SENTIMENTS

As the Hong Kong government continued to refuse to make additional concessions and police-protester clashes further escalated, protesters' anger and frustrations accumulated, and one could expect the exercise of collective restraint to become increasingly difficult. Into the later months of the movement, slogans directly expressing proindependence sentiments became more conspicuous on protest sites. The author's observation in a small-scale rally in the Tin Shui Wai district of the New Territories, held on January 20, 2020, and attended by around three hundred people, illustrates the atmosphere in some of the protest events at that stage. In a small park and with a stage set on one side, prominent activists took turns speaking. As the speakers shouted, "Five demands!" participants shouted, "Not one less!"

in response. "Disbanding the police force" was followed by "Can't delay for another moment." "Liberate Hong Kong" was followed by "Revolution of our time." Then, without any prompts from the stage, some participants at the back shouted: "Hong Kong independence, the only way out!"

The activists and politicians on stage went as far as "Liberate Hong Kong, revolution of our time!" This again illustrates the brokering function of the slogan: through the slogan, the activists and politicians on stage acknowledged the demand for fundamental changes of the society, without the need of specifying what fundamental changes are needed. The most militant protesters could feel that they were addressed. At the same time, the militant protesters standing at the back were free to shout the slogans they liked. The ethics of solidarity and tolerance toward diversity in tactical and ideological preferences remained intact.

But across the movement, how widespread was the discussion about Hong Kong independence? Figure 7.7 shows the daily number of posts on LIHKG that mentioned Hong Kong independence. The first major peak occurred from August 5 through 7, 2019, directly in response to government leaders' claim about the movement taking up the characteristics of a color revolution. Another peak occurred surrounding the National Day on October 1. Yet another peak appeared on December 23, one day after some protesters held a rally to support the Uygur in Xinjiang. However, the appearance of Hong Kong Independence does not necessarily signify

Figure 7.7. No. of posts on LIHKG mentioning Hong Kong independence. *Note:* The figure includes posts mentioning either the complete phrase *heung-gong-duk-laap* or its abbreviated version, *gong-duk. Source:* Created by the author.

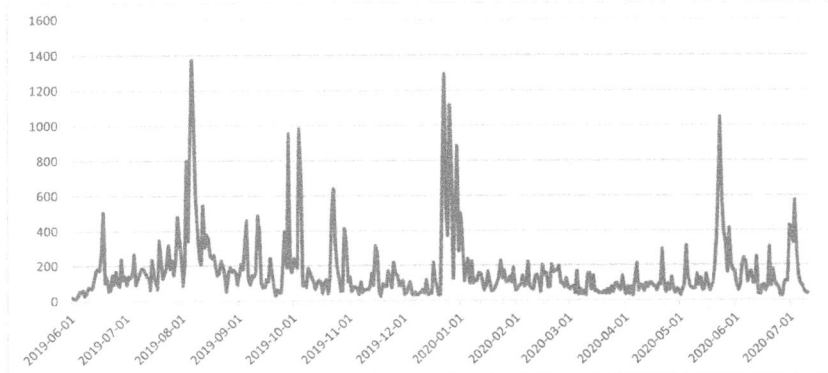

a call for independence. In the early August peak, for instance, the phrase *Hong Kong Independence* appeared probably partly because many movement supporters tried to counter the government's discourse by claiming that the movement did not aim at independence.

There was no linear and over-time increase in the frequencies of the invocation of the idea of independence. When June 1, 2019, through July 10, 2020, was taken as a whole period, the correlation between daily number of posts mentioning Hong Kong independence and a linear time variable (June 1, 2019 = 1, July 10, 2020 = 407) was even negative in sign (Pearson r = −.13). Moreover, even at the several peaks shown in figure 7.7, numbers of posts mentioning Hong Kong independence stood at only around thirteen hundred. The figure was substantially lower than the peak values for the other key words and movement slogans registered by the other graphs presented earlier in this chapter. These indicators showed that Hong Kong independence was by no means a dominant idea in the discussions among movement supporters.

Observers might wonder if the lack of mention of Hong Kong independence was only a result of the rhetorical restraint exercised by movement supporters. That is, one might suspect that movement supporters did not want to express the idea explicitly, yet they were expressing their proindependence sentiments in other ways. Government leaders, in particular, might insist that the slogan Liberate Hong Kong, Revolution of Our Time did refer to Hong Kong independence, and the multiplicity of interpretations discussed in the previous section was only a façade created by movement supporters to hide the "true meaning" of the slogan.

Analytically, whether the Liberate Hong Kong slogan was indeed tied to Hong Kong independence can be further examined through the association between daily mentions of the slogan and daily mentions of Hong Kong independence. If the two were indeed closely tied to each other, the mentioning of the two should fluctuate together in a time series.

To examine this issue, a regression analysis was conducted. The model uses daily percentages of posts mentioning *five demands* and daily percentages of posts mentioning *liberate Hong Kong* to predict daily percentages of posts mentioning *independence*. Since the variables are time series, an autoregressive term for mentioning of Hong Kong independence was controlled. A linear time variable was also controlled to rule out spurious correlation due merely to simultaneous over-time increase in mentioning of all the key phrases. If liberate Hong Kong and Hong Kong independence were largely equivalent in what they referred to, the relationship between mentioning of liberate Hong

Kong and mentioning of Hong Kong independence should be substantial, and it should be stronger than the correlation between mentioning of five demands and mentioning of Hong Kong independence.

Table 7.5a, however, shows that it was not the case. When June 1, 2019, to July 10, 2020, was taken as a single period, there was no correlation between mentioning of liberate Hong Kong and mentioning of Hong Kong independence. When the period was broken down into three phases,[11] mentioning of Hong Kong independence and mentioning of liberate Hong Kong was positively and significantly correlated in the second and third phases. Nonetheless, in each phase, the correlation between mentioning of liberate Hong Kong and mentioning of Hong Kong independence was not

Tables 7.5a–b. Predicting percentage of LIHKG posts mentioning Hong Kong independence. DV: percentage mentioning independence

Table 7.5a. By period

	Full	Period 1	Period 2	Period 3
Time	.14**	.09	.16*	.16*
HK independence.$_{t-1}$	.56***	.32***	.47***	.41***
Five demands	.11*	.09	.33***	.26***
Liberate HK	.02	.00	.15*	.24**
Adjusted R^2	.35***	.10**	.50***	.43***

Table 7.5b. Periods 2 & 3 only

	Model 1	Model 2	Model 3
Time	.63***	−.02	.57***
HK independence.$_{t-1}$	.47***	.53***	.44***
Five demands	.39***		.34***
Liberate HK		.39***	.22**
Time X Five demands	.39**		.38**
Liberate HK		−.21*	−.06
Adjusted R^2	.42***	.48***	.50***

Note: Entries are standardized regression coefficients. Period 1 = June 9 to October 31, 2019; Period 2 = November 1, 2019, to February 29, 2020; Period 3 = March 1 to July 10, 2020.

Source: Created by the author.

stronger than that between mentioning of five demands and mentioning of Hong Kong independence. In other words, there was no evidence for a particularly close linkage between the slogan Liberate Hong Kong, Revolution of Our Time and the idea of Hong Kong independence.

Despite such findings, some might wonder if the connection between liberate Hong Kong and Hong Kong independence was strengthened over time. That is, is it possible that the slogan was interpreted in a diverse manner at first, but the meanings became more centered on independence as the movement became more radical? To test this possibility, we created two interaction terms: (1) between the linear time variable and mentioning of liberate Hong Kong, and (2) between the linear time variable and mentioning of five demands. If a slogan or a notion became more closely tied to Hong Kong independence over time, the interaction term should obtain a positive coefficient. If a slogan or a notion became more detached from Hong Kong independence over time, the interaction term should obtain a negative coefficient.

Table 7.5b shows that the interaction term for mentioning of liberate Hong Kong and "time" actually obtained a negative coefficient. That is, as time went on, mentioning of liberate Hong Kong became less likely to lead to mentioning of Hong Kong independence. This finding, however, is understandable in relation to the dynamics discussed earlier: the slogan was originally adopted from proindependence activist Edward Leung, but it was developed into a broker frame during the Anti-ELAB Movement. It is therefore not surprising that the slogan could become relatively detached from Hong Kong independence as time went on. Table 7.5b shows the empirical evidence for this development.

Certainly, even if the slogan Liberate Hong Kong, Revolution of Our Time should not be taken as proindependence, many protesters did express proindependence sentiments in other indirect and covert means. For instance, in early September, "Glory to Hong Kong" became a highly popular movement song. In the onsite survey on September 15, 88.0 percent of the respondents agreed that "the song made me identify myself as a Hongkonger even more," and 69.5 percent agreed that "the song is Hong Kong people's national anthem." One way to understand the situation is to posit that many protesters exhibited a strong tendency to see Hong Kong as a distinctive nation other than "Chinese," but they were reluctant to call for political independence, probably due to the latter's perceived impossibility.

More broadly speaking, while movement supporters were deeply critical toward the implementation of one country, two systems, they might also find it difficult to conceive of a realistic alternative. Table 7.6 shows the results from the protest onsite surveys conducted on August 31 and December 8, respectively. Both surveys included several items to capture the protesters' attitudes toward one country, two systems. In both surveys, an absolute majority of the respondents strongly agreed that "if the movement fails, it means that one country, two systems is dead even if it nominally exists." Besides, more than 60 percent of the respondents strongly agreed with the statement "this movement makes me feel that Hong Kong people need to consider possibilities beyond one country, two systems."

However, when asked to respond to the statement "If the movement succeeds this time, there is still the possibility of repairing one country, two systems," more than 30 percent of the respondents in both surveys strongly agreed, whereas another 30 percent agreed. Agreement with the statement declined from August to December, probably reflecting the protesters' increasing frustration. Yet the mean score still stood at 3.70 on December 8. It is substantially higher than the midpoint of the scale and signifies an overall inclination to agree with the claim. Even at that stage, ideological self-restraint was still exercised by the majority of the protesters.

Table 7.6. Attitudes toward one country, two systems

	August 31	December 8
If the movement fails, it means one country, two systems is dead even if it nominally exists	80.1 (4.73)	75.6 (4.68)
This movement makes me feel that Hong Kong people need to consider possibilities beyond one country, two systems	63.6 (4.48)	65.5 (4.54)
If the movement succeeds this time, there is still the possibility of repairing one country, two systems	37.8 (3.83)	31.6 (3.70)
N	527	902

Note: Entries are percentages of "strongly agree" with the statements in a five-point Likert scale. Figures in parentheses are mean scores.

Source: Created by the author.

THE EXTENT OF LOCALIST IDENTIFICATION

The phenomenon of ideological self-restraint can be corroborated by surveys of the general public. In a series of polls conducted by the CCPOS of the Chinese University of Hong Kong between June 2019 and May 2020, respondents were asked whether they would support the continuation of one country, two systems, comprehensive and direct governance by mainland China, and Hong Kong independence after 2047. The specified time frame is important here. Respondents were not asked if they would push for a certain goal at the moment, but only about their preference for the constitutional arrangement of Hong Kong after the end of the first fifty years after the handover. The three possibilities were not offered as competing options. Rather, three questions asked the respondents about the three possibilities separately. Respondents could express agreement simultaneously with more than one arrangement.

In the survey in June 2019 (N = 1048), only 14.3 percent of the respondents supported Hong Kong independence, whereas 71.2 percent supported the continuation of one country, two systems. In October 2019 (N = 751), percentage of respondents supporting the continuation of one country, two systems declined to 60.3 percent, but percentage supporting Hong Kong independence increased only slightly to 17.7 percent. In late May 2020 (N = 810), percentage of respondents supporting independence increased slightly again to 19.7 percent, while percentage supporting the continuation of one country, two systems rebounded to 69.3 percent. Support for Hong Kong independence, even when framed as a matter of constitutional arrangement after 2047, had never registered support from more than a quarter of the public during the Anti-ELAB protests.

Admittedly, the percentage of people supporting Hong Kong independence could be higher if one focuses only on movement supporters. In the June 2020 survey, a question asked the respondents if they would support the Anti-ELAB Movement to continue. Only 39.1 percent of the respondents supported the continuation of the movement at that stage. These could be regarded as the hardcore supporters of the movement. Among these people, 41.5 percent would support Hong Kong independence after 2047, whereas 59.2 percent supported the continuation of one country, two systems. The percentage supporting independence after 2047 was substantial, but it was smaller than 50 percent and still lower than the percentage supporting the continuation of one country, two systems.

The same series of surveys also asked respondents about their political inclination, with localists, moderate democrats, radical democrats, centrists, proestablishment, probusiness, pro-China, and no inclination being the options. In June 2019, only 6.9 percent of the respondents claimed to be localists, whereas 30.0 percent and 2.4 percent claimed to be moderate and radical democrats, respectively. In October 2019, 13.6 percent of the respondents claimed to be localists, whereas 38.6 percent and 5.9 percent claimed to be moderate and radical democrats, respectively. In June 2020, the respective figures became 12.7 percent, 34.6 percent, and 4.6 percent. Percentage of respondents claiming to be localists increased over the course of the movement, but not in a linear manner. Besides, the percentage of respondents claiming to be moderate democrats also increased.

We can expect the percentage of self-identified localists to be higher among movement supporters and participants. In fact, in the protest onsite surveys, since all participants could be presumed to be supporters of the prodemocracy movement, the political inclination question adopted a more differentiating set of categories toward the "localist end" of the spectrum. Specifically, respondents were asked to choose among progovernment, centrists, moderate democrats, radical democrats, self-determinists, localists, proindependence, others, and no inclination. Table 7.7 summarizes the results from seven onsite surveys. Percentage of respondents claiming to be moderate democrats indeed declined from 43.0 percent in the July 1 protest to 31.1 percent on August 11 and 34.7 percent on September 8, respectively. There was no further decline, however, and the figures even jumped back to above 43 percent in October. In comparison, there was a largely linear increase in percentage of respondents claiming to be radical democrats, rising from 6.6 percent on July 1 to 15.5 percent on December 8.

Percentages of respondents claiming to be self-determinists, localists and proindependence also increased. If we combine the three percentages, 24.5 percent of the respondents in the July 1 protest onsite survey chose one of these three labels. The figure grew to the highest point of 39.1 percent on September 8. In the December 8 survey, the corresponding number still stood at 38.2 percent. When the three labels are considered separately, percentage of respondents claiming to be proindependence remained low. Only 3.7 percent of the July 1 protesters regarded themselves as proindependence. The figure grew only somewhat to 7.2 percent on December 8. Protesters identifying themselves as self-determinists also increased only slightly from 6.9 percent on July 1 to 9.2 percent on December 8. Respondents claiming

Table 7.7. Self-proclaimed political inclination among the protesters

	Jul. 1	Aug. 4	Aug. 11	Sept. 8	Oct. 1	Oct. 20	Dec. 8
Progovernment	0.2	0.2	0.2	0.3	0.2	0.1	0.0
Centrists	4.0	1.7	1.1	1.5	0.6	0.3	0.4
Moderate democrats	43.0	36.8	31.1	34.7	48.8	43.6	33.7
Radical democrats	6.6	8.4	10.5	9.8	9.2	11.5	15.5
Self-determinists	6.9	8.3	9.0	10.1	10.5	10.2	9.2
Localists	13.9	21.9	21.1	24.0	16.9	16.6	21.8
Proindependence	3.7	6.8	7.4	5.0	3.9	4.9	7.2
Others / no inclination	16.2	10.7	12.1	9.2	7.5	6.8	5.4
N	1169	1272	636	337	640	921	902

Note: Entries are column percentages. The totals do not add up to 100.0 percent because a small number of respondents in each survey answered, "Don't know."

Source: Created by the author.

themselves to be localists registered a larger increase: from 13.9 percent on July 1 to 21.8 percent on December 8.

In other words, when a set of more differentiating labels was used, the majority of movement participants who did not want to take up the label of *democrats* would choose the label of *localists*. While "proindependence" signifies a demand for a concrete constitutional arrangement, and self-determination involves the idea of a referendum for the city's future, localism remains a broader and more ambiguous label. What being a localist entails could be interpreted rather differently by different people, and this might be part of the reasons why it was adopted by more people when compared to self-determinists and proindependence.

Observers might question if there were substantive differences among people who chose to label themselves self-determinists, localists, and proindependence. Table 7.8 thus compared the attitudes exhibited by five groups of protest participants using the December 8 onsite survey, which contained a broader set of attitudinal questions. To simplify the analysis, a radicalism index was created by averaging people's agreement with items 1, 3, and 4 in table 7.2. An affective solidarity index was created by averaging people's agreement with items 6, 7, and 8 in table 7.3, and a guilt feeling index was created by averaging people's agreement with items 1 through 4 in table 7.3. An index on attitude toward one country, two systems was created by the third item in table 7.6 minus the average of the first and second items so that a larger value represents a more positive attitude toward repairing one country, two systems.

Table 7.8 summarizes the analysis. The moderate democrats constituted a distinctive group having relatively lower levels of acceptance toward radicalism, lower levels of affective solidarity with the militant protesters, lower degrees of guilt feelings, and less negative views toward one country, two systems. The other four groups did not significantly differ from each other in degrees of affective solidarity with the militant protesters and guilt feelings. Radical democrats, localists, and proindependence protesters did not differ from each other on acceptance of radicalism, with self-determinists accepting radicalism to a significantly lesser degree when compared to the three groups. More important for the present discussion, compared to the proindependence protesters, the localists had nominally lower mean scores on acceptance of radicalism, guilt feelings, and affective solidarity, and they were significantly less negative toward one country, two systems. Overall speaking, there were meaningful differences in attitudes among the self-determinists, localists, and proindependence protesters.

Table 7.8. Self-proclaimed political inclination and protest attitudes (December 8, 2019)

	Moderate democrats	Radical democrats	Self-determinists	Localists	Proindependence
Radicalism (F = 27.5, p < .001)	4.20	4.54_b	4.45	4.57_b	4.62_b
Affective solidarity (F = 26.8, p < .001)	4.39	4.76_a	4.69_a	4.78_a	4.78_a
Guilt feelings (F = 11.8, p < .001)	4.34	4.56_a	4.56_a	4.65_a	4.72_a
Attitude toward one country, two systems (F = 22.9, p < .00)	–.47	$-.88_a$	-1.07_{ab}	-1.29_b	–1.80

Notes: Entries are mean scores. Entries sharing the same subscript do not differ from each other significantly in posthoc LSD tests.

Source: Created by the author.

In sum, as the Anti-ELAB Movement evolved, tactical and ideological radicalization was accompanied by a slight increase in localist identification and even support for Hong Kong independence. Proindependence sentiments might have been particularly conspicuous on the protest sites due to the ways they were expressed. But when the "majority views" of the movement supporters are considered, the Anti-ELAB Movement had exercised a significant degree of collective self-restraint even into the later stages of the protests. Hong Kong independence, when understood strictly in terms of an active pursuit of secession from China, was not what the movement aimed at, though a gradual shift toward the idea could occur when, in face of a lack of positive response to the demand of democratization, more and more movement supporters abandoned the formula of one country, two systems.

Concluding Remarks

This chapter reviewed the evolution of the Anti-ELAB Movement, focusing particularly on the intertwined issues of solidarity maintenance, tactical and ideological radicalization, and degree and limits of radicalism. Given the analysis and data provided in this chapter, we may argue that the relational dynamics and mechanisms discussed between chapters 2 and 6 were discernible during the Anti-ELAB protests, though the dynamics and mechanisms might also take up distinctive features due to the character of the movement.

Chapter 5 highlighted the role of ideological bridge brokers in negotiating the relationship between the moderate and radical flanks of the prodemocracy movement. This chapter, in parallel, has highlighted the role of Liberate Hong Kong, Revolution of Our Time as a broker frame emerging in the Anti-ELAB Movement. The broker frame helped bring the moderates and militant protesters together under an open and inclusive symbol. It became the "common ground" for movement supporters who might otherwise hold different views regarding preferred tactics and movement goals.

Nonetheless, chapter 5 highlighted the role played by specific and identifiable brokers, such as the political party Demosisto and commentators such as Joseph Lian. These were prominent figures and groups in the public arena in Hong Kong. In contrast, one could not identify prominent activists or groups promoting Liberate Hong Kong, Revolution of Our Time as a broker frame. The activist who coined the slogan was serving his jail sentence, and his supporters might not favor the diversification of the meanings of the slogan. The brokering was accomplished by networked actors in a decentralized process, consistent with studies about the networked coordination of the Anti-ELAB movement (see Cheng & Yuen, 2024; Lee, Liang, et al., 2022; Lee & Fong, 2023; Ting, 2020). Even the state, through criticizing the slogan for indicating the subversive character of the movement, played a role in encouraging movement supporters to articulate alternative readings of "liberate" and "revolution."

Chapter 6 highlighted how indiscriminate state repression had contributed to affective depolarization between the democrats and the localists. In the Anti-ELAB Movement, the state also exercised legal and physical repression of the protests. The state's nonconciliatory approach followed the path it had already undertaken before 2019. And given China's strong suspicion about foreign intervention, the protesters' actions on the international front had probably further consolidated the state's resolve to take the hardline stance.

On the ground and during the months of the protests, repression was executed mainly by the police force. While the state and the police might regard their actions as targeting only the violent protesters, the moderate protesters also experienced the repression indirectly through various ways, including the witnessing of police violence via live broadcasting, the experience with tear gas being fired at their neighborhood, and participation in the "evacuation" at the end of peaceful protests. Although the experiences of the militant and moderate protesters cannot be equated with each other, there was a sense in which a common experience of repression existed. Besides, to the extent that the moderates did not suffer as much as the militant protesters did, the moderates developed feelings of guilt. It became an important basis of affective solidarity inside the movement.

At the same time, the relational dynamics were punctuated by important events. The Umbrella Movement and the Mongkok civil unrest, together with the elections held afterward, urged political actors to reevaluate public opinion and the political reality. During the Anti-ELAB protests, the charge into the LegCo Building on July 1 tested public sympathy toward militant protest actions. The absence of a strong backlash illustrated the force of the ethics of solidarity inside the movement. It also led to the realization that many movement supporters were sympathetic, if not necessarily supportive, toward militant actions. The Yuen Long Attack on July 21 diverted public attention from the CLO protests and pushed up public outrage to another level. It strengthened protesters' distrust against the police and perceived unreliability of the police force as an adjudicator of conflicts contributed directly to the emergence of vigilantism. The Prince Edward MTR station incident on August 31 galvanized public perception of police violence, even leading to rumors of fatalities due to police actions. In short, all these incidents played a role in consolidating or sometimes even broadening the movement's public support. They also played a role in urging the movement supporters and participants to reconsider the justifiability of various protest tactics and reevaluate the degree to which their fellow protesters and the public were receptive toward more militant forms of protests.

Chapters 4 to 6 discussed the trend of the mainstreaming of localism. The democrats-localists divide was not prominent during the Anti-ELAB Movement, but what we see is the widespread acceptance of militant protests. There was also an increasing percentage of people identifying themselves as "localists." As analyzed in previous chapters, the mainstreaming of localism involves the smoothening of localist ideas and discourses, as well as the gradual shifts in the moderates' and the general public's latitude of acceptance. In the Anti-ELAB Movement, the development of Liberate Hong Kong, Revolution of Our Time into a broker frame involved a certain degree of deradicalization of the slogan through the articulation of more moderate interpretations. Militant actions were promoted together with efforts to articulate the norms and principles governing them. These processes facilitated the moderates' uptake of the militant ideas and actions.

Ultimately, although proindependence sentiments found the space of expression in the Anti-ELAB protests, independence was not the aim of the majority of protesters. There were limits to ideological radicalization. The latitude of acceptance of the moderates could not be shifted too abruptly, and many of them remained uncomfortable with the idea of pursuing independence. The five demands remained the common denominator. Interestingly, although international lobbying might be seen by the Chinese state as a radical move, the international arena actually had a moderating impact on movement ideologies. Activists in the international front acknowledged that they had to refrain from talking in terms of independence and stick to the idea of democratization when engaging international actors, since foreign governments are unlikely to support an independence movement in a foreign country (F. Lee, 2023c).

To conclude, a set of relational dynamics parallel to those occurring in the period between 2016 and 2019 were in place in the Anti-ELAB protests, even though there can be other aspects and dynamics of the movement that are beyond the scope of the present analysis. The concrete and empirical manifestations of the dynamics and mechanisms inevitably differ from case to case, but the analysis should have shown that they constitute useful tools to make sense of the prodemocracy movement in Hong Kong.

Chapter 8

Conclusion

This book has examined the development of the prodemocracy movement in Hong Kong mainly between the Umbrella Movement in 2014 and the Anti-ELAB protests in 2019, with the aim of not only demonstrating the continuity between the two peaks of mobilization, but also explaining why the Anti-ELAB Movement emerged with a distinctive set of characteristics, including its much broader appeal, higher degree of tactical radicalism, and the emphasis on internal solidarity. The analysis follows a relational approach and focuses particularly on three arenas of interactions: the interaction between the state and the prodemocracy movement, the interaction among various factions and groups within the prodemocracy movement, and the interaction between the prodemocracy movement and the public. It also pays attention to the role of significant event clusters in shaping actors' perceptions of reality and strategies.

Without repeating the details of the analysis, we can summarize the main outcomes of the relational dynamics examined between chapter 2 and chapter 6 under two headings, namely, the mainstreaming of localism and affective depolarization within the prodemocracy movement. Other authors have also talked about the "mainstreaming" of localism in Hong Kong in the 2010s, but they typically referred merely to the entrance of localist ideas into the mainstream public arena (e.g., Kaeding & Wang-Kaeding, 2023). In this book, the term *mainstreaming* has a more substantive meaning: it refers to both (1) the mainstream society's increased receptivity toward localism and militant protests and (2) localist activists' and ideological brokers' attempts to develop relatively less radical versions of localism as they interacted with the state, the moderate democrats, and the public. Certainly, even tuned-down versions of localism are relatively more radical—in the sense of deviating from prevalent norms or demanding more fundamental change—than the views of the moderate democrats, for example, even tuned-down versions of localism could involve an urge for disruptive or even violent protests under certain conditions (as opposed to an emphasis on the principle of non-violence). But the tuning down helped localism to fall into the latitude of acceptance of more ordinary citizens.

Affective depolarization, meanwhile, refers to the process through which the radical and moderate camps of the prodemocracy movement became less antagonistic toward each other over time. When the localists emerged as a political force in the early to mid-2010s, they tended to engage in adversarial framing against the democrats. The Umbrella Movement and its aftermath witnessed increasing conflicts between the two camps. But the relationship started to become less antagonistic between 2016 and 2019 due to several dynamics and mechanisms, including the aforementioned mainstreaming of localism, the work of ideological brokers who constructed possible common grounds for the two sides, and indiscriminate state repression, which put the localists and the democrats into the same position of being victims of repression and outsiders of established institutions. Mainstreaming of localism and internal affective depolarization help explain certain key characteristics of the Anti-ELAB Movement, though the evolution of those key characteristics also needs to be understood with the dynamics within the Anti-ELAB Movement itself.

In social movement research, the relational approach is often contrasted with more structuralist accounts that emphasize the roles of opportunity and mobilizing structures. While some early studies of local social movements in Hong Kong have also drawn upon such key concepts (Lui & Chiu, 2000), more recent studies about the prodemocracy movement have generally rejected the adequacy of the structuralist approach (e.g., Lee & Chan, 2018). This is first and foremost due to the basic fact that Hong Kong experienced the rapid growth of social mobilization when the opportunity structure was significantly contracting. Therefore, without explicitly claiming to follow a relational perspective, various authors have also emphasized how prodemocracy protests evolved in Hong Kong in a dynamic and contingent manner based on the interactions among actors at the local, national, and international levels (Tang & Cheng, 2024). Against this background, to further explicate the distinctiveness and contribution of this book's analysis, we may compare the current analysis with two pieces of scholarly works that attempted to systematically relate the Anti-ELAB Movement to the Umbrella Movement.

In a journal article, Mingsho Ho (2020) linked the Umbrella Movement to the Anti-ELAB Movement through examining how the latter learned from the former. He identified three major mechanisms of learning. First, the occupation zones during the Umbrella Movement served as social laboratories in which new ideas about protest actions were conceived. Specifically, "the ideas of more evenly spreading the campaign spatially and escalating the confrontation physically and symbolically were already brewing during the Umbrella Movement" (Ho, 2020: 719). Second, the aftermath of the Umbrella Movement witnessed the formation of numerous post-Umbrella organizations, including professional groups, community organizations, and so on. These provided part of the mobilizing structures for the Anti-ELAB Movement. Third, movement activists, politicians, and supporters learned from the "failure" of the Umbrella Movement and recognized the significance of decentralized decision-making and solidarity. The ethos of "no division" between the moderates and the radicals emerged, which entailed greater tolerance for disruptive and even violent actions.

While Ho (2020) highlighted several linkages between the Umbrella Movement and the Anti-ELAB protests, the concept of "learning" begs the question of why certain ideas were articulated as the "lessons" from the Umbrella Movement. Take decentralized decision making as the example, various scholars examining the Umbrella Movement had commented on how the trend of decentralization undermined the movement's capability to effectively respond to the changing environment and negotiate with the government (A. Chow, 2019; Lee & Chan, 2018). Decentralization contributed to a tactical freeze (Tufekci, 2017). Hence, it is plausible for one to argue that, based on the experience of the Umbrella Movement, one actually needs centralized decision-making mechanisms, instead of even more decentralization. So, what made decentralization the takeaway from the Umbrella Movement?

Besides, even if a lesson is indisputable, there is still the question of what ensured learning. People can fail to learn even when the "lesson" is clear. For instance, most people probably would not argue against solidarity, but for a period of time after the Umbrella Movement, polarization between the democrats and the localists actually became more serious. People did not learn the lesson of solidarity automatically and immediately.

The above does not dismiss Ho's (2020) analysis. How movements learn from the past is a theoretically legitimate and important question. But even if we focus on what and how the Anti-ELAB Movement learned from the Umbrella Movement, one needs to pay attention to the relational dynamics happening between the two movements so as to understand why certain lessons were being constructed and taken up, whereas other plausible lessons were ignored or dismissed. The relational perspective and a more in-depth analysis of the years between the two movements could plug the gaps in the analysis.

In their book-length treatment of the Anti-ELAB Movement and its historical origin, Cheng and Yuen (2024) constructed a "theory of mediated threat" for understanding the evolution of the forms of prodemocracy protests in Hong Kong since the early 2000s. They emphasized that threats, instead of opportunities, were the main driver of prodemocracy protests in Hong Kong. Yet threats do not simply exist objectively; they have to be articulated, constructed, mediated, and perceived. Threats play two explanatory roles in their work. First, as generalized and existential threats increase, people perceive that the costs of doing nothing increase, hence they become more likely to take actions. That is, stronger threat perceptions lead to higher levels of social mobilization. Second and more important, whether supporters of different political groups and factions share similar threat perceptions is related to the degree of cohesion of protest actions. Protests are more cohesive when there is threat perception alignment among different factions. Following the second point, they argue that alignment in threat perceptions holds the key to understanding the difference between the Umbrella Movement and the Anti-ELAB Movement: the decline in disparity of threat perceptions held by various groups contributed to the cohesiveness of the latter.

One strength of the work by Cheng and Yuen (2024) is that their analysis covered a longer time period—the transformation of protest mobilization in posthandover Hong Kong as opposed to the present book's focus on the 2010s. Nevertheless, despite Cheng and Yuen's (2024) emphasis on the idea of constructed and mediated threats, their book offers relatively little analysis on the relevant discourses about the "threats" facing Hong Kong developed by the localists and the democrats both in the period between the Umbrella Movement and the Anti-ELAB Movement and during the Anti-ELAB Movement. The two authors did provide a brief examination of the aftermath of the Umbrella Movement and the happenings in the four years prior to the Anti-ELAB Movement. Several key points emphasized by the present book, such as indiscriminate repression by the state and changes in citizens' tactical inclination, were mentioned. But overall, their account on exactly why and how threat perceptions held by different factions within the prodemocracy movement started to align after 2014 is not particularly clear. Besides, from the perspective of the current book, it is also not entirely clear if "threat perception alignment" should be the most important out-come of the dynamics in the years between the Umbrella Movement and the Anti-ELAB Movement.

The current analysis puts more emphasis on the articulation of dis-courses and processes other than threat perception alignment. Mainstream-ing of localism is seen as shaping how people understand what "militant protests" refer to and preparing people for discussions about the norms that should constrain and/or guide militant actions. Common experience of state repression is seen as leading to the beginning of a trend of affective depolarization before 2019, which constituted the initial condition for soli-darity in the Anti-ELAB protests. All these do not mean that alignment of threat perceptions is irrelevant, but the relational dynamics between 2014 and 2019 and its outcomes were richer and more multifaceted.

In short, the current analysis does not completely overturn other authors' understandings of the relationship between the Umbrella Move-ment and the Anti-ELAB Movement (also see Tang & Cheng, 2024), but to borrow a metaphor used by Chiu and Siu (2020) in their overview of Hong Kong society, this book has provided a "high-definition account" of the development of the prodemocracy movement in Hong Kong in the 2010s.

In addition to the linkage between the Umbrella Movement and the Anti-ELAB Movement, this study provides a unique perspective on localism and movement radicalization in Hong Kong in the 2010s. Among scholars on Hong Kong politics, there is a consensus that the rise of localist sentiments in the early 2010s could be attributed to the threat of mainlandization under forceful assimilation by the state, as well as the negative consequences of social and economic integration on the Hong Kong society (Kong, 2017; So & Ip, 2019). These sentiments were then articulated into a range of localist perspectives by the cognitive praxis of various activists and groups. Yet none of the perspectives had achieved a hegemonic status among the localists. The "localists" remained a loosely defined faction.

Scholars had examined localism in several ways. Some focused on criticizing the most "toxic" form of right-wing localism (Ip, 2020), whereas others tried to explicate the range of perspectives articulated by prominent authors and groups (Carrico, 2022). Yet others tried to identify the themes commonly adopted by self-proclaimed localist groups (Ng & Kennedy, 2021), whereas some treated *localism* as a broad term, covering even the moderate democrats (Lam, 2018; Lo, 2019). While these approaches are useful for specific purposes, none seems to satisfactorily answer the question of how localism gained traction among more and more Hong Kong citizens over time. This book argues that the increasing positive attitude toward localism held by the Hong Kong public at large needs to be understood in terms of how various actors interacted with each other. In contrast to looking at the supposed "core content" of localist thinking and practices, this book examines the forms of localism articulated at the interfaces between the localists and other actors. Not many Hong Kong people were fervent followers of localist discourses in the online environment or had read the works of major localist authors. But people would be exposed to the forms of localism articulated at and communicated through the interfaces.

At the interface between the democrats and the localists, we saw the articulation of democratic self-determination by Demosisto. Demosisto was not the first to put forward the idea of self-determination in association with Hong Kong's future. However, their *democratic* self-determination was a softened version because it put relatively less emphasis on Hongkongers being a distinctive nation. With the timeline set at 2047, it was presented as a move not violating the Basic Law. Of course, the Chinese state refused to accept the distinction between self-determination and independence. But within the prodemocracy movement, democratic self-determination became an idea that even the moderate democrats found it hard to reject. Self-determination could be seen as a bridging or broker frame through which supporters of democratization could relate themselves to other localist ideas.

Key localist figures and groups also interacted with the public without the brokerage or mediation by other political groups. This book treats the public performance of Edward Leung as the most illustrative. In both his electoral campaign in 2016 and media representations of him (e.g., the documentary *Lost in the Fumes*), a powerful affective framing of young localists as "the weak" who were willing to fight against the giant and make sacrifices for their beloved city of Hong Kong was promulgated. At the same time, Edward Leung maintained a degree of strategic ambiguity on his political program when speaking in the electoral arena. He also adjusted his discourses in response to criticisms from others. Facing Edward Leung, the Hong Kong public was invited not to judge and agree with a fully developed perspective on Hong Kong politics; rather, the public was invited to sympathize with a youngster who was perhaps immature yet genuine and reflective.

At the interface with the state, localist activists—and the self-determinists too—were willing to compromise, such as by signing the form declaring one's allegiance to the Basic Law when running in elections. The concession did not stop the state from disqualifying them, but it further consolidated their positioning as "the weak," and it made the state's act of excluding them from the political institutions even more illegitimate in the eyes of the prodemocracy citizens. It could strengthen public perception of the impossibility of having genuine freedom and democracy unless there is a radical shift in China's approach to Hong Kong or a radical change in Hong Kong's political status.

Considering the above, we can see that what the public was exposed to were forms of localisms that had their radical edges smoothened to a certain extent. Besides, the affective appeal of localism was arguably stronger than its cognitive appeal. As Kaeding and Wang-Kaeding (2023) explained, the affective appeal was crucial to understanding how localist discourses could generate a sense of community among sympathetic citizens. Meanwhile, localism remained a broad notion that can be defined differently. People did not find it necessary to reject localism just because they found some forms of localism problematic. Instead, they could define localism in their own ways, just as protesters in the Anti-ELAB Movement adopted the slogan Liberate Hong Kong, Revolution of Our Time but interpreted it in various ways.

The above discussion has implications on how we understand radicalization of the prodemocracy movement in Hong Kong in the 2010s. In a typical protest cycle, radicalization is often led by the emergence of radical groups when protest groups proliferate and start to differentiate themselves (Tarrow, 1998). However, radicalization of the prodemocracy movement in Hong Kong in the 2010s was only partly driven by the rise of radical groups. The state's reluctance to make concessions on the issue of democratization led to the radicalization of the moderates, which was already apparent in the Umbrella Movement (Lee & Chan, 2018). Between 2016 and 2019, the state's indiscriminate repression led to further convergence between the democrats and the localists, though the moderate-radical distinction did not entirely disappear (Au et al., 2023).

Theoretically, della Porta (2018) distinguished among three pathways toward radicalization. Radicalization could be driven by the instrumental rationale of raising the costs for the powerholders when more moderate means are ineffective. It could be driven by ideological development, as more disruptive protest tactics could be seen as required for movements seeking more fundamental social and political changes. Radicalization could also be driven by the concern of solidarity, as people come to adopt more disruptive or even violent means in order to stand with others. In Hong Kong's prodemocracy movement, radicalization could be seen as originally driven by instrumental concerns. When Benny Tai proposed the idea of Occupy Central in early 2013, his writing focused on the need of a civil disobedience campaign largely in instrumental terms (Lee & Chan, 2018). The failure of the Umbrella Movement, however, led to the rise of localism and even calls for Hong Kong independence. At this stage, radicalization became partly driven by ideology. Nevertheless, facing indiscriminate state repression and with the efforts of ideological brokers, the prodemocracy movement became more cohesive. A high degree of solidarity emerged in the Anti-ELAB Movement. Radicalization proceeded through the solidaristic path (Tang & Cheng, 2021).

The relational dynamics among the state, actors inside the prodemocracy movement, and the public thus drove the process of radicalization through a combination of pathways. Nonetheless, radicalization at too quick a pace could still alienate the public. Hence, radicalization of protests was typically associated with the phenomenon of restraint. Lee and Chan (2018) argued that the proposal of Occupy Central was a case of radicalization with self-restraint: while the earliest writing by Benny Tai leaned toward the use of civil disobedience as a way to force the government to make concession, the rhetoric of OCLP quickly shifted toward persuasive civil obedience. In the Anti-ELAB protests, the phenomenon of collective restraint can be discerned when movement supporters tried to articulate norms and rules that militant tactics such as vigilantism and vandalism needed to follow. Between the Umbrella Movement and the Anti-ELAB protests, radicaliza-tion was also constrained by the need of localist activists to respond to the moderate democrats and the public, who were concerned about the perceived xenophobic character of some forms of localism and the seeming absence of any moral considerations underlying militant tactics.

Notably, as Lee, Yuen, and others (2021) pointed out, what demanded explanation in the Anti-ELAB Movement was not so much radicalization per se as public sympathy toward radical tactics. Part of the explanation resided in the stepwise radicalization process occurring before 2019. At any given point in time, the public would see a range of actions as acceptable and a range of actions as beyond the boundary of acceptability. But each major protest event since the early 2010s had led people to become familiar with or even sympathetic toward certain types of actions, thus shifting the latitude of acceptance gradually.

Similarly, there was a gradual shift toward acceptance of more radical ideas among the Hong Kong public. The Umbrella Movement called for genuine popular election of the chief executive of the Hong Kong govern-ment within the framework stipulated by the Basic Law. Its inability to force concession from the government triggered the growth of localism and the articulation of Hong Kong nationalism by young activists. Although the majority of the public between 2014 and 2019 did not support independence, they believed in the right of people to discuss the idea. Independence was treated by Hong Kong citizens as within the sphere of legitimate controversy.

The Anti-ELAB Movement began as a protest campaign against a specific bill. It evolved into a movement with five demands, including democratization and investigation of police abuse of power. Independence was neither the trigger nor the most common denominator among the protesters. Nonetheless, similar to the Umbrella Movement, people were pushed to consider alternatives when they found their demands falling onto deaf ears. Over the years, movement-state interaction made more and more people to see genuine democratization as impossible within the framework of one country, two systems. Each major protest event led more people to recognize the need for more fundamental change.

Up till this point, I have discussed how this book's analysis contributed to our understanding of social movement and politics in Hong Kong. But this book is not only about the Anti-ELAB Movement or the Hong Kong society. It also aims at engaging in dialogues with general theoretical issues in the study of social movements. The next section will discuss the theoretical lessons derivable from this study, especially on issues such as movement abeyance, relational dynamics, the relationship between protests and elections in hybrid regimes, and the idea of event clusters. Afterwards, the final section will return to the Hong Kong context and discuss how this book's approach might inform the analysis of Hong Kong society after the enactment of the National Security Law (NSL) in 2020.

Theoretical Reflections

This study begins with the premise that the years between the Umbrella Movement and the Anti-ELAB protests—especially the latter part between 2016 and 2019—constituted a period of abeyance during which public support for the prodemocracy camp and participation in protest actions declined significantly. Motivated by an attempt to explain continuity between peaks of mobilization, the concept of abeyance was originally proposed as a holding process by which resources, networks, values, and identities are preserved for the next wave of mobilization (Taylor, 1989). Over the years, research on movement abeyance has broadened its focus from the role of formal organizations and core activists to actors and processes in a more diverse range of arenas (e.g., Geha, 2019; Lee, Chan, & Chen, 2020; Yates, 2015; Zihnnioglu, 2023). However, there is still a presumption that social movements tend to turn inward and refrain from engaging in mobilizing the public or interacting with other agents (Sawyers & Meyers, 1999). This emphasis on abeyance as a holding process for preservation is shared by various researchers commenting on the linkage between the Umbrella Movement and the Anti-ELAB Movement in Hong Kong (Lam, 2018; Ma & Cheng, 2023).

This study differs from the above literature by seeing the abeyance period as involving not only a holding process but also a process of continual interactions and possible transformation. When an unfavorable environment sets in at the end of a protest wave or a major campaign, activists may reflect upon past experiences and reevaluate their strategies and frames. They may reassess their relationships with other actors, including the general public, the state, and other "factions" within the same movement. Therefore, abeyance can be a period during which tactical innovation occurs, new alliances are built, frames are transformed, and new cultural codes are produced (Fominaya, 2015; Jacobsson & Sorborn, 2015). As a result, the happenings during the period of abeyance not only provide the bases for a new wave of mobilization to occur when the environment changes; in cases where the new wave of mobilization differs from the previous wave significantly in its character, explanations for the differences could also be found from the happenings in the abeyance period. Hence a perspective emphasizing transformation amidst abeyance would be useful.

To facilitate a systematic analysis, this study adopts a relational approach, especially that articulated by Alimi and colleagues (2012), and emphasizes three intertwined arenas of interactions: interactions within a social movement, interactions between the movement and the public, and interactions between the movement and the state. For within-movement interactions, instead of having formal organizations at the center, movement abeyance in mid-2010s Hong Kong occurred alongside the trend of decentralization of the prodemocracy movement. The case differs from both the classic analysis of Taylor (1989) and Valiente's (2015) argument about the prevalence of new and networked actors in the abeyance processes in nondemocracies. For Valiente (2015), social movements are typically sustained by new groups and activists in authoritarian contexts because the most prominent organizations from the previous wave of protests are likely to have been suppressed by the state. This might correspond to the Hong Kong experience after 2020, as to be discussed later in this chapter, but for the period being analyzed in this book, the emergence of new political groups and the formation of a decentralized movement arena were driven by dynamics already set in place through earlier movement campaigns.

Theoretically, the present case illustrates how the previous wave of mobilization sets the stage for and feeds into the subsequent abeyance process. During the period of abeyance, movement actors are responding to both the unfavorable contemporary environment and the issues derived from the previous wave of protests. Jacobsson and Sorborn's (2015) analysis of Swedish left-libertarian activists, for example, emphasized how radical activists needed to reflect upon past experiences and learned from the failure of the previous protests. Similarly, the rise of localism in Hong Kong after 2014 was driven partly by the perceived failure of the Umbrella Movement. Nonetheless, the definition of localism was contested. Various groups—both old and new ones—had to consider their relationship with the emerging localist sentiments. The result was the remapping of the movement and political field.

In this process, movement actors tried to position themselves strategically in the political field under reconfiguration. This book's analysis discusses the interaction between the radical and moderate flanks of the prodemocracy movement. On the one hand, observers can indeed identify groups and activists that clearly belonged to one of the two camps. But on the other hand, this book highlights some of the actors who located themselves between the two camps. These actors played the role of ideological brokers. More specifically, they were mainly articulators who negotiated common positions for the two sides (von Bulow, 2011). Previous social movement research has pointed out the possibility of frame reconstruction and innovation during the period of movement abeyance (Geha, 2019). This study shows that frame innovation can result from discursive brokerage.

Although low levels of protest activities and participation are the defining characteristics of movement abeyance, this study argues that there could still be interactions between a movement and its supporters as well as the public at large during periods of low levels of mobilization. Even without participating actively in street politics, citizens can remain attentive spectators; that is, they pay attention to ongoing events and form their views about the events and the actors involved.[1] Schudson (1999) argued that conventional conceptions of the constantly active and informed citizenry can be unrealistic even in a democracy. Instead, many people in democratic societies act as monitorial citizens. They pay *some*, but not too much, attention to public affairs in order to monitor social happenings and the operation of powerful institutions. They are normally inactive, but they would act when the need arises. Therefore, the appearance of inactivity does not entail the lack of concern.

Whether the public can be effectively mobilized in the next wave of mobilization would depend on the evolution of public opinion during abeyance. If a movement is concerned about maintaining or even building public support, it would have to consider adjusting its performance and discourses in order to appeal to the general public. In the case of antiglobalization activism in Sweden analyzed by Jacobsson and Sorborn (2015), left-libertarian activists tried to regain public trust, and that required them to reconsider their militant tactics. In this book, the moderate democrats in the 2010s had to react to increasing level of public sympathy toward the localists, whereas the localists had to react to the overall preference for order among the mainstream public.

Other than participation in collective actions, public opinion can be expressed or represented through numerous means, including opinion polls, media reports, and elections. Elections can become particularly important when movement activists try to enter the formal political institutions. Activists may want to run in elections for various reasons, ranging from obtaining the political power and material resources associated with formal political positions, to gaining more chances to promote their views inside the formal political institutions and through the mass media. We will further discuss the significance of elections as part of event clusters below. Here, the important point to note is that an activist would be compelled to face the voting public when one runs in an election. The logic of electoral competition could affect the way the activist frames his/her messages. This, of course, could in turn depend on the electoral system in place (e.g., single-seat-single-vote vs. proportional representation) and the aim of the candidate (e.g., simply participating or actually trying to win as many votes as possible). But there is the possibility that activists running in elections need to make their messages more "mainstream" so as to appeal to a broader segment of the voting public.

The relational approach also emphasizes the interaction between the movement and the state. The state is sometimes treated in extant research as a relatively stable "context." For instance, in Valiente's (2015) discussion of movement abeyance in nondemocracies, the repressive state is largely a contextual parameter. Certainly, if the state consistently adopts a set of political and social control strategies over a period of time, then the state would look like a stable structure from the observer's perspective. But theoretically, the state is as an actor with its own agency (Bosi, 2008). In the Hong Kong experience, identifying the state's strategy is crucial for understanding specific movement campaigns and the prodemocracy movement at large. The ending of the Umbrella Movement cannot be properly understood without paying attention to the state's counterframing and strategy of attrition (Lee & Chan, 2018; Yuen & Cheng, 2017). The fact that the prodemocracy movement entered a period of abeyance before 2019 was itself the outcome of legal and electoral repression by the state. The perception that state repression of the prodemocracy movement was indiscriminate contributed to less antagonistic interactions within the prodemocracy movement.

Even if we restrict the focus to nondemocracies, it is important to acknowledge that different authoritarian states can employ different approaches to exercise political control, and the same authoritarian state may change its approach over time. Such differences and changes in state strategies have direct implications on the strength and characteristics of social movements. The Chinese state, for instance, had adopted a strategy of limited and controlled liberalization in the 2000s, which facilitated the growth of civil society organizations, investigative journalism, cause lawyering, and popular protests in mainland China. A contentious public sphere was formed as a result (Lei, 2018; Repnikova, 2017). But the development of a contentious public sphere could in turn impinge on state strategies. The trend of liberalization was reversed since the early 2010s, especially after Xi Jinping came to power. It led to new forms of individualized protests supported by civil society organizations in a covert manner (Fu, 2017). The relational approach provides a good way to examine such dynamic evolution of contentious politics.

The three arenas of interactions are interconnected and mutually influence each other. The state's strategies can shape the interactions within the movement as well as the movement-public relationship, and vice versa. The interactions can also be shaped by the occurrence of significant events. The interactional dynamic is therefore contingent. This book mainly covers the five-year period between two major movement campaigns. But as the beginning section of chapter 2 has illustrated, the occurrence of the Umbrella Movement could also be placed against the background of both within-movement interactions and movement-state interactions in the preceding years. Similarly, if the timeline is extended to after 2019, one can see how the Anti-ELAB protests and the subsequent enactment of the NSL altered the politics of social movement tremendously, yet the continual evolution of contentious politics in Hong Kong can still be examined through the relational approach.

Both the Umbrella Movement and the Anti-ELAB Movement are hugely important events for Hong Kong. Event is a key element in social movement analysis that emphasizes contingencies and ruptures. The concepts of critical events (Staggenborg, 1993) and transformative events (McAdam & Sewell, 2001) point toward unpredicted and shocking events that significantly alter people's perceptions of reality and lead to changes in social and cultural structures, thereby shaping the trajectory of history. What constitutes an event worthy of being singled out and analyzed is a matter of judgment and is probably tied to the temporal dimension adopted in an analysis. In the case of Hong Kong, if one examines the development from the 1960s to the 2020s, one might consider the 1967 urban riot, the 1989 mobilization to support the Beijing student movement, the 2003 July 1 protest, the 2014 Umbrella Movement, and the 2019 Anti-ELAB protests as the key transformative events (Lee, 2019). All of these are peaks of social mobilization. But if one zooms into a shorter period of time, one might identify additional events that played significant roles in the dynamics between two peaks of mobilization. This book sees the Mongkok civil unrest as such an event.

Theoretically, we may use primary and secondary critical events to refer to the two types of events respectively. The primary critical events, as the extant literature stresses, are typically unanticipated large-scale protests, disturbances, or uprisings that lead to fundamental shifts in the ways actors interact with each other in the relational field. The changes brought about are paradigmatic. The secondary critical events can also be unanticipated protests and disturbances, but they do not necessarily involve large-scale mobilization. Compared to the primary critical events, the secondary critical events are relatively less shocking. However, a secondary critical event can still lead to important adjustment in political actors' perceptions of reality and strategies. It can further strengthen or crystallize tendencies already set in place through the previous primary critical event. A secondary critical event has the capacity to shape the outcome of relational dynamics during a period of abeyance, thereby shaping the characteristics of the subsequent peak of mobilization.

Primary and secondary critical events are proposed as sensitizing concepts here. It is a matter of the researcher's judgment of what constitutes a primary or a secondary event in a specific study. However, the distinction between primary and secondary critical events should be helpful for constructing a richer eventful history of social development without compelling researchers to treat all events as having the same level of significance and influence. In the case of posthandover Hong Kong, the notion of secondary critical events should allow scholars to acknowledge the significance of protest events such as the Mongkok civil unrest, the Anti-National Education campaign in 2012, and the Antiexpress Rail Movement in 2010, without treating them as equivalent to the Umbrella Movement and the Anti-ELAB protests in terms of significance and impact. When analyzing a specific protest campaign, primary and secondary events may also be used to refer to the broader campaign itself and the subevents that significantly shaped the cause of the campaign, such as the role of the Yuen Long Attack (a secondary critical event) in the Anti-ELAB protests (a primary critical event).

Another aspect of this book's analysis of events is the prominent place of elections. There are at least three different ways to consider the relationship between protests and elections. The first is to treat them as parallel events having separate effects on people and society. Different from critical protest events, elections are preannounced and anticipated. Elections in specific social and political contexts can be framed in specific ways. In Hong Kong, LegCo elections—before the various "reforms" after 2019—were generally framed as a competition between the prodemocracy camp and the progovernment or pro-China camp (Ma, 2017). LegCo elections were therefore occasions when the struggle between Hong Kong and mainland China on the issue of democratization was foregrounded. Empirical research thus shows that elections could affect how Hong Kong people perceived the relationship between their Hong Kong and Chinese identities (Lee & Chan, 2024).

However, in the present study, significant protests and elections were not parallel events; they were related to each other in important ways. The election-protest nexus has received much research attention in the past two decades. Researchers have noted how elections might affect protest activities in different circumstances (e.g., Raisi, 2021; Trejo, 2014), and vice versa (e.g., El-Mallakh, 2020). Following the dynamics of contention approach, McAdam and Tarrow (2010) noted six mechanisms that can link movements and elections together, including the possibility of social movements "taking the electoral option."

For the prodemocracy movement in Hong Kong, "taking the electoral option" is arguably the "natural" strategy: the crux of democratization is the institutionalization of democratic elections, and once partial democratization had begun, it would be sensible for the prodemocracy movement to get into the formal political arena to push for further democratization. As a matter of fact, since the early 1990s, forming political parties to take part in such elections was the prodemocracy movement's primary strategy to push for further democratization (Sing, 2000). Street politics became more significant only after the transfer of sovereignty as the progress of democratization became stagnant and the capability of the democrats to effect political change via the legislature was undermined. Nonetheless, the electoral arena remained important because of the resources associated with seats in the legislature (and the District Council) as well as the recognition that changes in the political system would inevitably have to pass through the formal political institutions. Therefore, it was not surprising that both the young leaders of the Umbrella Movement and the localist groups emerged after the Umbrella Movement were active in the electoral arena in 2015 and 2016.

Movement participation in elections had two main consequences. First, movement activists have the strategic need to adjust the framing of their ideologies and demands to improve their electoral prospect. Przeworski and Sprague's (1986) study of European working-class parties in the early twentieth century noted that the parties found it impossible to win elections based on support from the working class alone. Hence the parties softened their programs. Yet such a move alienated some of their original supporters. In the present case, the "softened" presentation of localism by Edward Leung in the 2016 by-election did not damage his electoral prospect. It was, instead, a key for his surprisingly good vote return. This may be explained by three factors: (1) the absence of another "radical option" in the by-election, (2) Leung's softening of localism mainly involved an affective framing of the localists as the weak and the nonexpression, instead of rejection, of radical ideas such as Hong Kong independence, and (3) at the time of the 2016 by-election, the size of localist support was very small when compared to the size of the support for the prodemocracy movement as a whole. The first two factors mean that the localist supporters were unlikely to see Leung's discursive efforts as a betrayal, and the third factor implies that, even if the softening of localism might alienate some localist supporters, the loss was likely to be much smaller than the gain. In any case, the theoretical point here is that, while movement parties generally have the need to soften their ideologies in elections, various conditions can shape the impact of this move.

Second, the performance of movement activists in elections under nondemocratic settings may trigger state responses. The surprisingly good performance of Edward Leung in the 2016 by-election was followed by the state banning his participation in the LegCo election later in the same year. This opened the floodgate for disqualifying the candidacy of other candidates in an increasingly wider range of elections. Outside the period analyzed in this book, after prodemocracy politicians and activists won a landslide victory in the 2019 District Council elections and threatened to capture more than half of the seats of the legislature in 2020, the state took the more extreme measure of first postponing the 2020 elections (in the name of COVID-19 pandemic), and then put forward a "reform" of the election system which severely reduced the democratic character of the legislature. Even the most moderate prodemocracy parties were barred from participating in elections. The move changed the nature and significance of elections in Hong Kong.

Certainly, it does not mean that all nondemocratic states would respond to positive electoral performance of the opposition in the same way. In the literature on elections in hybrid regimes, many scholars are concerned with the conditions under which "electoral revolutions" might occur (Kadivar, 2017; Knutz & Thompson, 2009; Smith, 2014). It is commonly agreed that the introduction of even partially democratic elections could change the political dynamics inside electoral authoritarian regimes, leading to the growth of oppositional forces and the potential of democratization (Shirah, 2016). In one sense, the political development in Hong Kong up to 2020 was consistent with this argument: the democrats were highly unlikely to control the LegCo given the electoral rules, but the political dynamics in the 2010s generated unprecedentedly strong voter support for the oppositional forces in the 2019 District Council elections. Combined with the piecemeal progress the democrats had made in the functional constituencies of the LegCo, there was arguably a real possibility for the democrats to take control of the LegCo in year 2020. However, the Chinese state was both willing and strong enough to exercise a combination of legal and electoral repression to prevent an "electoral revolution" from happening.

In addition to movement participation in elections and how elections become another arena in which a social movement interacts with the state, this study illustrates one more possible way to understand the linkage between protests and elections; namely, an election can become an occasion for people to ascertain the significance and impact of a major protest event when the election is held within a short period of time after the protest. Lee and Chan's (2011) analysis of the 2003 District Council elections in Hong Kong, held a few months after the 2003 July 1 protest, had provided an earlier example. In the current study, the 2015 District Council elections, held about nine months after the Umbrella Movement, as well as the 2016 LegCo by-election, held only a few weeks after the Mongkok civil unrest, played the same role. In each case, the society was concerned with how the protest would affect the electoral outcome, and the electoral outcome was used as evidence of the impact of the earlier protest events.

Scholarly discussion on the role of events in social movement dynamics often emphasized the importance of interpretations. A political event does not have fixed and uncontested meanings and implications. Rather, critical events are essentially events interpreted as critical (McAdam & Sewell, 2001). The actual lesson to be learned from an event is dependent on the outcome of meaning-making processes (Alimi & Maney, 2018; Vicari, 2015). However, what the extant literature did not note is that the retrospective meaning-making process surrounding a major protest can be tied to subsequent political events. Elections, in particular, can powerfully shape how people understand previous protests because they facilitate the expression of public opinion with binding power. Certainly, even election outcomes can be subjected to interpretations (Hershey, 1992; Kelly, 1983), but the interpretations are constrained by the factual electoral outcome. Election results can close down the range of possible readings of the significance of the protest event that precedes the election.

To the extent that an event becomes critical only through how it is interpreted, one might argue that the Mongkok civil unrest could not be understood as a standalone (secondary) critical event, that is, without considering it together with the 2016 by-election. This is why the present study proposes the notion of event cluster to make sense of how several events occurring in close temporal proximity could determine the significance of the focal critical event. This study examines mainly the combination of a focal protest event and a subsequent election, and there are reasons why elections are particularly influential in shaping people's understanding of the prior protest. However, an event cluster might involve the combination of other types of political events and should be observable in various contexts. Paying attention to event clusters has the potential of enhancing our understanding of the impact of events on social movements and social change in general.

After the National Security Law

Although this book addresses the period between the Umbrella Movement and the Anti-ELAB protests, it would be appropriate to briefly comment on the relevance of the approach employed in this book's analysis to the post-2019 era. Mobilization for the Anti-ELAB Movement was first undermined by the COVID-19 outbreak in February 2020 and then by the enactment of the NSL in June 2020. The enactment of the NSL was followed by, among other developments, conviction of a large number of protesters in 2019 for rioting or other crimes, activation of the old colonial sedition law, disqualification of a large number of prodemocracy district councilors who won in the 2019 election, the aforementioned reform of the electoral systems for the LegCo and the District Council, prosecution of a couple of critical media outlets, and the disbanding of a substantial number of civil society organizations that used to be core members of the prodemocracy movement. Hong Kong's ranking or rating in major international indices such as the political rights and civil liberties indices in the Freedom House Report or the world press freedom index of Reporters without Borders had dropped substantially after 2020 (Lee & Chan, 2023; Wellman, 2023).

The Chinese and Hong Kong government would maintain that one country, two systems remains in place, and the clamp down on the "violent black mob" in 2019 has allowed the society to return to order from chaos, which would then allow the city's entering prosperity based on order. Hong Kong might still differ significantly from mainland China in various ways, but many citizens would feel that civil liberties had been scaled back so substantially that Hong Kong is no longer the city as people know it. When the right to hold protests and rallies is concerned, between 2020 and early 2023, collective actions were banned in the name of the pandemic. After the removal of pandemic control policies in early 2023, various groups attempted to obtain the "no objection letter" from the police for holding protest marches. In early March, 2023, a women's group canceled an approved demonstration after receiving the police's warning that "violent groups" might join the march and cause troubles. In late March 2023, the first authorized protest in three years, addressing the issue of land reclamation, was held. Although the police approved the protest, it implemented strict rules on it, including requiring participants to wear numbered tags. It made the march looked like a shame parade, and only eighty people joined (Hung & Kong, 2023). Protests will not be completely banned, but they are likely to be tightly regulated regarding time, place, manner, and topic.

Scholars of authoritarian rule have pointed toward the use of prophylaxis by governments (Dimitrov, 2023). Through sending out warnings to dissidents and oppositional groups, the state could maintain social stability without the need to employ legal measures too frequently, which could be costly. The Hong Kong government has apparently started the relevant practices. Up to June 2024, the prodemocracy political party League of Social Democrats still persisted. But right before the anniversary of the handover in 2022, the National Security Department of the Hong Kong police contacted key members of the party to have a "conversation." After the conversation, the political party announced that it would not conduct any protest actions on the anniversary day.

The tightening of social and political control signified by the establishment of the NSL and supported by the other measures described above was followed by societal quiescence. According to the polls conducted by the Public Opinion Research Institute, distrust toward the Hong Kong government declined from 64.8 percent in January 2020 to 29.0 percent in February 2023, whereas trust increased from 23.4 percent to 53.5 percent in the same period. The number of Hong Kong citizens trusting one country, two systems rose from 27.0 percent to 62.4 percent from February 2020 to February 2023, and those distrusting one country, two systems dropped from 67.9 percent to 33.5 percent. Such levels of trust are comparable to those registered in 2009 and 2010. Regarding identity, the number of Hong Kong citizens considering themselves merely as "Hongkongers" declined from 55.4 percent in December 2019 to 32.0 percent in December 2022, whereas those holding a mixed identity ("Hongkonger in China" or "Chinese in Hong Kong") increased from 32.3 percent to 45.9 percent in the period, and those seeing themselves as Chinese increased from 10.9 percent to 20.5 percent.[2] These figures are also similar to those registered in opinion polls in the early 2010s.

However, we do not know how much of such changes is a matter of statistical regression to the mean (i.e., a "natural" return to less extreme scores after an extraordinary period), how much represents real changes in public opinion, and how much is a matter of prodemocracy citizens selectively not participating in polls or even not expressing their true views due to the worsening political environment (Kobayashi & Chan, 2022a). In fact, self-censorship has become a society-wide phenomenon.

Nevertheless, one can see signs of the society's resilience in the post-NSL era. In the media arena, for instance, after the closure of critical news outlets such as the prodemocracy newspaper *Apple Daily* and the critical online news outlet *Stand News*, a range of small-scale online media outlets were established in 2022, often by former journalists at the two organizations and/or other professional journalists who had left the increasingly conservative mainstream media organizations. Numerous civil society organizations remain in operation, and some long-time activists of the prodemocracy movement are still serving in such organizations. While it might have become virtually impossible for groups to actively fight for human rights, civil society groups can still be playing important roles in serving as the third sector of social service provision. Meanwhile, observers have started to examine popular culture—Cantopop and films, and so on—as the arena where critical ideas can be expressed in more covert and nuanced ways, as well as where ordinary people can project their wishes and desires onto the "stars."

A survey conducted in February 2023 on twenty-five hundred people who had participated in the Anti-ELAB Movement found that a substantial proportion of them were still engaging in political consumption: 53.9 percent continued to buycott, and 68.3 percent continued to boycott.[3] In the family arena, Lui (2022) illustrated how prodemocracy parents in post-NSL Hong Kong practiced political parenting in face of national education in primary and secondary schools. Many parents were training their children to become acquiescent critical thinkers, preparing their children to be global citizens, and expressing discontent using depoliticized social discourses. Certainly, the maintenance of resilience entails adaptation. The parents in Lui's (2022) study trained their children to be acquiescent, instead of openly critical thinkers. In an interview-based study on professional journalism in Hong Kong after the NSL, Lee (2023a) explicated how journalists and news organizations developed methods of risk assessment and risk management in order to navigate the increasingly dense legal minefield. Journalism is certainly not the only institution that has a strong need to assess and manage risks in the post-NSL era. Civil society actors and professionals in various sectors are trying to continue their work as far as possible and in ways that would not invite the wrath of the state. For instance, while civil society groups with varying topical focus (e.g., environment, gender, etc.) often joined hands to work on broadly defined human rights and social justice issues in the past,[4] the surviving groups are nowadays restricting their work to their primary areas of expertise. Education and social services are prioritized over advocacy. When groups have to advocate or present their work in public, they also typically exercise higher levels of "care" in terms of choice of action format, wording, and arguments to be presented.[5]

Whether people can adapt to the new environment is related to their decisions to stay in Hong Kong or emigrate to other countries. The enactment of the NSL and the loosened immigration policies of the UK and several other countries had led to a new wave of emigration from the city since 2020. Britain's British National (Overseas) Visa scheme alone had attracted more than one hundred thousand Hong Kong citizens to leave the city and go to England by February 2023 (Westbrook, 2023). Studies had found that political attitudes were linked to the decision to emigrate among contemporary Hongkongers (Chan et al., 2022), whereas Kobayashi and Chan (2022b) found that people who were more capable of adapting to difficult environments exhibited lower levels of intention to emigrate. In any case, the current wave of emigration had contributed to the formation of an emerging Hong Kong diaspora. One unique feature of the Anti-ELAB Movement is the international front at which activists engaged in overseas mobilization, public diplomacy, and foreign government lobbying. Diasporic mobilization has continued in the post-NSL era and is likely to persist into the future (Fong, 2022).

While this chapter has described some of the most recent developments in the Hong Kong society, the continual evolution of the prodemocracy movement in Hong Kong could still be tracked following the relational approach adopted in this book, that is, by paying attention to within-movement interactions, movement-public interactions, and movement-state interactions (as well as their mutual influence). Certainly, given the circumstances, the "prodemocracy movement"—at least when what happens inside the city of Hong Kong is considered—may no longer be referring to groups and people aiming at proactively pursuing political change through organizing actions. If one can still speak of a prodemocracy movement inside Hong Kong, it may be referring to the presence of social forces holding onto the values of liberty and democracy, and some of these forces are still engaging, more or less consciously, in actions that attempt to preserve the social, cultural, and/or institutional elements that would be supportive of a liberal democratic system.

The state's forceful repression had compelled prodemocracy forces to go into deep abeyance. The post-NSL situation is much closer to Valiente's (2015) description of the typical abeyance process in authoritarian states, in which many old groups and activists are persecuted and/or find it hard to survive. Yet new groups and actors with a liberal-democratic orientation are still emerging, though the sustenance of goals, values, and networks often has to be conducted covertly, often involving a turn to cultural activities.

Given the continuation of indiscriminate repression and the lack of opportunities to carry out regime-challenging actions, the distinction between the moderates and the radicals has become ever less significant. This does not mean that there would be no internal dissension among supporters of democratization, but the dissension will probably be organized less along the cleavage between the democrats and the localists. Instead, one may observe if a local-overseas divide might be emerging in the future. Given the specter of the NSL, especially the charge against "collusion with foreign powers," activists and civil society actors who remain in Hong Kong would have to minimize their connections and interactions with overseas groups and activists. For instance, in July 2023, the National Security Police put eight overseas activists from Hong Kong (including former Demosisto chairperson Nathan Law) on their wanted list. Obviously, the Hong Kong police could not really arrest the activists who are already overseas, but within a couple of days, the police arrested five former core members of Demosisto for supporting the activities of the wanted overseas activists. This can be understood as part of a plan to cut off the connections between activists inside and outside the city.

In late March 2024, the Hong Kong government has passed additional national security legislation under Article 23 of the Basic Law. The legislation came after a one-month public consultation, and it covered additional crimes such as treason, espionage, publishing of state secrets, and crimes related to external interference. Such legal provisions are likely to lead Hong Kong citizens to further refrain from connecting themselves with foreign groups as well as overseas activists.

Meanwhile, activists who have gone overseas might lose touch with emerging local realities inside Hong Kong since they might have to refrain from traveling back to the city, and communication between local and overseas actors can be undermined by state actions. The difficulty for overseas actors to "read" the social atmosphere in Hong Kong is aggravated by the aforementioned point that the surviving groups and actors inside Hong Kong would probably need to restrict their actions, keep a low profile, and express themselves in covert ways. This means that the kind of adaptive resilience exhibited by a sector of the Hong Kong society can be rather invisible to people who stay in the city, let alone to people who have left. Moreover, overseas activists inevitably have to face and respond to the political situation of their host societies when they consider how to present and frame the Hong Kong situation. Put generally, local and overseas actors are facing different sets of constraints and opportunities. Their opinions regarding what can be and needs to be said and done might diverge. This is not to say that a split between local and overseas actors is a foregone conclusion. The point is that close attention to how local and overseas actors interact with each other is needed, and it has implications for the evolution of the prodemocracy forces of Hong Kong.

Regarding movement-public interactions, without major changes in the political environment, it would be difficult for civil society groups to mobilize the public to participate in collective actions. But it does not entail the absence of meaningful connections and interactions between civil society actors and the prodemocracy citizens. One interesting phenomenon emerging in the most recent years is the proliferation of "independent bookstores" across Hong Kong. Against the background of censorship by public libraries and major chain bookstores, independent bookstores become the places where more critical works can be found. Several independent bookstores also organize regular seminars and sharing by authors with strong liberal progressive orientations. The discussion in these seminars is often depoliticized, but certain values and ideas can still be shared and reaffirmed, and affective attachments can be built. In fact, one might argue that, instead of having a critical public sphere that exists in a society with sufficient freedom of expression, there is an emerging affective cultural sphere where likeminded people can still connect with each other.

Another interesting question related to movement-public interaction is how meanings and information can be communicated effectively yet covertly. Take political consumption as the example. When political consumption was promoted during the Anti-ELAB Movement in the name of the Yellow Economic Circle (Chan & Pun, 2020), citizen participation in the practice was aided by the proliferation of promovement shops and digital sites sharing information about the whereabouts of those shops (Lee & Fong, 2023). In the post-NSL era, the number of promovement shops inevitably declined, shops had to be more careful in expressing their political leanings, and many digital information-sharing sites were closed. Yet it is mentioned above that a significant proportion of the most committed participants of the Anti-ELAB Movement were still engaging in boycotting and buycotting even in early 2023. It suggests that there are still mechanisms for people to share relevant information.

More generally speaking, if we return to the idea of abeyance as a holding process preserving the values, identities, and networks of a movement, the sustenance of people's values and identities may require the continual presence of relevant cultural and discursive resources. Such resources would need to be provided by actors who are in the strategic positions to do so. In contemporary Hong Kong, these actors may not be restricted to movement activists as conventionally defined. These actors may include, among others, progressive cultural producers who try to embed their values and ideals into creative and imaginary visions, professional journalists who attempt to continue to practice their watchdog role, and civil society actors who offer opportunities for citizens to engage in nonconfrontational and socially meaningful actions.

Regarding state-movement interaction, it has already been noted that the government is apparently trying to cut off the ties between overseas activism and local civil society actions. More broadly speaking, it remains unknown how far the contraction of civil liberties in Hong Kong will go. On the one hand, the Chinese government is adamant about the overwhelming importance of national security. The government may still be in the process of establishing additional laws that would facilitate further social control. For instance, in summer 2023, the Hong Kong government proposed to legislate for regulating crowd funding. The details of such a law can have an important influence on the operations of online media and civil society groups. Besides, the state is aware of the prodemocracy forces' turn to cultural activities. After 2021, Chinese government officials coined the term "soft resistance" to refer to societal resistance to state power through "softer" means such as arts and culture. Hong Kong government officials had since then picked up the language and vowed to keep attempts of soft resistance under scrutiny and control. A pessimist might predict Hong Kong to become closer and closer to mainland China as time goes by.

But on the other hand, as the society is already largely "under control," China might still have a certain number of economic incentives to create a liberal façade for Hong Kong in order to pacify international businesses and foreign governments. This might lead China to refrain from the more extreme actions. Internet control can be the prime example here. When the NSL was established in June 2020, some Hong Kong citizens and the international media had speculated if China would impose the "Great Firewall" onto Hong Kong, thus making Hong Kong part of the mainland Chinese internet (which practically means that major platforms such as Facebook, YouTube, and Google would be inaccessible without the use of VPNs). Since then, Hong Kong had witnessed the blocking of individual websites, and in summer 2023, the Hong Kong government applied for a court injunction to ban the online circulation of the movement song "Glory to Hong Kong" (because the song is purportedly treated by many promovement citizens as Hong Kong's "national anthem"). The court granted the injunction in April 2024.

However, at least up to the time of finalizing this book, China still seems to be refraining from actually imposing the Great Firewall onto Hong Kong once and for all. This refrain from more extreme internet control is not difficult to understand: banning individual websites of interests only to prodemocracy citizens in Hong Kong would not arouse as much international attention or affect international businesses in the city, but imposing the Great Firewall will. An "optimist" might hope that such refrain would continue. Even maintaining a façade could entail the presence of space for an independent civil society to operate.

The relational approach emphasizes agency of actors as well as contingency of events, but there are certainly macro and structural forces—sustained by interactions among players at a "higher level"—determining the parameters of the field within which the relational interactions at the more local level play out. As Hung (2022) explained, ever since the handover, how to maintain control of a society that has developed its own identity while also utilizing the society and reaping the benefits from its international connections has always been the overarching question facing the Chinese state, and the state's priority and strategic choices have been shaped by its international status, foreign relations, and internal social, political, and economic conditions. What happens at the global and national level, including the evolution of rivalry between the United States and China, tensions across the Taiwan strait, and the health of the Chinese economy could change China's grand policy, thus also its policy toward Hong Kong. It is beyond the scope of this book to address such macrolevel dynamics. Suffice it to say that opportunities and threats may arise unpredictably. When the possibility for change arises, the prodemocracy movement in Hong Kong may reemerge, but its form, strength, and character will be shaped by the relational dynamics that transpire during the period of movement abeyance.

Appendix

Research Methodologies

This methodological appendix aims at providing background information about the methods of data collection related to the various empirical studies conducted over the years by the author (and his collaborators) and utilized in the course of writing this book. These methods range from protest-onsite surveys and population-opinion surveys to content and textual analysis of media materials. The methodological descriptions are organized by the type of method being utilized. It should be noted that the appendix aims only at providing basic information about the methods. In some cases, readers are directed to other published studies or publicly available sources for additional methodological details.

PROTEST-ONSITE SURVEYS

Parts of chapter 2 draw upon a protest-onsite survey conducted during the Umbrella Movement. Methodologically, the survey follows what was, by the time of the Umbrella Movement, a well-established approach in social movement studies for deriving samples of protesters from protest sites (Lee & Chan, 2011; Milkman et al., 2013; Walgrave & van Aelst, 2011). Specifically, teams of interviewers were ordered to walk along designated paths that would allow them to cover the occupied areas. They were asked to select every tenth person that they walked past as an interviewee. This procedure essentially treated the temporal-spatial distribution of the protesters in the occupied areas as the sampling frame and then employed a systematic sampling procedure to identify the target respondents. To minimize the introduction of interviewer bias, the interviewers were asked not to choose interviewees by their own predilections but to follow the procedure strictly and select the person who stood closest to them when several protesters were standing together. The selected interviewees were asked to fill out the questionnaires by themselves.

We were able to adopt this procedure largely because the occupied areas were usually peaceful and orderly throughout the Umbrella Movement. The participants were cooperative. The fieldwork was conducted in the Admiralty area on October 4 and 5. Later, it was clear to the author (and his collaborator) that the Mongkok occupation also played a significant role in the evolution of the Umbrella Movement. Fieldwork was therefore conducted in both Mongkok and Admiralty on November 2, when we fielded the survey for a second time. The sample sizes of the two surveys were 969 and 567, respectively, and the response rates of both were higher than 95 percent.

Parts of chapter 7 draw upon the protest-onsite surveys the author and his collaborators conducted during the Anti-ELAB Movement. The basic logic behind the data collection method is the same as the survey conducted during the Umbrella Movement. That is, to the extent that is possible, we tried to utilize the spatial-temporal distribution of the protesters as the sampling frame. However, protests during the Anti-ELAB Movement presented a few additional challenges. First, instead of people staying at or walking around a fixed occupied area, most of the protests during the Anti-ELAB Movement involved marches. In those cases, we distributed the interviewers both inside the area where a protest march started as well as alongside the route of the march. But the interviewers were given the same instruction to conduct a systematic sampling of protesters. Moreover, to enlarge sample size and to avoid asking all respondents to stay at a certain point for a period of time to complete the interview, we allowed the respondents to either respond through a face-to-face interview by our interviewers or to access an online questionnaire using their smartphones and a QR code.

Second and more challenging, protests in and after the second half of July became more fluid and riskier, as police-protester conflicts sometimes started earlier than expected, and in some cases, the protests did not obtain a letter of no objection from the police and were therefore technically illegal. Therefore, in some of the protests associated with higher levels of risks and uncertainties, we resorted to a post-hoc online survey approach. A small number of helpers were asked to help distribute leaflets onsite. The leaflets contained the QR codes for accessing an online questionnaire, and the protesters were expected to respond to the survey after the protest event. Admittedly, this approach implies the forfeiture of probability sampling, but it was necessitated by the character of the protest events. Another potential problem of this approach is that people may share the QR codes with nonparticipants of a protest. In order to ensure that all respondents were participants in a specific protest, the first question of the questionnaire asked the respondents about the location where they joined the protest on the day. "Not having joined the protest" is an answering option. This helped us screen out nonprotesters (who would not know that the question was actually serving a filtering function).

We conducted a total of twenty-seven onsite surveys between June 9, 2019, and January 1, 2020. Valid sample sizes range from 175 to 2,309. Yuen and colleagues (2022) provided a thorough analysis of the methodological choices and their implications on the data (e.g., the difference between the results derived from paper-based surveys and results from online surveys). Readers can refer to the article for additional information about the survey methods and the basic results.

POPULATION SURVEYS

Chapters 4 through 7 have drawn upon several population surveys conducted by the CCPOS at the Chinese University of Hong Kong. They include a survey conducted in March 2016, one conducted in March 2019, a couple conducted in summer 2016 and summer 2017, respectively, and a few surveys conducted during the months of the Anti-ELAB Movement in the second half of 2019. All surveys were conducted via telephone and followed standard probability sampling procedures adopted in Hong Kong. Specifically, for the March 2016 survey, sampling began by collecting all phone numbers from the most recent residential directories. To include nonlisted numbers, the last two digits of the numbers were replaced by the full set of one hundred double digits from 00 to 99. Specific numbers were randomly drawn by computers during the survey. The most recent birthday method was used to select the target respondent from a household. A total of 1,012 interviews were completed. The response rate was 32.0 percent according to formula AAPOR RR3.

The March 2019 survey followed basically the same approach. The sample size was 1,010, and the response rate was 39.0 percent following AAPOR RR3. A slight difference between the two surveys is that the former targeted Chinese-speaking Hong Kong residents aged fifteen or above, whereas the 2019 survey targeted Chinese-speaking Hong Kong residents aged eighteen or above. To keep the samples consistent, when comparing the results of the two surveys (in chapter 6), only respondents aged eighteen or above in the 2016 survey were analyzed. The effective sample size of the 2016 survey is 960. Meanwhile, as typical in surveys on political and public affairs in Hong Kong, citizens with high levels of income and education would be oversampled. The data sets were weighted according to the age x sex x education distribution of the corresponding Hong Kong population when conducting the analysis.

The other population surveys utilized in chapters 4 through 7 were part of the Hong Kong Public Opinion and Political Development Program at the CCPOS. The series of surveys employed the same methodological approach. The only major difference is that the surveys conducted during and after mid-2019 (i.e., the population surveys conducted during the Anti-ELAB protests) involved the use of both landline and mobile phone numbers for the purpose of sampling. Sampling proceeded by creating telephone number databases through combining all four-digit telephone prefixes in use in Hong Kong with the full set of possible four-digit suffixes (i.e., 0000 to 9999). Individual numbers were then randomly selected by computers during the fieldwork. The most recent birthday method was adopted to select a target respondent from a household (i.e., reached through landlines), whereas the person picking up the call was the target respondent in the case of a mobile number. Table A1 summarizes the basic information of the surveys belonging to the series. For further information, readers can

Table A1. Basic information about population surveys belonging to CCPOS's Hong Kong Public Opinion and Political Development Program

Time	Sample Size	Response Rate (RR3)
July 2016	1010	43%
May/June 2017	1028	37%
June 2019	635	43%
August 2019	842	46%
September 2019	623	41%
October 2019	751	44%
May 2020	815	44%

Source: Created by the author.

visit the webpage of the research program (https://ccpos.com.cuhk.edu.hk/hong-kong-public-opinion-and-political-development/).

IN-DEPTH INTERVIEWS

In-depth interview was the main data collection method for the study of the Mongkok civil unrest. The project was initiated and organized by a group of academics, civil society actors, legal professionals, and journalists. The study aimed to reconstruct the happenings in the night of the unrest. While the project team did refer to records of court proceedings and media materials, the team also recruited interviewees who were either participants or observers of the event. The recruitment of interviewees relied on personal referrals and snowballing. Given the sensitivity of the event and the possible lack of trust between the activists and the research team, not all potential interviewees agreed to participate in the project. Nevertheless, the project team was still capable of recruiting thirty-eight interviewees in the end, including twelve participants, twenty-one observers, and five journalists who worked in Mongkok that night. Table A2 summarizes the information of the interviews.

The interviews were semistructured, and the set of guiding questions differed somewhat depending on which category the interviewee belonged to. Most of the interviews were conducted by two interviewers, one of whom was an academic from a social science or humanities discipline, and the other was an assistant with some relevant research training. The interviews were mostly done in a "privatized" location, such as the room loaned by a civil society organization or a university classroom. The interviews lasted two hours on average. Most of the interviews were audio recorded and transcribed for the purpose of analysis. All interviewees were promised anonymity.

In-depth interviews were also conducted by the present author in association with his past projects on the Umbrella Movement, the Anti-ELAB protests, and Tiananmen commemoration. A couple of interviews from the Tiananmen commemoration project, for instance, were quoted in chapter 2 when discussing Mongkok as a site where some young people had their "first taste" of militant protests and developed their localist orientation. Information about the interview methods can be found in relevant works (Lee & Chan, 2021).

Moreover, eight interviews were conducted specifically for offering additional information directly pertinent to specific parts of the book. Six of the eight interviewees are the following: sociologist and initiator of the

Table A2. List of interviewees on the Mongkok civil unrest

Number	Date of interview	Remarks
A01	2019 / 3 / 21	
A02	2019 / 11 / 3	
A03	2020 / 1 / 16	Arrested due to the Mongkok civil unrest
A04	2020 / 1 / 22	Arrested due to the Mongkok civil unrest
A05	2020 / 1 / 23	Arrested due to the Mongkok civil unrest
A06	2020 / 4 / 29	
A07	2020 / 5 / 3	
A08	2020 / 6 / 15	
A09	2020 / 6 / 18	
A10	2020 / 6 / 22	
A11	2020 / 6 / 23	
A12	2020 / 6 / 26	
B01	2019 / 7 / 3	
B02	2019 / 7 / 10	Experienced participant in left-wing social movements
B03	2019 / 7 / 13	Experienced participant in left-wing social movements
B04	2019 / 11 / 23	
B05	2019 / 12 / 30	
B06	2020 / 1 / 14	
B07	2020 / 5 / 4	
B08	2020 / 5 / 15	
B09	2020 / 5 / 20	
B10	2020 / 5 / 30	A district councilor
B11	2020 / 6 / 6	
B12	2020 / 6 / 5	
B13	2020 / 6 / 6	
B14	2020 / 6 / 8	
B15	2020 / 6 / 17	
B16	2020 / 7 / 2	
B17	2020 / 7 / 22	Experienced participant in left-wing social movements
B18	2020 / 8 / 24	

Number	Date of interview	Remarks
B19	2020 / 9 / 2	
B20	2020 / 9 / 7	
B21	2020 / 9 / 7	Arrested due to the Mongkok civil unrest
C01	2019 / 7 / 30	News reporter
C02	2019 / 8 / 9	Freelance photojournalist
C03	2019 / 9 / 7	News reporter
C04	2019 / 9 / 20	Photojournalist
C05	2020 / 7 / 29	Photojournalist

Source: Created by the author.

Occupy Central campaign Chan Kinman, former chairperson of the Democratic Party Lee Wing-tat, prominent public affairs commentator Joseph Lian, former chairperson of Demosisto Nathan Law, veteran civil society organizer Fermi Wong, and Nora Lam, the director of the documentary *Lost in the Fumes*.

All of these interviews were conducted between October 2022 and January 2023. The first five were conducted via zoom, as the interviewees had left Hong Kong by the time, whereas the sixth interview was conducted in person in the interviewee's workspace. The interviews were recorded and transcribed. The interviewees are not kept anonymous because of the unique roles they played in the analysis of this book. Given the possible sensitivity of the materials, in some cases, the interviewees were offered the chance to edit the transcript. The audio recordings were deleted afterwards.

The two other interviewees were young activists who were active in the prodemocracy movement during the period under investigation (2016–2019). The interviews were conducted face-to-face in Hong Kong. The interview records were similarly handled, with the only difference being anonymization since their individual identity is unimportant to the analysis. The questions discussed in all eight interviews were specific to each interviewee. Each of the eight interviews lasted for about an hour to ninety minutes.

ANALYSIS OF NEWS MEDIA CONTENTS

Materials from the news media are crucial for reconstructing various events and happenings during the years being examined. But in addition to general usage of news media texts as records and information sources, a couple of chapters include systematic analyses of news media contents. First, chapter 4 begins with an analysis of mainstream news coverage of the Mongkok civil unrest. The Mongkok civil unrest occurred in the late night of February 8 and the early morning hours of February 9, 2016. The event happened too late at night on February 8 so that most daily newspapers did not cover the event on February 9. The analysis thus focuses on a ten-day period between February 10 and 19, 2016. The analysis relies on the electronic news archive Wise News and centers on ten Chinese-language newspapers: *Apple Daily*, *Hong Kong Economic Journal*, *Ming Pao*, *Hong Kong Economic Times*, *Sing Pao*, *Singtao Daily*, *Hong Kong Commercial Daily*, *Oriental Daily*, *Ta Kung Pao*, and *Wen Wei Po*. These ten papers covered the whole ideological spectrum of mainstream newspapers at the time. To identify relevant news reports and commentary articles, a keyword search was conducted using five possible labels of the event: the Chinese name of Mongkok + *bou-lyun* or *bou-dong* or *sou-lyun* or *chung-dat* or *sijin* (see chapter 4's explication of what these labels refer to). A total of 1,163 articles were derived.

Since a single article can use more than one of these labels, a research assistant then manually classified all articles into one of two categories: (1) those that primarily employed *bou-lyun* or *bou-dong* and (2) those that primarily employed *sou-lyun* or other names. In 102 articles, two types of labels were used more or less frequently, and they were dropped from further analysis. We then examined the appearance of a range of keywords in the two sets of news articles in order to illustrate the differences in how they framed the Mongkok civil unrest.

Part of chapter 4 presented an analysis of election forums during the 2016 LegCo by-election. The record on Wikipedia shows that there should have been a total of fourteen election forums organized by various media organizations or social organizations. Two were conducted in English, and twelve were conducted in Cantonese. The analysis focuses on the Cantonese forums. At the time of conducting the analysis, full records of ten of the twelve forums could be found on YouTube. They include two forums organized by the Commercial Radio, one by NOW TV, two by Radio Television Hong Kong, one by the independent online media Social Record Channel, one by online media outlet TVMost, one by Television Broadcasting Ltd., one by online radio station D100, and one by the campus TV of the Hong Kong University's Student Union. The lengths of the forums range from only fifteen minutes to two hours. To serve as a reference point, the video of Edward Leung's own campaign rally held on February 20, 2016, was also examined.

The analysis was conducted by a systematic and iterative viewing of the forums by a research assistant under the guidance of the present author. The assistant was instructed to identify and register the prognostic, diagnostic, adversarial, and affective framings employed by Edward Leung, while also marking significant conversational exchanges among the candidates. After having the initial results, the assistant was further instructed to pay attention to more specific issues, such as how the other candidates—and especially the main candidate from the prodemocracy camp Alvin Yeung—responded to Leung's discourses.

Chapter 5 included a systematic analysis of the writings of Joseph Lian, a prominent public affairs commentator who is treated as an ideological bridge broker in the present study. A search on the electronic news archive Wise News was conducted to derive newspaper articles written by Lian that contained the keywords of *bun-tou* (local), *goog-duk* (Hong Kong independence) or *ji-kyut* (self-determination). The time period was set to be between January 2014, about nine months before the occurrence of the Umbrella Movement, and November 2018, about one year before the onset of the Anti-ELAB protests. A total of 147 articles were derived, including 108 articles from the *Hong Kong Economic Journal* between January 2014 and August 2016 and 39 articles published by *Apple Daily* between September 2016 and November 2018. The present author read all the articles iteratively to identify the main themes included in his writings, especially regarding questions such as the justifiability of militant protests, the relationship between the localists and the democrats, possible future of the Hong Kong society, and the possibility of Hong Kong independence. The aim was to produce an account of Lian's discourse that could highlight the political import of his writings under the context of the time. As indicated above, the textual analysis was supplemented by an interview with Joseph Lian himself in October 2022.

ANALYSIS OF OTHER TEXTUAL MATERIALS

In addition to analyses of news media texts, the book also draws upon systematic analyses of other textual materials. The analysis of legal repression in chapter 6 is based on a study of court verdicts. The study was associated with the project on the Mongkok civil unrest. For the broader study, a corpus of twenty-one cases was compiled, including nine riot cases associated with the Mongkok civil unrest, the first ten riot cases associated with the Anti-ELAB Movement, and two high-profile cases associated with the Umbrella Movement. The analysis in this book focuses only on the nine riot cases of the Mongkok civil unrest and the "incitement" case against the leaders of the Umbrella Movement. We focus on these cases because they are most pertinent to the present book.

In the Hong Kong legal system, cases tried at the District Court or the High Court have their verdicts publicly available online.[1] The verdicts of all the sampled cases were downloaded from the site. A qualitative textual analysis was conducted by the author and three research assistants who had relevant academic training and good background understanding of the protest events. The texts were read in relation to the context of social protests in Hong Kong. The analysis is most tuned to ideas and assumptions about protests, protesters, and protest policing, though other recurrent themes were also identified.

The various "assumptions" could be stated explicitly by the judges in the texts, or they could serve as unstated assumptions that are nonetheless crucial for giving coherence to the arguments made in the verdict. The analysis also paid attention to what was absent from the texts. Notes were taken throughout the analysis. Several rounds of discussions were held among the author and the assistants in the process. Themes and ideas derived from the readings were iteratively categorized and recategorized as observations accumulated. Readers may see Lee (2023b) for more information about the analytical approach and results based on the larger corpus of twenty-one court cases.

Chapter 7 included information and results derived from analyzing the contents of the online forum LIHKG, generally regarded as the central communication platform used by protesters and movement supporters during the Anti-ELAB movement. LIHKG is often described as "Reddit-like." It is a typical online forum with a conventional design. Users can initiate discussion threads, post replies to existing threads, or "like or dislike" the threads posted by others. However, the forum does not allow users to become "friends" with others. That is, it does not afford the formation of individualized networks. There are various subforums known as channels. Most discussions related to the Anti-ELAB Movement appeared in the public affairs channels. Although the public affairs channel was supposed to host the discussions of a full range of public matters, throughout the second half of 2019 and most of early 2020, the Anti-ELAB Movement constituted the single overwhelmingly dominant topic of discussion in the forum's public affairs channel.

A computer program was therefore developed to scrape all posts and comments from the public affairs channel between June 1, 2019, and June 30, 2020. The total number of posts and comments reached 25 million. The scraped posts were stored, and analysis was conducted by writing computer commands. For the purpose of the present book, the analysis of LIHKG content is largely restricted to keyword-based content analysis and some additional statistical analysis based on the keyword-based content analysis results. Interested readers can see Liang and Lee (2023) for an example of a study that examines the LIHKG data in a more "advanced" manner to address the conceptual issue of opinion leadership in the forum.

Focus Group Study

Last, chapter 7 has cited data derived from a focus group study of the participants of the Anti-ELAB Movement. Specifically, ten focus groups were organized in August and September 2020, which included four groups of working adults, two groups of university students, two groups of tertiary students (nondegree), and two groups of upper secondary students. Each group comprised around six participants. The overall number of participants in the study was fifty-nine.

The focus group discussion covered three topical areas: (1) views toward peaceful and radical protests, (2) views toward radical protest tactics, and (3) views towards the idea of "mutual destruction." There were subquestions in each of these areas, such as questions regarding the participants' understanding of various key protest slogans. The focus groups were conducted in a semistructured manner which allowed participants to freely express and elaborate their thoughts surrounding the three designated topical areas. Each focus group discussion lasted for around two hours.

Normally, a focus group would require face-to-face discussion among the participants. But by the second half of 2020, the COVID-19 pandemic was already ongoing, and the Hong Kong government had put forward a range of measures regarding social distancing and the banning of gatherings. The ten focus groups were conducted online via the video communication platform Zoom. Both CCPOS researchers and the author's research assistant served as the moderators. The focus group discussions were transcribed for analysis.

Notes

Chapter 1

1. According to the original data (accessed by the author), an opinion poll conducted by the CCPOS in late May and early June of 2019, weeks before the first million-strong protest march of the Anti-ELAB Movement, showed that 66 percent of the respondents were against the amendment bill, whereas only 17 percent supported it. In contrast, various opinion polls conducted in early 2015 and reported by the news media showed that the percentages of people supporting and opposing the electoral framework set up by China's National People's Congress for the Chief Executive election do not differ from each other hugely.

2. Protesters criticized the Anti-Express Railway project for being overpriced and negligent of its impact on the environment and the livelihood of rural citizens who would be affected by the construction. The protest was part of Hong Kong's New Preservation Movement that arose in the mid-2000s (Chen & Szeto, 2015). Underlying the protest was the discontent toward the government's developmentalism (Law, 2018).

3. Also see Ku (2020) and Wang (2019) for how localist ideas may be articulated with Hong Kong's historical legacy as a British colony and contemporary reality as a global city.

Chapter 2

1. The protests were against the demolition of the piers, seen as important historical sites by the activists. They were part of the New Preservation Movement in Hong Kong arising in the 2000s.

2. The exception was 2011 when 138 protesters were arrested in the night of July 1 after a political group called for the "occupation" of the commercial district Central at the end of the annual July 1 protest in the afternoon. Besides, although

1,100 protesters were arrested during the Anti-WTO protest in 2005, they were primarily Korean protesters instead of local protesters. Aside from the Anti-WTO protest, only 58 protest-related arrests were made that year.

3. Personal interview conducted in January 2023. Unless otherwise stated, other materials from Lee Wing-tat quoted in this and the subsequent chapters also come from the same interview.

4. Personal interview conducted in January 2023. Unless otherwise stated, other materials from Chan Kinman quoted in this and the subsequent chapters also come from the same interview.

5. The moderate democrats pointed out that civil nomination violates the Basic Law, the miniconstitutional document for Hong Kong, and is extremely unlikely to be accepted by the Central Government. They prefer putting forward supposedly more realistic proposals. Critics argued that the voting results deprived the public a chance to select from a more meaningful range of options (Shen, 2020).

6. The OCLP initiators expressed this in media interviews and during the court trial in December 2018.

7. The space was originally accessible by the public, and it was "occupied" by protesters during the 2012 Anti-National Education Movement. The young protesters at the time called the space the Civic Square. The action on September 27, 2014, was undertaken in the name of "retaking the Civic Square."

8. The survey was conducted by the author and his colleague Joseph M. Chan. The findings were presented in Lee and Chan (2018). A version of the analysis of the differences between Admiralty and Mongkok based on these data was also presented in Yuen (2019). The analytical approach by Yuen (2019) and the approach adopted here differ slightly, but the major findings and conclusions remain the same. See appendix A for more information about the method.

9. The more radical occupiers were suspicious toward the idea of a square voting as they feared that the voting was merely a means to justify a decision to retreat from the occupied areas. The square voting was not conducted in the end due to both such suspicions and practical difficulties.

10. The notion of emotional imprint was used by Lee and Chan (2021) to describe the consequence of Hong Kong people's experience of the 1989 Beijing Student Movement. Similar to the usage here, what is foregrounded is how emotional experiences can leave a deep and long-lasting impact on people, significantly shaping the way they act and think in subsequent years.

11. There was no physical and violent resistance to police eviction in Mongkok in the end. Despite the Mongkok occupiers' emphasis on militant resistance, unlike the Admiralty activists, they were not committed to persuasive civil disobedience. Instead, given their law-defying attitude (Shen, 2019), fighting the police when the latter was determined to evict the occupation could be seen as "pointless sacrifice."

12. See https://www.facebook.com/9WuFreedom. The Cantonese pronunciation of the number 9 is close the pronounciation of *gau*. The page was still

accessible by the author on March 17, 2024, though the last post was published on July 2, 2015.

13. "Commemorating the 1000th day of Mongkok's Gauwu group," *Apple Daily*, August 22, 2017, p. A04.

14. The eight papers are *Apple Daily, Ming Pao, Sing Tao Daily, Hong Kong Economic Journal, Hong Kong Economic Times, Oriental Daily, Ta Kung Pao,* and *Wen Wei Po*. They encompassed newspapers ranging from the prodemocracy *Apple Daily* to the Communist-sponsored *Ta Kung Pao* and *Wen Wei Po*.

15. The candidates' platforms were available on the "introduction to candidates" page of the government's official website for the 2015 District Council elections (https://www.elections.gov.hk/dc2015/eng/intro_to_can.html). The whole page—and therefore the electoral platforms for all participating candidates—was no longer available by March 17, 2024.

16. "Localist terms not mentioned in the platform of Umbrella Soldiers; localists took the opportunity to promulgate radical ideas," *Ming Pao*, November 3, 2015.

17. Fong's (2015) count of additional seats won by the democrats in the 2015 District Council elections differed from Lam's (2017)—twenty-five versus twenty-two. This again illustrates the difficulties of clearly and definitively classifying all candidates into one camp or the other.

Chapter 3

1. The name of the group refers to Article 45 of the Basic Law, which is the article about democratization of the election of the chief executive in Hong Kong. The article reads:

> The Chief Executive of the Hong Kong Special Administrative Region shall be selected by election or through consultations held locally and be appointed by the Central People's Government.
>
> The method for selecting the Chief Executive shall be specified in the light of the actual situation in the Hong Kong Special Administrative Region and in accordance with the principle of gradual and orderly progress. The ultimate aim is the selection of the Chief Executive by universal suffrage upon nomination by a broadly representative nominating committee in accordance with democratic procedures.

The specific method for selecting the Chief Executive is prescribed in Annex I: Method for the Selection of the Chief Executive of the Hong Kong Special Administrative Region.

2. K was interviewed in 2019 for the project related to the Mongkok civil unrest. A separate pseudonym K—instead of the pseudonyms used in the analysis of the civil unrest later in this chapter—is used here to further protect the anonymity of the interviewee.

3. The description in this paragraph was summarized from news reports in local newspapers.

4. As of March 24, 2024, a version of the video clip, uploaded on March 10, 2015, was still available on YouTube at: https://www.youtube.com/watch?v=4J_TuKLJv-c&t=8s&ab_channel=AbrahamFord.

Chapter 4

1. It is worth noting here that, despite being the most strongly prodemocracy newspaper in Hong Kong at the time, the owner of *Apple Daily* Jimmy Lai, who had close connections with the moderate democrats, was also known to hold negative attitudes toward the localist camp. See Li (2022).

2. Social Record Channel was an online alternative media outlet established in 2010, and it professed to keep records of the voices of the minorities and marginal groups.

3. D100 is an online radio station with a clear prodemocracy orientation. Only Edward Leung and Alvin Yeung participated in the forum.

4. *Discourse on the Hong Kong Nation* emphasized the development of the Hong Kong nation and the right to national self-determination. It was named and criticized by then chief executive CY Leung in early 2015 for promoting Hong Kong independence. An analysis of the content of the book can be found in Carrico (2022).

5. TVMost is an online site producing infotainment content.

6. The speech was accessed on July 5, 2022, through: https://www.haaretz.com/israel-news/culture/2009-02-17/ty-article/always-on-the-side-of-the-egg/0000017f-db26-d3ff-a7ff-fba694020000.

Chapter 5

1. Unless indicated otherwise, opinions from Nora Lam were derived from an interview in October 2022.

2. Unless attributed to published writings, quotations from Nathan Law in this and the subsequent chapter come from a personal interview conducted online in October 2022.

3. *Derek* is a pseudonym. The interview was conducted in October 2022. Quotations from Derek below came from the same interview.

4. "Give the pro-democracy movement a future: Rally for democratic self-determination." https://www.facebook.com/demosisto/photos/a.497270963815 064/533220750220085/ (last accessed on March 18, 2024).

5. "Supplements on Q&A during the foundation press conference," April 11, 2016. From Facebook page of Demosisto, https://www.facebook.com/demosisto, last accessed on November 28, 2022.

6. "10 questions and 10 answers: On the positioning of Demosisto," June 23, 2016. From Facebook page of Demosisto, https://www.facebook.com/demosisto, last accessed on November 28, 2022.

7. The Alliance has been the organizer of the annual vigil since 1990. As the name suggests, the group proclaimed itself to be patriotic toward China and was a target of criticisms for many localist groups.

8. "10 questions and 10 answers: On Demosisto's stance regarding June 4," May 29, 2016. From Facebook page of Demosisto, https://www.facebook.com/ demosisto, last accessed on November 28, 2022.

9. Personal interview conducted in October 2022.

10. Politicians and activists called the question surrounding post-2047 political arrangement "the question of Hong Kong's future for a second time." "The first time" was in the 1980s when the society had to consider the future of Hong Kong after 1997. The social media page on which the Resolution was published was no longer available as of 2022, whereas the original text of the Resolution can still be located online. As of March 24, 2024, the full text of the Resolution was still available online through the commentary website News Lens (https://www.thenewslens.com/article/27944).

11. 'Supplements on Q&As during the press conference for the establishment of the party," April 11, 2016. From the official Facebook page of Demosisto, https:// www.facebook.com/demosisto (last accessed on November 28, 2022).

12. "Tam Chi-Yuen met the Chinese Liaison Office: Central Government is concerned about whether Hong Kong independence would spread," *Ming Pao*, April 23, 2016, p.A02.

13. *Terence* is a pseudonym. Personal interview in October 2022.

14. The vote coordination campaign, ThunderGo, was proposed and led by Occupy Central leader Benny Tai. The campaign aimed at providing information to voters about the degree of support of various prodemocracy candidates so as to facilitate strategic voting, thus maximizing the number of seats that the prodemocracy candidates could win in the proportional representation system.

15. Unless attributed to published writing, Lian's view cited in this chapter was derived from a personal interview conducted in 2022.

16. *Pan-democrats* is the term used in local public discourses to refer to the broad coalition of prodemocracy political parties and politicians. For the sake of simplicity and to avoid confusion, this book has mainly used the term *democrats* to refer to the prodemocracy parties and politicians.

17. "Joseph Lian: Theory of violence on the edge——a possible point of convergence of the route of resistance of the three camps," *The Initium*, September 28, 2015. https://theinitium.com/article/20150928-opinion-lianyizheng-evaluation/.

Chapter 6

1. As a comparison, Alvin Yeung of the Civic Party, who won the February by-election with more than 160,000 votes, returned to the LegCo in the September election with only 58,825 votes. Given the proportional representation system, and with nine seats in the New Territories East constituency, voters were aware of the fact that a candidate list was very likely to win a seat if it obtains 8 percent to 10 percent of the votes cast. The challenge for prodemocracy voters was how to spread their votes more evenly across various candidate lists belonging to the prodemocracy camp in order to maximize the number of seats won.

2. "Rebel Hong Kong politicians defy China at chaotic swearing-in ceremony," *The Guardian*, October 12, 2016.

3. See https://www.elegislation.gov.hk/hk/A115!en.assist.pdf.

4. Nonetheless, it was not the first time interpretation of the Basic Law by the NPC deviated from the stipulation of the Basic Law. See Jones (2015).

5. By 2023, the Democratic Party had become practically the only prodemocracy political party still in operation. But members of the district-level consultation bodies were appointed by the government. News reports indicated that even some progovernment politicians faced difficulties in obtaining enough nominations.

6. https://www.elegislation.gov.hk/hk/cap245.

7. Paragraph 92, DCCC901/2016 [2018] HKDC 225. The verdict was in Chinese. The current translation was done by the author. In the subsequent footnotes of this chapter, "(translated)" and "(original)" are used to mark if the verdict was originally in Chinese (thus translated by the author) or English.

8. Paragraph 111, DCCC901/2016 [2018] HKDC 225. (translated)

9. Paragraph 50, DCCC 200/2019 [2020] HKDC 1184. (translated)

10. Paragraph 26, DCCC 200/2019 [2020] HKDC 1184. (translated)

11. Paragraph 8, DCCC 783/2019 ([2020] HKDC 337. (original)

12. Paragraph 9 of the verdict, DCCC 783/2019 [2020] HKDC 337. (original)

13. Paragraph 45 of the verdict, DCCC 783/2019 [2020] HKDC 337. (original)

14. Paragraph 34 of the verdict, DCCC 125/2020 [2020] HKDC 1311. (original)

15. Paragraphs 80 and 81, respectively, DCCC 480/2017 [2019] HKDC 450. (original)

16. Paragraphs 390 to 392, DCCC 480/2017 [2019] HKDC 450.

17. Paragraphs 562, DCCC 480/2017 [2019] HKDC 450. (original)

18. Paragraph 393, DCCC 480/2017 [2019] HKDC 450. (original)
19. Paragraph 197, DCCC 480/2017 [2019] HKDC 450. (original)

Chapter 7

1. All posts and comments on the "public affairs channel" of the forum published between June 1, 2019, and July, 2020, were scraped. This created an archive of more than 26 million posts and comments. See methodological appendix for more information about the methods.

2. After the incident, movement supporters felt the need to further emphasize the necessity of standing together. In online discussions, movement supporters upgraded the command to "no severing of ties even in a nuclear blast."

3. Movement supporters were not the only ones using dehumanizing speech. Throughout the movement period, many government supporters also called movement supporters "cockroaches." Both before and during the movement, progovernment senior citizens and prodemocracy young people often called each other "rubbish old guys" and "rubbish youths," respectively.

4. See https://lihkg.com/thread/1465135/page/1 (last accessed on March 28, 2024).

5. There was no direct evidence supporting the rumor even after media outlets attempted to investigate the matter. The police argued that they were intervening in the situation where the protesters on the metro train were threatening other fellow riders. Movement supporters rejected the police's explanation and remained suspicious about what eventually happened that night. "August 31, beating people to death" would become part of a prominent slogan shouted in protest events between September and December 2019.

6. At one point along the route, a protester stood in front of the entrance of a shopping mall, urging the "escaping" protesters not to go inside because the police had entered the mall. The author did not follow the protester's advice and entered the mall, which was entirely quiet and peaceful, without any sign of the presence of police officers.

7. In the opinion poll conducted by the CCPOS of the Chinese University of Hong Kong in October 2019 (N = 751), 87.6 percent of the respondents believed that a COI should be established. The figure implies that the idea of a COI was supported by even a substantial proportion of citizens who otherwise did not support the movement.

8. Edward Leung himself was in prison at the time of the 2019 protests due to the Mongkok civil unrest

9. See https://t.me/hkstandstrong_promo. Together with LIHKG, Telegram was regarded as another major online platform that has played a significant role in

social mobilization and coordination of actions during the 2019 protest movement. See Urman et al. (2021) and Su et al. (2022).

10. See https://www.rfa.org/cantonese/commentaries/dcwatcher/dcwatcher-08132019110318.html.

11. The whole period of the Anti-ELAB Movement was broken down into three phases because the slogans and claims emerged at different times. Hence their intercorrelations at the early phase of the movement were not particularly telling. In fact, this explains the absence of significant relationships in the first phase as shown in table 7.5. The correlations in later phrases—that is, after all the slogans and ideas had already emerged and become part of movement discourses—would be more meaningful.

Chapter 8

1. In Hong Kong research, the notion of the attentive spectator was coined by Kuan and Lau (1995) to describe the change in political culture in Hong Kong in the early 1990s, when citizens became more attentive to public affairs, though level of political participation remained relatively low.

2. The findings are available at https://www.pori.hk/. But in June 2023, the Public Opinion Research Institute announced that it would no longer publicize the results of several types of opinion surveys after discussion with the authorities. The surveys that would no longer be made publicly available include those on Hong Kong people's identity, trust toward the Central Government, and so on.

3. The survey was conducted by Dr. Samson Yuen and Dr. Gary Tang. The author has access to the original data.

4. The Civil Human Rights Front, for instance, was formed as a coalition of civil society and political groups, including groups working on labor, feminist, LBGTQ, and ethnic minority issues, among others.

5. Personal conversations with core members of civil society organizations.

Appendix

1. See https://legalref.judiciary.hk/lrs/common/ju/judgment.jsp.

References

Accornero, G. (2013). Contentious politics and student dissent in the twilight of the Portuguese dictatorship: Analysis of a protest cycle. *Democratization, 20*(6), 1036–55.

Ah-Guo (2019). *Hong Kong's loss of voice.* Hong Kong: Breakthrough. [in Chinese]

Alimi, E. Y. (2007). The Israeli political arena and Palestinian contention: The case of the "first" Intifada. *British Journal of Political Science, 37*, 433–453.

Alimi, E. Y. (2016). The relational contexts of radicalization: The case of Jewish settler contention before and after the Gaza pullout. *Political Studies, 64*(4), 910–29.

Alimi, E. Y., Bosi, L., & Demetriou, C. (2012). Relational dynamics and processes of radicalization: A comparative framework. *Mobilization, 17*(1), 7–26.

Alimi, E. Y., & Maney, G. M. (2018). Focusing on focusing events: Event selection, media coverage, and the dynamics of contentious meaning-making. *Sociological Forum, 33*(3), 757–82.

Almeida, P. (2019). *Social movements: The structure of collective mobilization.* Oakland: University of California Press.

Alvarez, R. M., & Brehm, J. (2002). *Hard choices, easy answers.* Princeton: Princeton University Press.

Anisin, A. (2016). Repression, spontaneity, and collective action: The 2013 Turkish Gezi protests. *Journal of Civil Society, 12*(4), 411–29.

Anonymous (2021). Hong Kong unraveled: Social media and the 2019 protest movement. *Global Storytelling: Journal of Digital and Moving Images, 1*(1), doi: 10.3998/gs.830.

Aslandis, P. (2018). Populism as a collective action master frame for transnational mobilization. *Sociological Forum, 33*(2), 443–64.

Au, A. K. L. (2017). *Freedom under 20 shades of grey.* Hong Kong: Chinese University of Hong Kong Press. [in Chinese]

Au, N. H., Chan, K. M., & Ng, K. L. (2024). Cooperate but divided at heart: Analysis of an opposition elite survey during autocratization. *Political Studies Review, 22*(1), 156–173.

Aytaç, S. E., Schiumerini, L., & Stokes, S. (2018). Why Do People Join Backlash Protests? Lessons from Turkey. *Journal of Conflict Resolution, 62*(6), 1205–28

Bagguley, P. (2002). Contemporary British feminism: A social movement in abeyance? *Social Movement Studies, 1*(2), 169–85.

Basinger, S. J., & Lavine, H. (2005). Ambivalence, information, and electoral choice. *American Political Science Review, 99*(2), 169–84.

Beck, C. J. (2015). *Radicals, revolutionaries, and terrorists.* Cambridge: Polity.

Beja, J. P. (2019). Xi Jinping's China: On the road to neo-totalitarianism. *Social Research: An International Quarterly, 86*(1), 203–30.

Benford, R. D., & Snow, D. A. (2000). Framing processes and social movements: An overview and assessment. *Annual Review of Sociology, 26*, 611–39.

Bennett, W. L. (2008). Changing citizenship in the digital age. In W. L. Bennett (ed.), *Civic life online: Learning how digital media can engage youth* (pp. 1–24). Cambridge, MA: MIT Press.

Bennett, W. L., & Segerberg, A. (2013). *The logic of connective action.* Cambridge University Press.

Benson, J. (2023). Democracy and the epistemic problems of political polarization. *American Political Science Review*, advanced online publication, doi: 10.1017/S0003055423001089.

Bernardi, L., Morales, L., Luhiste, M., & Bischof, D. (2018). The effects of the Fukushima disaster on nuclear energy debates and policies: A two-step comparative examination. *Environmental Politics, 27*(1), 42–68.

Bosi, L. (2008). Explaining the emergence process of the civil rights protest in Northern Ireland (1945–968): Insights from a relational social movement approach. *Journal of Historical Sociology, 21*(2–3), 242–71.

Bosi, L., & Davis, D. (2017). What is to be done? Agency and the causation of transformative events in Ireland's 1916 rising and 1969 Long March. *Mobilization, 22*(2), 223–43.

Bosi, L., & della Porta, D. (2012). Micro-mobilization into armed groups: Ideological, instrumental and solidaristic paths. *Qualitative Sociology, 35*(4), 361–83.

Boxell, L., Gentzkow, M., & Shapiro, J. M. (2024). Cross-country trends in affective polarization. *The Review of Economics and Statistics, 106*(2), 557–65.

Bray, L. A., Shriver, T. E., & Adams, A. E. (2019). Mobilizing grievances in an authoritarian setting: Threat and emotion in the 1953 Plzen Uprising. *Sociological Perspective, 62*(1), 77–95.

Buechler, S. M. (2011). *Understanding social movements.* Boulder: Paradigm.

Burns, K. (2016). Judges, "common sense" and judicial cognition. *Griffith Law Review, 25*(3), 319–51.

Burns, K. (2018). "In this day and age": Social facts, common sense and cognition in tort law judging in the United Kingdom. *Journal of Law and Society, 45*(2), 226–53.

Burstein, P. (1991). Legal mobilization as a social movement tactic: The struggle for equal employment opportunity. *American Journal of Sociology, 96*(5), 1201–25.

Cai, Y. S. (2017). *The Occupy Movement in Hong Kong: Sustaining decentralized protest*. London: Routledge.

Cai, Y. S. (2020). Protesters and tactical escalation. In E. W. Cheng & N. Ma (eds.), *The Umbrella Movement: Civil resistance and contentious space in Hong Kong* (pp. 209–31). Amsterdam: Amsterdam University Press.

Carey, J. M. (2017). Electoral formula and fragmentation in Hong Kong. *Journal of East Asian Studies, 17*(2), 215–31.

Carrico, K. (2022). *Two systems, two countries: A nationalist guide to Hong Kong*. Oakland: University of California Press.

Cassegard, C. (2023). The recovery of protest in Japan: From the "ice age" to the post-2011 movements. *Social Movement Studies, 22*(5), 751–66.

Castells, M. (2012). *Networks of outrage and hope*. Polity.

CCPOS (Center for Communication and Public Opinion Survey) (2014). *Public Opinion & Political Development in Hong Kong*. Press release on December 18, 2014. http://www.com.cuhk.edu.hk/ccpos/images/news/TaskForce_Press-Release_141218_English.pdf.

CCPOS (Center for Communication and Public Opinion Survey) (2020). *Research Report on Public Opinion During the Anti-Extradition Bill (Fugitive Offenders Bill) Movement in Hong Kong*. Report submitted to the Independent Police Complaints Commission, May 2020. http://www.com.cuhk.edu.hk/ccpos/en/pdf/202005PublicOpinionSurveyReport-ENG.pdf.

Chan, A. (2020). From unorganized street protests to organizing unions: The birth of a new trade union movement in Hong Kong. *Made in China Journal, 5*(2), 89–96.

Chan, A. K. W., Cheung, L. T. O., Chong, E. K. M., Lee, M. Y. K., & Wong, M. Y. H. (2022). Hong Kong's new wave of migration: Socio-political factors of individuals' intention to emigrate. *Comparative Migration Studies, 10*, article no. 49, doi: 10.1186/s40878-022-00323-y.

Chan, C. S. C., & Junker, A. (2021). Anti-activism and its impact on civil society in Hong Kong: A case study of the anti-Falun Gong campaign. *Modern China, 47*(6), 765–94.

Chan, D. S. W. (2022). The consumption power of the politically powerless: The Yellow Economy in Hong Kong. *Journal of Civil Society, 18*(1), 69–86.

Chan, D. S. W., & Pun, N. (2020). Economic power of the politically powerless in the 2019 Hong Kong pro-democracy movement. *Critical Asian Studies, 52*(1), 33–43.

Chan, E., & Chan, J. (2017). Hong Kong 2007–2017: A backlash in civil society. *Asia Pacific Journal of Public Administration, 39*(2), 135–52.

Chan, J. M., & Lee, C. C. (1984). Journalistic paradigms on civil protests: A case study of Hong Kong. In A. Arno & W. Dissanayake (eds.), *The news media in national and international conflict. Boulder*. Colorado: Westview.

Chan, J. M., & Yau, S. M. (2019). The real meanings of slogans: Government's immature definition of the movement. *Ming Pao*, August 8, 2019, A23. [in Chinese]

Chan, K. F. (2016a). Resistance without bottom line is barbaric. *Ming Pao*, February 18, 2016, A32. [in Chinese]

Chan, K. F. (2016b). When some eggs hurt the other eggs. *Ming Pao*, February 26, 2016, A31. [in Chinese]

Chan, N. K. (2018). Place-making and communication practice: Everyday precarity in a night market in Hong Kong. *Space and Culture, 21*(4), 439–54.

Chan, S. C. K. (2020). Some thoughts on the endgame of resistance: *Ngo-yiu Naam-chaau* as terminal reciprocity. *Inter-Asia Cultural Studies, 21*(1), 99–110.

Chandler, C. (2000). Discontent afflicts Hong Kong. *Washington Post*, June 28, 2000.

Chen, X. (2012). *Social protest and contentious authoritarianism in China*. New York: Cambridge University Press.

Chen, Y. C., & Szeto, M. M. (2015). The forgotten road of progressive localism: The New Preservation Movement in Hong Kong. *Inter-Asia Cultural Studies, 16*(3), 436–53.

Cheng, E. W. (2016). Street politics in a hybrid regime: The diffusion of political activism in post-colonial Hong Kong. *China Quarterly, 226*, 383–406.

Cheng, E. W. (2020). United front work and mechanisms of countermobilization in Hong Kong. *China Journal, 83*, 1–33.

Cheng, E. W., & Chan, W. Y. (2017). Explaining spontaneous occupation: Antecedents, contingencies and spaces in the Umbrella Movement. *Social Movement Studies, 16*(2), 222–239.

Cheng, E. W., & Lee, F. L. F. (2023). Hybrid protest logics and relational dynamics against institutional decay: Networked movements in Asia. *Social Movement Studies, 22*(5–6), 607–627.

Cheng, E. W., Lee, F. L. F., Yuen, S., & Tang, G. (2022). Total mobilization from below: Hong Kong's freedom summer. *China Quarterly, 251*, 629–59.

Cheng, E. W., & Ma, N. (eds.) (2020). *The Umbrella Movement: Civil disobedience and contentious space in Hong Kong*. Amsterdam: Amsterdam University Press.

Cheng, E. W., & Yuen, S. (2024). *The making of leaderful mobilization: Power and contention in Hong Kong*. New York: Cambridge University Press.

Cheng, J. Y. (2023). Beijing's changing Hong Kong policy: The rise and fall of pragmatism. *Journal of Contemporary Asia, 53*(4), 626–47.

Cheng, J. Y. S. (2014). The emergence of radical politics in Hong Kong: Causes and impact. *China Review, 14*(1), 199–232.

Cheung, T. (2015). "Father" of Hong Kong nationalism? A critical review of Wan Chin's city-state theory. *Asian Education and Development Studies, 4*(4), 460–70.

Choi, S. Y. (2018). The politics of depoliticization in Lost in the Fumes. *Ming Pao*, February 11, 2018. [in Chinese]

Chow, A. (2019). Prefigurative politics of the Umbrella Movement: An ethnography of its promise and predicament. In C. K. Lee and M. Sing (eds.), *Take back our future* (pp. 34–51). Ithaca: Cornell University Press.

Chow, V. (2019). Umbrella Movement 2.0 exposes flaws in "one country, two systems." *The Interpreter*, June 14, 2019. https://www.lowyinstitute.org/the-interpreter/umbrella-movement-20-exposes-flaws-one-country-two-systems.

Choy, I. C. K. (2015). The District Council election results are likely to lead to adjustment of political stance by the pan-democrats. *Ming Pao*, November 24, 2015. [in Chinese]

Chung, H. F. (2015). A tale of two societies: Fragments of an ethnography of Umbrella Revolution. *Hong Kong Anthropologist, 7*. https://www.arts.cuhk.edu.hk/~ant/hka/documents/2015/HKA7_CHUNG.pdf

Chung, H. F. (2021). Taking "community" to its end: From movement abeyance to community activism. In F. Lee (ed.), *Actors in the contention of our time* (pp. 105–20). Oxford: Oxford University Press. [in Chinese]

Chung, K., & Cheung, T. (2018). Political storm in Hong Kong as activist Agnes Chow banned from by-election over party's call for city's "self-determination. *South China Morning Post*, January 27, 2018.

Chung, K., & Cheung, T. (2019). Hong Kong protests have "obvious characteristics of colour revolution," top Beijing official warns amid "worst crisis since 1997 handover." *South China Morning Post*, August 8, 2019.

Cochran, P. (2017). *Common sense and legal judgment*. Kingston: McGill-Queen's University Press.

Cottle, S. (2008). Reporting demonstrations: The changing media politics of dissent. *Media, Culture & Society, 30*(6), 853–72.

della Porta, D. (2014). On violence and repression: A relational approach. *Government & Opposition, 49*(2), 159–87.

della Porta, D. (2018). Radicalization: A relational perspective. *Annual Review of Political Science, 21*(1), 461–74.

della Porta, D. (2020). Protests as critical junctures: Some reflections towards a momentous approach to social movements. *Social Movement Studies, 19*, 556–75.

Demirel-Pegg, T., & Rasler, K. (2021). The effects of selective and indiscriminate repression on the 2013 Gezi Park non-violent resistance campaign. *Sociological Perspectives, 64*(1), 58–81.

DiMaggio, P., Evans, J., & Bryson, B. (1996). Have American's social attitudes more polarized? *The American Journal of Sociology, 102*(3), 690–755.

Dimitrov, M. K. (2023). *Information and dictatorship*. Oxford: Oxford University Press.

Dirks, E., & Fu, D. (2023). Governing "untrustworthy" civil society in China. *The China Journal, 89*, 24–44.

Drago, A. (2021). Strikes, general assemblies and institutional insurgency: Explaining the persistence of the Quebec student movement. *Social Movement Studies, 20*(6), 652–68.

Eagly, A. H., & Telaak, K. (1972). Width of the latitude of acceptance as a determinant of attitude change. *Journal of Personality and Social Psychology, 23*(3), 388–97.

Earl, J. & J. M., Braithwaite (2022). Layers of political repression: Integrating research on social movement repression. *Annual Review of Law and Social Science, 18*, 227–48.

Ellefsen, R. (2016). Judicial opportunities and the death of SHAC: Legal repression along a cycle of contention. *Social Movement Studies, 15*(5), 441–56.

Ellefsen, R. (2018). Deepening the explanation of radical flank effects: Tracing contingent outcomes of destructive capacity. *Qualitative Sociology, 41*(1), 111–33.

El-Mallakh, N. (2020). How do protests affect electoral choices? Evidence from Egypt. *Journal of Economic Behavior and Organization, 179*, 299–322.

Espeland, C. E., & Rogstad, J. (2013). Antiracism and social movements in Norway: The importance of critical events. *Journal of Ethnic and Migration Studies, 39*(1), 125–42.

Fang, K. C., & Cheng, C. Y. (2022). Social media live streaming as affective news in the Anti-ELAB Movement in Hong Kong. *Chinese Journal of Communication, 15*(3), 401–14.

Feldman, S., & Zaller, J. (1992). The political culture of ambivalence: Ideological responses to the welfare state. *American Journal of Political Science, 36*(1), 268–307.

Fishkin, J. (1995). *The voice of the people: Public opinion and democracy.* New Haven: Yale University Press.

Flesher Fominaya, C. (2015). Debunking spontaneity: Spain's 15-M/Indignados as autonomous movement. *Social Movement Studies, 14*(2), 142–63.

Flesher Fominaya, C. (2020). *Democracy reloaded.* Oxford: Oxford University Press.

Fong, B. C. H. (2017). One country, two nationalisms: Center-periphery relations between mainland China and Hong Kong. *Modern China, 43*(5), 523–56.

Fong, B. C. H. (2021). Exporting autocracy: How China's extra-jurisdictional autocratic influence caused democratic backsliding in Hong Kong. *Democratization, 28*(1), 198–218.

Fong, B. C. H. (2022). Diaspora formation and mobilization: The emerging Hong Kong diaspora in the anti-extradition bill movement. *Nations and Nationalism, 28*(3), 1061–79.

Fong, G. C. (2015). Umbrella Soldiers and democrats should not be complacent despite the small win. *Hong Kong Economic Journal*, November 24, 2015. [in Chinese]

Fong, I. W. Y., & Lee, F. L. F. (2023). Disagreement resolution on digital communication platform in a self-directed political consumerism campaign. *Information, Communication & Society, 26*(15), 3035–53.

Fraser, N. (1985). What's critical about critical theory? The case of Habermas and gender. *New German Critique, 35*, 97–31.

Freeman, J. (1972). The tyranny of structurelessness. *Berkeley Journal of Sociology, 17*, 151–64. https://www.jstor.org/stable/41035187.

Fu, D. (2017). *Mobilization without the masses.* New York: Cambridge University Press.

Fung, A. Y. H. (2007). Political economy of Hong Kong media: Producing a hegemonic voice. *Asian Journal of Communication, 17*(2), 159–71.

Gade, T. (2019). Together all the way? Abeyance and co-optation of Sunni networks in Lebanon. *Social Movement Studies, 18*(1), 56–77.

Gamson, W. (1992). *Talking politics.* Cambridge: Cambridge University Press.

Gamson, W. (1995) Constructing social protest. In H. Johnston and B. Klandermans (eds.), *Social movements and culture* (pp. 85–106). Minneapolis: University of Minnesota Press.

Gamson, W. A., & Herzog, H. (1999). Living with contradictions: The taken-for-granted in Israeli political discourse. *Political Psychology, 20*(2), 247–66.

Gan, W. (2017). Puckish protesting in the Umbrella Movement. *International Journal of Cultural Studies, 20*(2), 162–76.

Geha, C. (2019). Politics of a garbage crisis: Social networks, narratives, and frames of Lebanon's 2015 protests and their aftermath. *Social Movement Studies, 18*(1), 78–92.

Grimm, J., & Harders, C. (2018). Unpacking the effects of repression: The evolution of Islamist repertoires of contention in Egypt after the fall of President Morsi. *Social Movement Studies, 17*(1), 1–18.

Gube, J. & Halse, C. (2023). Precarity of belonging? Belongingness and race of ethnically diverse young people in Hong Kong. *Ethnic and Racial Studies, 46*(12), 2591–11.

Gyimesi, M. (2021). Reclaim, occupy, pillow fight! Movement continuity in the Urban Playground Movement's Budapest scene. *Social Movement Studies, 20*(4), 417–38.

Haines, H. H. (1984). Black radicalization and the funding of civil rights: 1957–1970. *Social Problems, 32*(1), 31–43.

Hallin, D. (1986). *The uncensored war.* New York: Oxford University Press.

Hargreaves, S. (2015). From the fragrant harbour to Occupy Central: Hong Kong's democratic development & "rule of law" discourse. *Journal of Parliamentary & Political Law, 9*(3), 519–67.

Harlow, S., & Johnson, T.J. (2011). Overthrowing the protest paradigm? How the New York Times, Global Voices, and Twitter covered the Egyptian Revolution. *International Journal of Communication, 5*, 1359–74.

Haydu, J. (2012). Frame brokerage in the pure food movement, 1879–1906. *Social Movement Studies, 11*(1), 97–112.

Hershey, M. R. (1992). The constructed explanation: Interpreting election results in the 1984 Presidential race. *Journal of Politics, 54*(4), 943–76.

Hetherington, M. J., & Rudolph, T. J. (2015). *Why Washington won't work.* Chicago: University of Chicago Press.

Hiroko, N. (2020). Legalization of the Chinese Communist Party's governance over Hong Kong. *Journal of Contemporary East Asia Studies, 9*(2), 157–174.

Ho, J. C. T. (2022). Understanding Hong Kong nationalism: A topic network approach. *Nations and Nationalism, 28*(4), 1249–66.

Ho. J. C. T. (2023). The internationalism of stateless nations: The case of Hong Kong. *Nations and Nationalism, 29*(1), 346–363.

Ho, K. K. L. (2019). Policing transnational protests in an Asian context: The WTO sixth ministerial conference in Hong Kong. *Contemporary Chinese Political Economy and Strategic Relations: An International Journal,* 5(1), 211–49.

Ho, K. K. L. (2021). A government-society confrontation: Policing protests in postcolonial China's Hong Kong SAR. Interventions: *International Journal of Postcolonial Studies, 23*(4), 481–505.

Ho, M. S. (2018). From mobilization to improvisation: The lessons from Taiwan's 2014 Sunflower Movement. *Social Movement Studies, 17*(2), 189–202.

Ho, M. S. (2019). *Challenging Beijing's mandate of heaven.* Temple University Press.

Ho, M. S. (2020). How protesters evolve: Hong Kong's anti-extradition movement learned the lesson of the Umbrella Movement. *Mobilization, 25*(SI), 711–28.

Ho, M. S. (2023). Aiming for Achilles' heel: A relational explanation of the ascendency of pro-nuclear activism in Taiwan, 2013–2020. *Social Movement Studies, 22*(5–6), 628–47.

Ho, M. S. (2024). Hongkongers' international front: Diaspora activism during and after the 2019 Anti-Extradition protest. *Journal of Contemporary Asia, 54*(2), 238–59.

Ho, P. S. Y. (2020). Queering the valiant: An alternative perspective on the Hong Kong protest movement. *Feminista,* May 8, 2020. https://feministajournal. com/queering-the-valiant-an-alternative-perspective-on-the-hong-kong-protest-movement/.

Ho, P. S. Y. (2021). A feminist snap: Has feminism in Hong Kong been defeated? *Made in China Journal,* March 8, 2022. https://madeinchinajournal.com/ 2022/03/08/a-feminist-snap-feminism-in-hong-kong/.

Holland, L., & Cable, S. (2002). Reconceptualizing social movement abeyance: The role of internal processes and culture in cycles of movement abeyance and resurgence. *Sociological Focus, 35*(2), 297–314.

Huang, V. G., & Li, X. (2024). Diffusion-proofing protest paradigm: Mass media and China's prevention of social movement spillover during the Hong Kong Anti-Extradition Law Amendment Bill Movement. *The International Journal of Press/Politics, 29*(2), 328–50.

Hughes, R. (1968). *Hong Kong: Borrowed place, borrowed time.* London: Deutsch.

Hui, P. K., & Lau, K. C. (2015). "Living in truth" versus realpolitik: Limitations and potentials of the Umbrella Movement. *Inter-Asia Cultural Studies, 16*(3), 348–66.

Hung, E., & Kong, H. (2023). Hong Kong marks first authorized protest in 3 years as 80 homeowners march against Tseung Kwan O reclamation plan. *South China Morning Post*, March 26, 2023.

Hung, H. F. (2022). *City on the edge: Hong Kong under Chinese rule*. New York: Cambridge University Press.

Ingham, M., & Ng. K. K. K. (2022). Introduction: Hong Kong independent documentaries and their visibility. *Asian Cinema, 33*(2), 132–45.

Ip, I. C. (2020). *Hong Kong's new identity politics*. London: Routledge.

Ives, B., & Lewis, J. S. (2020). From rallies to riots: Why some protests become violent. *Journal of Conflict Resolution, 64*(5), 958–86.

Jacobsson, K., & Sorborn, A. (2015). After a cycle of contention: Post-Gothenburg strategies of left-libertarian activists in Sweden. *Social Movement Studies, 14*(6), 713–32.

Jamte, J., & Ellefsen, R. (2020). The consequences of soft repression. *Mobilization, 25*(3), 383–404.

Jasanoff, S. (2018). Science, common sense, and judicial power in U.S. courts. *Daedalus 147*(4), 15–27.

Jasper, J. M. (1998). The emotions of protest Affective and reactive emotions in and around social movements. *Sociological Forum, 13*(3), 397–424.

Jones, C. A. G. (2015). *Lost in China? Law, culture and identity in post-1997 Hong Kong*. New York: Cambridge University Press.

Juris, J. S. (2008). Performing politics: Image, embodiment, and affective solidarity during anti-corporate globalization protests. *Ethnography, 9*(1), 61–97.

Kadivar, M. A. (2017). Preelection mobilization and electoral outcome in authoritarian regimes. *Mobilization, 22*(3), 293–310.

Kaeding, M. P. (2016). The rise of "localism" in Hong Kong. *Journal of Democracy, 28*(1), 157–71.

Kaeding, M. P., & Wang-Kaeding, H. (2023). Coping with international politics: A case study of Hong Kong. *Review of International Studies*, advanced online publication, https://doi.org/10.1017/S0260210523000591.

Kay, E., & Ramos, H. (2017). Do subnational governments fund organizations in neoliberal times? The role of critical events in provincial funding of women's organizations. *American Behavioral Scientist, 61*(13), 1658–77.

Kelly, S. (1983). *Interpreting elections*. Princeton: Princeton University Press.

Kitschelt, H. (2006). Movement parties. In R. S. Katz & W. Crotty (eds.), *Handbook of party politics* (pp. 278–90). Thousand Oaks, CA: Sage.

Klandermans, P. G., & de Weerd, M. (1999). Injustice and adversarial frames in a supranational political context: Farmer's protest in the Netherlands and Spain. In D. della Porta, H. Kriesi, & D. Rucht (eds.), *Social Movements in a Globalizing World* (pp. 134–47). Macmillan.

Knight, G., & Greenberg, J. (2011). Talk of the enemy: Adversarial framing and climate change discourse. *Social Movement Studies, 10*(4), 323–40.

Kobayashi, T. (2020). Depolarization through social media use: Evidence from dual identifiers in Hong Kong. *New Media & Society, 22*(8), 1339–58.

Kobayashi, T., & Chan, P. (2022a). Political sensitivity bias in autocratizing Hong Kong. *International Journal of Public Opinion Research, 34*(4), edac028, https://doi.org/10.1093/ijpor/edac028.

Kobayashi, T., & Chan, P. (2022b). Psychological underpinnings of self-censorship in post-NSL Hong Kong. Paper presented at the Hong Kong: Interrupted Revolutionary Movements Workshop, Australian National University, Australia, December 2022.

Koinova, M. (2018). Critical junctures and transformative events in diaspora mobilisation for Kosovo and Palestinian statehood. *Journal of Ethnic and Migration Studies, 44*(8), 1289–1308.

Kong, T. G. (2017). Mainlandization: How the Communist Party works to control and assimilate Hong Kong. https://hongkongfp.com/2017/10/15/mainlandization-communist-party-works-control-assimilate-hong-kong/, October 15, 2017.

Ku, A. S. (2007). Constructing and contesting the "order" imagery in media discourse: Implications for civil society in Hong Kong. *Asian Journal of Communication, 17*(2), 186–200.

Ku, A. S. (2012). Remaking places and fashioning an opposition discourse: Struggle over the Star Ferry Pier and the Queen's Pier in Hong Kong. *Environment and Planning D, 30*(1), 5–22.

Ku, A. S. (2019). In search of a new political subjectivity in Hong Kong: The Umbrella Movement as a street theater of generational change. *The China Journal, 82*, 111–32.

Ku, A. S. (2020). New forms of youth activism: Hong Kong's anti-extradition bill movement in the local-national-global nexus. *Space and Polity, 24*(1), 111–17.

Kuan, H. C. (1998). Escape from politics: Hong Kong's predicament of political development? *International Journal of Public Administration, 21*(10), 1423–48.

Kuan, H. C., & Lau, S. K. (1995). The partial vision of democracy in Hong Kong: A survey of popular opinion. *The China Journal, 34*, 239–63.

Kuntz, P., & Thompson, M. R. (2009). More than just the final straw: Stolen elections as revolutionary triggers. *Comparative Politics, 41*(3), 253–72.

Kwok, C., & Chan, N. K. (2017). Legitimacy and forced democratization in social movements: A case study of the Umbrella Movement in Hong Kong. *China Perspectives, 2017*(3), 7–16.

Kwong, Y. H. (2016). State-society conflict radicalization in Hong Kong: The rise of "anti-China" sentiment and radical localism. *Asian Affairs, 47*(3), 428–42.

Lai, B. (2018). Want to draw your sympathy and provoke you too: Somewhere beyond the mist and lost in the fumes. *Ming Pao*, February 11, 2018. [in Chinese]

Lai, J. F. (2015). Those who follow the public live; those who go against the public die. *Hong Kong Economic Journal*, November 25, 2015. [in Chinese]

Lai, R. Y. S. (2021). From #MeToo to #ProtestToo: How a feminist movement converged with a pro-democracy protest in Hong Kong. *Politics & Gender*, *17*(3), 500–7.

Lai, Y. H., & Sing, M. (2020). Solidarity and implications of a leaderless movement in Hong Kong: Its strength and limitations. *Communist & Post-Communist Studies*, 53(4), 41–67.

Lam, J. (2019). "Liberate Hong Kong; revolution of our times": Who came up with this protest chant and why is the government worried? *South China Morning Post*, August 6, 2019.

Lam, J. T. M. (2017). Hong Kong District Council elections 2015: A political litmus test for the Occupy Central Movement. *Asian Education and Development Studies*, 6(4), 354–71.

Lam, J. T. M. (2020). Localist challenges and the fragmentation of the pan-democratic camp in Hong Kong. *Asian Education and Development Studies*, 9(4), 279–89.

Lam, W. M. (2004) *Understanding the political culture of Hong Kong*. New York: M. E. Sharpe.

Lam, W. M. (2018). Hong Kong's fragmented soul: Exploring brands of localism. In L. Cooper & W. M. Lam (eds.), *Citizenship, identity and social movements in the new Hong Kong* (pp. 72–93). London: Routledge.

Laugerud, S. (2020). Common sense, (ab)normality and bodies in Norwegian rape verdicts. *NORA: Nordic Journal of Feminist and Gender Reesearch*, *28*(1), 18–29.

Lavine, H, Borgida, E., & Sullivan, J. L. (2000). On the relationship between attitude involvement and attitude accessibility: Toward a cognitive-motivational model of political information processing. *Political Psychology*, *21*(1), 81–106.

Law, N. (2016). On self-determination and Hong Kong independence: Responding to Rita Fan. *Ming Pao*, May 9, 2016. [in Chinese]

Law, W. S. (2018). Decolonisation deferred: Hong Kong identity in historical perspective. In L. Cooper & W. M. Lam (eds.), *Citizenship, identity and social movements in the new Hong Kong* (pp. 13–33). London: Routledge.

Law, W. S. (2019). The spectrum of frames and disputes in the Umbrella Movement. In C. K. Lee and M. Sing (eds.), *Take back our future* (pp. 74–99). Ithaca: Cornell University Press.

Le Bon, G. (2001/1895). *The crowd*. New York: Dover.

Lee, C. K. (2019). Take back our future: An eventful sociology of the Hong Kong Umbrella Movement. In C. K. Lee and M. Sing (eds.), *Take back our future* (pp. 1–33). Ithaca: Cornell University Press.

Lee, C. K., & Sing, M. (eds.) (2019). *Take back our future*. Ithaca: Cornell University Press.

Lee, E. W. Y. (2020a). United front organizations as a political machine: Political clientelism, authoritarian election, and electoral breakthrough. *Taiwan Journal of Democracy, 16*(2), 101–20.

Lee, E. W. Y. (2020b). United front, clientelism, and indirect rule: Theorizing the role of the "liaison office" in Hong Kong. *Journal of Contemporary China, 29*(125), 763–75.

Lee, F. L. F. (2006). Collective efficacy, support for democratization, and political participation in Hong Kong. *International Journal of Public Opinion Research, 18*(3), 297–317.

Lee, F. L. F. (2008). Local press meets transnational activism: News dynamics in an anti-WTO protest. *Chinese Journal of Communication, 1*(1), 57–78.

Lee, F. L. F. (2014). Triggering the protest paradigm: Examining factors affecting news coverage of protests. *International Journal of Communication, 8*, 2725–46.

Lee, F. L. F. (2018a). Internet alternative media, movement experience, and radicalism: The case of post-Umbrella Movement Hong Kong. *Social Movement Studies, 17*(2), 219–33.

Lee, F. L. F. (2018b). On Hong Kong people's collective powerlessness. *Ming Pao*, August 16, 2018. [in Chinese]

Lee, F. L. F. (2018c). The role of perceived social reality in the adoption of postmaterial value: The case of Hong Kong. *Social Science Journal, 55*(2), 139–48.

Lee, F. L. F. (2020). Solidarity in the Anti-Extradition Bill movement in Hong Kong. *Critical Asian Studies, 52*(1), 18–32.

Lee, F. L. F. (2023a). Beyond self-censorship: Emergence of journalistic risk cultures in Hong Kong under the National Security Law. *The China Journal*, 90, 129–53.

Lee, F. L. F. (2023b). Judges' understanding of protests and cultural underpinnings of legal repression: Examining Hong Kong court verdicts. *Social & Legal Studies, 32*(3), 464–84.

Lee, F. L. F. (2023c). Proactive internationalization and diasporic mobilization in a networked movement: The case of Hong Kong's Anti-Extradition Bill protests. *Social Movement Studies, 22*(2), 232–49.

Lee, F. L. F., & Chan, C. K. (2023). Legalization of press control under democratic backsliding: The case of post-national security law Hong Kong. *Media, Culture & Society, 45*(5), 916–31.

Lee, F. L. F., & Chan, C. K. (2024). Political events and cultural othering: Impact of protests and elections on identities in post-handover Hong Kong, 1997–2021. *Journal of Contemporary China, 33*(147), 417–31.

Lee, F. L. F., & Chan, J. M. (2011). *Media, social mobilization, and mass protests in post-colonial Hong Kong*. Routledge.

Lee, F. L. F., & Chan, J. M. (2013). Exploring Hong Kong's "movement society": Analyzing the formation and development of collective contentious actions in Hong Kong. In S. K. Cheung & K. C. Leung (eds.), *Hong Kong, society, culture*. Hong Kong: Oxford University Press. [in Chinese]

Lee, F. L. F., & Chan, J. M. (2018). *Media and protest logics in the digital era: The Umbrella Movement in Hong Kong.* Oxford: Oxford University Press.

Lee, F. L. F., & Chan, J. M. (2021). *Memories of Tiananmen: Politics and processes of collective remembering in Hong Kong, 1989–2019.* Amsterdam: Amsterdam University Press.

Lee, F. L. F., Chan, M., & Chen, H. T. (2020). Social media and protest attitudes during movement abeyance: A study of Hong Kong university students. *International Journal of Communication, 14*(2020), 4932–51.

Lee, F. L. F., & Fong, I. (2023). The construction and mobilization of political consumerism through digital media in a networked social movement. *New Media & Society, 25*(12), 3573–92.

Lee, F. L. F., Liang, H., Cheng, E. W., Tang, G. K. Y., & Yuen, S. (2022). Affordances, movement dynamics, and a centralized digital communication platform in a networked movement. *Information, Communication & Society, 25*(12), 1699–1716.

Lee, F. L. F., Yuen, S., Tang, G. K. Y., & Cheng, E. (2019). Hong Kong's summer of uprising: From anti-extradition to anti-authoritarian protests. *China Review, 19*(4), 1–32.

Lee, F. L. F., Yuen, S., Tang, G. K. Y., Cheng, E. W., & Liang, H. (2022). Dynamics of tactical radicalization and public receptiveness in Hong Kong's Anti-Extradition Bill Movement. *Journal of Contemporary Asia, 52*(3), 429–51.

Lee, M. Y. K. (2017). Lawyers and Hong Kong's democracy movement: From electoral politics to civil disobedience. *Asian Journal of Political Science, 25*(1), 89–108.

Lee, Y. (2023). Meso-level leaders as brokers of horizontal and vertical linkages in feminist networked social movements. *Information, Communication & Society, 26*(10), 2015–32.

Lei, Y. W. (2018). *The contentious public sphere in China: Law, media, and authoritarian rule in China.* Princeton: Princeton University Press.

Leung, D. K. K. (2015). Alternative Internet radio, press freedom and contentious politics in Hong Kong, 2004–2014. *Javnost-the Public, 22*(2), 196–212.

Leung, L. (2009). Mediated violence as "global news": Co-opted performance in the framing of the WTO. *Media, Culture & Society, 31*(2), 251–69.

Lewis, J. S. (2023). Repression and bystander mobilization in Africa. *Social Movement Studies, 22*(4), 494–512.

Li, M., Adra, A., Yuen, S., Salfate, S. V., Chan, K. M., & Baumert, A. (2024). Understanding non-normative civil resistance under repression: Evidence from Hong Kong and Chile. *Political Psychology, 45*(3), 493–515.

Li, Y. (2022). *Memoir of a loser*, volume II. Taipei: Ink. [in Chinese]

Li, Y. T., & Whitworth, K. (2023a). Contentious repertoires: Examining Lennon Walls in Hong Kong's social unrest of 2019. *Journal of Contemporary Asia, 53*(1), 124–45.

Li, Y. T., & Whitworth, K. (2023b). Data as a weapon: The evolution of Hong Kong protesters' doxing strategies. *Social Science Computer Review, 41*(5), 1650–70.

Lian, J. (2014a). Detailed discussions of the loss of democracy and the changing paths and changing formation of social movements. *Hong Kong Economic Journal,* September 1, 2014. [in Chinese]

Lian, J. (2014b). Thought clearly about the serious long-term consequences of "pocket-it-first"? *Hong Kong Economic Journal,* August 22, 2014. [in Chinese]

Lian, J. (2014c). Talking about Hongkonger and Hong Kong consciousness with students from Undergrad. *Hong Kong Economic Journal,* June 9, 2014. [in Chinese]

Lian, J. (2015a). After Tianjin, Shenzhen; looking at the handover, when will the dusk arrive? *Hong Kong Economic Journal,* December 24, 2015. [in Chinese]

Lian, J. (2015b). Very dark in the past three years; ultra-moderates are ok; aging of voters is a good thing. *Hong Kong Economic Journal,* August 3, 2015. [in Chinese]

Lian, J. (2016a). Three breakthroughs in two years: The formation of the democrats under layers of contradictions. *Hong Kong Economic Journal,* February 29, 2016. [in Chinese]

Lian, J. (2016b). Fishball Revolution prevents Hong Kong from becoming the mainland; continual repression would create the 228 incident. *Hong Kong Economic Journal,* February 11, 2016. [in Chinese]

Lian, J. (2016c). The warm wind of criticisms against Hong Kong independence turns cold; strange logic criminalizes everyone. *Hong Kong Economic Journal,* April 25, 2016. [in Chinese]

Lian, J. (2016d). The whole city focuses on Hong Kong independence; the eggs seep into the wall. *Hong Kong Economic Journal,* July 25, 2014. [in Chinese]

Liang, H., & Lee, F. L. F. (2023). Opinion leadership in a leaderless movement: Discussion of the anti-extradition bill movement in the "LIHKG" web forum. *Social Movement Studies, 22*(5–6), 670–88.

Liang, H., & Zhang, X. Z. (2021). Partisan bias of perceived incivility and its political consequences: Evidence from survey experiments in Hong Kong. *Journal of Communication, 71*(3), 357–79.

Lichbach, M. I. (1987). Deterrence or Escalation? The Puzzle of Aggregate Studies of Repression and Dissent. *Journal of Conflict Resolution, 31*(2), 266–97.

Liu, J. (2017). From "moments of madness" to "the politics of mundanity": Researching digital media and contentious collective actions in China. *Social Movement Studies, 16*(4), 418–32.

Lo, S. S. H. (2016). *The politics of policing in Greater China.* New York: Palgrave Macmillan.

Lo, S. S. H. (2018). Ideologies and factionalism in Beijing-Hong Kong relations. *Asian Survey, 58*(3), 392–415.

Lui, L. (2022). National security education and the infrapolitical resistance of parent-stayers in Hong Kong. *Journal of Asian and African Studies, 58*(1), 86–100.

Lui, T. L. (2003). Rearguard politics: Hong Kong's middle class. *Development Economy, 42*(2), 161–83.

Lui, T. L. (2020). *Embarrassment*. Hong Kong: Oxford University Press. [in Chinese]

Lui, T. L., & Chiu, S. W. K. (eds.) (2000). *The dynamics of social movements in Hong Kong*. Hong Kong: Hong Kong University Press.

Luqiu, L. R. (2021). *Covering the 2019 Hong Kong protests*. Palgrave Macmillan.

Ma, E. K. W. (1999). *Culture, politics, and television in Hong Kong*. New York: Routledge.

Ma, M. L. Y. (2017). Affective framing and dramaturgical actions in social movements. *Journal of Communication Inquiry, 41*(1), 5–21.

Ma, N. (2001). The decline of the Democratic Party in Hong Kong: The second legislative election in the HKSAR. *Asian Survey, 41*(4), 564–83.

Ma, N. (2005). Civil society in self-defense: The struggle against national security legislation in Hong Kong. *Journal of Contemporary China, 14*(4), 456–82.

Ma, N. (2011). Value changes and legitimacy crisis in post-industrial Hong Kong. *Asian Survey, 51*(4), 683–712.

Ma, N. (2015). District Council elections: A test for umbrellas entering the community. *Ming Pa*o, November 9, 2015. [in Chinese]

Ma, N. (2017). The China factor in Hong Kong elections: 1991 to 2016. *China Perspectives, 2017*(3), 17–26.

Ma, N. (2020). Parties without power: Disabled governance and disarticulated participation in Hong Kong. *Communist and Post-Communist Studies, 53*(4), 118–35.

Ma, N., & Cheng, E. W. (2023). Professionals in revolt: Specialized networks and sectoral mobilization in Hong Kong. *Social Movement Studies, 22*(5–6), 648–69.

Marinelli, M. (2018). From street hawkers to public markets: Modernity and sanitization made in Hong Kong. In Y. Cabannes, M. Douglass, & R. Padawangi (eds.), *Cities in Asia by and for the people* (pp. 229–58). Amsterdam: Amsterdam University Press.

Martin, B. (2007). *Justice ignited: The dynamics of backfire*. Lanham, MD: Rowman & Littlefield.

Marullo, S., Pagnucco, R., & Smith, J. (1996). Frame changes and social movement contraction: US peace movement framing after the Cold War. *Sociological Inquiry, 66*(1), 1–28.

Mathews, G. (1997). Heunggongyahn: On the past, present and future of Hong Kong identity. *Bulletin of Concerned Asian Scholars, 29*(3), 3–13.

Mayer, B. (2009). Cross-movement coalition formation: Bridging the labor-environment divide. *Sociological Inquiry, 79*(2), 219–39.

McAdam, D. (1982). *The political process and the development of black insurgency*. Chicago: University of Chicago Press.

McAdam, D., & Sewell, Jr., W. H. (2001). It's about time: Temporality in the study of contentious politics. R. R. Aminzade, J. A. Goldstone, D. McAdam, E.

J. Perry, W. H. Sewell, S. Tarrow, & C. Tilly (pp. 89–125). *Silence and Voice in the Study of Contentious Politics*. Cambridge: Cambridge University Press.

McAdam, D., & Tarrow, S. (2010). Ballots and barricades: On the reciprocal relationship between elections and social movements. *Perspectives on Politics, 8*(2), 529–42.

McAdam, D., Tarrow, S., & Tilly, C. (2001). *Dynamics of contention*. New York: Cambridge University Press

McAdam, D., Tarrow, S., & Tilly, C. (2008). Methods for measuring mechanisms of contention. *Qualitative Sociology, 31*(4), 307–31.

McCammon, H. J., Bergner, E. M., & Arch, S. C. (2015). "Are you one of those women?" Within-movement conflict, radical flank effects, and social movement political outcomes. *Mobilization, 20*(2), 157–78.

McCarthy, J. D., & Zald, M. N. (1977). Resource mobilization and social movements: A partial theory. *American Journal of Sociology, 82*, 1212–41.

McLeod, D. M., & Hertog, J. K. (1998). Social control and the mass media's role in the regulation of protest groups: The communicative acts perspective. In D. Demers and K. Viswanath (eds.), *Mass media, social control and social change*. Ames: Iowa State University Press.

Melucci, A. (1989). *Nomads of the present: Social movements and individual needs in contemporary society*. London: Hutchinson.

Mendelsohn, M. (1998). The construction of electoral mandates: Media coverage of election results in Canada. *Political Communication, 15*(2), 239–53.

Meyer, D. S., & Staggenborg, S. (1996). Movements, countermovements, and the structure of political opportunity. *American Journal of Sociology, 101*(6), 1628–60.

Meyer, D. S., & Tarrow, S. (1998). A movement society: Contentious politics for a new century. In D. S. Meyer & S. Tarrow (eds.), *The social movement society* (pp. 1–28). Lanham: Rowman & Littlefield.

Mische, A. (2008). *Partisan publics: Communication and contention across Brazilian youth activist networks*. Princeton, NJ: Princeton University Press.

Mok, C. W. J. (2020). Why and how Umbrella Movement participants ran in the authoritarian elections in Hong Kong: Bringing umbrellas indoors. *Asian Survey, 60*(6), 1142–71.

Mooney, P. H., & Hunt, S. A. (1996). A repertoire of interpretations: Master frames and ideological continuity in US agrarian mobilization. *Sociological Quarterly, 37*(1), 177–97.

Nam (2016). An organization "without the townhall": Interviewing Wong Toi-Yeung of the Hong Kong Indigenous. *Stand News*, March 18, 2016. [in Chinese]

Newth, G. (2022). Populism in abeyance: The survival of populist repertoires of contention in North Italy. *Social Movement Studies, 21*(4), 511–29.

Ng, E. (2018). Defense says Hong Kong democracy activists face "unconstitutional, unnecessary charges in Umbrella Movement in trial. *Hong Kong Free Press*, January 9, 2018.

Ng, H. Y., & Kennedy, K. J. (2019). Localist groups and populist radical regionalism in Hong Kong. *China: An International Journal, 17*(4), 111–34.

Ng, M., Ko, J., & Lau, K. (2019). Is Hong Kong's riot law "respectable"? *Hong Kong Law Journal, 50*(3), 935–60.

O'Brien, K. J. & Deng, Y. (2015). Repression backfires: Tactical radicalization and protest spectacle in rural China. *Journal of Contemporary China, 24*(93), 457–70.

Oktavianus, J., Davidson, B., & Guan, L. (2023). Framing and counter-framing in online collective actions: The case of LGBT protests in a Muslim nation. *Information, Communication & Society, 26*(3), 479–95.

Ong, A. (2006). *Neoliberalism as exception.* Durham: Duke University Press.

Opp, K.-D., Voss, P., & Gern, C. (1995). *Origins of a spontaneous revolution: East Germany, 1989.* Ann Arbor: University of Michigan Press.

Over, D., & Taraktas, B. (2017). When does repression trigger mass protest? The 2013 Gezi protests. *Research in Social Movements, Conflicts and Change, 41*, 205–39.

Pang, L. K. (2020). *The appearing demos.* Ann Arbor: Michigan University Press.

Petty, R. E., & Cacioppo, J. T. (1996). *Attitudes and persuasion.* London: Routledge.

Pilati, K., Acconcia, G., Suber, D. L. & Chennaoui, H. (2019). Between organization and spontaneity of protests: The 2010–2011 Tunisian and Egyptian uprisings. *Social Movement Studies, 18*(4), 463–81.

Powell, F. A. (1966). Latitudes of acceptance and rejection and the belief-disbelief dimension: A correlational comparison. *Journal of Personality and Social Psychology, 4*(4), 453–57.

Przeworski, A., & Sprague, J. (1986). *Paper stones: A history of electoral socialism.* Chicago: University of Chicago Press.

Pubrick, M. (2019). A report of the 2019 Hong Kong protests. *Asian Affairs, 50*(4), 465–87.

Raisi, A. (2021). The reciprocal impact of electoral turnout on protest participation in developing countries: Evidence from Iran's 2018 uprising. *Democratization, 28*(4), 703–22.

Ramos, H. (2008). Opportunity for whom? Political opportunity and critical events in Canadian aboriginal mobilization, 1951–2000. *Social Forces, 87*(2), 795–823.

Repnikova, M. (2017). *Media politics in China.* New York: Cambridge University Press.

Rewal, P. (2018). Hawkers in Hong Kong: The informal sector in a contemporary city. *Journal of Royal Asiatic Society China, 78*(1), 285–319.

Robin-D'Cruz, B. (2019). Social brokers and leftist-Sadrist cooperation in Iraq's reform protest movement: Beyond instrumental action. *International Journal of Middle East Studies, 51*(2), 257–80.

Robnett, B., Glasser, C. L., & Trammell, R. (2015). Waves of contention: Relations among radical, moderate, and conservative movement organizations. *Research in Social Movements, Conflicts and Change, 38*, 69–101.

Romanos, E. (2016). Immigrants as brokers: Dialogical diffusion from Spanish indignados to Occupy Wall Street. *Social Movement Studies, 15*(3), 247–62.

Ruiz-Junco, N. (2013). Feeling social movements: theoretical contributions to social movement research on emotions. *Sociology Compass, 7*(1), 45–54.

Sanches, E. R. (2022). Introduction: Zooming in on protest and change in Africa. In E. R. Sanches (ed.), *Popular protest, political opportunities, and change in Africa* (pp. 1–18). London: Routledge.

Sauer, B. (2019). Mobilizing shame and disgust: Abolitionist affective frames in Austrian and German anti-sex-work movements. *Journal of Political Power, 12*(3), 318–38.

Sawyers, T. M., & Meyer, D. S. (1999). Missed opportunities: Social movement abeyance and public policy. *Social Problems, 46*(2), 187–206.

Schedler, A. (2023). Rethinking political polarization. *Political Science Quarterly, 138*(3), 335–59.

Schifeling, T., & Hoffman, A. J. (2017). Bill McKibben's influence on US climate change discourse: Shifting field-level debates through radical flank effects. *Organization & Environment, 32*(3), 213–33.

Schock, K. (1999). People power and political opportunities: Social movement mobilization and outcomes in the Philippines and Burma. *Social Problems, 46*(3), 355–75.

Schudson, M. (1998). *The good citizen.* Harvard: Harvard University Press.

Scott, I. (2017). "One country, two systems": The end of a legitimating ideology? *Asia Pacific Journal of Public Administration, 39*(2), 83–99.

Sewell, W. (1996). Historical events as transformations of structures: Inventing revolution at the Bastille. *Theory and Society, 25*, 841–81.

Sewell, W. (2005). *Logics of history.* Chicago: University of Chicago Press.

Shen, Y. (2019). In the name of the law: Legal frames and the ending of the Occupy Movement in Hong Kong. *Law and Social Inquiry, 44*(2), 468–90.

Shen, Y. (2020). Enclave deliberation and social movement mobilization: The DDays in Occupy Central. *Social Movement Studies, 19*(2), 144–59.

Shirah, R. (2016). Electoral authoritarianism and political unrest. *International Political Science Review, 37*(4), 470–84.

Shultziner, D. (2018). Transformative events, repression, and regime change: Theoretical and psychological aspects. In L. R. Kurtz & L. A. Smithey (eds.), The paradox of repression and nonviolent movement (pp. 52–73). New York: Syracuse University Press.

Shum, M. (2021). When voting turnout becomes contentious repertoire: How anti-ELAB protest overtook the District Council election in Hong Kong 2019. *Japanese Journal of Political Science, 22*(4), 248–67.

Sing, M. (2000). Mobilization for political change: The pro-democracy movement in Hong Kong (1980s–1994). In T. L. Lui & S. W. K. Chiu (eds.), *The dynamics of social movements in Hong Kong* (pp. 21–54). Hong Kong: Hong Kong University Press.

Smart, A. (2006). *The Shek Kip Mei myth: Squatters, fires and colonial rule in Hong Kong, 1950–1963*. Hong Kong: Hong Kong University Press.

Smart, A., & Smart, J. (2017). Formalization as confinement in colonial Hong Kong. *International Sociology, 32*(4), 437–53.

Smart, J. (1989). *The political economy of street hawkers in Hong Kong*. Hong Kong: Hong Kong University Press.

Smith, I. O. (2014). Election boycotts and hybrid regime survival. *Comparative Political Studies, 47*(5), 743–65.

Snow, D. A., & Benford, R. D. (1988). Ideology, frame resonance, and participant mobilization. *International Social Movement Research, 1*, 197–218.

Snow, D. A., & Moss, D. M. (2014). Protest on the fly: Toward a theory of spontaneity in the dynamics of protest and social movements. *American Sociological Review, 79*(6), 1122–43.

So, A. Y., & Ip, P. L. (2019). Civic localism, anti-mainland localism, and independence: The changing pattern of identity politics in Hong Kong special administrative region. *Asian Education and Development Studies, 9*(2), 255–67.

Sokefeld, M. (2006). Mobilizing in transnational space: A social movement approach to the formation of diaspora. *Global Networks, 6*(3), 265–84.

Soule, S. A., & Roggeband, C. (2018). Diffusion processes within and across movements. In D. A. Snow, S. A. Soule, H. Kriesi, & H. J. McCammon (eds.), *The Wiley Blackwell companion to social movements*. https://doi.org/10.1002/9781119168577.ch13.

Staggenborg, S. (1993). Critical events and the mobilization of the pro-choice movement. *Research in Political Sociology, 6*, 319–45.

Steinhardt, H. C., Li, L. C. L., & Jiang, Y. H. (2018). The identity shift in Hong Kong since 1997: Measurement and explanation. *Journal of Contemporary China, 27*(110), 261–76.

Stott, C., Ho, L., Radburn, M., Chan, Y. T., Kyprianides, A., & Morales, P. S. (2020). Patterns of "disorder" during the 2019 protests in Hong Kong: Policing, social identity, intergroup dynamics, and radicalization. *Policing: A Journal of Policy and Practice, 14*(4–5), 814–35.

Su, C., Chan, M., & Paik, S. (2022). Telegraph and the anti-ELAB movement in Hong Kong: Reshaping networked social movement through symbolic participation and spontaneous interaction. *Chinse Journal of Communication, 15*(3), 431–48.

Tai, B. Y. T. (2007). The judiciary. In W. M. Lam, P. L. T. Lui, W. Wong, & I. Holliday (eds.), *Contemporary Hong Kong politics* (pp. 59–74). Hong Kong: Hong Kong University Press.

Tai, B. Y. T. (2009). An unexpected chapter two of Hong Kong's constitution: New players and new strategies. In M. Sing (ed.), *Politics and government in Hong Kong: Crisis under Chinese sovereignty* (pp. 220–45). London: Routledge.

Tam, W. K. (2013). *Legal mobilization under authoritarianism*. New York: Cambridge University Press.

Tang, G., & Cheng, E. W. (2021). Affective solidarity: How guilt enables cross-generational support for political radicalization in Hong Kong. *Japanese Journal of Political Science, 22*(4), 198–214.

Tang, G., & Chung, H. F. (2018). Localist young people do not necessarily reject mainstream social movements. *Ming Pao*, June 28, 2018, A26. [in Chinese]

Tang, G., & Lee, F. L. F. (2018). Social media campaigns, electoral momentum, and vote shares: Evidence from the 2016 Hong Kong Legislative Council election. *Asian Journal of Communication, 28*(6), 579–97.

Tang, G. K. Y. (2015). Mobilization of images: Effects of TV screen and mediated instant grievances in the Umbrella Movement. *Chinese Journal of Communication, 8*(4), 338–355.

Tang, T. Y. T., & Cheng, M. M. T. (2024). The road to electoral authoritarianism: Tracing three phases of state-society contention in post-colonial Hong Kong, 2003–2020. *Journal of Contemporary Asia, 54*(2), 210–237.

Tarrow, S. (1998). *The power in movement*. New York: Cambridge University Press.

Taylor, V. (1989). Social movement continuity: The women's movement in abeyance. *American Sociological Review, 54*(5), 761–75.

Thompson, M., and Cheng, E. W. (2023). Transgressing taboos: Relational dynamics of claim radicalization in Hong Kong and Thailand. *Social Movement Studies, 22*(5–6), 802–21.

Thompson, M., Zanna, M. P., & Griffin, D. W. (1995). Let's not be indifferent about (attitudinal) ambivalence. In R. E. Petty & J. Krosnick (Eds.), *Attitude strength: Antecedents and consequences* (pp. 361–86). Mahwah, NJ: LEA.

Ting, T. Y. (2020). From "be water" to "be fire": Nascent smart mob and networked protests in Hong Kong. *Social Movement Studies, 19*(3), 362–68.

Tong, J. R. (2011). *Investigative journalism in China*. London: Continuum.

Trejo, G. (2014). The ballot and the street: An electoral theory of social protest in autocracies. *Perspectives on Politics, 12*(2), 332–52.

Tsang, S. (2003). The rise of a Hong Kong identity. In T. Fisac & L. Fernýndez-Stembridge (eds.), *China Today: Economics reforms, social cohesion and collective identities* (pp. 222–39) London: Routledge.

Tsang, S., & Cheung, O. (2022). Has Xi Jinping made China's political system more resilient and enduring? *Third World Quarterly, 43*(1), 225–43.

Tufekci, Z. (2013). "Not this one": Social movements, the attention economy, and microcelebrity networked activism. *American Behavioral Scientist, 57*(7), 848–70.

Tufekci, Z. (2017). *Twitter and tear gas*. Yale University Press.

Tweets, J. C. (2014). *Civil society under authoritarianism: The China model*. New York: Cambridge University Press.

Uncu, B. A. (2016). From a conflictual coalition to a social movement? The transformative capacity of the Gezi protests. *Southeastern Europe, 40*(2), 188–216.

Urman, A., Ho, J. C. T., & Katz, S. (2021). Analyzing protest mobilization on Telegram: The case of 2019 anti-extradition bill movement in Hong Kong. *Plos One, 16*(10), e0256675.

Valiente, C. (2015). Social movements in abeyance in non-democracies: The women's movement in Franco's Spain. *Research in Social Movements, Conflicts and Change, 38,* 259–90.

Varese, F., & Wong, R. W. Y. (2017). Resurgent triads? Democratic mobilization and organized crime in Hong Kong. *Australian & New Zealand Journal of Criminology, 51*(1), 23–39.

Vasi, I. B. (2011). Brokerage, miscibility and the spread of contention. *Mobilization, 16*(1), 11–24.

Veg, S. (2017). The rise of "localism" and civic identity in post-handover Hong Kong: Questioning the Chinese nation-state. *China Quarterly, 230,* 323–347.

Veugelers, J. W. P. (2011). Dissenting families and social movement abeyance: The transmission of neo-fascist frames in postwar Italy. *British Journal of Sociology, 62*(2), 241–61.

Vicari, S. (2015). The interpretative dimension of transformative events: Outrage management and collective action framing after the 2001 Anti-G8 summit in Genoa. *Social Movement Studies, 14*(5), 596–614.

Vittori, D. (2017). Podemos and the Five-Star Movement: Populist, nationalist, or what? *Contemporary Italian Politics, 9*(2), 142–61.

Von Bulow, M. (2011). Brokers in action: Transnational coalitions and trade agreements in the Americas. *Mobilization, 16*(2), 165–80.

Von Scheve, C., Zink, V., & Ismer, S. (2016). The blame game: Economic crisis responsibility, discourse, and affective framings. *Sociology, 50*(4), 635–51.

Wagner, M. (2021). Affective polarization in multiparty systems. *Electoral Studies, 69.* https://doi.org/10.1016/j.electstud.2020.102199.

Walsh, E. (1988). *Democracy in the shadows.* New York: Greenwood.

Walsh-Russo, C. (2014). Diffusion of protest. *Sociology Compass, 8*(1), 31–42.

Wang, K. J. Y. (2017). Mobilizing resources to the square: Hong Kong's anti-moral and national education movement as precursor to the Umbrella Movement. *International Journal of Cultural Studies, 20*(2), 127–45.

Wang, X., Ye, Y., & Chan, C. K. C. (2019). Space in a social movement: A case study of Occupy Central in Hong Kong in 2014. *Space and Culture, 22*(4), 434–48.

Wang, Y., & Wong, S. H. W. (2021). Electoral impacts of a failed uprising: Evidence from Hong Kong's Umbrella Movement. *Electoral Studies, 71,* 102336.

Wang, Y. D. (2019). Local identity in a global city: Hong Kong localist movement on social media. *Critical Studies in Media Communication, 36*(5), 419–33.

Wellman, B. (2023). Fall of democratic dreams in Hong Kong. Democratic Erosion Consortium, December 5, 2023. https://www.democratic-erosion.com/2023/12/05/fall-of-democratic-dreams-in-hong-kong/

Westbrook, L. (2023). 105,000 Hongkongers start new lives in UK since BN(O) visa scheme began 2 years ago. *South China Morning Post*, February 23, 2023.

Wong, J. (2015). Facing the question of Hong Kong's future. *Ming Pao*, June 15, 2015. [in Chinese]

Wong, K. Y., & Wan, P. S. (2009). New evidence of the postmaterialist shift: The experience of Hong Kong. *Social Indicators Research, 92*(3), 497–515.

Wong, S. H. W. (2019). Gerrymandering in electoral autocracies: Evidence from Hong Kong. *British Journal of Political Science, 49*(2), 579–610.

Wong, S. H. W. (2020). Correlates of public attitudes toward the Umbrella Movement. In E. W. Cheng and N. Ma (eds.), *The Umbrella Movement: Civil disobedience and contentious space in Hong Kong* (pp. 251–76). Amsterdam: Amsterdam University Press.

Wong, W. L. (2019). In the end, the business sector's legislator will, with tears . . . *Ming Pao*, April 7, 2019, P02. [in Chinese]

Wong, W. P. (2016). 15% voters supported "thug" Leung Tin-kei. *AM730*, March 1, 2016, A04. [in Chinese]

Wu, H. (2022). The making of the citizen-spectator in postmillennial Hong Kong: Authorial and spectatorial engagement with independent documentary films. *Asian Cinema, 33*(2), 191–207.

Yang, G. (2009). *The power of the Internet in China*. New York: Columbia University Press.

Yap, P. J., & Chan, E. (2017). Legislative oaths and judicial intervention in Hong Kong. *Hong Kong Law Journal, 47*, 1–15.

Yates, L. (2015). Everyday politics, social practices and movement networks: daily life in Barcelona's social centres. *British Journal of Sociology, 66*(2), 236–58.

Yaziji, M., & Doh, J. P. (2013). The role of ideological radicalism and resource homogeneity in social movement Organization campaigns against corporations. *Organization Studies, 34*(5–6), 755–80.

Yep, K. M. (2015). The public's heart might want to seek change but there are full of worries. *Ming Pao*, November 27, 2015. [in Chinese]

Yeung, K. C. (2016). The Hong Kong Indigenous actually does not exist. *Stand News*, February 24, 2016. [in Chinese]

Young, L., & Cross, W. (2002). Incentives to membership in Canadian political parties. *Political Research Quarterly, 55*(3), 547–69.

Yuen, S. (2018). Contesting middle-class civility: Place-based collective identity in Hong Kong's Occupy Mongkok. *Social Movement Studies, 17*(4), 393–407.

Yuen, S. (2019). Transgressive politics in Occupy Mongkok. In C. K. Lee and M. Sing (eds.), *Take back our future* (pp. 52–73). Ithaca: Cornell University Press.

Yuen, S., & Cheng, E. W. (2017). Neither repression nor concession? A regime's attrition against mass protests. *Political Studies, 65*(3), 611–30.

Yuen, S., & Cheng, E. W. (2020). Deepening the state: The dynamics of China's United Front work in post-handover Hong Kong. *Communist and Post-Communist Studies, 53*(4), 136–54.

Yuen, S., & Chung, S. (2018). Explaining localism in post-handover Hong Kong: An eventful approach. *China Perspectives, 2018*(3), 19–29.

Yuen, S., & Mok, C. W. J. (2023). Groundwork for democracy? Community abeyance and lived citizenship in Hong Kong. *The China Journal, 90,* 78–103.

Yuen, S., & Tong, K. L. (2021). Solidarity in diversity: Online petitions and collective identity in Hong Kong's Anti-Extradition Bill Movement. *Japanese Journal of Political Science, 22*(4), 215–32.

Yung, B., & Leung, L. Y. M. (2014). Diverse roles of alternative media in Hong Kong civil society: From public discourse initiation to social activism. *Journal of Asian Public Policy, 7*(1), 83–101.

Yung, E. H., & Chan, E. H. (2011). Problem issues of public participation in built-heritage conservation: Two controversial cases in Hong Kong. *Habitat International, 35*(3), 457–66.

Zaller, J. (1992). *The nature and origin of mass opinion.* New York: Cambridge University Press.

Zhao, D. X. (2001). *The power of Tiananmen: State-society relations and the 1989 Beijing student movement.* Chicago: University of Chicago Press.

Zhao, S. (2017). Oath-taking antics: The acts that got six Hong Kong lawmakers disqualified. *South China Morning Post,* July 14, 2017.

Zhu, H. (2019). Beijing's "rule of law" strategy for governing Hong Kong. *China Perspectives, 2019*(1), 23–34.

Zihnnioglu, O. (2023). Strategizing post-protest activism in abeyance: Retaining activist capital under political constraint. *Social Movement Studies, 22*(1), 122–37.

Index

Abeyance, 6–10, 11, 16, 239–244, 252, 254, 256
  networked abeyance structure, 8
Agnes Chow, 167
Alex Chow, 45, 169
Alliance in Support for Patriotic Democracy
  Movement in China, 134, 273
alternative media, 120, 121, 153, 154, 155, 272
Alvin Yeung, 63, 91, 100, 104, 106, 110, 111, 112, 265, 272, 274
ambivalence, 24, 92, 113, 119, 120, 121, 122, 191
Anti-Express Railway protests, 4, 30, 269
Anti-National Education Movement, 4, 30, 132, 245, 270
Anti-WTO protests, 30, 31, 270
Apple Daily, 93, 94, 95, 98, 102, 250, 264, 265, 271, 272
Article 45 Concern Group, 63
articulator, 130, 141, 155, 241
attentive spectator, 241, 276
attrition, 1, 10, 48, 243
autocratization, 187

backfire / backfiring, 15, 37, 160, 161, 291, 293
Baggio Leung, 55, 164–166

Basic Law, 4, 102, 104, 109, 125, 129, 130, 135, 139, 145, 163, 165, 166, 210, 236, 238, 253, 270, 271, 274
  NPC interpretation, 165, 166
Benny Tai, 34, 49, 174, 237, 238, 273
boundary deactivation, 131, 161, 178
boycotting, 201, 254
Brian Fong, 131
broker, 12, 17, 24, 25, 128, 130, 134, 135, 138, 139, 142, 146, 147, 155–157, 188, 191, 192, 206, 212, 216, 220, 227, 229, 231, 232, 236, 238, 241, 265
  broker frame, 25, 138, 139, 142, 147, 192, 206, 212, 216, 220, 227, 229, 236
  bridge broker, 128, 130, 131, 134, 135, 141, 142, 146, 227
  ideological brokers, 12, 17, 24, 25, 128, 130, 147, 155, 156, 159, 188, 191, 231, 232, 238, 241
boycotting, 201, 254

Carrie Lam, 207, 208, 212
Center for Communication and Public Opinion Survey / CCPOS, 2, 3, 26, 49, 114 147, 148, 222, 259, 260, 261, 267, 269, 275
Chan Ho-tin, 187

301

Chan Kinman, 33, 34, 36, 162, 174, 175, 179, 263, 270
Chin Wan, 130
Chinese Liaison Office / CLO, 34, 212, 228, 273
Christine Fong, 100
Chu Yiu-ming, 34, 174
city-state theory, 129, 130
Civic Party, 31, 32, 38, 63, 91, 100, 104, 105, 138, 140, 156, 168, 274
Civic Passion, 38, 39, 57, 67, 109
civil disobedience, 1, 2, 27, 35, 49, 50, 58, 105, 174, 238, 270
Civil Human Rights Front / CHRF, xi, 189, 207–209, 211, 276
civil nomination, 35, 270
collective efficacy, 29, 153
collective restraint (*also see* self-restraint), 200, 201, 216, 238
color revolution, 48, 213, 217
Commercial Radio, 100, 105, 108, 264
Commission of Inquiry / COI, 98, 208, 209, 210, 275
common sense, 127, 169, 170, 172, 174, 178
Confederation of Trade Union, 31, 38
connective action, 65, 215
counterframe / counterframing, 1, 48, 191, 243
countermobilization / countermovement, 11, 198
COVID-19, 2, 167, 190, 247, 248, 267
CY Leung / Leung Chun-ying, 51, 98, 113, 129, 272

D100, 104, 105, 107, 108, 110, 264, 272
decentralization / decentralized movement, 8, 40, 58, 192, 233, 240, 241

Democratic Alliance for the Betterment and Progress of Hong Kong, 100
Democratic Party / DP, 31, 38, 100, 106, 139, 140, 156, 160–162, 168, 179, 186, 263, 274
Demosisto, 24, 63, 128, 130–140, 147, 150, 155–157, 164, 166, 167, 227, 236, 253, 263, 273
derogatory speech, 194, 196, 197
diasporic mobilization / Hong Kong diaspora, 252
direct action, 30, 133
disciplinary tropes, 196, 197
Discourse on the Hong Kong Nation, 109, 129, 272
disqualification, 24, 163, 164, 166, 167, 249
Donald Tsang, 32

Eddie Chu, 167
Edward Leung, 24, 26, 62, 71, 75, 79, 80, 81, 82, 89, 91, 92, 96, 99, 100, 101–106, 109, 110, 112, 113, 122, 123, 125–127, 133, 140, 156, 163, 164, 169, 171, 210, 220, 236, 246, 265, 272, 275
Edward Yiu, 166, 167
eggs versus wall, 110–112
election
    District Council election, 15, 16, 23, 28, 53–59, 61, 87, 101, 122, 168, 190, 247, 271
    2003 District Council election, 15, 53, 58, 247
    2015 District Council election, 16, 23, 28, 53–58, 59, 61, 87, 101, 122, 247, 271
    2019 District Council election, 190, 247
    2023 District Council election, 168

Legislative Council elections / LegCo elections, 16, 24, 26, 31, 32, 34, 61, 62, 74, 79, 89, 91, 99–113, 125, 131, 140, 156, 163–166, 167, 245, 246, 247, 264
  2012 LegCo elections, 32, 34
  2016 LegCo by-election, 16, 24, 26, 34, 61, 62, 74, 79, 89, 91, 99–113, 247, 264
  2016 LegCo elections, 125, 131, 140, 156, 163–166, 246
  2020 Legislative Council elections, 247
election-protest nexus, 245
electoral revolution, 247
emotional contagion, 173
emotional imprint, 47, 270
emotional priming, 87
ethics of solidarity (see solidarity), 192, 193, 206, 217, 228
event
  critical, 6, 13, 14, 15, 17, 19, 25, 27, 58, 282, 285, 293, 295
  secondary critical, 244, 245, 248
  transformative, 13, 14, 244 297
event cluster, 6, 16, 17, 53, 122, 231, 239, 242, 248

Facebook, 22, 52, 75, 79, 132, 133, 163, 255, 270, 273
Fermi Wong, 135, 263
filibuster, 104, 105
five demands, 207–212, 214, 216, 218–220, 229, 239
Five-District Referendum campaign, 32
Foreign Correspondents Club, 187
frame /framing
  adversarial, 3, 19, 59, 101, 103, 106, 113
  affective, 24, 25, 92, 101, 110–112, 113, 236, 246, 265
  diagnostic, 97, 100, 101, 101–103, 113

law-abiding, 49
law-defying, 49
personal action, 216
prognostic, 97, 98, 101, 103–107, 113
retention, 8
frame innovation, 241
Freedom House, 249

gauwu, 48, 51, 52, 58, 59, 87, 271
Gezi protests, 14, 161
Glory to Hong Kong, 220, 255

Haruki Murakami, 110
Hawkers Control Team / HCT, 73, 74, 76, 85
Holden Chow, 100
Hong Kong Connection, 214
Hong Kong Economic Journal, 95, 142, 264, 265, 271
Hong Kong Economic Times, 164, 271
Hong Kong Federation of Students, 36, 45, 50, 127, 132, 169
Hong Kong Human Rights and Democracy Act, 192
Hong Kong independence
  legalistic, 145, 146, 147, 156
  pragmatic objection against, 149–153
  principled objection against, 149–153
  pro-independence sentiments in anti-ELAB, 216–227
  public attitude toward, 148–155
Hong Kong Indigenous / HKI, 19, 23, 24, 62, 63–69, 70, 73, 74, 75, 76, 77, 78, 79, 80, 82, 84, 85, 88, 89, 92, 95, 96, 99, 100, 102, 103, 107, 109, 110, 156, 163, 164
Hong Kong National Party, 63, 187

Hong Kong University's Student
Union, 108, 109, 129, 135, 164,
264
Hu Jintao, 186
Hung Ho-fung, 213

identity
Chinese identity, 17, 18, 245, 250
Hong Kong identity, 18, 22, 41,
245, 250
local identity, 17, 18
improvise / improvisation, 1, 16, 27,
37, 66, 68, 85, 86, 88,
incitement, 174, 175, 266
international lobbying, 137, 190, 229
internet, 20, 67, 86, 255
Ivan Choy, 56, 57

Jimmy Lai, 272
Joseph Lian, 26, 128, 131, 141–147,
154, 155, 156, 157, 227, 263,
265, 274
Joshua Wong, 127, 132, 136, 167,
169
July 1 protest, 14, 15, 18, 29, 30, 53,
58, 63,
105, 119, 120, 150, 152, 153, 247
July 1 protest (in 2019), 200, 208,
223, 225, 228, 244
June 4, 105, 119, 120, 134, 150, 152,
153, 273

Labor Party, 38
Lau Siu-lai, 47, 75, 76, 140, 164, 166
leadership, 7, 19, 24, 35, 39, 40, 49,
64, 65, 68, 85, 89, 176–178,
186, 192, 193, 209, 267
League of Social Democrats / LSD,
31, 32, 38, 226, 249
Lee Wing-tat, 33, 34, 162, 178, 179,
263, 270
leftard, 52

legal mobilization, 168
legalization, 168
Lennon Walls, 190, 201
Leung Kwok-hung, 166
Lewis Loud, 141
Li Yee, 131, 142
Liberate Hong Kong, Revolution of
Our Time, 25, 192, 195, 210,
211, 212, 214–218, 220, 227,
229, 237
LIHKG, 193, 194, 196, 197, 200,
208, 209, 211, 217, 219, 266,
267, 275
localism
as a floating signifier, 22–23
mainstreaming of, 23, 25, 113, 123,
127, 128, 143, 146, 156, 192,
229, 231, 232, 235
Nativism / nativist, 20, 21
Progressive localism / localist, 18,
19, 30
Lost in the Fumes, 125, 127, 236, 263

Ma Ngok, 55
mainlandization (also see reddening),
19, 56, 63, 101–103, 113, 235
militant resistance
bottom lines, 82, 107, 108, 111,
112, 133
conditional acceptance, 117,
119–121
latitude of acceptance, 123, 124,
229, 232, 238
principled opposition, 119, 120, 121
Ming Pao, 93–95, 98, 102, 112, 136,
264, 271, 273
mobilizing structure, 8, 29, 232, 233
Mongkok civil unrest, 16, 17, 24, 25,
59, 61–90, 91–94, 96, 99, 100,
104, 107, 108, 110, 113–117,
119–122, 125, 141, 143, 144,
150, 151, 155, 160, 169, 170,

171, 173, 178, 191, 193, 228, 244, 245, 247, 248, 261–266, 272, 275
Mongkok occupation, 27, 28, 37, 40, 42, 45–51, 58, 84, 87, 258

Nathan Law, 127, 131, 132, 134, 138–140, 164, 166, 169, 253, 263, 272
national anthem, 220, 255
national emblem, 212
National People's Congress, 4, 31
National Security Law / NSL, 2, 25, 139, 167, 190, 239, 243, 248–252, 254, 255
nationalism, 22, 128, 239
Neo Democrat, 56, 57, 131, 156
networked social movement, 2, 22, 65
New Preservation Movement, 18, 30, 63, 269
New Tim Mei Village, 50
news coverage of the Mongkok civil unrest, 92–99
newspaper, 34, 53, 55, 58, 83, 93, 94, 95, 108, 136, 139, 142, 213, 214, 250, 264, 265, 271, 272
Nora Lam, 126, 127, 263, 272
NOW TV, 102, 104, 106, 109, 264

oath-taking, 164–167
Occupy Central for Love and Peace / OCLP, 1, 27, 34–36, 49–51, 238, 270
one country two systems, 20, 102, 109, 136, 147–150, 186, 210, 212, 215, 221, 222, 225–227, 239, 249, 250
onsite surveys, 26, 37–44, 194–196, 198–200, 205–206, 221–227, 257–258
opportunity structure, 10, 232
order imagery, 2

Oriental Daily, 94, 264, 271

People Power, 38, 294
planning vs. preparation / preparedness, 16, 24, 65, 75, 86, 88, 175, 177
polarization
  affective depolarization, 24, 159, 162, 179–185, 188, 191, 206, 228, 231, 232, 235
  affective polarization, 179, 180, 182, 183, 197, 278, 297
  external affective polarization, 180, 183
  internal affective polarization, 180, 183
police violence, 204–205, 208, 209, 210, 228
  surrogate experiences of, 204–205
political consumerism, 190
prefigurative politics, 1, 45, 50
Priscilla Leung, 54
protest cycle, 237
Public Opinion Research Institute, 250, 276
Public Order Ordinance, 168, 170, 171
public nuisance, 1, 48, 49, 174, 175

radical flank effect, 12–13, 159, 160
radicalization, 2, 3, 11, 27, 35, 58, 87, 110, 124, 143, 144, 161, 185, 188, 191, 192, 193, 198, 206, 207, 216, 227, 229, 235, 237, 238
  ideological radicalization, 191, 192, 206, 207, 216, 227, 229
  tactical radicalization, 191, 192, 198, 216
Radio Free Asia, 213
Radio Television Hong Kong / RTHK, 83, 103, 214, 264

Reclaim Hong Kong, Revolution of
    Our Time, 62
reclamation protests / reclaim actions
    Defend Shatin, 67
    Reclaim Sheung Shui, 66, 213
    Reclaim Tuen Mun, 67
    Reclaim Yuen Long, 67, 213
reddening (*also see* mainlandization),
    102, 143
relational approach, 6, 10, 13, 16, 24,
    28, 191, 231, 232, 240, 242,
    243, 252, 256
    arenas of interactions, 11, 231, 240,
    243
Reporters without Borders, 249
repression
    discriminate, 24, 161, 163, 164,
        185, 188, 234, 237, 252
    electoral, 24, 163, 168, 178, 243, 247
    indiscriminate, 24, 161, 163, 185,
        188, 234, 237, 252
    legal, 24, 25, 168, 169, 178, 187, 265
    selective, 161
    social movement 160
resisting the communists by democracy,
    143
Resolution for Hong Kong's Future,
    130, 135, 136, 138, 273
Returnism, 129
reunion in democracy, 135
rhetorical restraint, 218
rule of law, 1, 48, 49, 145, 165, 169

Scholarism, 36, 50, 75, 127, 132
script dissolution, 85
self-censorship, 125, 154, 250
self-determination
    democratic, 130–132, 135, 136,
        138–141, 147, 150, 155, 156,
        164, 166, 167, 236, 273
    Internal, 136, 138
    national, 129, 135, 272

self-mobilization, 39, 40
self-restraint, 2, 54, 57, 61, 92, 101,
    106, 108, 109, 122, 123, 192,
    221, 222, 227, 238
Sing Tao Daily, 94, 95, 264, 271
social media, 7, 46, 87, 120, 121,
    135, 153, 180, 204, 273
Social Record Channel, 102, 264, 272
solidarity
    affective solidarity, 203, 205, 225,
        226, 228
    in the anti-ELAB Movement, 3, 5,
        24, 25, 190, 191, 192–197
    ethics of solidarity, 192, 193, 206,
        217, 228
    solidarity slogan, 193, 194, 195,
        197
sphere of legitimate controversy, 138,
    239
spontaneity, 24, 62, 65, 66, 69, 84,
    85, 88
    Mongkok Civil Unrest as a
        spontaneous protest, 84–87
Stand News, 250
strategic ambiguity, 109, 140, 236

Ta Kung Pao, 93, 94, 95, 214, 264,
    271
tactical freeze, 45, 49, 233
Taiwan, 1, 10, 16, 125, 189, 256
Tanya Chan, 138
Telegram, 211, 275
television, 37, 48, 51, 84, 193, 204,
    264
Television Broadcasting Ltd., 83, 106,
    111, 112, 264
threat, 5, 14, 18, 19, 31, 54, 57, 145,
    163, 172, 198, 204, 212, 234,
    235, 247, 256, 275
Tiananmen, 14, 26, 45, 65, 133, 134,
    189, 261
TVMost, 109, 110, 264, 272

Umbrella Movement, 1–5, 7, 8, 14, 16, 17, 19, 20, 23–26, 27–60, 61–63, 65–67, 77, 87, 110, 120–122, 126, 127, 131, 132, 143, 144, 150, 152–155, 160–162, 169, 170, 174, 175, 177–179, 185, 190, 191, 204, 208, 214, 228, 231–235, 237–241, 243–248, 257, 261

Umbrella Soldiers, 23, 28, 53–58, 271, 282

united front, 11, 18, 162, 186

United States, 35, 92, 179, 256

universal suffrage, 1, 195, 271

vandalism, 133, 190, 201, 238

vigilantism, 190, 198, 201, 228, 238

violence on the edge, 144–146, 156, 274

Wen Wei Po, 57, 93–95, 264, 271

woleifei, 29

Wong Shing-chi, 100, 106

Wong Wing-ping, 113

Wong Toi-yeung, 62, 64, 67, 75–80, 82, 96, 109

Wong Yuk-man, 164

xenophobia, 20, 133

Xi Jinping, 186, 243

Xinjiang, 217

Yau Wai-ching, 54, 164, 165, 166

Yep Kinman, 57

Youngspiration, 19, 54, 55, 63, 156, 164, 166, 185

YouTube, 65, 255, 264, 272

Yuen Long Attack, 198, 212, 228, 245